CCBS REFERENCE LIBRARY

TO BE RETURNED TO THE CENTRE AT THE END OF YOUR COURSE.

CORPORATE GOVERNANCE, FINANCIAL MARKETS AND GLOBAL CONVERGENCE

FINANCIAL AND MONETARY POLICY STUDIES

Volume 33

Published on behalf of the
Société Universitaire Européenne de Recherches Financières (SUERF)

This volume contains selected lectures from those given at the 20th Colloquium of SUERF, arranged in conjunction with the Robert Triffin-Szirak Foundation and held in Budapest, Hungary, in May 1997.

The titles published in this series are listed at the end of this volume.

Corporate Governance, Financial Markets and Global Convergence

Edited by

MORTEN BALLING
Rector, Aarhus School of Business, Aarhus, Denmark

ELIZABETH HENNESSY
Managing Editor, *Central Banking*, London, United Kingdom

and **RICHARD O'BRIEN**
Global Business Network, London, United Kingdom

Published on behalf of the Société Universitaire Européenne de Recherches Financières (SUERF)

with contributions from

Ana Isobel Fernández Álvarez
Silvia Gómez Ansón
Morten Balling
Fabrizio Barca
Marco Battaglini
Hans J. Blommestein
Tito Boeri
Wilko Bolt
Jenny Corbett
Guido Ferrarini
Giovanni Ferri

Francesco Giavazzi
Karel Lannoo
Chris Mallin
Colin Mayer
Carlos Fernández Méndez
Marga Peeters
Giancarlo Perasso
Nicola Pesaresi
Luc Renneboog
Arend J. Vermaat

KLUWER ACADEMIC PUBLISHERS
DORDRECHT / BOSTON / LONDON

Cataloging-in-Publication Data is available from the Library of Congress

ISBN 0-7923-4825-7

Published by Kluwer Academic Publishers,
P.O. Box 17, 3300 AA Dordrecht, The Netherlands.

Sold and distributed in the U.S.A. and Canada
by Kluwer Academic Publishers,
101 Philip Drive, Norwell, MA 02061, U.S.A.

In all other countries, sold and distributed
by Kluwer Academic Publishers,
P.O. Box 322, 3300 AH Dordrecht, The Netherlands.

Printed on acid-free paper

All Rights Reserved
© 1998 Kluwer Academic Publishers
No part of the material protected by this copyright notice may be reproduced or
utilized in any form or by any means, electronic or mechanical,
including photocopying, recording or by any information storage and
retrieval system, without written permission from the copyright owner.

Printed in Great Britain

Table of Contents

Introduction
by *Morten Balling*   i

Corporate Governance: A Keynote Speech
by *Morten Balling*   xi

Chapter I   The Effect of Board Size and Composition on
Corporate Performance
by *Ana Isabel Fernández Álvarez, Silvia Gómez Ansón and
Carlos Fernández Méndez*   1

Chapter II   Banks and Corporate Governance in Italy:
A Two-Tier System
by *Fabrizio Barca, Giovanni Ferri and Nicola Pesaresi*   17

Chapter III   The New Financial Landscape and its Impact on
Corporate Governance
by *Hans J. Blommestein*   41

Chapter IV   Privatization and Corporate Governance:
Some Lessons from the Experience of Transitional Economies
by *Tito Boeri and Giancarlo Perasso*   73

Chapter V   Corporate Governance in the Netherlands
by *Wilko Bolt and Marga Peeters*   89

Chapter VI   Changing Corporate Governance in Japan
by *Jenny Corbett*   113

Chapter VII   Stock Exchange Governance in the European Union
by *Guido Ferrarini* 139

Chapter VIII   Should We Trust Banks When They Sit on the
Board of Directors?
by *Francesco Giavazzi and Marco Battaglini* 163

Chapter IX   Corporate Governance, West and East: A Synthesis
of the EU Framework in the Perspective of Enlargement
by *Karel Lannoo* 199

Chapter X   The Role of Institutional Investors in the Corporate
Governance of Financial Institutions: The UK Case
by *Chris Mallin* 217

Chapter XI   Corporate Governance, Competition and Performance
by *Colin Mayer* 235

Chapter XII   Shareholding Concentration and Pyramidal
Ownership Structure in Belgium
by *Luc Renneboog* 263

Chapter XIII   Insurance Company Ownership in the Netherlands:
Implications for Corporate Governance and Competition
by *Arend J. Vermaat* 301

Index 323

Introduction

MORTEN BALLING

The studies in this volume were presented at a Colloquium in Budapest arranged by SUERF and the Robert Triffin-Szirak Foundation in May 1997. All contributions deal with characteristics and trends in corporate governance systems. The structure of financial markets and institutions has a strong impact on the ways in which the power to manage corporate resources is allocated. The relative roles of different types of owners and the legal framework for their behaviour are changing all over Europe. Financial integration in the European Union and transition to open market economies in Central and Eastern Europe have a profound effect on the allocation of influence and on enterprise behaviour, and so has privatization, which is taking place in almost all European countries. The present collection of papers gives an impression of how many interesting corporate governance aspects researchers and practitioners have to deal with in a world characterized by rapid technological, political and institutional change.

The first paper in the volume is the text of a keynote speech by Morten Balling. In the speech, he gives a general survey of the corporate governance problems to be discussed at the Colloquium. By referring to a so called 'Matrix of Governance by sector', he points out characteristics and trends in the interplay between different types of owners of equity and managers of financial and non-financial companies and institutions.

In the paper by Ana Isabel Fernández Álvarez, Silvia Gómez Ansón and Carlos Fernández Méndez, the role played by the board of directors and the influence of the board on company performance is analysed. The authors use data from non-financial companies listed on the Madrid Stock Exchange. By applying a series of regressions they are able to observe statistically significant relationships between board size and firm performance. Their analysis indicates also that outsiders on the board are doing an effective job, which contributes in a positive way to company performance.

In the paper by Fabrizio Barca, Giovanni Ferri and Nicola Pesaresi, the corporate governance role played by banks in Italy is analysed. In the first part of the paper, the authors take a historical perspective in which they discuss the implications of state ownership and the relatively close ties between political leaders and managers of banks and industrial conglomerates. Later they emphasize the importance of the distinction between large Italian banks, which in their view have not exercised effective corporate governance and the smaller but much more active local banks. Due to that distinction they find it appropriate to recommend a two-tier model for understanding the Italian corporate governance system.

Hans J. Blommestein's paper analyses the impact of structural changes in financial systems on financial governance channels. He emphasizes in particular the growing role of institutional investors in the OECD area. These investors have become major shareholders almost everywhere, and from year to year they tend to be more active. They are very much interested in market liquidity, and their desire to carry out large transactions means that they demand a market infrastructure characterized by specialized wholesale markets. In general, the institutional investors support efforts to improve public disclosure standards and other measures to increase market transparency.

In the paper by Tito Boeri and Giancarlo Perasso a comparison is made between the privatization methods and experiences of the Czech Republic and Poland. In the Czech Republic ownership changes were mainly achieved via a mass privatization scheme, while in Poland there was a strong involvement of insiders – i.e. managers and employees. The speed of the privatization was much greater in the Czech Republic, but speed should not be the most important concern. What really matters is the creation of an effective governance structure, which makes managers accountable and gives them strong incentives to be efficient.

In their paper, Wilko Bolt and Marga Peeters analyze the Dutch corporate governance system. The Dutch economy is one of the most open economies in the world, and one reflection of this is the very high proportion (40 per cent) of Dutch shares owned by foreign investors. In addition to this strong representation of foreigners in the ownership structure, statistics show a strong increase in share holdings by funds and banks. In the paper, the authors summarize an intense recent discussion concerning proposals to change the Dutch corporate governance system towards the Anglo-Saxon model with more shareholder influence.

Jenny Corbett gives in her paper a survey of evidence on the characteristics of the corporate governance system in Japan. Based on ownership statistics and other available evidence, she concludes that large institutional shareholders with concentrated shareholdings have a direct effect on the behaviour of Japanese firms. Among the large shareholders, banks play a particularly important governance role. In spite of recent concerns about the health of the banking sector, the author expects the banks to be at the centre of the Japanese corporate governance system for some time to come. The corporate sector has for many years been heavily dependent on bank financing, and this situation has not changed fundamentally.

In his paper on stock exchange governance in the European Union Guido Ferrarini discusses the relative merits of member and investor ownership and compares stock exchange regulation in a number of EU countries. Faced with increasing competition amongst themselves and against other enterprises that offer transaction services, such as proprietary trading systems, it is essential for European stock exchanges to improve their efficiency and to generate volume. Large investments in new information technology are necessary in order to preserve competitiveness in a global financial market. The implementation of the ISD has accelerated cross-border transaction activity of member firms and investors and strengthened the pressure for convergence of national stock exchange laws in the EU.

In their paper, Francesco Giavazzi and Marco Battaglini look at the role played by banks in privatization processes. Banks can be involved in such processes in several ways. They may themselves be the objects of privatization since in many countries a significant fraction of the banking industry is publicly owned. This is the case in France, Spain and Italy. But banks can also be important buyers of the equity of industrial firms sold by the government if they are allowed to do so. The authors characterize privatizations as a very good opportunity to set up the right environment for the development of new financial intermediaries and in general for a sound corporate governance system.

In his paper, Karel Lannoo brings what he calls a European approach to the corporate governance discussion. The institutional framework in Central and Eastern European countries is in a process of transition to market systems with current adaptation of regulatory systems with reference to the EU legislative framework. Institutional shareholdings are growing in almost all European countries, but there seems to be a need to strengthen the monitoring activity and governance role played by institutional investors. The portfolios of the institutions are becoming more and more international, but cross-border governance remains weak. Maybe European industry should take the initiative to establish a European-wide Code of Good Practice in Corporate Control.

The role of institutional investors is also the subject of Chris Mallin's paper. Based on empirical material concerning the structure of ownership of British financial institutions and on interviews, she concludes that best practice in corporate governance is generally being followed. The institutional owners of banks and insurance companies have in general a healthy influence on the management of these financial firms.

Colin Mayer's paper is an overview of the interrelation between corporate governance, competition and performance. His stated purpose is to review what is known about the relation of corporate governance and corporate performance. In order to illuminate the relation, he looks carefully at five topics: incentives, disciplining, restructuring, finance/investment, and commitment/trust. In spite of the existence of an extensive academic literature and systematic comparative studies of different institutional arrangements, the author characterizes the state of the art as 'ignorance', and he warns us not to try to look for optimal governance arrangements. Concentration of ownership encourages more active corporate governance and the development of long-term relations, but concentration may also cause conflicts of interest. All in all he concludes that there are no easy solutions and that we still have a lot to learn.

Luc Renneboog's paper addresses the question as to how corporate control is exerted in poorly performing listed Belgian companies. The analysis shows that in Belgium disciplining of underperforming management is more frequent in companies with a high non-executive board representation and highly concentrated ownership. Institutional shareholders are not very often actively involved in efforts to improve managerial performance, but there are in Belgium other shareholder classes with a high monitoring ability. Shareholders who increase their ownership in companies which demonstrate poor performance tend to be high quality monitors who press for restructurings and other measures, which can improve profitability.

The paper by A. J. Vermaat deals with insurance company ownership in the Netherlands. In his capacity as Chairman of the Dutch Insurance Supervisory Board, the author is in a very good position to analyse the ownership structure and its implications for governance and competition in the market for insurance services. Due to the strong foreign presence in this market, the corporate governance arrangements in the Netherlands cannot be separated from the European and other international forces and developments. The author emphasizes the need to apply a long-term investment perspective.

THE PRIX MARJOLIN

The Council of SUERF awarded the Prix Marjolin to Dr Luc Renneboog of the Catholic University of Leuven for the best contribution to the Colloquium by an author of less than forty years of age. The award was presented by Alexandre Lamfalussy, then President of the European Monetary Institute, who delivered the 1997 Marjolin Lecture at the Colloquium.

Corporate Governance: A Keynote Speech*

MORTEN BALLING

1. Introduction

Ladies and Gentlemen,

Let me start by thanking my colleagues in the SUERF Council of Management for asking me to give one of the keynote speeches today.

I consider it to be a great honour to be given the opportunity to talk to such a distinctive group of European people from the academic world, the financial world and the political world, and to do it in this impressive historical building.

According to my dictionary, a keynote is a fundamental note, a central principle, or a controlling thought.

In French, the term is *note dominante* and in German *Grundton*.

The concept obviously has its origin in music, and if we continue to seek inspiration in the world of music and choose to consider all the speakers at this Colloquium as musicians in a symphony orchestra, we can say that it is the task of the keynote-speaker to try to strike a tone, which all the following speakers can listen to and to some extent build their contribution on.

I hope you will allow me to continue a little longer with this introductory 'semantic exercise'.

I intend, if I may, to subject the two words in the title 'Governance' and 'Corporate' to a similar exercise.

The concept 'Governance' is related to words like influence, power, ruling, leading, guiding, directing and inspiring.

The concept 'Corporate' refers to ways of organizing business, the formation and management of joint stock companies, company law provisions on capital, regulation by laws and statutes of manager/shareholder relations, procedures for the appointment of supervisory boards, definition of the respective responsibilities of managers, board members, auditors etc.

---

* Speech given by Professor Morten Balling at the opening session of the 20th Colloquium of the Société Universitaire Européenne de Recherches Financières (SUERF) and the 7th Conference of the Robert Triffin-Szirák Foundation (RTSF), May 15 1997, Budapest.

So, in the Commissions of this Colloquium we are supposed at the company level to discuss the appropriate way of building organizations and at the systemic level to consider the proper design of the structure of financial markets with a view to the implications for the efficiency with which owners and other stakeholders can exert influence on corporate managers with operational responsibilities.

We shall discuss what we consider to be good (or bad) managerial performance, efficient ways of monitoring, what different ownership structures imply for the efficiency of Corporate Governance, how best to enforce accountability, obligations to disclose information on company results, incentives for managers, the proper ways of carrying out privatization, mergers and acquisitions and other types of restructuring.

2. SHAREHOLDERS AND STAKEHOLDERS

The concept 'stakeholder' is broader than the concept 'owner' or 'shareholder'. Employees, trade unions, suppliers, tax authorities and other public authorities can be important stakeholders in companies, but they will not normally be shareholders. To have something 'at stake' means in this connection having a direct interest in the proper conduct of the affairs of the business.

Most stakeholders want to play a role in the 'Governance' structure – they want to influence corporate decision making in accordance with their own interests, and some of the stakeholders who are not owners do have the power to exert a certain influence. In some countries, for instance Germany, The Netherlands, Luxembourg and Denmark, employees of big companies have the right to elect members of the supervisory boards, and in Scandinavia the government has the right to appoint one board member in banks and other financial institutions.

But in most cases, it is through ownership that people and institutions acquire influence over business management.

Managers are hired by boards of directors, which in turn are elected in stockholder meetings, where the owners can exercise their voting power.

3. OWNERSHIP STRUCTURE AND MATRIX OF GOVERNANCE

Ownership structures vary considerably from country to country. But I think it is appropriate to say that enterprises in almost all countries in Western Europe, in Central Europe and in Eastern Europe have mixed ownership in the sense that there are everywhere examples of companies owned by the government, by banks and other financial institutions, by institutional investors, by non-financial companies, by personal investors and by foreign companies and investors.

It seems in fact to be difficult to find a country, in which one single type of owner completely dominates the company ownership structure.

The relative roles of the different types of owner vary, but representatives of each type have some influence on managers and have from time to time some activity in each country's 'Market for Corporate Control'.

A 'Matrix of Governance by sector' is shown in Appendix A on p. xxvii. Within the two-dimensional framework of the Matrix I will point out some important features and trends in the institutional background of Corporate Governance in Europe. Simplification is always risky, but as you all know, economists can conclude nothing if they do not draw simplified pictures of the world. So, I have simplified the world by assuming that in all European countries it is meaningful in a Corporate Governance context to classify all participants in the business community and in the financial markets into seven sectors.

The names of the sectors, which can be found both at the top of the columns and to the left at the beginning of the rows in the Matrix, are so general that they should be applicable in almost all national Corporate Governance environments.

If we move into the Matrix from the top and follow a column, we look at the business world from the point of view of people and institutions, who are owners and have influence in their capacity of owners. If we go into the Matrix of Governance from the left and follow a row, we look at the world from the point of view of market participants that are under influence. Thus the two-dimensional framework allows us to observe that the same financial institution or non-financial company is in some respects able to exercise governance on others, while in other respects it is subject to influence from other market participants or authorities.

The division of labour between the Commissions at this Colloquium is based on this way of classifying the direction of influence.

4. FOCUS IN COMMISSION I

The title of Commission I is 'Corporate Governance of financial institutions, East and West'. The focus in Commission I corresponds accordingly to the perspective in row b in the Matrix of Governance by sector.

Banks and other financial institutions are owned by different types of owners such as the government (b,G-cell), institutional investors (b,I-cell), non-financial companies (b,N-cell), personal investors (b,P-cell) or by foreign investors (b,F-cell).

Commission I will therefore participate in discussions about the influence exerted by these owners and by the supervisory authority (b,C-cell) on bank management all over Europe.

Questions to discuss could be: What does institutional and foreign bank share ownership imply for bank management and competition among banks in the country? Should institutional investors be more active in bank shareholder meetings? Should there be a limit on the share of equity ownership in a bank or on the share of the votes exercised by one single shareholder? What implications do capital adequacy requirements and other prudential rules have for governance of financial institutions? According to what criteria should different stock exchange ownership structures be evaluated?

These questions exemplify what we mean when we say 'Corporate Governance of Financial Institutions, East and West'.

5. Focus in Commission II

The title of Commission II is 'Corporate Governance as exerted by financial institutions, East and West'. The focus in Commission II corresponds to the perspective in the B-column in the Matrix of Governance.

Banks own shares in other financial institutions (b,B), in subsidiaries and funds of different kinds (i,B), in non-financial companies (n,B) – and to a certain extent also in foreign companies (f,B-cell). So banks can, in addition to the influence they have in their capacity as lenders, have influence in their capacity as shareholders. In Commission II excellent lecturers discuss the role of banks in Corporate Governance in different banking systems.

A very fundamental question is: should transition economies seek inspiration in Japan or in Germany where banks and non-financial companies for many years have played an important role in Corporate Governance as major shareholders, or should they rather look at the Corporate Governance environment in the US or the UK where insurance companies and pension funds are relatively more important as shareholders?

Other important subjects to discuss within the framework of Commission II are economies of scope in banking, universal banking, the access of bank managers to boards of industrial companies and the desirability of separation of owner and creditor interests.

Banks communicate literally with their big corporate clients on a daily basis. They are therefore in general much better informed about the financial condition of these clients than most of the other investors, who own shares in the client companies. If the corporate clients are in financial difficulties, the officials of the bank will normally be in a much better position to evaluate the prospects for recovery than other market participants are. In Commission II we should accordingly discuss how carefully the bank must operate as a shareholder or as an advisor to fellow shareholders in order to avoid the risk of being accused of taking advantage of its informational lead due to its position as a creditor.

6. Focus in Commission III

The title of Commission III is 'Financial Institutions as participants in the transfer of Corporate Governance, East and West'. This title reminds us that ownership structures and influence structures are always subject to change. Managers are appointed, they work for a number of years for the company and then they quit or retire.

Investors buy shares, they can use the voting right attached to the shares and subsequently they sell their shares or swap them for shares in other companies or maybe for bonds. The frequency with which shares are traded in equity markets seems, however, to be much higher for shares with ordinary voting rights than for shares with multiple voting rights.

Transfer of control over a company can take place in a deliberate way. For instance when managers retire because they reach a certain age and their responsibilities are taken over by younger people who have been given time to prepare themselves for the job.

Transfer of control, however, can also result from more dramatic events such as deaths of managers, dismissals due to unsatisfactory performance or violations of ethical principles, major share transactions (privatizations or takeovers), mergers, financial difficulties, restructurings or even bankruptcies.

Banks and other financial institutions almost always play a crucial role when transfer of control – also in non-financial companies – takes place. Banks and investment banks give advice, they may act as brokers between old owners, issuers, managers in search of new owners on one side and institutional investors in their capacity of potential new owners on the other side. The bank may underwrite securities, assist in listing on stock exchanges, provide sales facilities directed towards interested personal investors etc.

So, in Commission III questions to discuss could be: How can banks and other financial institutions evaluate the prospects of a proposed acquisition or merger? What are the risks involved from the bank's point of view? What implications has a legal commitment for the buyer of major blocks of shares in a company to offer equal treatment to owners of small shareholdings? What effects can be expected in the market for corporate control, if the EU Commission's new proposal for a 13th Company Law Directive on takeover bids is adopted and subsequently implemented in the member countries? Does it improve the performance of incumbent managers, if they are constantly exposed to the threat of being fired by potential new more profit oriented owners? What are the prospects of success with respect to the initiatives from the EU Commission with the aim of removing remaining takeover barriers?

7. FOCUS IN COMMISSION IV

Privatization is an important topic in Commission III, but it is in fact also important in Commission IV, whose title is 'Global monetary and Economic Convergence, East and West'.

In addition to the macroeconomic aspects of convergence, there are institutional aspects. Thus, the expression convergence can also be assumed to cover convergence of legal and financial systems.

Countries in the process of building and improving market economies can probably benefit from studying the experience of other countries which in the 1990s are forced to reevaluate the efficiency of their own governance systems in the light of the ongoing European integration process, c.f. the implementation of the Internal Market Programme.

In Commission IV, several papers deal with privatization experiences in transition economies, but there are certainly also important cases of privatization to study in EU-member countries. In several older market economies, for instance, telecommunications companies have recently been privatized or are in the process of being privatized.

Within the framework of the Matrix of Governance, privatization implies a movement of share ownership from the left to the right, i.e. from the G-column to some of the other columns.

I understand that it has been a major goal for many of the mass privatization programmes in Central and Eastern Europe to involve as many private citizens as possible as shareholders, i.e. it is considered desirable by the authorities to stimulate a movement from the (n,G-cell) to the (n,P-cell). But foreign investors have also been invited as new owners, for instance in Hungary and in the Czech Republic, and this implies, of course, a movement from the (n,G-cell) to the (n,F-cell).

The Treaty on European Union contains several provisions concerning the legal framework for Corporate Governance. Important examples are the articles on the right of establishment and approximization of laws according to which company law harmonization and harmonization of banking laws and stock exchange regulations have taken place. It is, however, interesting to observe that the Treaty is 'neutral' towards member states' choices as to the private or public character of their national economies. According to article 222, the Treaty shall in no way prejudice the rules in Member States governing the system of property ownership. The article calls for a neutral treatment of private, public and mixed ownership structures.

At the time of the adoption of the Treaty of Rome, Article 222 was designed to protect nationalization programmes in the Member States from undue interference by other Member States or by the Community Institutions.

Political thinking about the advantages and disadvantages of private and public ownership has changed considerably since the 1950s.

I find it in some way comforting that an old Treaty provision, which was originally formulated in order to protect the right of EU Member States to nationalize i.e. to move the structure of ownership of enterprises from the right to the left in the 'Matrix of Governance', can today be used to protect the right of the Member States to privatize i.e. to move from the left to the right !

8. FEATURES OF AND TRENDS IN SHARE OWNERSHIP

Let me now with reference to the Matrix of Governance try to point out some other characteristic features of the ownership structure in Europe and identify some further trends with implications for the overall pattern of Corporate Governance in the years to come.

Several of the Colloquium papers contain or refer to empirical analysis of corporate ownership structures.

Let me mention one important source: 'Share ownership structure in Europe, 1995', a study which was undertaken by the Oslo Stock Exchange on behalf of the Federation of European Stock Exchanges.

One very important structural feature is that corporate managers in general own only a very small fraction of the share capital of the company in which they work. Cases of management buy-outs, in which the managers buy controlling ownership stakes in their company, are rare in Europe, but they deserve attention because they represent a radical solution to the principal-agent problem.

Corporate managers are normally well paid wage earners, who are working at some distance from the owners of the company and with only limited knowledge about the demands and wishes of the individual shareholders. The separation of management and ownership is, of course, more characteristic in big listed companies than in smaller companies. That was true in 1932, when Berle and Means published their classic book *The Modern Corporation and Private Property* – and it is still true in 1997. But it is also part of the overall picture in Europe that the great majority of non-financial companies are small unlisted firms, for instance farms, workshops, retail shops, which are owned by one person or by a limited number of personal investors (often family members) or by other non-financial companies.

Let me again indicate where we are in the Matrix of Governance.

Non-financial companies owned by personal investors and households belong to the (n,P-cell). In France and Italy this group of owners is still relatively important, also for quite large companies.

Non-financial companies owned by other non-financial companies belong to the (n,N-cell). In continental Europe – in particular in Germany – groups of companies owned by industrial parent companies play a very important role. Ownership of controlling blocks of shares by industrial parents or by foundations often lasts for decades.

In Western Europe, and to an increasing extent also in Central and Eastern Europe, the biggest non-financial companies are listed on stock exchanges and have in addition to the big owners also several thousands of shareholders, most of whom own very few shares.

Distribution of information from big listed companies to their shareholders takes place through annual reports, semi-annual reports and announcements through the press. The content of these information sources is regulated by legal disclosure requirements, which reflect political investor protection goals. The aim is to reduce problems arising from asymmetric information and the risk of insider trading.

Several EU-directives contain provisions concerning the disclosure of accounting information. Let me mention explicitly the Fourth Company Law Directive (78/660/EEC) on annual accounts, and the Seventh Company Law Directive (83/349/EEC) on consolidated accounts. Listed companies must comply with stricter disclosure regulations due to implementation of the directives on admission to stock exchanges, on listing particulars, on interim reports, on major holdings transactions, and on insider trading. Directive (88/627/EEC) on major holdings is often referred to as the 'Transparency Directive' because it provides an obligation for the companies to disclose which investors own more than 10 per cent of the share capital and voting rights. Several member countries have chosen a lower percentage in their disclosure provisions in order to make the ownership structure more visible to the public.

In most of Western Europe, we have in the last 25 years seen remarkable structural changes in stock ownership.

Partly for tax reasons, but also because of strong growth in the percentage of the population who are wage-earners and participants in private or collective retirement schemes, an ever increasing share of the savings is channelled through pension funds, insurance companies and mutual funds, and consequently these institutional investors accumulate very considerable portfolios of bonds, real estate and equity. Their shareholdings comprise in particular ownership of listed companies, partly due to legal requirements concerning the structure of their portfolios.

In London, insurance companies and pension funds own approximately 60 per cent of the listed shares.

There are still some wealthy and influential individuals on the Corporate Governance scene, who sit on boards of directors or at least influence the composition of these boards, but on the whole the influence of wealthy individuals is diminishing, while the influence of institutional investors is growing.

Personal investors seem to have significantly reduced their relative importance as share owners in all European markets for which figures are available.

In the Matrix of Governance, this important trend is reflected in a movement of the focus away from the (n,P-cell), which indicates personal investor ownership and influence on the management of non-financial companies and to the (n,I-cell), which points to institutional investor ownership and influence on non-financial companies. Where cross ownership of shares is common among non-financial companies, there is what has been called an 'insider system of corporate control', where company managers are members of each others' boards and monitor each other. In the Commissions we can discuss what cross ownership implies for the management expertise of the monitors and as a possible protection against hostile takeovers.

In Central and Eastern Europe, there has also been an interesting development towards institutional investor ownership of companies, the so-called Privatization Investment Funds (PIFs).

In several mass privatization programmes, individuals received special privatization vouchers which could be used to purchase shares of privatized enterprises.

Governments allowed the creation of special intermediaries, which would compete for the vouchers received by the citizens offering their own PIF-shares in exchange and investing the vouchers on the citizens' behalf.

It seems to have been the idea that the new PIF-intermediaries would function in the financial system both as a kind of mutual funds providing the citizens the option of diversification plus special investment expertise for their shareholders, and as active shareholders holding significant stakes in the companies, sitting on boards of directors, monitoring corporate performance and contributing to the restructuring process.

The experience with the PIF-intermediaries, which must belong to the I-column in the Matrix, has been mixed. It seems that some cases of abuse and publishing of misleading information have caused political measures to strengthen the regulation of big share transactions.

9. WHAT BEHAVIOUR CAN WE EXPECT FROM THE STAKEHOLDER?

In a market economy the managers, the banks, the institutional investors and the personal investors share the responsibility for the functioning and efficiency of the governance system.

Taken together, their decisions are crucial for investment, production, employment and other aspects of the business development in the country.

We must therefore ask what we can realistically expect them to do.

Can we expect them to behave in a way which contributes in a constructive way to the growth of the national economy and the welfare of the population? Can we expect them to intervene promptly in cases of financial difficulty?

We must also ask how parliaments in co-operation with governments should design the legal and regulatory framework in order to support constructive behaviour in the corporate governance system. We can improve our understanding of the division of labour between managers, banks and investors by looking closer at the concept 'Incorporation'. Incorporation means that the risk of the owners is limited to the sums they have invested in companies characterized by limited liability. Incorporation also means that companies can have a stable equity base at the same time as the owners have a liquid portfolio.

If many owners decide to restructure their portfolios and to walk away and sell their shares in a particular company, the share price may come down, but the financial situation of the company does not immediately change.

Incorporation in combination with organized equity markets makes it therefore possible to overcome the fundamental mismatch between the interest of the company managers and boards of directors in a stable equity base and the investors' interest in having liquid portfolios.

Incorporation also implies portfolio diversification opportunities to risk averse investors, who are more interested in protecting their wealth and future dividend income than in exercising influence on corporate managers.

Maybe the great majority of the personal investors (in the P-column) can be supposed to have risk reduction and income protection as prime motives. If that is the case, what role can we then realistically expect them to play in the Corporate Governance system? An important factor to keep in mind here is that serious monitoring of corporate performance is hard work. It takes time to study and analyse company accounts and other types of disclosed company information. It also takes time to acquire necessary knowledge about market conditions in the industry in question, about relevant accounting principles and about the general business environment of the companies.

We should therefore not be surprised if most shareholders decide that they do not have the time or do not want to invest the time and the effort, which is necessary for monitoring.

Typically, if their holdings of shares in individual companies are relatively small, it may be due to deliberate portfolio diversification, and they therefore do not feel that it is worthwhile for them to attend shareholder meetings, to ask critical questions to the board and to exercise their voting power.

The low attendance at shareholder meetings seems to be a common European phenomenon, and that may indicate that we should expect personal shareholders to be relatively passive owners.

The monitoring task is, however, important and the question is then: Who is going to do the job?

10. THE IMPORTANT ROLE OF THE INSTITUTIONAL INVESTORS

Let me here refer to the answers given in the British Cadbury (1992) and Greenbury (1995) Reports, in the French Viénot and Marini Reports, in the Report on Corporate Governance 1995 from the Centre for European Policy Studies (CEPS) in Brussels and in several other reports on Corporate Governance.

It seems to be a common feature of most reports that the big institutional shareholders are called upon to remember their responsibilities and to involve themselves in systematic analysis of company information, to participate in shareholder meetings and to criticize weak corporate performance.

These recommendations are, of course, reinforced by the fact that institutional share ownership has been rising all over Europe. It should also be kept in mind that foreign shareholders in many cases are institutional investors.

So, in the Commissions we should discuss how active we can expect institutional investors to be, and what the framework for monitoring by them should look like.

Several Colloquium papers deal with the role of institutional investors. Some of them leave the impression that European institutional investors in spite of their growing role as owners are not too active at shareholder meetings. On the Corporate Governance scene in Germany, some authors suggest that corporate investors are more active than institutional investors.

Several institutional portfolio managers follow a diversification strategy and consequently they own only a very small fraction of each individual listed company. Some indicate that it is their policy not to get involved in meetings with corporate managers.

Pension funds with international equity portfolios may as a rule use their voting power in domestic companies, but there seems to be a tendency to stop voting at national frontiers. Costs and practical difficulties are often referred to as explanations of this relatively passive investor behaviour. There seems to be no single European equity market in the EU area as far as share voting is concerned!

If it is considered politically desirable to activate institutional investors more on the European corporate governance scene, measures could be taken to improve the flow of company information prior to shareholder meetings and to make it easier for foreign investors to vote by mail.

Some of the investment portfolio managers interviewed by researchers from CEPS indicated that when they used their voting power at stockholder meetings, they generally voted in favour of management.

This does, of course, not mean that their presence at shareholder meetings and their interest in corporate affairs cannot affect managerial performance in a positive way.

There has recently been discussion about the internal governance structure of pension funds. The current European trend seems to be that individuals with pension rights demand influence on the selection of pension fund managers and want to have the option to move their savings from one fund to another. In the Commissions we can discuss whether pressures of that kind perhaps supported by legislative initiatives may stimulate the interest by pension fund managers to involve themselves more in Corporate Governance.

11. PROXY VOTING TRADITIONS

In several European companies, registered shareholders who are unable to come to general meetings are automatically asked by the company to transfer their votes to the board of directors. If the performance of the company is considered to be satisfactory, and the shareholders accordingly have confidence in the board, many of them do that to such an extent that the board continuously has sufficient voting power to control decisions at the shareholder meeting.

Typical items on the agenda of shareholder meetings include approval of company accounts, election of supervisory board members, appointment of auditors, approval of the dividend and authorization of the issue of new shares. The Third Company Law Directive (78/855/EEC) on mergers of public limited liability companies has for several years been implemented in the EU countries. The Third Directive prescribes a number of minimum requirements for the documents and information on which merger decisions are made, and specifies that merger decisions as a rule are to be made by the general meeting of the shareholders of each of the merging companies. So from time to time, merger proposals appear on the agenda. Transfer of voting rights often therefore involves decisions with far-reaching implications for the company.

In Germany, it is customary for personal shareholders to transfer their voting rights to banks or to shareholder associations who send their representatives to the meetings.

In view of its importance, the extent and Corporate Governance implications of proxy voting as an organized process should be discussed in the Commissions.

12. MANAGER INCENTIVES AND BEHAVIOUR

Let us now focus on the role of corporate managers.

In view of the fact that crucial decisions are made by them, their motives and efficiency deserve analysis. It is very important not only from the stakeholders' point of view, but also from a political point of view, that the best available corporate managers are trained, hired and given strong incentives to demonstrate good management performance. Principal-agent models suggest that there should be a close relation between corporate performance and management remuneration.

Managers' contracts with the boards of directors should induce them to be led primarily by company profitability and shareholder wealth maximization prospects when they evaluate the business opportunities arising from the development in relevant markets and technologies.

Business opportunities are always somewhat uncertain so the managers must be given the incentive to take calculated risks. There seems to have been a substantial increase in the use of stock options as a form of manager remuneration. The ability of such schemes to align the interests of managers and shareholders and the effect of stock options on managers' risk taking behaviour deserves discussion.

The proficiency of managers should not be measured by their ability to avoid mistakes and losses on projects: no corporate manager can avoid mistakes if he takes initiatives.

Their managerial proficiency should rather be measured by their ability to make decisions which on average improve the profitability and value of the company over a certain period. It is the task of the board of directors to monitor the performance of the managers, to participate in major corporate decisions, and to discuss strategic opportunities during board meetings. As long as they demonstrate good performance, the managers should be paid well and be allowed to stay.

The board of directors should be prepared to accept some mistakes and some losses due to bad management decisions, but there should also be a limit on the patience of the board of directors. If a manager makes too many mistakes, he must leave the company. It is one of the most difficult tasks of a board to decide when a manager exceeds the limit.

So managers should know that they are continuously monitored and that their ability to run the company profitably determines whether they will be rewarded or punished by the board. To be continuously monitored is not necessarily a pleasant experience. Managers' concern for their own job security, earnings prospects and pension benefits is natural. So is the concern of employees. When you can see a potential threat to your professional and financial position, it is also natural that you try to build up a system of defence. Golden parachutes in contracts, anti-takeover defences, and poison pills are examples of such defences. But resistance from managers and employees to privatization plans that will remove close links to the political system and reduce the likelihood of taxpayer financing of deficits is also an example of defence.

Defensive management behaviour of that kind is often called 'entrenchment'. Entrenchment is as I said natural, but is it also defensible from the point of view of other stakeholders?

One argument in favour is that entrenchment allows the incumbent managers to follow long-term goals, to restructure the company gradually in a careful way and to avoid takeovers by raiders who seek short-term capital gains.

An argument against is that entrenchment may be used to protect inefficient managers, and that this violates the principle that managerial inefficiency should be punished, and that poor managers should be replaced by good ones, when they have exhausted the board's limit of patience.

Thus, managers can under certain circumstances be forced to leave. They can, however, also themselves decide to leave the company. There is a market for professional managers. Executives with a good track record and reputation can seek or be offered positions in other companies. A board of directors must, of course, keep this in mind in its monitoring behaviour in relation to the managers in their company.

In a constantly changing world, the ability to reallocate resources is an important feature of an economy. I have earlier referred to reallocation of financial capital through equity markets, and now I have had the opportunity to mention reallocation of 'human managerial capital' through the market for professional managers. I could add that there is also a market for professional non-executive directors, who have an important role to play in Corporate Governance.

An obvious subject to discuss at this Colloquium is what can be done in order to improve the reallocation ability of different Corporate Governance systems. We could also discuss the strong financial incentives for managers as well as for directors to build up a reputation for good performance and integrity. Is it not likely that they care at least as much for that reputation as they care for the wealth of the shareholders?

13. Keynote Conclusions

In my brief conclusion, I want to repeat a few observations and to make a couple of new statements which may hopefully impact on the following discussion.

Corporate Governance systems create a framework for some of the most important decision makers in the society.

It is not an exaggeration to say that the decisions of managers of companies and banks strongly affect the corporate and financial landscape of Europe.

It is therefore a matter of great political concern how the managers are selected, what their motives are, what incentives they have when they make decisions concerning production and investment, and how effectively their performance is monitored.

In short, Corporate Governance systems are a matter of great political importance.

Several Colloquium papers clearly demonstrate that the institutional structure and the governance systems vary from country to country and they vary through time.

There are, however, clear signs of system convergence. In Western Europe, the implementation of the Single Market and international financial integration stimulate the convergence process. The impact of international competition and integration is also felt in Central and Eastern Europe, and financial regulatory systems in that region seem to be gradually adapted to the principles reflected in EU directives.

In part, the adjustments may be seen as preparatory steps in the movement of these countries towards EU membership. Against this background I suggest that we should not in our subsequent discussions exaggerate the differences between Corporate Governance systems in the EU countries and in the transition economies.

There are several similarities and common features. In all parts of Europe, we can find countries which are moving towards governance systems in which financial markets can be expected to play a stronger disciplining role on corporate managers. And in all parts of Europe, we can observe cases of privatization, in which it is a main goal for efficiency reasons to expose managers to tougher monitoring from different categories of private investors, whose interest in corporate performance lies in the fact that they will suffer losses, if companies are mismanaged.

Take also the increasing role of institutional investors. When plans in Central and Eastern Europe to establish fully-funded pension systems are carried out, pension funds will gradually develop into big investors and shareholders and will to an increasing extent become important players on the Corporate Governance scene.

Our understanding of Corporate Governance systems is not so deep that we can realistically try to design an optimal system: a perfect or an optimal Corporate Governance system does not exist. Each country must build on its own historical experience and business traditions and gradually adapt the system to changes in the European and global environment.

Political concern for the competitiveness of domestic enterprises is natural here.

The presence of foreign owned branches and subsidiaries implies as a rule strong competition in product markets, but it also implies inspiration with respect to management and governance. By looking at the best performing enterprises, stakeholders of all kinds can obtain ideas about how to improve the functioning of their own companies. In the university world the subject 'lifelong learning' is topical, but it can easily be transferred to the corporate world. Stakeholders should also see themselves as participants in a lifelong learning process and currently improve their understanding of the important role they have to play.

Allow me to conclude with a remark on involvement.

It seems to me that irrespective of Corporate Governance systems, it is essential that there are stakeholders who are seriously involved in company affairs.

Corporate Governance does not work unless there are some people present who are really engaged in efficiency and performance. Somebody must stand ready to intervene and take an initiative, when business opportunities develop or corrective action is needed.

Somebody must at the same time be willing to praise managers, when they demonstrate good performance, and to criticize them or remove them, when they make mistakes.

In Corporate Governance stakeholder indifference is understandable but deplorable, stakeholder politeness is all right but secondary, stakeholder involvement, however, is crucial.

APPENDIX A

MATRIX OF GOVERNANCE BY SECTOR

M. Balling
The Aarhus School of Business, Denmark
Feb. 1996

		In capacity as owner with influence						
		G Government	C Central bank and supervisory authority	B Banks and other financial institutions	I Institutional investors, pension funds etc.	N Non-financial companies	P Personal investors, households and others	F Foreign companies and investors etc.
In capacity as owned and under influence	g Government							
	c Central bank and supervisory authority	c.G						
	b Banks and other financial institutions	b.G	b.C	b.B	b.I	b.N	b.P	b.F
	i Institutional investors, pension funds etc.	i.G	i.C	i.B	i.I	i.N	i.P	i.F
	n Non-financial companies	n.G	n.C	n.B	n.I	n.N	n.P	n.F
	p Personal investors, households and others							
	f Foreign companies and investors etc.	f.G	f.C	f.B	f.I	f.N	f.P	

NOTE: Upper case letter indicates owner with influence
Lower case letter indicates market participant under influence

☐ Not relevant

Board Size and Composition

ABSTRACT

This paper studies the effect of Board features on Board efficiency and corporate performance. We specifically focus on Board size and the proportion of non-executive directors on the Board. Our findings show that non-executive directors enhance Board capabilities to control and evaluate managerial actions, and therefore, influences positively corporate performance. Our results relating to Board size suggests the existence of a double relationship between Board size and corporate performance, resulting in a non-linear relationship between these two variables.

Ana Isabel Fernández Álvarez: PHD in Finance from the University of Oviedo. Professor of Finance in the Department of Finance at the University of Oviedo.

Silvia Gómez Ansón: Bachelor degree in Business administration from the Complutense University (Madrid). Bachelor degree in International Economics form the University of Konstanz. PHD in Finance from the University of Oviedo. Assistant in the Department of Finance at the University of Oviedo.

Carlos Fernández Méndez: Bachelor degree in Business administration from the University of Oviedo. Assistant in the Department of Finance at the University of Oviedo.

I. The Effect of Board Size and Composition on Corporate Performance

ANA ISABEL FERNÁNDEZ ÁLVAREZ, SILVIA GÓMEZ ANSÓN AND
CARLOS FERNÁNDEZ MÉNDEZ

1. INTRODUCTION

The modern corporation is characterized by the separation between shareholders, the owners of the company, and managers who control the assets and activities of the firm (Berle and Means, 1932). This separation implies the existence of conflicts of interests between managers and shareholders as managers may have the power to pursue their own objectives at the cost of shareholders. In order to lower the negative impact of managerial discretion on shareholders' wealth, several devices are intended to control managerial actions. These devices include the market for corporate control (Jensen and Ruback, 1983), managerial compensation systems, based on incentives that tie managers' wealth to corporate performance (Jensen and Murphy, 1990b) and the monitoring exercised by major shareholders (Shleifer and Vishny, 1986) and the Board of Directors (Fama, 1980; Baysinger and Butler, 1985). The Board of Directors is an internal governance mechanism, one of its functions being to control divergences between managerial and shareholders' interests and to discipline managers who indulge in opportunistic behaviour. In this sense, the efficiency of the Board of Directors is crucial, especially, when the conflicts of interests between managers and equity holders are severe.

In this paper we analyze, for the Spanish market, the role played by the Board of Directors, as a device to control managerial behaviour, and the relevance of its features for company performance. We specifically investigate, controlling for managerial ownership, how Board size and composition measured, respectively, through the number of directors seated on the Board, and by the proportion of outside directors, influence a firm's performance, measured by Tobin's q ratio and market to book value of common equity ratio.

The results of this study indicate the relevance of Board size and Board composition on the firm's overall performance. We find evidence of a positive influence of outside directors on firm performance and, also, of a non-linear relationship between Board size and firm performance.

The remainder of this paper is organized as follows. Section 2 reviews the literature related to Board effectiveness and control, exposes the paper's theoretical basis and the hypotheses that are tested. Section 3 describes the sample, the set of variables and empirical methods used in the study. Section 4 presents and discusses the empirical results. Finally, in Section 5, implications of the results are discussed and conclusions for the Spanish market are offered.

2. Theoretical Background and Testable Hypotheses

Modern corporations are formed mainly by two separate parties: the shareholders and the managers. This principal-agent relationship implies the existence of conflicts of interest between these two parties and, therefore, of agency costs (Jensen and Meckling, 1976). As owners of modern corporations are mostly small shareholders, whose stake is not large enough to make the direct benefits of monitoring counterbalance its costs, they will not be interested in the monitoring and control of managerial actions. According to this free rider problem, no single small shareholder will exercise direct control over managers (Grossman and Hart, 1980). Therefore, shareholders delegate to the Board of Directors the task of controlling and disciplining managers.

2.1. Board Composition and Corporate Performance

The Board of Directors has the task of contracting new managers, establishing their compensating scheme and disciplining them. The Board is formed by executive (insiders) and non-executive directors (outsiders). As executive, or insider, directors' careers are often tied to those of other senior managers, they are usually unwilling to discipline managers (Weisbach, 1988) and, therefore, the task of evaluating senior managers and removing them when they fail to perform well, will fall mainly on the non-executive directors.

Outside directors may have incentives, such as their reputation in the directors' labour market and the possible legal implications derived from poor monitoring (Fama, 1980; Fama and Jensen, 1983) to control managerial actions. In this sense, the empirical evidence suggests that the labour market rewards good professional reputation with a higher number of directorships and that directors of poorly performing corporations often lose directorships and are rarely offered additional ones (Kaplan and Reishus, 1990).[1]

Different studies also suggest that outsiders play an important role as monitors of senior managers. Weisbach (1988) finds that the removal of CEOs, caused by poor performance is more likely to occur in outsider dominated Boards, than in insider dominated ones. Byrd and Hickman (1992) find that abnormal returns are significantly higher in bidding firms with outsider dominated Boards. According to these arguments, we test the following hypothesis:

Hypothesis 1: The proportion of outsiders seated on the Board, and therefore its composition, increase the efficiency of its monitoring role. Thus, a higher proportion of non-executive directors increases a firm's performance.

2.2. Board Size and Corporate Performance

Board size may also influence the effectiveness of Board decisions intended to discipline managers. On the one hand, initially, a higher number of directors may provide wider criticism of a manager's actions. On the other hand, Board size may slow down the Board's decision making and increase politeness and courtesy, lowering, therefore, the level of criticism towards top manager policies (Lipton and Lorsch, 1992; Jensen, 1993; Yermarck, 1996).

Thus, increases in Board size may have two opposite effects on Board effectiveness. On the one hand, it enhances Board capabilities as the number of critics of managerial policies grow and, on the other hand, it facilitates the existence of certain norms of courtesy that prevent directors from actively controlling managerial actions which, in turn, erases the Board's capability to protect shareholder's interests. These two effects combine resulting in a non-linear relationship between Board size and firm performance. According to these arguments we test the following hypothesis:

Hypothesis 2: There is a non-linear relationship between Board size and company's performance. Initially, increases in Board size enhance Board effectiveness and company's performance but, after a certain Board size is reached, dysfunctional behaviour of the Board, arising from an excessive amount of members, outweighs the positive effects of Board size, giving way to a negative relationship between a firm's performance and Board size.

3. DATA AND VARIABLES

3.1. Data

The data used in this study is composed of 70 non-financial companies listed on the Madrid Stock Exchange in 1993. Companies included in the sample are grouped in seven different industrial sectors as defined by the Madrid Stock Exchange. Accounting data was collected from the annual reports and from the CMNV (Spanish SEC) databases. Stock ownership data was obtained from the CMNV data tapes and from the directory *Spain: The Shareholder's Directory*. Stock prices were collected from the Madrid Stock Exchange's data tapes. Data referring to the composition and size of the Board of Directors was obtained from the CMNV tapes. This data was compared with the data contained in the annual reports. Directors' personal data referring to their present and past jobs, and their family ties with other relevant members of the company, were obtained from the following directories: *Who's Who in Spain*, *Duns 50,000* and *Dicodi*.

3.2. Variables Selection

We measure a firm's performance using Tobin's q^2 (Q), the ratio of the firm's market value to the replacement cost of its assets. Values of this ratio above one indicate that the firm has valuable intangible assets such as market power or any other kind of competitive advantage. One of these intangible and valuable assets is its internal organization and the low level of agency costs that specific organizational forms can generate. Thus, as far as Board composition and size may influence a firm's organization, they will be considered valuable intangible assets. We also use the ratio of market to book value of a firm's equity as an alternative measure of company's performance.[3]

We use the proportion of outside directors (OUT) to measure Board composition and the degree of independence between the Board and the managerial team. For that purpose, we define outside directors as those who have never been executives of the company.[4,5]

Board size (BDSIZE) is defined as the number of directors sitting on each company's Board at the annual meeting as stated in each firm's annual report.

We also control for different factors that may affect Tobin's q and market to book value of common equity. For that purpose, we include dummy variables, representing the industrial sectors of the sample firms.

We also control for a firm's leverage (LEVERAGE) including in the analysis the ratio of debt to total assets. Firm's leverage may have a positive effect on Tobin's q as it decreases the level of free cash flows that can be used by managers to satisfy their own objectives at the expense of shareholders' wealth (Jensen, 1986).

We include the logarithm of a firm's total assets' book value (SIZE) to control for the positive effect on Tobin's q of intangible assets related to a firm's size. This way, we control for the possible systematic divergences in Tobin's q ratio between small and large companies. This fact is especially important as we found that firm's and Board's sizes are strongly and positively correlated The relationship between the Board's size and the firm's performance, without controlling for firm's size, could be, therefore, the result of an underlying relationship between the firm's performance and the firm's size.

Managerial ownership (OWN) may also affect Tobin's q. Different studies have found non-linear relations between managerial ownership and market value of the firm (Mork et al., 1988; Barnhat et al., 1994; Hermalin and

TABLE 1
Descriptive statistics

	Q	MB	OUT	BDSIZE	OWN	LEVERAGE	SIZE
Mean	1.158	1.287	0.686	10.857	7.216%	0.476	10.588
Median	0.99	1.217	0.714	10	0.736%	0.479	10.455
Mode	1.04	0.107	0.75	12	0	0.019	7.876
Std dev	0.763	0.728	0.178	5.063	14.728	0.256	1.544
Maximum	5.02	3.279	0.923	29	74.23%	1.463	15.179
Minimum	0.26	0.107	0	3	0	0.019	7.876

Q	Tobin's q ratio
MB	Market to book ratio of common equity
OUT	Proportion of non-executive members of the Board
BDSIZE	Number of members of the Board
OWN	Stock ownership of Board directors
LEVERAGE	Total debt to total assets ratio
SIZE	Logarithm of Book value of total assets

Weisbach, 1991). On the one hand, managers' stock ownership may have a positive effect on market value since it ties managerial wealth to that of shareholders. On the other hand, managerial stock ownership may have a negative effect on the firm's market value if managerial stock ownership is high enough to allow managers to isolate themselves from control devices such as the market for corporate control and the Board of directors. These two opposite effects combine in a non-linear relationship between managerial stock ownership and firm's performance. For that reason, we include linear, quadratic and cubic terms for directors' stock ownership.

3.3. Variables Summary Statistics

Table 1 presents the summary statistics (mean, mode, median, maximum and minimum and standard deviation) related to Tobin's q ratio, market to book value of common equity, Board size, proportion of outside directors, directors' stock ownership, firm's leverage and company's size.

Tables 2 and 3 display, respectively, the bivariate correlations between these variables. P values correspond to the probability of not rejecting the null hypothesis.

Tobin's q (Q) ranges from 0.26 to 5.02. The mean is 1.15. Market to book value of common equity (MB) has a minimum and maximum value of 0.107 and 3.279 respectively and it presents a mean of 1.287. Board size (BDSIZE) ranges from 3 to 29 members and has a mean value of approximately 11. The proportion of outside directors (OUT) has a minimum value of 0 and a maximum of 0.923, its mean value being 0.686. Directors' stock ownership

TABLE 2

Correlations between Tobin's q and independent variable set

	Q	OUT	BDSIZE	OWN	LEVERAGE	SIZE
Q	1	0.1457	0.111	−0.0649	−0.0778	−0.0347
	$P=0.000$	$P=0.229$	$P=0.360$	$P=0.593$	$P=0.522$	$P=0.775$
OUT	0.1457	1	0.4076	−0.4074	−0.0077	0.3118
	$P=0.229$	$P=0.000$	$P=0.000$	$P=0.000$	$P=0.950$	$P=0.009$
BDSIZE	0.111	0.4076	1	−0.293	−0.1869	0.6289
	$P=0.360$	$P=0.000$	$P=0.000$	$P=0.014$	$P=0.121$	$P=0.000$
OWN	−0.0649	−0.4074	−0.293	1	−0.0676	−0.3607
	$P=0.593$	$P=0.000$	$P=0.014$	$P=0.000$	$P=0.578$	$P=0.002$
LEVERAGE	−0.0778	−0.0077	−0.1869	−0.0676	1	0.1374
	$P=0.522$	$P=0.950$	$P=0.121$	$P=0.578$	$P=0.000$	$P=0.257$
SIZE	−0.0347	0.3118	0.6289	−0.3607	0.1374	1
	$P=0.775$	$P=0.009$	$P=0.000$	$P=0.002$	$P=0.257$	$P=0.000$

TABLE 3

Correlations between market to book value of common equity and independent variable set

	MB	OUT	BDSIZE	OWN	LEVERAGE	SIZE
Q	1	0.114	0.0665	−0.1362	−0.0657	0.148
	$P=0.000$	$P=0.378$	$P=0.607$	$P=0.291$	$P=0.612$	$P=0.251$
OUT	0.114	1	0.4076	−0.4074	−0.0077	0.3118
	$P=0.378$	$P=0.000$	$P=0.000$	$P=0.000$	$P=0.950$	$P=0.009$
BDSIZE	0.0665	0.4076	1	−0.293	−0.1869	0.6289
	$P=0.607$	$P=0.000$	$P=0.000$	$P=0.014$	$P=0.121$	$P=0.000$
OWN	−0.1362	−0.4074	−0.293	1	−0.0676	−0.3607
	$P=0.291$	$P=0.000$	$P=0.014$	$P=0.000$	$P=0.578$	$P=0.002$
LEVERAGE	−0.0657	−0.0077	−0.1869	−0.0676	1	0.1374
	$P=0.612$	$P=0.950$	$P=0.121$	$P=0.578$	$P=0.000$	$P=0.257$
SIZE	0.148	0.3118	0.6289	−0.3607	0.1374	1
	$P=0.251$	$P=0.009$	$P=0.000$	$P=0.002$	$P=0.257$	$P=0.000$

(OWN) ranges from 0 to 74.23 per cent, and has a mean value of 7.216 per cent. Firm's size (SIZE) presents minimum and maximum values of 7.876 and 15.179 respectively. The mean value of a firm's size is 10.588. Finally a firm's debt to total assets (LEVERAGE) presents a minimum value of 0.019 and a maximum value of 1.463.[6] The mean value of a firm's leverage is 0.476.

4. Empirical Methods and Results

We estimate the relationships between a firm's performance and Board composition and size using OLS regression models. Two different sets of models are

TABLE 4

Mean value of a firm's performance depending on the proportion (below or above the average) of outsiders seated on the Board of Directors

Variable	Mean value in Subsample with OUT below the average	Mean value in Subsample with OUT above the average	t significance (P value)
Q	0.8995	1.17	0.009
MB	1.1125	1.3439	0.15

Q   Tobin's q ratio
MB Market to book value of common equity
OUT Proportion of non-executive members of the Board

estimated. The first set analyzes the relationship between firm's performance and Board composition and, the second one studies the relationship between a firm's performance and Board size. Each of these two sets is calculated for two different measures of firm performance, Tobin's q and the ratio of market to book value of common equity.

4.1. Board Composition and Corporate Performance

Firstly, taking the proportion of outsiders on the Board as a factor to separate two different subsamples, we checked for statistically significant differences in means in Tobin's q. As expected, we find a higher Tobin's q mean in the subsample with the higher proportion of outsiders. Firms that present a proportion of outsiders above the mean have a higher Tobin's q mean value than firms with an under average outsider representation on the Board (q mean of 1.1752 compared to q mean of 0.8995). These differences are statistically significant with a p value above 0.01. Using market to book value of a firm's equity as a measure of a firm's performance, we obtain a mean value of 1.3439 for the over average outsider proportion sample, and 1.1125 for the under average outsider proportion sample, but, in this case, the difference is not statistically significant.

These results partially indicate the positive influence of outsiders on a company's performance. We also check this relation in a set of regression models that include the variables mentioned before that control for spurious correlations between the proportion of outsiders and firm's performance.

Table 5 displays the results for these models based on Board composition. Regressions one to four use Tobin's q as the dependent variable and regressions five to eight include, instead, market to book value of firm's equity.

In the first model, considering only the proportion of outsiders on the Board, we found no statistically significant relationship between a firm's performance and this proportion (OUT). The second model includes a set of dummy

TABLE 5

Board composition and firm's performance

	REG 1	REG 2	REG 3	REG 4	REG 5	REG 6	REG 7	REG 8
OUT	0.446602	1.702964	1.76211	0.826947	0.791136	1.020337	0.983259	0.826818
T	1.34	2.753	2.724	2.278	1.769	2.245	2.06	1.662
SIG T	0.1852	0.0083	0.0092	0.0268	0.0825	0.0293	0.0451	0.1035
OWN			−0.019258	−0.019174			0.016559	0.007712
T			−0.472	−0.7			0.506	0.213
SIG T			0.6395	0.4871			0.6156	0.8322
OWN2			2.27E−04	3.80E−04			−0.001659	−0.001329
T			0.138	0.35			−1.257	−0.94
SIG T			0.8907	0.7281			0.215	0.3522
OWN3			2.86E−06	1.60E−07			2.17E−05	1.89E−05
T			0.18	0.015			1.698	1.399
SIG T			0.858	0.9879			0.0962	0.1687
LEVERAGE				0.049894				−0.506393
T				0.197				−1.356
SIG T				0.8448				0.1819
SIZE				−0.009076				0.02549
T				−0.203				0.433
SIG T				0.8397				0.6669
INDUSTRY DUMMIES	NO	YES	YES	YES	NO	YES	YES	YES
F	1.79474	2.6111	2.1994	2.00159	3.13005	1.99245	2.53163	2.23139
SIG F	0.1852	0.0228	0.0353	0.0471	0.0825	0.0847	0.0189	0.0296
ADJUSTED R^2	0.01246	0.17016	0.17903	0.14885	0.03728	0.09769	0.2004	0.19761

Q   Tobin's q ratio
MB   Market to book ratio of common equity
OUT   Proportion of non-executive members of the Board
BDSIZE   Number of members of the Board
OWN   Stock ownership of Board directors
LEVERAGE   Total debt to total assets ratio
SIZE   Logarithm of Book value of total assets

variables that control for industry specific effects that may affect Tobin's q. This model shows a positive and statistically significant relationship (p value of 0.008) between the proportion of outsiders and Tobin's q. The third model controls for specific industrial effects on Tobin's q and also for the effect of director's stock ownership. To do this, we include linear quadratic and cubic terms of directors' stock ownership as was exposed in the variable selection point. Even after including these control variables we found a positive and statistically significant relationship between OUT and Tobin's q. Finally, in the fourth model we add two more control variables to account for a firm's size and leverage effects on Tobin's q. Still, after adding these control variables, the positive and statistically significant relationship between OUT and Tobin's q holds good, although the statistical significance of the relationship falls very slightly and its p value nears 0.01.

Regressions five to eight are similar to those described before, only now market to book value of a firm's equity is used as dependent variable. These models show a consistent and statistically significant relationship, even after including the whole set of control variables, between the proportion of outsiders seated on the Board and the market to book value ratio. The significance of the OUT coefficients are slightly lower than they were in the case of the models where Tobin's q was used as dependant variable, but they are still statistically significant at the 5 per cent level in almost all cases. However, in the model which includes the whole set of control variables, the coefficient of OUT is only statistically significant at the 10 per cent level.

These results indicate, therefore, the existence of a positive relationship between the proportion of outsiders seated on the Board of Directors and a firm's performance as was proposed in H1. According to this hypothesis and to the empirical results obtained we can conclude that outsiders, in the Spanish market, make an effective job of evaluating and monitoring managerial actions, enhancing, in that way, a firm's performance.

4.2. Board Size and Corporate Performance

Models one to eight in Table 6 test the relationship between Board size and a firm's performance. The first four models use, as dependant variables, Tobin's q and the last four include market to book value of the firm's equity.

Model 1 presents a positive and statistically significant relationship between the linear term of Board size (BDSIZE) and Tobin's q and a negative and statistically significant one between the quadratic term of Board size and Tobin's q. This two terms jointly form a non-linear relationship between BDSIZE and firm performance. So, these results suggest that, initially, an additional member on the Board has a global positive effect on a firm's

TABLE 6

Board size and firm's performance

	REG 1	REG 2	REG 3	REG 4	REG 5	REG 6	REG 7	REG 8
BDSIZE	0.0903	0.088764	0.096989	0.110228	0.117567	0.152651	0.152968	0.132173
T	2.195	2.187	2.355	2.431	2.188	2.807	2.884	2.216
T significance	0.032	0.0329	0.0223	0.0187	0.0331	0.0072	0.006	0.0321
BDSIZE2	−0.002838	−0.002553	−0.002826	−0.003104	−0.003398	−0.004718	−0.004814	−0.004324
T	−2.036	−1.876	−2.077	−2.15	−1.904	−2.625	−2.818	−2.31
T significance	0.0461	0.0659	0.0426	0.0364	0.0623	0.0116	0.0071	0.0259
OWN			−0.022834	−0.019459			1.36E−02	0.010495
T			−0.906	−0.707			0.423	0.292
T significance			0.3688	0.483			0.6744	0.7717
OWN2			5.15E−04	3.82E−04			−1.60E−03	−0.00146
T			0.504	0.349			−1.23E+00	−1.037
T significance			0.6163	0.7284			0.2234	0.3055
OWN3			−1.16E−06	2.00E−07			2.13E−05	2.01E−05
T			−0.116	0.019			1.706	1.494
T significance			0.9082	0.985			0.0948	0.1427
LEVERAGE				2.47E−01				−0.33186
T				0.895				−0.817
T significance				0.3749				0.4187
SIZE				−0.042627				3.60E−02
T				−0.759				0.485
T significance				0.4517				0.6305
IND SECTOR	NO	YES	YES	YES	NO	YES	YES	YES
F	2.44379	2.56338	2.30603	1.7983	2.66022	2.15523	2.80607	2.10904
SIG F	0.0953	0.0231	0.0247	0.0695	0.0793	0.0553	0.0086	0.0342
ADJUSTED R^2	0.04383	0.148	0.17171	0.14143	0.05693	0.12818	0.2472	0.20769

Q Tobin's q ratio
MB Market to book ratio of common equity
OUT Proportion of non-executive members of the Board
BDSIZE Number of members of the Board
OWN Stock ownership of Board directors
LEVERAGE Total debt to total assets ratio
SIZE Logarithm of Book value of total assets

performance, but when the Board's size grows this relationship reverses and an additional member has a negative effect on the firm's performance.

In model 2, when we include dummy variables to account for specific industry effects on a firm's performance, the positive and negative relationships between the linear and quadratic terms of Board size and firm performance still hold, but P values fall slightly after including dummy variables. The coefficient on the linear and quadratic term of Board size are statistically significant at the 10 per cent and 5 per cent level, respectively.

In model 3 we control for the effect of directors' stock ownership on a firm's performance. After including a linear, quadratic and cubic terms of directors' shareholdings the coefficient signs of the variables representing Board size remain unchanged and are statistically significant at the 5 per cent level.

In the fourth regression model we test the effect of Board's size on a firm's performance controlling for industry effects, directors' stock ownership, financial leverage and firm's size. Even after including these control variables the positive and negative relationships between the linear and quadratic term of a Board's size and Tobin's q are statistically significant with a p value above 5 per cent.

Models five to eight explore the relationship between Board size and corporate performance using equity market to book value to measure the firm's overall performance including the same control variables as models one to four. The relationship between a Board's size and equity's market to book value ratio are similar to those obtained for a Board's size and Tobin's q. The coefficients of the linear and quadratic terms of a Board's size are, respectively, positive and negative respectively and both are statistically significant at conventional levels of significance.

So, the results from this set of regression models suggest the existence of a non-linear relationship between a Board's size and a firm's performance in the Spanish market. This result confirms our second hypothesis. According to that hypothesis Board size determines the quality of monitoring and decision making of the Board which, in turn, determines the quality of a firm's policies. Our results show that when the number of members of the Board rises, coordination problems and slow decision making erases Board capability to control managerial actions. These negative effects can offset the positive effect derived from an additional person to draw on and make the overall effect of an additional member of the Board to be negative.

5. Conclusions

This paper studies the effects of Board features on a firm's performance in the Spanish market. We specifically focus on Board size and composition, defined as the proportion of non-executive directors. Our results indicate that a Board of directors' characteristics influence a firm's performance. This empirical evidence indicates that outsider non-executive directors influence positively a Board's capabilities to evaluate and discipline managers supporting thus, the view that the task of disciplining managerial actions falls mainly on the Board's non-executive members since executive members tend to avoid disciplinary actions because their careers depend greatly on those of managers.

Our results relating to a Board's size suggests the existence of a non-linear relationship between this variable and Board effectiveness. They show that, initially, increases in Board size enhance a Board's effectiveness and a firm's performance, but after a certain point, increases in a Board's size decreases a firm's performance. As a consequence, the relationship found between a Board's size and a firm's performance is non-linear, suggesting that, in firms with small Boards, the positive effect of an additional member (having an additional member to evaluate managerial actions) offsets the potential negative effects (problems of lack of co-ordination and slow decision making) which derive from an increase in Board size. But, when the Board is large, this negative effect outweigts the positive one, resulting in an overall negative relationship between a Board's size and a firm's performance.

NOTES

1. See also Gilson (1989).
2. Several studies in the field of corporate governance also measure firm performance using Tobin's q. See McConnel and Servaes (1990); Morck et al. (1988); Hermallin and Weisbach (1992).
3. See Barnhart et al. (1994).
4. See Borokhovich et al. (1996).
5. This classification scheme differs from the one used by Weisbach (1988) or Byrd and Hickman (1992), where there is a third class of outside dependent directors, or grey directors, composed by members of the Board, such as lawyers or commercial and investment bankers, who are not officers of the firm, but have a close relationship with it. We chose this classification as it was difficult to obtain data on the activities of some members of the Boards. In any case, we suppose that this noisy measure of the proportion of independent directors in the Board would be against our hypothesis of positive relationship between outside directors proportion in the Board and Tobin's q.
6. This value above one corresponds to a bankrupted firm.

REFERENCES

Barnhart, S. W., M. W. Marr and Rosenstein, S. (1994) 'Firm Performance and Board Composition: Some New Evidence', *Managerial and Decision Economics*, Vol. 15, pp. 329–340.

Baysinger, B. and H. Butler (1985) 'Corporate governance and the Board of Directors: Performance effects of changes in board composition', *Journal of Law, Economics and Organization*, Vol. 1, pp. 101–124.

Berle, A. and G. C. Means (1932) *The Modern Corporation and Private Property*, Ed. Macmillan, New York, NY.

Borokhovich, Kenneth A., R. Parrino and T. Trapanni (1996) 'Outside directors and CEO selection', *Journal of Financial and Quantitative Analysis*, Vol. 31.

Brickley, J. A., R. C. Lease and C. W. Smith (1988) 'Ownership Structure and Voting on Antitakeover Amendments', *Journal of Financial Economics*, Vol. 20, pp. 267–292.

Byrd. W. and K. Hickman (1992) 'Do outside directors monitor managers?' *Journal of Financial Economics*, Vol. 32, pp.195–221.

Curcio, R. (1994) 'The effect of managerial ownership of shares and concentration of voting power', Discussion Paper No. 185, Centre for Economic Performance, LSE.

Fama, E. (1980) 'Agency problems and the theory of the firm', *Journal of Political Economy*, Vol. 88, pp. 288–307.

Fama, E. and M. C. Jensen (1983) 'Separation of Ownership and Control', *Journal of Law and Economics*, Vol. 27, pp. 301–325.

Gilson, S. C. (1989) 'Management turnover and financial distress', *Journal of Financial Economics*, Vol. 25, pp. 241–262.

Grossman, S. J. and O. D. Hart (1980) 'Takeover Bids, the Free-Rider Problem, and the Theory of the Corporation', *Bell Journal of Economics*, Vol. 11, pp.42–64.

Hermalin, B. E. and M. S. Weisbach (1988) 'The determinants of board composition', *Rand Journal of Economics*, Vol. 19, pp. 95–112.

Hermalin, B. E. and M. S. Weisbach (1991) 'The effects of board composition and direct incentives on firm performance', *Financial Management*, Vol. 20, pp. 101–112.

Jensen, M. (1986) 'Agency Costs of Free Cash Flow, Corporate Finance and Takeovers', *American Economic Review*, Vol. 76, pp. 323–339.

Jensen, M. (1993) 'The modern industrial revolution, Exit, and the failure of internal control systems', *Journal of Finance*, Vol. 48, pp. 831–880

Jensen, M. C. and W. H. Meckling (1976) 'Theory of the Firm; Managerial Behavior, Agency costs and Ownership Structure', *Journal of Financial Economics*, pp. 305–360.

Jensen, M. C. and K. J. Murphy (1990a) 'CEO Incentives – It's not how much you pay, but how', *Journal of Applied Corporate Finance*, pp. 36–49.

Jensen, M. C. and K. J. Murphy (1990b) 'Performance pay and top management incentives', *Journal of Political Economy*, Vol. 98, No. 21, pp. 225–263.

Jensen, M. C. and R. S. Ruback (1983) 'The market for corporate control: The Scientific Evidence', *Journal of Financial Economics*, Vol. 11, pp 5–50.

Kaplan, S. and D. Reishus (1990) 'Outside directorships and corporate performance', *Journal of Financial Economics*, Vol. 27, pp 389–410.

Linderberg, E. B. and S. A. Ross (1981) 'Tobin's q ratio and industrial organization', *Journal of Business*, Vol. 54, pp. 1–32.

Lipton, M. and J. W. Lorsch (1992) 'A modest proposal for improved corporate governance', *Business Lawyer*, Vol. 48, pp 59–77.

McConnell, J. J. and H. Servaes (1990) 'Additional evidence on equity ownership and corporate value', *Journal of Financial Economics*, Vol. 27, pp. 595–612.

Morck, R., A. Shleifer and R. W. Vishny (1988a) 'Management ownership and market valuation: an empirical analysis', *Journal of Financial Economics*, Vol. 20, pp. 293–315.

Perfect, S. W. and K. Wiles (1994) 'Alternative constructions of Tobin's q: An empirical comparison', *Journal of Empirical Finance*, Vol. 1, pp. 313–341.

Rosenstein, S. and J. Wyatt, (1990) 'Outside directors, board independence, and shareholder wealth', *Journal of Financial Economics*, Vol. 26, pp. 175–191.

Shleifer, A. and R. W. Vishny (1986) 'Large Shareholder and Corporate Control', *Journal of Political Economy*, Vol. 94, pp. 461–488.

Scott, K. and W. Kleidon (1994) 'CEO performance, board types and board performance: A first cut', in *Institutional Investors and Corporate Governance*, Edited by Baums Theodor, pp. 181–199

Weisbach, M. S. (1988) 'Outside directors and CEO turnover', *Journal of Financial Economics*, Vol. 20, pp. 431–460.

Yermack, D. (1996) 'Higher market vauation of companies with a small board of directors', *Journal of Financial Economics*, Vol. 40, pp. 185–211.

Banks and Corporate Governance in Italy

ABSTRACT

The paper analyzes the role of banks in corporate governance in Italy. We first describe the corporate governance system that prevailed in Italy in the post-war period: a mix of devices which assigned a large role to State ownership, implicit rules based on trust and family relations. With the sole exception of Mediobanca, the role of banks in the governance of large sized firms was modest, despite the remarkable share of bank loans in corporate external financing. A major role in corporate governance was attributed to *Enti pubblici* (quasi-State administrative entities). This institutional setting allowed Italy to fully participate in the extraordinary growth of Europe through the 1950s–1960s. Thereafter, however, this system progressively degenerated, and Italy could maintain high economic growth mostly thanks to the success of small firms, frequently structured in Marshallian industrial districts. By drawing on ongoing research, we suggest that, together with financial links within extended families and local communities, small local banks (often organized as co-operatives) and individual business consultants (*commercialisti*) played an active role in governance of small firms in industrial districts.

Fabrizio Barca (1954–), M.Phil in Economics at the University of Cambridge (UK) in 1979, Division Chief at the Research Department of Bank of Italy since 1991.

Giovanni Ferri (1957–) joined the Research Department of the Bank of Italy in 1987 after completing his PhD at New York University. Since 1991 he has headed the Credit intermediaries Office. He specializes in monetary and credit economics and policy.

Nicola Pesaresi (1963–) joined the Banking and Financial Supervision Department of the Bank of Italy in 1991 after gaining his M.A. in Economics at Yale University. In 1994 he was seconded as a national expert to the European Commission (Directorate General IV – Competition) where he currently deals with the issue of State aid to financial institutions.

II. Banks and Corporate Governance in Italy: A Two-Tier Model

FABRIZIO BARCA, GIOVANNI FERRI AND NICOLA PESARESI

1. INTRODUCTION[1]

In most countries today, whether industrial, fast developing or transitional there is a growing awareness that the competitiveness of the economy depends, among other institutions, on 'corporate governance systems', namely on the rules and the institutions that take care of financing and allocating control over firms. Several factors help explain this trend: growing capital mobility offering alternatives for the investment of national savings, emergence of new technological paradigms demanding changes in the allocation of control, and the transformation process in Eastern Europe. In Italy, as in other European countries, further reasons for the current debate and for a growing pressure to reform existing institutions are the need to privatize State-owned corporations, due to their growing failure to deliver good performance, and the obstacles that small firms encounter in financing very fast growth.

In this paper, partly drawing on a growing body of empirical investigation,[2] we analyze the role played by banks in Italian corporate governance. In a world where contracts are incomplete, a conflict of interest arises between entrepreneurs – whether majority-stakeholders or managers; and investors – whether lenders or shareholders; the former needing certainty of control for their irreversible investments in human capital to be justified, the latter needing the opportunity to monitor entrepreneurs and to prevent them from 'abusing' their power of control. Banks can help in tackling this conflict, either by exerting some kind of monitoring as lenders and/or shareholders or by providing corporate finance services (e.g. as underwriters, fund managers, etc.) or by a combination of the two.

To understand the role of banks in the Italian corporate governance, we first take an historical perspective. We show that, in the post-war period, a mix of devices prevailed which assigned a large role to State ownership, implicit rules based on trust and family relations and contracts, especially in the form of pyramidal groups. The role of financial institutions, particularly of banks, in the governance of large sized firms was modest, despite the remarkable share of bank loans in corporate external financing (Section 2). We argue that the failure of large banks to play a relevant role in corporate governance was largely the result of the separation between bank and industry, introduced in the 1930s (Section 2.1): a large role in corporate governance was attributed to *Enti pubblici* (quasi-State administrative entities) endowed with a large influence on the design and implementation of economic policy measures (Section 2.2.1). The only exception was Mediobanca: established immediately after the war inside the framework of *Enti pubblici* as a medium-term lending institution, it soon became a major independent actor in preserving corporate control in large private industrial conglomerates (Section 2.2.2). It is then argued that this institutional setting allowed Italy to fully participate in the extraordinary growth of Europe in the fifteen years after the war. Thereafter, however, the system progressively degenerated: *Enti pubblici* and most State controlled banks became more and more subjugated to a political spoil system. At the same time, private conglomerates underwent a progressive downsizing *vis-à-vis* both the world markets and Italian manufacturing, and relying more and more on hierarchical group links to keep a stable control, they were mostly immune from the scrutiny of financial markets, even in the face of recurring crises (Section 2.3).

But this is hardly the whole story. It would indeed be difficult to gauge how, with such a system, Italy could have maintained a very high growth of GDP and productivity, even through the 1970s and 1980s. To explain that we need to bring into the picture small firms. During the 1960s, in fact, a system of small, innovative and export oriented manufacturing firms evolved, mostly in the North-Eastern and Central regions of the country, away from the North-West, the first area of industrialization at the turn of the century. By drawing on ongoing research we suggest that, together with financial links within extended families and local communities, local banks (often organized as co-operatives) played a relevant role in such development (Section 3).

In Section 4 we report evidence to support our claim that large banks have not exerted a proper monitoring role in the corporate governance of large firms (Section 4.1) but that, at the same time, individual business consultants (*commercialisti*) and local banks played a more active role *vis-à-vis* small firms in industrial districts (Section 4.2).

2. A Quasi-State System Of Large Banks

Almost all large Italian banks have long been owned or controlled by the State, mostly through *Enti pubblici*, the quasi-State entities to which, since the 1930s, a large power was entrusted to allocate scarce capital to strategic sectors.

Because of their ancillary role, we will label large banks the 'entendance suivante' of *Enti pubblici*.

2.1. *The Backlash of the 1930s on Universal Banks: State Control on Large Banks*

At the end of the nineteenth century and until the Great Crash of the 1930s, a few German-style universal banks – operating through a mix of credit relations and equity subscriptions – were at the core of corporate governance in Italy. They acted to overcome the scanty primitive accumulation of capital, and later as the channel through which diffuse, fragmented savings could be funnelled into equity. During the prolonged industrial crisis of the late 1920s and early 1930s, this universal bank-based corporate governance degenerated: a progressive intermingling of interests between banks and large industrial corporations took place. Corporate crises were regularly dealt with and resolved by the banks themselves. The stock market failed to take off. Corporate control became more and more concentrated, while large industrial and financial conglomerates grew based on cross shareholdings.

With the stock market crash of 1929 and the following financial instability, the State took over the leading universal banks in order to prevent a major breakdown of the entire economy. This paved the way for the most sweeping reallocation of ownership and control in the history of Italy, and above all for the State to assume a central role in Italian capitalism. At the same time the banking law was deeply changed: (a) banks were prevented from holding shares in industrial companies; (b) short-term credit, assigned to commercial banks, was separated from long-term financing, which was assigned to special credit institutions. The end of the universal bank experience was not accompanied by any attempt to revive the stock market: a primary role in corporate financing remained with the banks, now mostly under State control.

2.2. *The Post-War Model: Conception and Success*[3]

The end of the war, the liberation of the nation from fascism, the drafting of a new constitution did not significantly alter the institutional structure of Italian capitalism. Lack of a market for corporate control, an inadequate system of directors' duties, lack of monitoring of their behavior – especially in the face of pyramidal groups – inadequate monitoring by the banking system: the Economic Committee of the Constitutional Assembly clearly perceived all of these features of the Italian corporate governance, but no reform was implemented.[4] Unlike the other two powers defeated in the war, Germany and Japan, no significant change took place within Italy, either in the public administration, or in the 'rules of the game' of the labour, product and financial markets.[5]

The working of institutions, however, also depends on the social and political context in which they operate: in Italy the change of this context allowed the pre-war institutions to perform a very different role. Democracy, the rise of a new governing class and the choice in favour of European integration and of free trade, together with the persistence of low wages, allowed the corporate governance model created in the 1930s to fully express its potential. In particular, the pre-existing system of State control based on *Enti pubblici* played a crucial role: it gave a new generation of managers, mostly untainted by involvement with the fascist regime, the chance to acquire control of large, emerging enterprises. A sense of mission linked to the post-war reconstruction climate helped to make up for the lack of a monitoring mechanism in the model. The fact that the main strategic choices were rather clear-cut (e.g. providing the country with an adequate and stable supply of energy, developing and modernizing the steel industry to suit the needs of the engineering sector, building a highway system, etc.) helped the system to deliver good results.

2.2.1. *Enti pubblici:* Large Banks as 'entendance suivante' for their Economic Policy

In the immediate aftermath of the war an intense debate took place over which function IRI – the largest State industrial and financial holding, controlling 216 companies and more than 135,000 employees – should play. In July 1944, facing US representatives' doubts on IRI, Donato Menichella, one of the designers of IRI back in 1933 who would soon become governor of the Bank of Italy, addressed a report to Captain Andrew Kamark, the representative for IRI of the Finance Sub-Commission of the Allied Control Commission. In arguing that the public ownership of banks and industries did not reflect the fascist regime's bent for planning but could serve the purpose of reconstruction, he offered a severe judgement on Italian financiers as a group: 'Italy has never had a class of financiers who loved banking for banking's sake; that is, who were disposed to invest their money in bank shares and to operate banks with the sole aim of earning the largest possible dividends from those shares. Only industrial groups have manifested any interest, at various times, in acquiring stakes in the leading banks'.[6] Menichella maintained that the impossibility of finding skillful hands to run IRI's banks and industrial firms through private ownership, had compelled the government to transform IRI into a permanent structure.

The view prevailed that *Enti pubblici* were an indispensable tool to mobilize capital and allocate it to capable hands in order to make up at once for the failure of other governance institutions and of the Italian public administration. It had already done so at the end of 1945, when a plan had to be devised on how to make use of the funds and resources unilaterally provided by the US government; it was up to IRI experts to draw the plan. Similarly, later in 1945 and in 1948, they wrote the preliminary framework for the Italian implementation of the Marshall plan. In February 1948 a decree law restored IRI to its operational status and above all strengthened its independence from the government.

In IRI's corporate governance it was management who exercised the power of control, and no monitoring was performed. IRI was formally subject to the control of a Committee of Ministers mandated to set general strategy, to approve any increase in endowment funds and to elect the group's chairman, its deputy chairman and its director general. The purchase or sale of equity participation beyond a given ceiling no longer required the authorization of the Finance Ministry. The group's financial statement had to be approved by the government and be later communicated to Parliament, but the latter had no power to intervene in operations. The 13-member IRI board of directors included representatives of several ministries (Treasury, Finance, Industry), of the Bank of Italy and the Accountant General. IRI's statute specified no purposes or objectives, but in practice during these years the Institute acted as a technical advisory body on economic policy. Memos produced by IRI bureaus reveal top-management's clear awareness of the main investment priorities for national reconstruction, focusing on basic industry, capital goods and infrastructure.[7] The 'residual right of control' was tightly in the hands of the management. It was up to them, not to political tutors, to devise the strategies for rebuilding a modern industrial apparatus in steel, ship-building and engineering, and to develop major infrastructure (e.g. highways, the telephone network, etc.).

In 1953 a new State holding company, the National Hydrocarbon Agency (ENI), to operate in the oil, petrochemical and, later, the chemical sector, was created mostly as the result of the efforts of Enrico Mattei (a self-made businessman, formerly a commander of Catholic partisan units in the Resistance). Mattei's programme was strongly opposed by private industry and by the major international oil companies. In Mattei's view, earnings from the exploitation of natural resources could be devoted to the development of an advanced energy industry; but, for that to be feasible, resources had to be managed neither by small, private businessmen with narrow interests nor by government bureaucrats (as under a regime of State-regulated concessions to private firms), but by technicians at the helm of 'State-owned public companies'.

Politicians were receptive enough to approve *Enti pubblici*'s plans. Even more importantly, in these early years they neither tried to extract private benefits from their power, nor interfered with the managers' decisions by pursuing their own agenda. Influential politicians, mostly from the ruling Christian Democrat (DC) party, aimed, instead, at the general goal of making use of *Enti pubblici* to achieve as high growth and development as possible, which in turn would have consolidated their power.

In conclusion, with the post-war development, *Enti pubblici* came to play a much greater role than before: they were no longer devised 'just' to make up for the weakness of the financial system; they had become at the same time institutions which entrusted capital in the hands of 'public managers' and directly set strategies for the industrial system. Two relevant issues were left open by this framework, which would later negatively impinge on the Italian economy. The first one had to do with the lack of monitoring of the system of *Enti pubblici* and with its inherent bias towards management's tyranny; the second with the link between *Enti pubblici* and the banking system. We will consider the former in the next section. Let us now briefly discuss the latter.

Together with broadening the role of *Enti pubblici*, the choice was made not to introduce major changes in the role of banks, as formulated in the 1930s. The negative assessment of the entrepreneurial skills of the 'class of financiers' (see Menichella above), went together with the strong belief that the risk was still present in Italy of a degeneration of bank/industry relations and that banks retained the potential to provide the financing for 'barbaric' takeovers of private companies. IRI and ENI themselves were then considered to be very important stabilizing factors of the ownership and control structure through their direct holding of about half of all medium and large enterprises of the country.[8] Stabilization was further pursued by retaining separation between short-term and medium/long-term lending, and by basically preventing commercial banks from developing the capability to become involved in corporate long-term investments.

Strong links between *Enti pubblici* and the banks were assured by the fact that IRI directly controlled the three largest former universal banks rescued in the 1930s, and by interlocking directorates (Ferri, Trento, 1997). Besides, *Enti pubblici* enjoyed a large autonomy in obtaining financing on the financial markets by issuing bonds practically assimilated to government securities. *Enti pubblici*'s managers, largely immune from political control, had a grip on large banks, while the reverse seldom happened: large banks were like an 'entendance suivante', a tool used by *Enti pubblici* to finance their industrial strategies.

It is hard to assess whether the great concern for stabilization was well-founded. There is no doubt, though, that the choice of retaining separation between bank and industry, while not making any move towards building alternative institutions of corporate governance, kept the banking industry in an infant state, in which very little 'corporate' or 'financial'[9] credit was offered. This failure, particularly detrimental for new and/or fast-growing firms, had only limited negative effects during the 1950s. A very high and steady economic growth provided firms with a stable cash-flow and with certain prospects. Furthermore, as we shall see in Section 3, informal institutions (families and communities built around shared values) yielded diffuse monitoring and local banks provided the means for financing a growing number of small-size firms.

But the limits of the banking system came to the fore later on, as soon as rising wages and exogenous shocks on relative prices shrank and made corporate cash-flows more volatile. These features of the financial system are underscored by the largest attempt ever made to fill the gap: the creation of Mediobanca.

2.2.2. *Mediobanca and the Financing of the Large Private Corporations*[10]

There is one notable exception to the general picture of major banks in Italy. Mediobanca, a large investment bank, was originally established as a satellite of public banks but soon gained full independence and managed to complement and support the mix of family, coalition and group control of large private firms. The initial lack of competition, self-perpetuating via reputation and the slackness of State-owned banks, created a strong incentive for Mediobanca to invest in monitoring, but, at the same time, provided little incentive for it to step in when signals of corporate distress arose. This situation also biased Mediobanca's function towards preserving and consolidating the implicit rules that hold together the existing corporate ownership and control structures, rather than opening them up.

The blueprint of Mediobanca was Mattioli's (Comit's CEO) idea. Having experienced the hard times of the 1920-1930s when even Comit had to beg for State rescue, and foretelling that it might soon need again to transform short into long-term corporate loans, Mattioli further predicted that the help of a friendly long-term lending bank would be needed. It would then be best to establish a sister long-term bank controlled by Comit. With the help of this bank Comit would have continued offering firms a whole range of corporate finance services spanning from short- and long-term loans to advice and to underwriting in the stock exchange. The final decision to make Mediobanca owned not only by Comit but also by Credit and Banco di Roma partly spoiled Mattioli's plan, ruling out a full integration between Comit and Mediobanca. If the imperfect integration meant for Mattioli devising the in-house strategy of rolling over short-term credit, it also implied that Mediobanca had to rely more on information acquired as a shareholder rather than on daily information gained by managing borrowing firms' payments. The lack of vertical integration with Comit, because of the missing strong fiduciary link between the two, also induced Mediobanca to re-focus its business, by establishing its own links with selected customers.

Mediobanca, under the guidance of Enrico Cuccia, would inevitably deviate from the original blueprint to become over time a merchant bank of the French type. Its specialization as a care-taker for few large private industrial groups and its attempts to guarantee their stability of control with as little capital as possible can easily be explained by the scarcity of Mediobanca's capital endowment.

2.3. Degeneration of the Post-war Model: Failure[11]

At the end of the 1950s changes took place revealing the weakness of the corporate governance system, and particularly the inadequate role played by banks. Since 1958, rapidly rising wages steadily reduced profit margins and corporate cash-flows; the stability of ownership and control of private corporations were increasingly challenged, often through the use of financing provided by the banking system, in spite of existing regulation;[12] rather than enacting monitoring devices, the party in power, namely the ruling DC, slowly turned *Enti pubblici* into its tools for achieving 'public targets', such as the development of the Southern regions, the reduction of unemployment and changes in industrial relations.

Already in the early 1950s, in conferences and studies by leaders of the CISL, the Catholic trade union linked to DC, it had been argued that IRI should withdraw from the Italian industrial employers' confederation, Confindustria, in order to better promote 'new industrial relations', with greater workers' involvement. It had been maintained that public enterprises should also aim at promoting the economic development of backward Southern Italy.[13] Between 1955 and 1963, in the long years during which the alliance between DC and the Socialist party (PSI) was conceived and shaped, major changes were indeed introduced in the system of *Enti pubblici* which paved the way for their degeneration. In December 1954 a governmental plan was approved which assigned State-owned companies a major role in developing the South. In 1956, a Ministry for State Shareholding was created to exercise political oversight over IRI and ENI. Rather than providing clear-cut *ex-ante* monitoring rules, the Ministry turned out to be the locus for carrying on a continuous bargaining among the interests of various politicians and those of 'public mangers'. In 1957, IRI companies left Confindustria: from then onwards, two entities, one for IRI and one for ENI, engaged in collective bargaining with the trade unions. Since 1957, ENI and IRI were also compelled by law 675 to invest 40 per cent of resources in Southern Italy.

Decelerating economic growth, the persistent backwardness of the South and the problems caused in the economic structure by abrupt changes in relative prices (in both wages and raw materials) further helped tilt the guidelines for *Enti pubblici* from getting as high a return as possible from long-term investments, to 'public interest' objectives such as employment, developing Southern regions and rescuing ailing private firms. According to the new model, as rationalized by Saraceno (1975), 'public managers' were assigned these exogenous goals (or 'improper costs' as they were called) and were asked to achieve them in the most efficient way. As a result of that, the task of truly monitoring their choices, rather than of being properly organized, was made even more difficult than before – by the difficulties inherent in discriminating between the negative effects on returns stemming from those 'improper costs' and those stemming from the lack of care or lack of diligence of managers. As debt and losses mounted, it was hard to discriminate between the costs of the social objectives imposed by the government and those due to mismanagement.

The degeneration of the new monitoring mechanism was exacerbated by the growing failure of the market to gain political control. From 1948 to 1992 the government was permanently controlled by alliances among an unchanging group of parties. In the first 10–15 years governing parties had an attitude of 'benign neglect' towards the top management of State-owned enterprises; but since the end of the 1950s top managers were chosen or promoted mostly thanks to their political links; a system of loyalty developed based on the exchange of monetary and non-monetary benefits.[14] Nor did the opposition perform its function as a watchdog over public enterprises; indeed most measures on behalf of the public enterprises, including subsidies, were approved unanimously in Parliament.[15]

The crisis that these two factors provoked in State-owned corporations also affected the private sector. It upset the equilibrium of the overall system of corporate governance in large enterprise. Relations between public and private enterprise, which were competitive in the 1950s, also became collusive: the government would rush to rescue private companies that threatened to fail. The shortcomings of Italy's system of private corporate governance, emerging at the end of an exceptional period of low wages, were increasingly dealt with by reallocating to the State the ownership of ailing companies. This 'controller of last resort' function would take on added importance in the course of the crisis of the 1970s.

Banks were indirectly protected by the increasing extension of implicit or explicit State guarantees behind large enterprises. Relations between banks and enterprises became looser, as banks adopted the approach of the 'insurer', by splitting among them the financing needs of a single borrower. Banks also relied to a large extent on collateral guarantees being provided by borrowers. Limited competition allowed banks for the most part to stay profitable. Even though large firms were becoming more and more leveraged, State interventions were expected to rescue endangered companies to which banks had wrongly lent. The most serious crisis was that of the chemical industry. Two among the largest long-term lending banks (IMI and Icipu) came to be heavily exposed *vis-à-vis* ailing private chemical conglomerates that had launched untimely investment, before the oil shocks hit the world economy. IMI was rescued by a special intervention on the part of the National Postal Savings Bank; Icipu was merged into the better capitalized Crediop. Even the crisis of the 1970s was thus solved owing to over-stretched State interventions; the time for banks to become actors of corporate governance was again postponed.

Only with the deep recession of the early 1990s had banks had to tackle wide corporate distress, with no help from the State. Taking unprecedented steps, many banks acquired joint control of companies in distress. Before commenting on such recent events in the final section, we must turn to the other component of the Italian banking system: local banks.

3. The 'Unexpected' Second Tier: Local Banks

With the bulk of large banks under State ownership or control, private banking in Italy has come to be identified more and more with local banks. The evolution of these banks is not only relevant *per se* but also for its possible links with the parallel evolution of a decentralized industry based on small- and medium-sized enterprises (SMEs). While growing attention has been devoted, both at home and abroad, to the sparkling growth of the Italian SMEs since the late 1960s, especially in the industrial districts, the likely interactions with local banks have so far been disregarded. Yet shared values and traditions which reportedly proved so important in allowing exceptional flexibility to the Italian SMEs, both in the labour market and in various stages of production and trade, seem to give rise to fiduciary networks which are hardly irrelevant for the operation of a local bank. As Giacomo Becattini (1991) remarks: "The local bank is an organism born and bred in the district, that is very closely linked with local entrepreneurs (and often with other local and political lobbies) and deeply involved in local life, which it knows in detail, and to which it gives direction to a considerable extent. An institution of this sort can give a much greater weight to personal qualities of whoever demands credit, and to the specific prospects of a given investment, than can a bank which is less well rooted in the local environment. Hence, there is an extra thrust to accumulation in the district, whatever forms – usually short-term – the credit may take" (p. 71). It is time to follow Becattini's suggestion. In order to do so, let us first consider the main features of Italian small firms.

3.1. *Small Flexible Firms: A Local Community Business*

SMEs have always been an important part of Italian manufacturing, since the post-war reconstruction. During the 1950s, owing to both domestic and international investments, within the Italian industry there was a strengthening of large production units, featuring universal application of the Fordist organization of labour. Yet this expansion did not produce an increase in the share of industrial employment accounted for by large plants: the share at plants with more than 500 employees declined from 25.4 per cent in 1951 to 21.5 per cent in 1961. Thus the development of large firms was accompanied by the significant growth of small firms with 10–50 employees, whose employment share rose from 14.1 to 18.9 per cent during that decade and continued to rise in the 1960s.

By the end of this period, union militancy shook the whole of Europe. The move was especially powerful in Italy, chiefly in large factories that had grown up during the boom years. These trends were accompanied by others that radically altered entrepreneurs' economic frame of reference:

(i) *an increasing specialization/diversification of demand*, with growing consumer demand for differentiated, quality products, fostering market entry of new firms (Scherer, 1980).

(ii) *a greater potential flexibility of capital due to technical progress* shortening the actual length of the individual production phases and thus reducing the 'minimum efficient scale'.

(iii) *greater diffusion of individual-specific skills* making the efficient allocation of control more widespread, i.e. the optimal firm size smaller (Brynjolfsson, 1990; Barca, 1994).

Accordingly, Brusco, Sabel (1981), Sabel (1982) and Piore, Sabel (1984) interpret the Italian case as one of flexible specialization, arguing that the development of SMEs in the 1970s was not a residual phenomenon stemming from the crisis of large corporations but, rather, the result of an emergent model of work organization. Individual work phases, even highly specialized ones, are assigned to separate plants run by independent SMEs, which become part of a large number of different production processes. Thus, for the same aggregate demand, average capacity utilization is higher. The goal of manufacturing a given product at the minimum cost is replaced by that of manufacturing a given selection of products at the lowest cumulative cost.

Examining the systematic component in the increasing share of output produced by SMEs reveals that such a rise was indeed due to a growing advantage of the small scale. The growth of smaller firms in the 1970s is found to have involved both 'traditional' sectors producing consumer goods and the rest of industry, while it was largely independent of the decentralization of large production units. These results fit the flexible specialization model. Further support for this interpretation is provided by the following facts: in contrast with the downward trend of larger firms' investment, that of SMEs expanded continuously throughout the period; a large part (20 per cent for firms with more than 20 but less than 200 employees) of SMEs' output is sold on foreign markets; the sustained growth of SMEs in the period has been coupled with a continuous expansion of employment; a wage gap exists between small and large companies of the same industrial sector which can be linked to factors such as lower job dissatisfaction and a trade-off between current wages and learning on the job (Barca, Magnani, 1989).

Although SMEs do not require, except when growing very fast, a degree of separation between ownership and control of the kind needed by large firms, a degree of separation is still necessary in the small business sector. This has been achieved mostly through informal corporate governance institutions: capital of enlarged families is often gathered by the entrepreneur, and trust is relied upon as the main tool to cope with the potential conflict of interest between the entrepreneur and the investors; 'coalition control' models are also spread, whereby the entrepreneur and non-controlling owners share common values. But that capital provided by banks has also played a substantial role, through monitoring devices idiosyncratic to each local district.

3.2. Community Business and Community Finance: Banks and Commercialisti

According to the mainstream theory of intermediation, banks' very role is to partly overcome the asymmetric information problems of borrowers who would not otherwise qualify for funding from external lenders. If it were not for banks, such borrowers would be forced to abandon even profitable investment projects or start only those for which self-financing suffices.[16] By collecting private information on potential and actual customers, banks specialize in screening credit-worthy applicants. They therefore perform an important role *vis-à-vis* little publicly known entrepreneurs, a role that would prove prohibitively expensive to non-specialists. Furthermore, exerting continuous monitoring over borrowers, banks are well placed to ensure that borrowers put funds to good use.

SMEs, which are usually younger than average firms, are natural candidates to suffer from lack of external finance due to inadequate information. Local banks, when belonging to the same community in which SMEs are established, may have an advantage in screening such firms. In particular, they could benefit from the fact that members of the local community consider themselves as effective 'stakeholders' in the bank and help the local bank better perform screening, monitoring and enforcement. According to Banerjee, Besley, Guinnane (1994), Besley, Coate (1995), owing to information spillovers, the members of a local community enjoy an informational advantage *vis-à-vis* external agents with regard to other members of their own community. They stress that this incentive mechanism may prove more effective when community members are also shareholders in the bank – typically a credit cooperative – thereby undergoing joint liability.

When banks fail to play a monitoring role, an alternative monitoring mechanism might have been at work based on skilled workers complementing arm's-length oriented banks. According to this hypothesis – a 'trilateral agency system' – banks, lacking adequate in-house monitoring capabilities, have relied on worker and community monitoring to decide whether to step in and force reallocation. In dense industrial areas, the existence of potential alternative entrepreneurs (possibly inside the firm) would have allowed banks to minimize losses resulting from firm bankruptcy. Stability of control assured by governance according to implicit rules, in turn, would have given workers an incentive to accept low wages in exchange for medium-term training. Workers, in their turn, would have had an incentive to signal bad performance insofar as bad performance was firm-specific and it did not affect other firms of the area where they could have been employed.

Available information on Italy indeed provides some confirmation of a preferential link between SMEs and local banks. In the very same geographic areas in which flexible SMEs of industrial districts have been particularly successful, local banks have also been particularly active: in particular, the industrial districts of the North-East have had the largest diffusion of rural credit coops of the Raiffeisen type (*casse rurali ed artigiane*) together with that of other larger urban mutual banks (*banche popolari*), while districts of the Centre have seen the largest presence of local savings banks (*casse di risparmio*). North-Eastern and Central regions had smaller sized firms and much smaller sized banks (Conti, Ferri, 1997). As Cesarini, Ferri, Giardino (1997) and Conti, Ferri (1997) document, there is also evidence that such networks of local banks may have exerted a positive effect on the SME-centred model of economic growth. In particular, municipal areas in industrial districts appear to have been endowed with a larger presence of banks at the time or even before their takeoff (in the 1960s and 1970s) and local banks gave a particularly high contribution to build such endowment.[17] Furthermore, Ferri, Mattesini (1997) show that, after controlling for other factors, growth of *per capita* income was higher in the Italian provinces possessing a larger presence of credit cooperatives.

But further direct evidence is needed to show that small banks do indeed exert tighter monitoring on firms. This is what we do in the next section, by contrasting the behaviour of large and small banks.

4. Empirical Evidence on Banks in the Market for Corporate Control[18]

It is our contention that, while as a whole the Italian financial structure is more similar to those of Germany and Japan than to the US one, the actual relationship between large Italian banks and firms resembles more the US situation than the German–Japanese one. The following section presents evidence on this and evaluates the negligible role of banks in the market for corporate control. On the contrary, as we argued above, there are good reasons to expect that the involvement of local banks in the corporate governance of

TABLE 1

Direct ownership of listed companies in major industrial countries (percentage on national total)

	USA	Japan	Germany	Italy		UK
				All listed companies	Listed co.s except banks	
Financial institutions	39.8	47.0	19.5	12.0	4.0	60.8
Banks	0.3	25.2	8.9	10.9	2.8	0.9
Insurance companies	5.2	17.3	10.6	0.8	0.8	18.4
Pension funds	24.8	0.9	–	–	–	30.4
Other financial co.s	9.5	3.6	–	0.3	0.4	11.1
Non-financial owners	53.5	48.8	62.8	83.7	90.6	26.9
Non-financial comp.s	–	25.1	39.2	21.6	27.3	3.6
State	–	0.6	6.8	28.0	26.8	2.0
Households and unidentified	53.5	23.1	16.8	34.1	36.6	21.3
Foreign owners	6.7	4.2	17.7	4.3	5.3	12.3
Total	100.0	100.0	100.0	100.0	100.0	100.0

Source: Barca, Bianchi, et al. (1994).

small firms, to which they specialize their lending, is not negligible; to this issue we will turn in Section 4.2.

4.1. *The Feeble Relationship Between Large Banks and Large Firms*

The deep involvement of banks in corporate financing is clear in view of the large share of bank loans in corporate external finance. As of the end of 1992, bank debt reached 33.4 per cent of firms' liabilities. Excluding shares from the total, a little part of which is traded in organized markets, bank financing reaches 60 per cent of external funds accruing to firms. In spite of the relevance of bank financing in firms' liabilities in Italy *vis-à-vis* other countries (Mayer, 1990), customer relationships tend to be weak and banks are seldom insider to firms. In our view, four main features of the Italian system account for such a situation:

1. *Negligible banks' shareholding in non-financial firms.* Up to 1994, shareholding in non-financial firms was substantially banned for commercial banks. The fact that corporate shareholding by banks and by other financial institutions is relatively small in Italy clearly emerges from Table 1, reporting the distribution of direct ownership of listed companies in the five major industrial countries. All financial institutions hold between 40 and 60 per cent in the USA, Japan and the UK – and some 20 per cent in Germany, where

proxy-voting helps sustain banks' corporate governance – while in Italy the percentage drops to 12 per cent and even to 4 per cent once shareholding in listed banks (over-represented in the stock exchange with respect to other countries) is properly excluded. Overall, shareholding by Italian banks comes closer to the situation in the US and UK than to Germany and Japan. In addition, proxy-voting is not allowed in Italy. The minor role of banks (2.8 per cent, excluding shares held in other banks) is not compensated, as elsewhere (e.g. USA), by other financial institutions.[19]

2. *Multiple banking.* Multiple bank borrowing is a long-standing feature for Italian firms. After taking the weighted average across classes of borrowers ranked by size of total loans granted to them by all banks, it turns out that each lira lent in 1987 was granted on average by 21 banks, while this number declined to 14 in 1994, mainly as the result of the shrinking average number of banks for larger size classes of borrowers.

3. *Large use of current account overdrafts and separation of short from long-term financing.* Whereas special credit institutions lent mostly in the form of mortgage loans, current account lending is the most common contract for loans at commercial banks. At the end of 1992, the total share of loans granted on current account loans reached 84.3 per cent (summing up current account advances and overdraft current account loans). Current accounts allow banks to call back loans. This type of contract is therefore particularly conducive to exit and banks may expect to be able to timely call back loans to firms facing bad times. Of course, this reasoning suffers from a fallacy of composition, but the readily available option for exit offered by this type of contract provides no strong individual incentive to monitoring to the various banks engaged in lending to a firm. This, combined with the large extent of multiple bank borrowing, makes an explosive mix against building strong long-term bank/firm relations. In addition, until 1994, the regulatory-induced divide of the market between short-term lending by commercial banks and long-term loans by special credit institutions traditionally segmented information between the two categories of intermediaries.

4. *Large extent of loan collateralization.* Collateralization was almost full at special credit institutions and sizable (about half) at commercial banks. According to Borio (1995) the share of collateralized loans in Italy is high compared to other G-10 countries. From our perspective, high collateral may put less pressure on banks to monitor borrowers.

These four main features show that banks had very little incentive to develop stable long-term ties with firms and to become insiders. In fact, building such ties is costly for a bank and doing this with firms that will likely turn soon to other banking partners is discouraged by the expectation of sunk costs.

To assess the involvement of banks in corporate governance in Italy, three questionnaires were also devised in the 1993 Bank of Italy research project:

the first submitted to all banks (but the small credit cooperative banks; see Capra et al. (1994)), the second addressed to a group of merchant banks (see Capra et al. (1994)) and the third submitted to a group of SMEs (see Barca, Bianco et al., 1994). The bank survey allows us to assess the involvement of the average bank in ownership changes for customers and contrast it with the behaviour of a group of 'more active' banks.[20] The modest involvement of banks in corporate changes is confirmed by several factors. First, only one bank out of four holds a database keeping track of customer's ownership changes. Second, rather than knowing of it in advance, over 60 per cent of banks in more than one third of occurrences learn of ownership changes after the contract has been signed.

In addition banks reportedly do not revise loan contracts when control over the firm shifts from the hands of the old entrepreneur to another member of the family exercising control. Such behaviour appears unwarranted, considering that there is no guarantee that the firm's performance will continue to be the same when its control shifts from father to son. It is also a noticeable feature that 'more active' banks are readier to do the revision. Furthermore, banks offer limited consulting services to firms undergoing ownership change. In more than 1/3 of the cases, only 6 per cent of the banks search for a buyer, only 5 per cent are given responsibility to evaluate the firm, only 4 per cent are given responsibility to take care of bargaining (or to write prospectuses), only 3 per cent organize buy-out deals and only 1 per cent supply fiscal/legal advice or help search for new managers.

Additional evidence on the weakness of bank/firm relations derives from observing that Italian banks seldom contribute to choose administrators and finance managers at borrowing firms: almost 90 per cent of them have never done this; on the contrary, some 6 per cent of the banks are most active in this respect. Furthermore, banks were asked to report what they normally do when firms come under stress. The answers are in line with our expectation: Italian banks are not particularly active in trying to take the firm out of the crisis as much as they are active in attempting to recover their loans. When a temporary crisis occurs, banks generally suggest financial restructuring to the firm, but seldom offer consulting for share issuing of the firm by incumbent shareholders, gather funds to support the sale, suggest share-capital restructuring, find a possible buyer, and almost never suggest new managers able to carry out restructuring or offer consulting for intergenerational transfers of control or for the outright sale of the firm (Table 2).

In the case of possibly terminal crises, banks' propensity to start action against borrower firms is sensitive to the amount and type of collateral. The share of banks starting legal procedures, leading to firms' bankruptcy, is low when loans are backed by collateral, and strongly increases otherwise. Finally, banks do not seem to play an active role in the efficient reallocation of control

TABLE 2

What do banks do when borrowing firms undergo a temporary crisis? (percentages on total)

	Suggest financial restruct.	Suggest share-cap restruct.	Suggest new managers	Advise intergener. transfers	Advise outright sale	Find buyer	Finance sale	Advise to recap.
(Almost) never	17.1	70.9	85.1	89.3	84.4	79.1	50.4	53.7
Less than 1/3 of the cases	22.6	21.1	12.8	8.0	11.8	17.2	40.1	30.7
1/3 to 2/3 of the cases	22.1	4.5	2.1	2.4	3.1	2.7	6.5	7.8
More than 2/3 of the cases	15.1	1.4	0.0	0.0	0.0	0.7	2.7	2.7
(Almost) always	23.1	2.1	0.0	0.3	0.7	0.3	0.3	5.1
Total	100.0	100.0	100.0	100.0	100.0	100.0	100.0	100.0

Source: Questionnaire to banks, Capra et al. (1994).

TABLE 3

How often do banks do the following against bankrupt firms? (percentages on total)

	Search for buyer		Finance acquisition	
	More active	All	More active	All
(Almost) never	62.5	72.2	58.3	44.7
(<1/3)	25.0	23.5	29.2	44.5
(1/3–2/3)	8.3	2.0	12.5	8.4
(>2/3)	4.2	1.0	0.0	1.7
(Almost) always	0.0	1.3	0.0	0.7
Total	100.0	100.0	100.0	100.0
t-statistic	1.3		1.1	
% rejection level	10		14	

Source: Questionnaire to banks, Capra et al. (1994).

over bankrupt firms. Almost three banks out of four never search for a buyer, although one bank out of two declares it often finances the acquisition (Table 3).[21]

The survey questionnaire directed to firms (some 280 SMEs selected in five Italian regions[22]) confirms the extremely limited involvement of banks in soliciting and financing ownership changes: they would be active only in the case of a liquidity crisis. As to the financing of acquisitions, bank credit, although the most important source of external funds (9.9 per cent of total financing), plays a minor part (17 per cent) of total financing.

TABLE 4

Consulting services for ownership changes to a group of SMEs (percentage on total)

Institutions	Search for buyer–seller	Evaluate target firm	Legal and fiscal consult.	Bargain	Financial plan for acquisit.	Using at least one intermed.
Banks	0.7	0.0	0.0	0.7	0.7	2.2
Special credit institutions	0.0	0.0	0.0	0.0	0.7	0.7
Other financial intermediaries	2.2	1.5	1.5	1.5	1.5	3.7
Legal and fiscal consultants	7.4	16.3	44.4	14.8	0.7	50.4
Public instit. and consortia	0.0	0.7	0.0	0.0	0.0	0.7
Auditing firms	0.0	3.0	1.5	0.0	0.0	3.7
Using at least one service	10.4	20.0	45.2	16.3	3.7	52.6

Source: Barca, Bianco et al. (1994).

Only 52.6 per cent of firms involved (actively or passively) in ownership changes avail themselves of even one service among a large number of consulting services potentially supplied by intermediaries and institutions (Table 4). *Commercialisti* (individual business consultants) rather than banks are by far the most involved: 50.4 per cent of firms involved in ownership change use at least one service supplied by them. Not surprisingly, the bulk of the *commercialisti*'s lead stems from fiscal and legal consulting (used by 44.4 per cent of firms). It is instead surprising that *commercialisti* play a much more active role than banks and other financial intermediaries in supplying services such as: searching for buyer/seller; evaluating target firms; bargaining during the acquisition.

4.2. The Strength Of Local Banks

We now turn to analyzing the special features of the 26 'more active' banks. This group consists of 12 small-sized (local) banks, 10 Italian subsidiaries of foreign banks, 1 major private long-term bank and only 3 medium-large commercial banks. Subsidiaries of foreign banks and small local banks are greatly over-represented in the group.

Our working hypothesis is that more active banks are more involved in ownership changes because they perform some type of corporate governance on borrowing firms. In turn, this likely requires stronger bank/firm relations than at the other banks. Indeed, we have already come across some interesting indications suggesting that these banks possess more information on customers and use it better. As we have seen, more active banks are readier to revise the loan contract in the face of ownership changes; we also know that they more frequently start non-judiciary procedures against firms in crisis, which may be

TABLE 5

Leadership in debt restructuring of industrial groups*

Type of leader	Number of institutions	Number of industrial groups
Domestic origin/control	20	24
– Commercial banks	9	12
– Law and account. firms, non-fin. institutions	6	6
– Merchant banks	5	7
– privately controlled	3	4
– bank controlled	2	3
Foreign origin/control	2	6
– Bank	1	3
– Merchant banks	1	3
Total	22	30

* Restructuring plans undertaken or being set by the end of 1993 with known leader. The discrepancy between the sum of items and the total for industrial groups is due to co-leaderships.
Source: Capra et al. (1994).

associated with debt restructuring (Generale, Gobbi, 1995); from Table 3 we see that they search more frequently for buyers of bankrupt firms, although they are not more active in financing the acquisition. In addition, data on leaderships of major corporate debt restructurings during the 1992–3 economic recession show that the banks of this group were quite active. It turns out that banking groups led 17 out of the 30 in debt restructuring for which a leader was specified: 12 Italian commercial banks, 3 foreign banks and 2 merchant banking subsidiaries of Italian banks. The four more active banking groups in debt restructuring all belong to our group and led 13 out of the 17 restructuring (Table 5).

Furthermore, we know that more active banks issue more loan guarantees than other banks and grant a larger share of loans without collateral, suggesting that they rely more on corporate governance (Table 6). In addition, more active banks tend to require less collateral when they finance buy-outs and buy-ins: the share of banks accepting to provide such finance without collateral in 30 per cent of the cases or above is approximately 30 per cent among more active banks whereas it is only 16 per cent among other banks; the average share of such financing not backed by collateral is 13.0 for the former banks and 7.0 for the latter.

Considering finally that the lead of the more active banks on the others could also depend on human capital endowments, we asked banks for information on their personnel's skill and level of education. It turns out that bank management holds a higher degree of education at more active banks.

TABLE 6

Bank collateralization of loans (percentage on total as of December 1992)

Extent of collateral backing					
Full collateral		Partial collateral		No collateral	
More active	All	More active	All	More active	All
27.2	32.5	15.1	15.7	57.7	51.8
t-statistic	4.5		1.3		3.7
% rejection lev.	1		11		1

Source: Capra et al. (1994).

5. Whither Banks Now?

We have seen that the role of banks and other financial institutions in the Italian corporate governance system has been traditionally very limited. It is our contention that weak bank/firm relations were consistent with the system of corporate governance which prevailed in Italy after the second world war. Family and coalition devices of corporate control both reduced corporate transparency and, most likely, demanded more confidential services than banks were able to provide. A regulation substantially banning banks' corporate shareholding, to avoid the past failures of the universal banks, also weakened incentives for banks to ever become truly insider to firms. State control over banks and over a substantial part of large firms reduced too the incentive for banks to develop any true monitoring skill. That, in turn, made banks rely on collateralized loans and State guarantees, on short-term overdraft credit, on multiple bank borrowing. The only exceptions were Mediobanca and local banks: the former specialized in preserving family and coalition control at large private corporations and relied more on ex-post than on interim monitoring; local banks, thanks to fiduciary networks in local communities, appear to have fostered the development of small firms which benefit to a large extent from flexible local labour markets.

For many years after the war, probably until the early 1960s, weak bank/firm relations did not prevent fast growth, which was indeed warranted by the working of the other corporate governance institutions. High corporate profits, mission-driven *Enti pubblici*, local district cross-monitoring also helped to achieve such results. The shortcoming, however, was that lack of monitoring and arm's length banking were encouraged by the existing institutional framework. When the self-sustained growth of the reconstruction came to an end, fast rising wages squeezed corporate profits and *Enti pubblici* were burdened with the constraints to achieve social goals, then the existing corporate governance became inadequate and the negative consequences of weak bank/firm relations came to the fore. More and more State resources were then put at the disposal of these enterprises, to cope with worsening corporate governance failures. They induced a relaxation of budget constraints as well as waste and mismanagement, while collusion between majority and opposition at the political level poisoned the selection process of top State managers. In the same years, corporate governance of small firms remained largely unchanged. While the lack of venture capital and of adequate capital markets prevented many small firms from fully catching growth opportunities, the general system of small firms, mostly specialized in traditional sectors, was not shaken by growing competition from fast developing countries: local, diffuse monitoring generally favoured quick adjustment of these firms to external shocks.

Today, consensus is growing on the need for the Italian system of corporate control to undergo a revision; together with the privatization of State-owned companies – with a partial redrawing of corporate law and of the system of directors' duties[23] – pressure is mounting for the banking system to change too. In implementing these reforms great care will have to be used in fully taking into account complementarities among the different institutions of corporate governance. This note suggests that the new setting should likely preserve the distinctive features of the existing two-tier banking system that the Italian economy carved out of its experience and needs.

NOTES

1. The views presented here do not involve the Institutions of affiliation.
2. See in particular Barca, Bianchi, et al. (1994), Barca, Bianco, et al. (1994), Capra, et al. (1994) – reporting on the results of a large Bank of Italy project on corporate governance – Barca, Ferri, Parigi (1994), Ferri, Pesaresi (1995), de Cecco, Ferri (1996), Barca, Trento (1996), Barca (1996).
3. This Section and Section 2.2.1 partly draw on Barca, Trento (1996).
4. See Barca (1994, chapter VIII).
5. On this issue see Barca, Pagano, Trento (1996).
6. See Menichella (1944), pp. 127–128.
7. See La Bella (1983), p. 36.
8. See Mattioli (1962).
9. By financial credit we mean, following Mattioli, credit whose repayment should come about not through the business turn-over but through the medium/long-term returns of investments.
10. This section partly draws on de Cecco, Ferri (1996).
11. This section is partly drawn on Barca, Trento (1996).
12. See Barca (1997).
13. See Bottiglieri (1981).
14. See, for example, Osti (1993); in particular pp. 219–230 and 279–286.
15. See Maraffi (1990).
16. See Bhattacharya, Thakor (1993).

17. Small banks focus lending to SMEs not only in Italy: for the USA, see Berger, Kashyap, Scalise (1995).
18. This section partly draws on Ferri, Pesaresi (1995).
19. See Bianco, Signorini (1994).
20. 'More active' banks satisfy all of the following conditions: (1) they hold a data-base on the ownership structure of borrowing firms; (2) if they are large banks, they have a merchant bank subsidiary; (3) they declare having made income on consulting related to ownership changes; or to have contributed, in more than 1/3 of the cases, to choose administrators and/or finance managers of borrowing firms; or to know early of ownership changes at borrowing firms and to have done at least some consulting to firms in crisis.
21. T-statistics for difference between sample means (between 'more active' banks and the other banks) and the associated rejection levels are reported in the last row of the table.
22. For a full description of the sample, see Barca, Bianco et al. (1994).
23. See Associazione Disiano Preite (1996).

REFERENCES

Associazione Disiano Preite (1996) *Rapporto sulla società aperta*, mimeo.

Banerjee, A. V., T. Besley and T. W. Guinnane (1994) Thy neighbor's keeper: The design of a credit cooperative with theory and a test, *Quarterly Journal of Economics*, May, 490–515.

Barca, F. (1994) *Imprese in cerca di padrone. Proprietà e controllo nel capitalismo italiano*, Laterza, Bari.

Barca, F. (1996) *On Corporate Governance in Italy: Issues, Facts and Agenda*, Fondazione Eni Enrico Mattei, working paper No. 10.96.

Barca, F. (1997) *Compromesso senza riforme nel capitalismo italiano: 1945–1962*, mimeo.

Barca, F. and M. Magnani (1989) *L'industria fra capitale e lavoro: piccole e grandi imprese dall'autunno caldo alla ristrutturazione*, Il Mulino, Bologna.

Barca, F., G. Ferri and G. Parigi (1993) *Growth, Financing and the Reallocation of Corporate Control: Theory and Initial Empirical Findings for Italy*, paper presented at the CEPR Conference on 'Corporate Finance', Sesimbra, Portugal, 29–30 October.

Barca, F., M. Bianchi, F. Brioschi, L. Buzzacchi, P. Casavola, L. Filippa and M. Pagnini (1994) *Assetti proprietari e mercato delle imprese. Gruppo, proprietà e controllo nelle imprese italiane medio-grandi*, Vol. II, Il Mulino, Bologna.

Barca, F., M. Bianco, L. Cannari, R. Cesari, C. Gola, G. Manitta, G. Salvo and L. F. Signorini (1994) *Assetti proprietari e mercato delle imprese. Proprietà, modelli di controllo e riallocazione nelle imprese industriali italiane*, Vol. I, Il Mulino, Bologna.

Barca, F. and S. Trento (1996) *State ownership and the evolution of Italian corporate governance*, mimeo.

Barca, F., U. Pagano and S. Trento (1996) *Post-War Property Right Shocks: an Interpretation of the Diverging Italian and Japanese Governance Models*, mimeo.

Becattini, G. (1991) *The Mershallian district as a socio-economic notion*, in F. Pyke, G. Becattini and W. Sengerberger (eds.), *Industrial districts and inter-firm cooperation in Italy*, International Institute for Labour Studies, Geneva.

Berger, A. N., A. K. Kashyap and J. M. Scalise (1995) *The transformation of the US banking industry: What a long, strange trip it's been*, Brooking Papers on Economic Activity 2, 55–218.

Besley, T. and S. Coate (1995) *Group lending, repayment incentives and social collateral*, Journal of Development Economics Vol. 46, 1–18.

Bhattacharya, S. and A. V. Thakor (1993) *Contemporary Banking Theory*, Journal of Financial Intermediation, Vol. 3, No. 1, 2–50.

Bianco, M. and P. E. Signorini (1994) *Evoluzione degli assetti di controllo: gli investitori istituzionali*, Banca d'Italia, Temi di discussione, No. 243.

Borio, C. E. V. (1995) *The Structure of Credit to the Non-Government Sector and the Transmission Mechanism of Monetary Policy: A Cross-Country Comparison*, in Bank for International Settlements, Edited by *Financial Structure and the Monetary Policy Transmission Mechanism*, Basle.

Bottiglieri, B. (1984) 'Linee interpretative del dibattito sulle partecipazioni statali nel secondo dopoguerra', in *Economia Pubblica*, April-May, pp. 239–244.

Brusco, S. and C. F. Sabel (1981) *Artisan Production and Economic Growth*, in F. Wilkinson (ed.), *The Dynamics of Labour Market Segmentation*, Academy Press, New York.

Brynjolfsson E. (1990) *Information Technology and the New Organization of Work: an Agency Theory Perspective*, mimeo, MIT.

Capra, L., N. D'Amico, G. Ferri and N. Pesaresi (1994) *Assetti proprietari e mercato delle imprese. Gli intermediari della riallocazione proprietaria in Italia*, Vol. III, Il Mulino, Bologna.

Cesarini F., G. Ferri and M. Giardino (1997) (eds.), *Credito e sviluppo. Banche locali cooperative e imprese minori*, forthcoming, Il Mulino, Bologna.

Conti G. and G. Ferri (1996) *Banche locali e sviluppo economico decentrato*, mimeo.

de Cecco, M. and G. Ferri (1996) *Le banche d'affari in Italia*, Il Mulino, Bologna.

Ferri, G. and F. Mattesini (1995) *Finance, Human Capital and Infrastructure: an Empirical Investigation of Post-War Italian Growth*, Banca d'Italia, Temi di discussione, forthcoming.

Ferri, G. and N. Pesaresi (1995) *The Missing Link: Banking and non-banking Financial Institutions in Italian Corporate Governance*, ENI nota di lavoro, No. 4.

Ferri, G. and S. Trento (1997) *Stabilità, ricambio e interconnessioni tra gli amministratori delle maggiori banche e imprese: un'indagine preliminare*, mimeo.

Generale, A. and G. Gobbi (1995) *Loan Repossession and Credit Markets: Evidence from Italian Bank Survey Data*, Banca d'Italia, mimeo.

La Bella, G. (1983) *L'IRI nel dopoguerra*, Roma, Edizioni Studium.

Maraffi, M. (1990) *Politica ed economia in Italia. La vicenda dell'impresa pubblica dagli anni trenta agli anni cinquanta*, Il Mulino, Bologna.

Mattioli, R. (1962) *I problemi attuali del credito*, in 'Mondo Economico', reprinted in L. Villari (ed.) (1972), *Il Capitalismo italiano del novecento*, Laterza, Bari.

Mayer, C. (1990) *Financial Systems, Corporate Finance and Economic Development*, in R. G. Hubbard (ed.), *Asymmetric Information, Corporate Finance and Investment*, The University of Chicago Press, Chicago, IL.

Menichella, D. (1944) *Le origini dell'IRI e la sua azione nei confronti della situazione bancaria*, reprinted in Banca d'Italia, Edited by Donato Menichella, *Scritti e discorsi scelti, 1933–1966*, Rome, 1986.

Osti G. L. (1993) *L'industria di stato dall'ascesa al degrado*, Il Mulino, Bologna.

Piore, M. J. and C. F. Sabel (1984) *The Second Industrial Divide*, Basic Books, New York.

Sabel, C. (1982) *Work and Politics – The Division of Labour in Industry*, Cambridge, CUP.

Saraceno, P. (1975) *Il sistema delle imprese a partecipazione statale nell'esperienza italiana*, Giuffré, Milano.

Scherer, F. M. (1976) *Industrial Structure, Scale Economies and Worker Alienation*, in R. T. Masson amd P. D. Qualls, *Essays on Industrial Organization*, Ballinger Publishing Company, Cambridge (Mass.).

The New Financial Landscape

ABSTRACT

The new financial landscape is having an important impact on corporate governance. The growth of the institutional sector (pension funds, insurance companies, investment companies) has been a driving force behind structural changes in both the process of corporate governance and the structure and *modus operandi* of OECD capital markets. Institutional investors have been growing in size dramatically over the past decade or so. The continued expansion of the institutional sector has had a growing influence on financial governance channels, including the market for corporate control.

Hendrikus J. Blommestein is a Senior Financial Economist at the Organisation for Economic Co-operation and Development (OECD), Paris, France. In the period 1991–1995, he was the CSCE Professor of Economics, Department of Public Administration and Public Policies, University of Twente, Enschede, The Netherlands. He participated as Advisor in many IMF missions to Central and Eastern Europe and the Former Soviet Union. Before joining the OECD, he served as Deputy Head of the International Monetary Affairs Division of the Netherlands Ministry of Finance and as a personal assistant of and advisor to Dr H. O. Ruding in his capacity as the Chairman of the Interim Committee of the IMF. He has been the Netherlands member of the OECD Committee on Capital Movements and Invisible Transactions (CMIT) and a temporary alternate Member of the Monetary Committee of the EC. Prior to that, Dr Blommestein held positions as an Associate Professor of Economics at the University of Twente, Visiting Professor at the University of Akron, and Visiting Scientist at the Smithsonian Institution. Dr Blommestein has published numerous articles on econometric methodology, spatial economics, financial markets and the transformation process in former socialist countries. He (co-)edited a number of books: *Handboek Beleidevaluatie* (1984, Samson Publishers), *The Reality of International Economic Policy Co-ordination* (1991, North-Holland Publishing Cy), *Transformation of Planned Economies* (1991, OECD), *Methods of Privatising Large Enterprises* (1993, OECD), *Transformation of the Banking System* (1993, OECD), *Government and Markets* (1994, Kluwer Academic Publishers), *The New Financial Landscape* (1995, OECD), *Coordination of Monetary and Public Debt Management* (1997, IMF), *Institutional Investors in the New Financial Landscape* (1997, OECD).

III. The New Financial Landscape and its Impact on Corporate Governance*

HANS J. BLOMMESTEIN

1. INTRODUCTION

Corporate governance structures are essential for shaping enterprise behavior, including the response by enterprises to these pressures and the associated new investment and growth opportunities. Improving the understanding of corporate governance is therefore of utmost importance. Enhanced understanding will permit the identification of policy priorities and tradeoffs as regards the regulatory and institutional environment which conditions corporate governance structures.

In this paper, the impact of structural changes in financial systems on financial governance channels – with the emphasis on the market for corporate control – will be examined. It will be argued that the growth of the institutional sector (pension funds, insurance companies, investment companies) has been the driving force behind structural changes in both the process of corporate governance and the structure and *modus operandi* of OECD capital markets. The expansion and growing sophistication of capital market operations have been a leading force in shaping the financial landscape.[1] Indeed, the growing role of institutional investors is perhaps the most important factor in changing the financial structure and behavior in the OECD area.[2] Institutional investors have been growing in size dramatically over the past two decades or so.

The increasing importance of institutional investors as holders of assets means that their impact on the functioning of financial markets is steadily growing. In most OECD countries, institutional saving institutions now play a key role in domestic financial systems. The involvement of institutional investors in capital market transactions is increasing in tandem with their growing financial clout. Institutional investors have been the main source of investment in securities markets. A strong community of institutional investors

---

* The views expressed in this paper are those of the author and do not necessarily represent those of the OECD.

seems to be a precondition for the development of liquid securities markets with sophisticated financial vehicles.

In a static sense, corporate governance can be defined as the outcome of the relationships and interaction between the different economic agents that operate within a corporate, limited-liability institution. Corporate governance determines both the long-term strategy of this institution and the use of its income. Typically, shareholders, management, employees, creditors and suppliers/customers are the main actors and, to varying degrees, exert influence on the corporation within a framework given by existing laws, regulations and institutions, as well as firm-specific governance structures. This paper focuses on the dynamic aspects of financial governance channels by analyzing the impact of institutional investors on structural changes in OECD financial systems.

The expansion of the institutional sector has had a growing influence on financial governance channels, including the market for corporate control. First, institutional investors have enhanced their corporate governance role in the form of an increase in market control via equity and debt. Second, an increase of direct control via equity in the form of an increase in shareholder activism by institutional investors has been an important characteristic of the change in corporate governance in the past decade. Third, direct control via debt is an important mechanism of corporate control in Continental Europe and Japan, although the corporate governance role of institutional investors is far from uniform in these countries.

The paper is organized as follows. Section 2 provides an overview of the growing financial importance of institutional investors in OECD countries. Forces shaping the *modus operandi* of institutional investors and financial governance channels are summarized in Section 3. The impact of institutional investors on financial markets is analyzed in Section 4. The relationship between institutional investors, financial markets and corporate governance is studied in Section 5. Section 6 focuses on the role by institutional investors in the market for corporate control. Final remarks and conclusions are summarized in the last section. The annex contains statistical information on securities holdings by institutional investors in the G-7 countries.[3]

2. Growth of Institutional Assets in the Main OECD Regions

The importance of institutional investors is steadily increasing. Total assets of the main regions in the OECD area rose from $2.5 trillion in 1981 (i.e. 36 per cent of GDP), to $14.6 trillion in 1991 (85 per cent of GDP), to more than $22.1 trillion in 1995 (102.0 per cent of GDP) (Table 1). The average annual rate of growth of institutional assets for the OECD area as a whole was strongest for investment companies (23 per cent), followed by insurance

TABLE 1

Institutional Investor's Holdings of securities issued by non-residents
(in per cent of total assets)

	1980	1988	1990	1991	1992	1993	1994	1995
Pension funds								
Canada[1]	4.6	5.9	6.4	8.6	10.2	11.6	12.9	13.4
Germany[2]	–	3.8	4.5	4.5	4.3	4.5	5.0[3]	–
Japan[2]	0.5	6.3	7.2	8.4	8.4	9.0	–	–
United Kingdom	7.9	16.3	17.8	20.6	19.5	20.0	19.8	19.8
USA[2]	0.7	2.7	4.2	4.1	4.6	5.7	–	–
Life insurance companies								
Canada[1]	0.3	1.5	1.1	1.2	0.7	0.5	0.5	0.3
Germany[2]	0.6	0.6	1.0	1.0	–	–	–	–
Japan[4]	–	–	13.5	12.5	11.4	9.0	6.7	6.9
United Kingdom	4.1	9.4	10.7	12.2	12.4	13.3	13.5	14.2
USA[2]	4.1	3.6	3.6	3.6	3.7	–	–	–
Mutual funds								
Canada[1]	19.9	19.4	17.5	16.1	17.0	20.4	23.6	23.4
Germany	–	–	–	–	–	24.8	20.3	20.2
Japan[2,5]	–	9.1	7.9	13.0	9.9	–	–	–
United Kingdom	17.9	33.0	31.0	34.3	35.2	35.8	36.4	34.5
USA[2]	–	–	6.6	–	10.1	–	–	–

[1] Non-resident investment.
[2] *Source:* International Capital Markets, IMF, Washington, D.C. 1995.
[3] *Source:* EFRP.
[4] Only bills and bonds.
[5] Investment trusts.
Sources: Statistics Canada, Deutsche Bundesbank, Bank of Japan, Office for National Statistics, and OECD staff estimates.

companies (12 per cent) and pension funds (10 per cent). This aggregate picture changes somewhat when one considers the three major sub-regions (see Figure 1). In Europe and North America investment companies record the highest growth (25 and 24 per cent, respectively), while in the Asia and the Pacific region pension funds have had the highest rate of growth (18 per cent).

The total share of assets held by the different types of institutional investors has changed over time: the holdings of investment companies increased from 18 per cent in 1991 to 23 per cent in 1995.

Institutional Holdings of Foreign Assets

Another noteworthy trend, is the gradual but clear shift toward internationally diversified portfolios of pension funds. The behaviour of life insurance companies

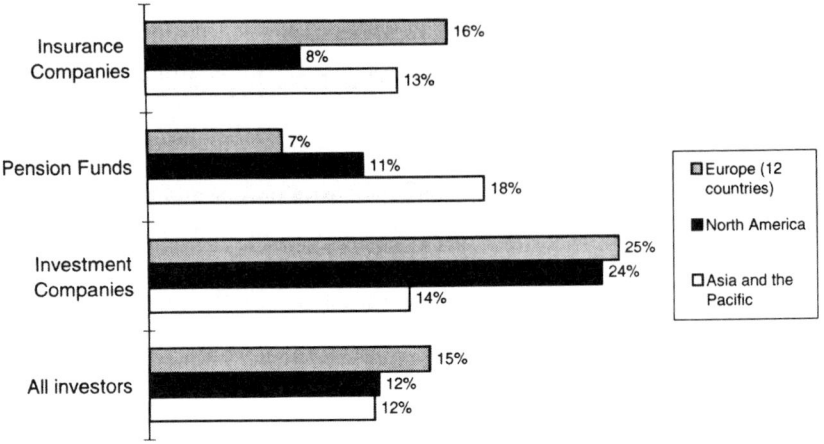

Fig. 1. Average annual rate of growth of institutional investors in OECD regions 1991–1995.

and investment companies is less clear (Table 1). The portfolios of insurance companies are less diversified than those of pension funds. In fact, their international diversification shows some decrease in the 1990s. There are important differences in the share of foreign securities in the portfolio of OECD investment companies: (a) the portfolios of mutual funds in Canada, Germany and the United Kingdom are more internationally diversified than in the United States and Japan; (b) possibly related to the previous point, US mutual funds show a clear trend toward increased international diversification, while in other countries this trend has levelled off or even declined somewhat (Table 1); (c) mutual funds in the larger OECD countries – except Japan – are significantly more diversified than insurance companies and pension funds.

3. Forces Shaping the *Modus Operandi* of Institutional Investors and Financial Governance Channels

The overview in the previous paragraph shows very clearly that institutional investors as a group have vastly expanded their economic sphere of influence. Yet, institutional investors are by no means a monolithic group, since they have different investment objectives and fiduciary mandates, operate under different regulatory and tax regimes, and have a different tolerance to risk. Partly due to these differences, the corporate governance role of the different types of institutional investors varies significantly. Nonetheless, it is possible to identify a number of structural factors driving the growth of institutional investors as a group. These factors are also influencing directly (i.e. other than via the influence of the institutional sector; e.g. by stimulating the growth of the capital market) the different financial governance channels:

(a) Deregulation of the banking and securities industries since the beginning 1980s has heightened competition between and among banks and other financial institutions. Abolishment of cross-border capital flow restrictions has further increased competition. New capital standards for banks were introduced in the same period. In response to these pressures, banks have massively expanded, or moved into, the insurance and investment fund business in search of new activities that generate earnings in the form of commissions and fees, while they do not necessarily absorb additional capital. To a certain degree, these developments have diminished the corporate governance role of banks in the form of less emphasis on direct control via debt. Moreover, banks in countries with insider systems (e.g. Germany) are reducing their equity stakes in non-financial enterprises. The latter development is driven by pressures by investors on bank management to increase the value of the shares of the banks.

(b) Liberalization of the activities of institutional investors, both in terms of the production and distribution of their respective products and the investment of their assets. An important aspect of the liberalization process is the relaxation of regulatory constraints on cross-border activities and investments. More freedom for pension funds and insurance companies to buy equity has increased the scope for equity-based control.

(c) The rising needs for retirement benefits of a rapidly aging population in conjunction with more sophisticated and wealthier private investors have had a significant impact on the growth of demand by private households for retirement benefit products offered by the different types of financial institutions – banks, insurance companies, and investment funds. This development is contributing to the creation of an 'equity culture', including greater scope for the market for corporate control and direct control via equity.

(d) Spectacular technological advances in communications and information technology enhanced the capacity of the financial sector, the professional fund managers, and the institutional investor community to use the opportunities offered by the liberalized environment. Advances in technology have enabled funds to be managed at lower costs. More reliable and efficient clearing and settlements systems for securities and payments, the creation and use of complex new financial products for risk management purposes, and the integration of capital markets have been important factors underpinning the spectacular growth of the managed assets of institutional investors, in particular, mutual fund assets. These structural changes have made equity transactions cheaper, thereby strengthening the so-called 'exit option' for institutional investors and others.

(e) The increasingly active role of the fund or money management profession has made important contributions to the transformation and dramatic expansion of the institutional investor industry. The management of funds by these professionals has common, technical features on the operational side, but the exact strategy and specific objectives are adapted to the specific institutional set-up.

4. THE IMPACT OF INSTITUTIONAL INVESTORS ON FINANCIAL MARKETS

In this section some aspects of the influence of institutional investors on the functioning of financial markets will be examined.

The Size of the Institutional Sector and the Development of the Capital Market

Institutional investors are likely to have an important impact on the functioning of the financial markets via different financial intermediation functions. The strong rise in crossborder transactions by institutional investors means that these intermediation functions are increasingly performed on an international scale. Institutional investors can have an overriding effect on the evolution of capital markets and corporate finance: the larger the institutional sector, the greater the influence on the development of the capital markets. At the same time, a dynamic community of institutional investors seems to be a precondition for the development of liquid securities markets with sophisticated financial vehicles. However, an extensive debate about the question of which comes first is not relevant. Institutional investors need well-developed securities markets for the efficient execution of their investment strategies. *Vice versa*, a dynamic institutional sector encourages the development of capital markets.

Market Liquidity

The growth of the institutional sector has had a profound effect on capital market structure. Institutional investors are very much interested in market liquidity – i.e. the ability to transact in large size without moving the price against them and at low transaction costs. They demand therefore a market infrastructure characterized by specialized wholesale markets which can process large transactions very rapidly and contribute to liquidity. This in turn requires the existence of well-capitalized market makers that are ready and able to execute large transactions. Advanced communications and information systems in conjunction with efficient and reliable clearing and settlement systems[4] and an efficient micro-structure for trading securities are also important components of liquid capital markets because they provide the ground for more efficient arbitrage activities and diversification of investment portfolios. Both activities create additional liquidity in the market. Other factors that are crucial for the development of a stable and liquid market infrastructure include: adequate public disclosure standards, an adequate (i.e. a market-oriented) accounting system and a proper legal framework for the institutional and financial sectors.[5] Finally, a healthy banking sector is a *sine qua non* for the emergence and development of capital markets, given its role as an important intermediary of liquid longer-term funds.[6]

Liquidity is a form of economy of scale and therefore the larger financial centres have a competitive edge, even with similar technology. Relative liquidity is reflected in transaction sizes.[7] In some countries, the growth of institutional investors – in particular pension funds – has encouraged the development of off exchange 'block trading'. This in turn may entail a tiering of markets, with order-driven and heavily regulated domestic markets dedicated to retail investors and small company stocks. Institutional investors have more power than small investors to press for the lowest possible transaction costs, thereby boosting liquidity.[8] Total transaction costs consist of indirect trading costs (determined by the liquidity of the market: the higher market liquidity, the lower indirect trading costs) and direct trading costs (determined by the structure of transaction fees). Institutional investors will seek to minimize total trading costs. Changes in the micro-structure of financial markets to improve one or more dimensions of market liquidity have lowered indirect trading costs. The search for more efficient ways of trading is also fostering the growth of alternative or non-traditional trading systems – in particular proprietary trading systems (PTSs). This has resulted in the bypassing of brokers by institutional investors from securities transactions (disintermediation) and pressure on transaction fees, thereby lowering direct transaction costs.[9] These liquidity-boosting changes have made equity transactions cheaper, thereby facilitating the exit option for equity holders.

Financial System Structure

Institutional investors have also had an impact on the overall structure of financial markets. Countries with large funded pension schemes (e.g. United Kingdom, United States) tend to have highly developed securities markets, while capital markets are relatively underdeveloped in countries with small pension-fund sectors (e.g. Germany, Italy). Table 2 gives an international overview of listed companies and market capitalization. Given their focus on real returns, pension funds should be particularly beneficial to the development of equity markets.[10] Although pension funds could in principle also develop by

TABLE 2

Listed companies and market capitalization (end 1994)

	Quoted companies		Market capitalization		Turnover Per cent of market value
	Number Units	Size $ million	$ billion	Per cent of GDP	
Singapore	240	1142	274	397	29
Malaysia	475	403	192	271	59
Luxembourg	55	518	29	204	1
United Kingdom	2070	585	1210	119	38
Switzerland	215	1321	284	111	81
Netherlands	320	884	283	85	66
Japan	2205	1673	3688	80	32
Australia	1144	192	219	68	34
United States[1]	2353	1802	4240	64	52
Canada[2]	1185	266	315	58	42
Korea	699	274	192	50	174
Belgium	155	542	84	37	14
France	459	919	422	32	45
Spain	372	331	123	26	44
Germany	417	1106	461	23	128
Italy	219	822	180	18	72

[1] NYSE only.
[2] Toronto only.
Source: Annual Security Statistics (1995).

providing loans and investments in real estate, their greatest comparative advantage is in the capital markets. Loans require monitoring, so the customer relationship probably gives banks a competitive edge. In contrast, trading and the pooling of risks are more efficiently undertaken in capital markets, where transactions costs are lower.

The growth of a dynamic institutional sector may contribute to a stronger role of capital market intermediation in so-called bank-based financial systems (e.g. Germany and Japan). In particular, pension funds that are investing significant parts of their portfolios in equities would pressure for changes in laws and regulations of companies that usually can be found in 'bank dominated' financial systems. For example, in the Netherlands, traditionally classified as a bank-based financial system, most people participate in funded pension systems, including civil servants. Stock market capitalization is relatively high and capital market intermediation has grown in importance. Consequently, equity-based control has also been strengthened in the Netherlands. In contrast, pension systems in France, Germany and Italy rely predominantly on unfunded (i.e. pay-as-you-go) schemes. Although capital market intermediation and equity-based control have grown in importance, stock markets are still relatively small in these countries. Although privatizations have been contributing to the development of an equity culture, a major switch to a funded pension system would probably give a bigger boost to both the development of the capital market and equity-based corporate governance channels.

In addition to a modernization of the capital market infrastructure, pension funds can be expected to push for a move to laws and practices that would better protect the interests of equity holders. These include takeover codes, insider information restrictions, limits on dual classes of shares which seek to protect minority shareholders, as well as equal treatment of creditors in bankruptcy to protect their holdings of corporate bonds.

The resulting modernization of the capital market might further encourage the larger corporations to shift from bank financing to securities markets. However, similar access to capital markets is not available for the smaller enterprises. This in turn may reinforce the development that bank lending is being increasingly concentrated in the smaller and medium-size enterprise sector, even in so-called bank dominated OECD countries.

The Role of Investment and Trading Strategies

Professional portfolio managers also have an important influence on the operational aspects of financial institutions and markets through trading strategies. In a competitive environment, fund management can be described as a two-stage decision-making process: (i) a strategic decision regarding the allocation of funds to different assets (equity, bonds, derivatives, real estate, cash) and countries; and (ii) a tactical decision about the size of specific assets within each category of assets determined at the strategic level.

The main factors influencing the strategic decisions are the investment objectives of the institutional investor, fiduciary mandate, regulatory and tax regime, and risk preference. The basic strategic decision concerns the desired mix of return and risk, whereby portfolio diversification plays a key role. This requires appropriate measures of risk-adjusted returns and the identification of portfolio performance in order to evaluate fund managers' performance.[11] Performance measurement systems should be in line with the policy objectives of the institutional investor. In other words, market exposure should be consistent with the benchmarks appropriate to the investment policies of an individual institutional investor. For example, proper asset allocation by pension plan sponsors requires alignment with plans' future liabilities. The next step is to establish appropriate benchmarks and a measurement system that best fits the actual portfolio.

Investment strategies provide institutional investors with a focused framework for conducting their corporate governance activities. The authorities need to put into place the proper capital market infrastructure in order to allow equity investors to exercise efficiently their control function.

5. INSTITUTIONAL INVESTORS, FINANCIAL MARKETS AND CORPORATE GOVERNANCE

Salient Features of Different Corporate Governance 'Models'

There are no national models of corporate governance in the sense that governance structures are similar across different firms in different industries within a country but different within the same industries across countries. Indeed, variation is considerable between firms operating within a given industry in a given country reflecting, *inter alia*, the ways in which individual firms position themselves strategically *vis-à-vis* parameters such as R&D intensity, vertical integration, human capital intensity etc. Nevertheless, with a lot of variation around them, there are some common tendencies within countries and differences between them which have fed the notions of shareholder vs. stakeholder governance, outsider vs. insider, or market-based vs. relations-based systems.

Traditional company legislation generally gives owners/shareholders mastery of the firm. However, other agents have staked claims to exercise some control. In Anglo-Saxon countries, company management has emerged as a powerful control agent. In continental Europe, employees and banks have acquired an important say in how firms are run. In several countries, including Japan, there is a pattern of interlocking control between large industrial companies and in some countries public-sector ownership plays a significant role, particularly in sectors deemed to be 'sensitive' or 'strategic'. Table 3 provides an international comparison of ownership of common stock in a sample of OECD countries. Attempts to identify such national characteristics should, however, not obscure the wide variation of governance structures within individual countries depending on the kind of activity firms are engaged in as well as more firm-specific idiosyncrasies. The information in Table 3 shows that there are large differences in institutional ownership.

Keeping the above diversity in mind, national corporate governance characteristics can be described in OECD countries by two stylized models: an 'insider model' and an 'outsider' model.[12] These two models in turn can be used to analyze the role of financial markets in corporate governance (see box: Corporate governance models and financial governance channels). The two models can also be used to characterize and describe the corporate governance process in OECD countries. However, it should be kept in mind that the 'actual' process has many idiosyncrasies, making the corporate governance process in individual countries in several important respects (e.g. the cultural

TABLE 3

Ownership of common stock: an international comparison (per cent at year-end)

	United States (1994)	Japan (FY 1994)	Germany (1993)	France (1993)	United Kingdom (1993)	Italy (1993)	Sweden (1993)
Financial sector	45	44	29	8	62	19	24
of which:							
Banks	3	26	14	3	1	10	1
Insurance companies	4	16	7	1	17	2	8
Pension funds	26	0	0	0	34	0	0
Mutual funds	12	0	8	2	7	6	6
Other financial institutions	4	2	0	2	3	1	8
Non-financial sector							
of which:							
Non-financial enterprises	0	24	39	59	2	32	34
Public authorities	0	1	4	4	1	28	7
Individuals	48	24	17	19	18	17	16
Foreign	6	7	12	11	16	5	9
Other	1	0	0	0	2	0	10
Total	100	100	100	100	100	100	100

Note: Due to rounding, the figures may not add up to the total. Pension funds in Japan are managed by trust banks and insurance companies. The assets in these funds are included under banks and insurance companies. No data are available on the extent to which mutual funds own shares. Security houses do manage such funds. These companies are included under other financial institutions.

Source: Flow of Funds, Board of the Federal Reserve System. Round Table of National Stock Exchanges, 'Survey of Stock Ownership Distribution', August 1995. Deutsche Bundesbank, Banque de France, CSO, Consob, Banca d'Italia, Statistika Centralbyran, Sweden. Quoted in OECD (1995b). Annual Security Statistics (1995).

and political dimensions) 'unique'. The range of potential governance factors which influence differences in economic performance across firms and countries is considerable. There is no consensus among analysts how to identify the effects of changes in governance on performance. Moreover, evidence on the effects of different governance systems is very sparse. A final complication is that in practice the corporate governance process in OECD countries is changing and there are indications that some 'convergence' in governance has taken place, stimulated by the internationalization of product – and factor (notably financial) markets as well as a more important role in capital markets by institutional investors.

TABLE 4

Financial structure of industrial companies (per cent of balance-sheet total)

	Own funds[1]			Debt[2]			Provisions		
	1985	1990	1994	1985	1990	1994	1985	1990	1994
France	20.5	33.0	36.2	73.6	61.8	57.5	4.9	4.6	5.6
Germany	30.3[3]	29.6	31.6	38.3[3]	38.6	34.3	31.5[3]	31.6	33.9
Italy	26.8	28.3	26.5	63.6	62.5	64.5	7.3	7.1	8.0
UK	47.8	37.1	36.8	47.8	50.9	46.1	4.4	12.1	17.0
EU(10)	31.6	32.6	33.3	60.8	51.7	49.5	5.8	16.6	17.1
United States	45.8	39.8	37.4	50.3	55.5	54.9	–	–	–
Japan	26.4	31.1	32.7	67.8	63.7	62.1	4.8	4.1	4.0

[1] Share capital and retained profits.
[2] Bank loans, bond issues and short-term loans between companies.
[3] 1987.
Source: EU (1996).

A broad indicator of convergence is the change in the financial structure of industrial companies. Companies in Europe have as a whole reduced their debt, while the own funds ratio (equity/total assets) has increased. The latter ratio has moved very closely to that of enterprises in Anglo-Saxon economies (see Table 4). It is likely that this change is having an impact on European corporate governance practices, including greater emphasis on transparency and the promotion of shareholder value. For example, in the wake of major privatizations, the French system of 'noyaux durs' (core investors) has been criticized as being incompatible with the promotion of an open equity culture characterized by a liquid equity market that enhances shareholder value and at the same time is not unduly restricting the influence of small shareholders.

Main Determinants of Corporate Governance Structures

Many factors influence the development of an enterprise's governance structure. A large number of these are either under direct policy control or indirectly linked to the setting of policy instruments. Regarding policy instruments, the following are among the most important: financial market regulation including stock market regulation, take-over legislation, prudential regulation and banking supervision, disclosure requirements, and regulations on institutional investors; bankruptcy legislation; accounting conventions; taxation; factors affecting venture capital; legislation concerning employee relationships, including representation, and restriction on hiring and firing. Table 5 provides an overview of important portfolio restrictions on large financial institutions in view of their major influence on financial governance channels.

TABLE 5

Important portfolio restrictions on large financial institutions (continued)

A. United States

Institution	Assets Year-end 1994	Restriction	Source
Banks Bank holding companies Bank trust funds	$4.2 trillion $411 billion $656 billion	Stock ownership prohibited. No more than 5 per cent of the voting stock of any non-bank. 1. No more than 10 per cent of assets in any one company. 2. Active bank control could trigger bank liability to controlled company.	Glass-Steagall National Bank Act Bank Holding Company Act of 1956 Comptroller regulations Bankruptcy case law
Insurers (total) Life insurers Property and casualty insurers	$2.6 trillion $1.9 trillion $670 billion	No more than 2 per cent of assets can go into a single company, no more than 20 per cent of assets can go into stock. No control of non-insurer.	New York Insurance Law (for insurers doing business in New York) Same
Open-end mutual funds	$1.3 trillion	1. For half of portfolio: No more than 5 per cent of fund's assets can go into stock of any one issuer and fund may not purchase more than 10 per cent stock of any company, otherwise tax penalties apply 2. Must get SEC approval prior to joint action with affiliate, i.e. a fund needs SEC approval before acting jointly to control a company of which it and its partner own more than 5 per cent.	Investment Company Act of 1940; subchapter M of the Internal Revenue Code Investment Company Act of 1940
Private pension funds	$2.4 trillion	1. Must diversify unless clearly sensible not to. 2. Enhanced duty of care to beneficiaries probably retained if pension fund designee sits on portfolio company board (directors usually subject only to low-level business judgment rule).	ERISA ERISA
State and local pension funds	$1.2 trillion	Economic control of private pension funds usually held by operating company managers.	Structural

TABLE 5 Continued
Important portfolio restrictions on large financial institutions

B. Other major OECD countries

Institution	Germany	United Kingdom	Japan	Italy
Commercial banks	No restrictions, apart from prudential rules: sum of shareholdings not to exceed 60 per cent of bank's own capital; no single shareholding to exceed 15 per cent of own capital	Bank of England may discourage ownership on prudential grouns. Capital adequacy rules discourage large stakes.	Prior to 1987 banks could hold up to 10 per cent of a firm's stock. After 1987 can hold up to 5 per cent.	Priori to 1993, stock ownership was prohibited or required prior approval (in special cases) by the Bank of Italy; proxy voting is still prohibited, while the presence of banks' employees on non-financial firms boards is allowed since 1992.
Life insurance companies	Can hold up to 20 per cent of total assets in equities.	Self-imposed limits on fund assets invested in any one company stemming from fiduciary requirement of liquidity.	Can hold up to 10 per cent of a firm's stock.	Can hold up to 5 per cent of a firm's stock.
Mutual funds	No more than 5 per cent of fund assets in one company; no more than 10 per cent of the total voting rights from the stock of the same issuer.	Cannot take large stakes in firms		No more than 5 per cent of a listed firm's stock (10 per cent if unlisted). Proxy voting prohibited.
Pension funds		Self-imposed limits on fund assets invested in one company stemming from fiduciary requirement of liquidity.		Limits on fund assets invested in one company (5 per cent if quoted, 10 per cent otherwise) and in the sponsoring company and its subsidiaries (20 per cent).
General	Regulatory notification required for ownership in listed companies from 5 per cent and upwards.	Insider trading laws discourage large stakeholders from exerting control. Regulatory notification required for 3 per cent ownership.		Consob[1] notification required for 2 per cent ownership in listed firms and 10 per cent ownership in unlisted firms by listed ones.

[1] Stock exchange commission.
Source: Roe (1990) and OECD.

However, other important determinants are outside the direct or indirect influence of structural policies, such as for example the kind of economic activity an enterprise engages in which is bound to significantly influence its governance structure, or the macroeconomic environment which through factors like inflation proneness may impact on the financing structure and thereby the governance of an enterprise. Moreover, less concrete factors may be significant such as when implicit social rules and expectations are reflected in standard business practices.

Existing institutional arrangements and the governance structures based on these, are likely to be profoundly affected by recent and prospective economic developments:

- Increased internationalization of businesses and the desire by enterprises to tap international capital markets highlight the risks of conflicts between different regulatory structures and traditions in areas such as company law, accounting and public disclosure with wider implications for governance structures.
- Structural changes in financial markets have led to the emergence of new financial instruments, increased integration of markets, stronger competition and new or radically changed financial institutions. These developments are having an important impact on the functioning of financial governance channels, although not all consequences are well understood.
- Increased reliance on private-sector solutions to issues previously addressed through public social security systems also have an important influence on both financial institutions and governance structures. Changing demographic patterns and increased strain on government-run unfunded pensions systems are likely to lead to increased private saving for pension purposes and to strengthen the role of institutional investors as a potential source of financing for, and agents for control of, enterprises. Pension reform, deregulation of institutional investment activities and privatization are expected to continue to contribute to the development of an 'equity culture' in insiders' systems and a further strengthening of equity-based control.
- Technological developments raise specific issues related to enterprise financing and corporate governance not least in cases where business assets have a largely intangible character. Technological developments may also enhance the importance of conditions for new firm creation.

Such developments increase the need for a better understanding of the mechanisms guiding corporate governance outcomes so as to be better prepared to respond to the new challenges.

The Impact of Institutional Investors on Financial Governance Channels

There is a growing perception in the last decade that managers have become insufficiently accountable to shareholders. In other words, it is argued that the conflict between owners and managers – a principal-agent problem – has increased or at least has become more acute. At the same time, institutional ownership has grown rapidly. The rise in institutional private securities holdings and the decline of the market for corporate control at the beginning of the 1990s[13] have focused attention on the role and importance of institutional investors as monitors of corporate management.[14]

In response, there is increased pressure on management of companies to maximize shareholder value by institutional investors and other shareholders. 'Shareholder activism' by traditionally passive institutional investors has increased. Shareholder activism includes monitoring and attempting to bring about changes in the organizational control structure of enterprises (the 'targets') not perceived to be pursuing share-holder-wealth-maximizing goals.[15] In essence, the larger institutional investors are seeking to enhance the return on capital through improvements in corporate governance systems so as to increase the accountability of managers.

In sum, the financial importance of the institutional sector is increasing while its influence on both the process of corporate governance and financial markets is growing. A good starting-point for analyzing this impact is to distinguish the following financial governance channels: (1) market control via equity, (2) market control via debt, (3) direct control via equity, and (4) direct control via debt.

CORPORATE GOVERNANCE MODELS AND FINANCIAL GOVERNANCE CHANNELS

Insider model

1. The 'insider model' can be found in many OECD countries (e.g. Japan, Germany, the Netherlands, Switzerland, Sweden). This model relies on the direct representation of specific interests on the board of directors. Monitoring and disciplining of management relies heavily on the accountability of board members to the stakeholders they represent, including banks, non-financial companies with close ties to the corporation, government representatives, and workers. Management discipline via securities markets is not the rule. Insider systems are also often characterized by concentrated shareholding, with cross-holding among companies being fairly common. Markets in corporate control (i.e. hostile and friendly takeovers) are weak. Banks play an important role in most countries with insider models.

Outsider model

2. In the 'outsider model' of the English-speaking countries, managers are weakly controlled by the board of directors, which may be even allied

with management. Monitoring and disciplining of management is done via the capital market. If the company is run badly and/or shareholder value is not being maximized, investors may react by selling shares. This will depress the share price, making the company vulnerable to a hostile takeover. This model presumes market-oriented accounting rules, adequate public disclosure standards, strict trading rules, and liquid stock markets.

ROLE OF CORPORATE FINANCE AND FINANCIAL MARKETS

The following four governance channels in financial markets can be distinguished:[16]

(i) *Market control via equity*
3. This corporate governance channel relies on selling shares and/or takeover activities. The principal advantage of takeover activity is that it can reduce the conflict between management and shareholders. This assumes that managers perceive takeovers as a personal cost. Institutional investors, both directly and via non-executive directors, can play an important role, both in complementing takeover pressure, and in evaluating takeover proposals. In practice, however, takeovers are not always effective; they may be a weak disciplinary tool because it is relatively easy for managers to protect themselves against personal losses due to takeovers (e.g. through golden parachutes). It has also been argued that the costs of a takeover may be high. Losses in welfare to stakeholders such as employees may be higher than gains to shareholders.

(ii) *Market control via debt*
4. Debt issues can exert a disciplining effect on management since a manager of a highly-indebted firm who wants to avoid bankruptcy (by failing to make regular interest payments) will expend more effort in avoiding low-profit outcomes. An increase in debt decreases the free cash flow, thereby reducing the extent to which managers can appropriate earnings to increase their own welfare. However, high leverage may also have negative economic consequences in the form of a higher incidence of dead-weight bankruptcy costs and increased financial fragility of the corporate sector which may lead to a chain of bankruptcies during a recession.

(iii) *Direct control via equity*
5. Boards of directors act as shareholders' representatives in monitoring management and ensuring that the business is run in their interest. Shareholders' influence is ensured by their right to vote on policy proposals

of management or shareholders (including the choice of directors). This mechanism may be supplemented by direct links from investors such as pension funds (see below) to management, either formally at annual meeting, or informally at other times.

(iv) *Direct control via debt*
6. Relationship banking along the lines of the German and Japanese models give banks an incentive and the opportunity to monitor managers. Bankers wish to ensure that loans are repaid and to avoid circumstances in which they are forced to continue lending to large firms who threaten to default on their obligations. The effectiveness of debt in controlling managerial behavior is limited however since the manger of a highly-indebted firm has an incentive to engage in asset substitution. The influence of institutional shareholders is often limited by voting restrictions and lack of detailed financial information.

The first three financial governance channels are typical of the outsider models largely used in Anglo-Saxon countries, which emphasize the liquidity of shareholdings and adequate public disclosure of financial information. The fourth channel is more common in the insider models of Continental Europe and Japan, where liquidity is less emphasized and information not so widely distributed. The insider model is further characterized by large shareholdings between non-financial companies and between companies and banks since they often form the basis of long-term business relationships. It is suggested that the role of institutional investors is more central in the case of outsider systems with equity-based control than in insider-systems relying on debt-based controls.

Evidence about which financial governance system leads to superior results is inconclusive. What emerges from studies is that differences in such systems are primarily concerned with the formulation, implementation and adaptation of corporate strategy and not simply with incentives, disciplining, finance and investment.[17] Insider systems are superior at implementing policies which require the development of relationships with several stakeholders; for example, it has been argued that the Japanese insider system is better at assuring the commitment to stability needed to ensure proper levels of employee firm specific investment.[18] Yet, it is not very clear that outsider systems are clearly beneficial to shareholders. Outsider systems seem to be superior at responding to change; for example, the US outsider system has been credited with an excellent ability to adapt to technological change.[19] Nevertheless, as identified above there are some signs of convergence which, in part, may be related to some features of different models being superior in a given environment but also by the environments for the different corporate governance models being exposed to some of the same shocks.

The Growing Corporate Governance Role of Institutional Investors

The relationship between the functioning of financial markets and other governance channels needs to be further explored to get more conclusive answers. In addition, the impact of structural changes in OECD financial markets on governance needs to be taken into account, in particular the growing role of institutional investors.

The growing corporate governance role of institutional investors manifest itself in several ways:
- First, institutional investors have enhanced their corporate governance role in the form of an increase in market control via equity and debt. Institutional investors are major shareholders, so that their role in take-overs is a central one. Regular performance checks on fund managers against 'the market' may induce heightened willingness of institutional investors to sell shares in take-over battles to maintain or improve performance. Market control via debt has also been enhanced by the growing financial clout of institutional investors. In some countries, institutional investors (mainly banks and insurance companies) have been important financiers of leveraged buy-outs (LBOs). In addition, if pension funds are willing to accept cash for leveraged takeovers and buy-outs, they can facilitate the process of gearing and, in this way, are linked to the takeover mechanism.
- Second, an increase of direct control via equity in the form of an increase in shareholder activism by institutional investors has been an important characteristic of the change in corporate governance in the 1980s. There has been a growing concentration of institutional assets in OECD countries. For example, it has been estimated that institutions as a whole own an average 50 per cent of the top fifty US companies, while the top twenty US pension funds hold 8 per cent of the stock of the ten largest companies. Thus, institutional investors as shareholders are in a potentially strong position to exert pressure on the management of enterprises.[20] Although institutional ownership of equities has increased sharply, institutional investors are, for the most part, passive investors. Thus, institutional ownership per se has no clear implications for corporate governance. Institutional investors in several OECD countries have a fiduciary responsibility to participate in a nominal way in corporate governance activities, such as reading proxy statements, making careful voting decisions, and so forth. However, in most instances, they have not tried to participate more actively.

– Third, direct control via debt is an important mechanism of corporate control in Continental Europe and Japan. Pension funds' role via this mechanism is a passive one in Germany and Japan; most of the loans by pension funds are to the banks or arranged by the banks, leaving banks in the controlling position to provide monitoring of management on the part of all external financiers. In other countries where bank loans are important, the nature of the pension fund's relation to the borrower differs. In the Netherlands, private loans are the major component of pension funds' portfolios. In Sweden, many of the loans are retroverse loans to firms that are major contributors to the various schemes – implicitly a form of self-investment. On the other hand, Anglo-Saxon countries tend not to invest significant amounts in corporate debt. United States pension funds, unlike life insurers, have not been significant investors in private placements.

The Fiduciary Responsibilities of Institutional Investors

In tandem with the increase in institutional holdings of private securities, pension funds and other institutional investors increasingly grapple with the issues of corporate governance. In order to meet *fiduciary* responsibilities, they are simultaneously seeking ways to improve systems of corporate accountability. For example, it has been argued that fiduciary duty may now include the duty to balance index fund strategies with active monitoring and relationship investing.[21] Under the recently enacted 'lead plaintiff' provision of the US Private Securities Litigation Act of 1995,[22] large shareholders can now seek to be named controlling parties in class-action shareholders suits. New forms of monitoring and collaboration between corporations and institutional investors are required for both governance activities. Both activities have the potential to increase the accountability of corporations to owners and to reduce agency costs.

Thus far, corporate governance guidelines have mainly concerned pension funds and insurance companies. Guidelines for mutual funds along the same lines as for pension funds, making it explicit that exercise of ownership rights, including proxy voting and evaluating more activist alternatives, must be undertaken as a part of fiduciary obligation, seem not to exist in OECD countries. For example, no provision of the US federal securities laws nor any SEC rule thereunder specifically addresses the responsibilities of fund investment advisers regarding the voting of proxies or shareholder activism. However, in 1992, the SEC adopted new rules that have significantly lowered the cost of proxy activism for institutional investors and have facilitated increased activism by institutional investors. Under the new rules, a mutual fund or other institutional investor, without making any filings with the SEC or any mailings, may discuss voting issues with an unlimited number of other shareholders as long as the fund does not solicit proxies from any of the other shareholders.

The normalization of the corporate governance process, through a commitment to exercise fiduciary responsibilities (e.g. voting) in accordance with published guidelines, represents a major change from situations in which governance activities were exclusively conducted in an informal fashion (e.g. private conversations between fund managers and the management of companies). Corporate governance guidelines may or may not be mandatory. In the US, governance guidelines tend to be compulsory. For example, under the Employee Retirement Income Security Act (ERISA) a plan fiduciary is required to discharge his or her duties with respect to a plan solely in the interests of the participants and beneficiaries. This standard applies to all duties charged to a fiduciary including the voting of proxies. In contrast, government guidelines in the UK tend to be voluntary. For example, the National Association of Pension Funds (NAPF) is opposed to compulsory voting. NAPF argues that institutional investors should be allowed to exercise appropriate judgment on corporate governance issues to take account of a company's individual circumstances. Nonetheless, NAPF and other UK institutions have demanded better accounting and auditing procedures and support the Cadbury and Greenbury Codes of Best Practice as well as the work of the Financial Reporting Council.

As a general matter, an investment advisor to an investment fund has a fiduciary responsibility to vote proxies of the fund's portfolio companies and, perhaps, to take additional actions with respect to those companies when it determines that doing so would promote the best interests of the fund. The nature and extent of an adviser's duties with respect to voting proxies and taking other actions regarding the corporate governance of portfolio companies, however, must be determined by reference to the adviser's contract with the fund, as well as the fund's specified investment objectives and policies, and an analysis of the surrounding circumstances.

Many mutual funds have a stated investment policy that the fund will not invest for the purpose of controlling or influencing the management of portfolio companies. A fund that has such a policy has elected, in effect, to remain a passive investor. Consequently, the ability of its investment adviser to go beyond the simple voting of proxies and engage in shareholder activism on the fund's behalf may be quite limited. Other funds may have a stated policy (disclosed in the fund's prospectus) of attempting to control or influence the management of portfolio companies. If a fund has such a policy, its advisers would not be prohibited from engaging in shareholder activism on its behalf.

Long-Term versus Short-Term Institutional Investment Strategies

It has been noted above that institutional investors demand market liquidity. Consequently, many improvements in the financial market infrastructure have been made to make it easier to trade. Critics have argued that by placing a premium on liquidity, a 'short-term' bias is being built into the economic system. Similarly, institutional investors have been criticized for their short term outlook.[23]

The conclusion that institutional investors have a short-term investment horizon has been questioned by several analysts. It is argued that institutions own such a large percentage of the market that two of the factors driving short-term orientation – the need for liquidity and the competitive advantages of active fund management – are no longer important, or even prudent. The massive size of some funds substantially removes the option of full disinvestment from a company due to the potential adverse impact on share price. In addition, the growth of indexed portfolios also means that funds are obliged to follow the view of the market. In effect, the large institutional investors are already 'patient investors'.[24]

In analyzing the average holding period of institutional assets it is important to distinguish the core portfolio – representing the bulk of a fund's assets – from the satellite portfolio (i.e. the remainder of the fund's assets). The core portfolio will normally be invested in a manner to provide stable returns (possibly as an index fund), while the satellite portfolio can then be managed more flexibly, in search of higher returns. The holding period of the core portfolio is normally much longer than that of the satellite portfolio.

Shareholder Activism and Shareholder Value

Shareholder activism by institutional investors is seen as a way of restoring the balance in the direction of a longer-term perspective by restoring the basis of 'relationship investing'. Advocates of this view point out that this mode of ownership leads to superior returns over a longer time period because relationship investors act as better informed and interested shareholders insisting on competitiveness.

Several analysts have pointed out that large institutions can enhance the value of their investments better through shareholder activism than through trading. They argue that the evidence is clear enough that activism is a highly competitive investment strategy and, therefore, governance activities should be merged into the mainstream of asset management.

Several empirical studies of the impact of shareholder activism by institutional investors demonstrate that institutional investor monitoring of management is associated with significant value gains, including stock price appreciation and increased financial performance.[25]

6. INSTITUTIONAL INVESTORS AND THE MARKET FOR CORPORATE CONTROL

In the last decade, monitoring by the capital market has become a more important disciplinary device in OECD governance processes – by the capital markets in general and 'the market for corporate control' in particular. Institutional investors, both directly and via non-executive directors, can play an important role, both in complementary takeover pressure and in evaluating takeover proposals.[26]

In a broad sense, the market for corporate control encompasses all mechanisms, financial instruments and institutional features that contribute to the efficient functioning of market-based methods of corporate governance, including shareholder voting procedures, the role of boards in representing the interest of shareholders, the takeover mechanisms, 'relationship investing' and capital market control via debt (loans, bonds) and equity.

Institutional investors are having an increasingly important influence on all of these factors affecting the market for corporate control. Institutional investors have become more active in using their voting rights and in communicating with corporate management (i.e., 'relationship investing'). They have also been instrumental in changing the role and structure of boards of directors, as well as the relationship between the board, the annual shareholders meeting (AGM) and the management of corporations. In making boards more active and AGMs more meaningful voting fora, institutional investors have improved the accountability of managers to shareholders generally.

The pressure of institutional investors to reduce barriers to shareholder control (special voting rights, non-voting shares, capped voting, obligations for banks or other custodians to support management, limits on proxy voting excessive requirements for attending AGMs) have made the market for corporate control more efficient. The changing financial landscape with a larger influence of institutional investors and a greater role for equity-based control is also slowly having an impact on insider systems characterized by widespread inter-company holdings (e.g., in France and Japan) and complex capital structures (such as pyramids; e.g., in Italy). These more general, deeply embedded features of insider systems also tend to entrench the management of corporations, thereby hampering the market for corporate control.

In a narrow sense, the market for corporate control can be equated with takeover activities. In outsider systems, takeovers are the primary disciplinary device to force managers to seek good corporate governance. Takeover activity various significantly across OECD countries, with US mergers more than twice the share for UK firms and about 15 times the levels recorded in Japan and Germany (Table 6).

After a slowdown at the beginning of the 1990s, the number and values of mergers and acquisition have accelerated in recent years (Table 7).

TABLE 6

Completed domestic mergers and acquisitions, 1986–89[1]

	United States	United Kingdom	Japan	Germany
Volume (in $ billion)	1070.0	107.6	61.3	4.2
As percentage of total market capitalization	41.1	18.7	3.1	2.3

[1] Only those with disclosed values.
Source: Prowse (1994).

TABLE 7

Mergers and acquisitions in four major countries

	United States	United Kingdom	Germany	France
1988	801	106	16	21
1989	677	250	28	72
1990	589	282	66	159
1991	367	187	55	116
1992	463	177	48	91
1993	615	203	59	81
1994	735	233	62	90
Average	607	205	48	90

Source: Morgan Stanley M&A Transaction Database, 'Announced and Completed Transactions over US$35 million in Aggregate Value or More'.

The equity holdings of institutions are increasing in many OECD countries and, therefore, institutional investors can be expected to play an increasingly important role in takeovers. Figure 2 shows that the equity holdings of OECD institutional investors have increased in the period 1990–1995.

Institutional shareholders, both directly and via non-executive directors, can add to takeover pressure by evaluating takeover proposals when they arise or by facilitating the reaching of the critical momentum for a successful bid. Although takeovers play a relatively more important role in outsider systems, they have become more prominent in insider systems (Table 7).

Institutional investors may act as key agents of change in this respect. An interesting recent example is the first large-scale hostile take-over bid in Germany, structured on the basis of Anglo-Saxon capital market standards.[27] It was reported that the bidder secured 30 per cent of the target company from institutional investors.[28]

Institutional investors have also been active in the removal of takeover protections in both insider and outsider systems (pension pills, greenmail, shark repellents, preferential shares, etc.). They have argued that the widespread use

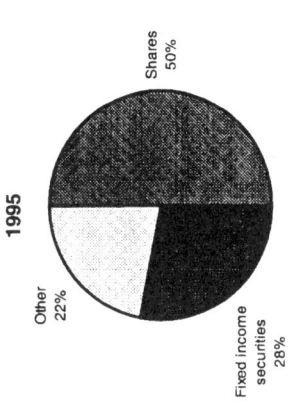
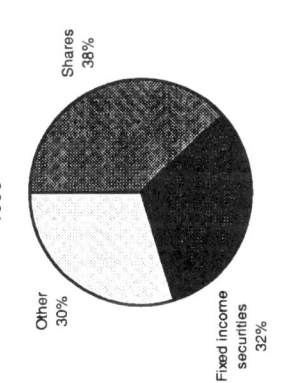

Fig. 2. Portfolio composition of institutional investors in OECD insurance companies.

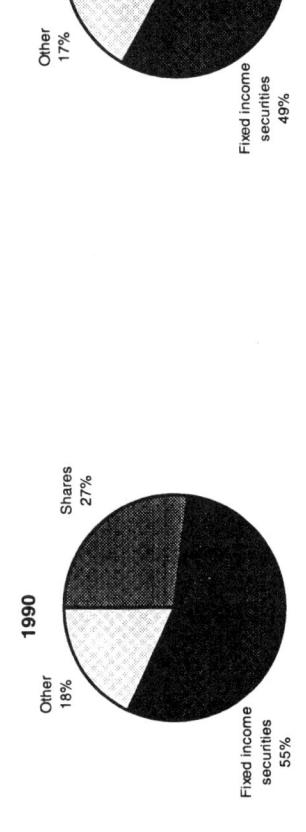
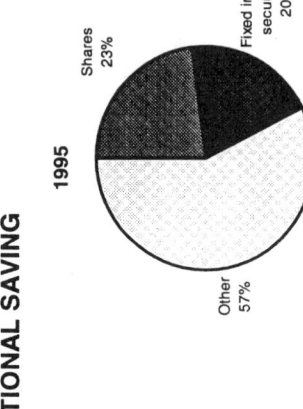
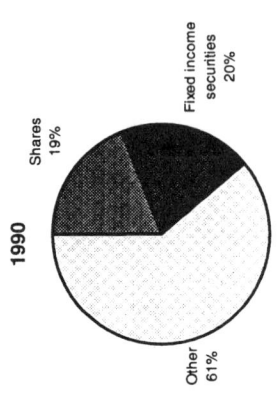

Fig. 2. *Continued.*

of anti-takeover devices is an unacceptable obstacle for the efficient functioning of the market for corporate control. Many countries with insider systems have introduced (or are planning to introduce) regulations for orderly takeovers, including a fair treatment of minority shareholders.

The takeover boom of the 1980s was primarily targeted at underperforming enterprises. In many cases junk bonds were used to finance hostile takeovers with the objective to restructure and downsize companies in order 'to squeeze out the fat'. In the 1990s, the driving force is to have an adequate corporate scale of operations and to form strategic alliances, that will enable enterprises to withstand globalization and deregulation. Institutional investors have been a major factor behind the new wave of mergers and acquisitions with their emphasis on getting the fastest possible large return.[29] Hostile bids, however, represent only a minority of the record-breaking number of mergers in 1995–1997: there were 97 hostile bids announced in 1995 in the USA and only 73 in 1996, with a combined value $155 billion. In 1988, however, there were 168 hostile bids with a total value of $222 billion.[30]

7. Conclusions

Institutional investors play an ever-increasing role as: collectors of savings; investors in securities and other financial assets; operators in the securities markets; major owners of publicly-held companies. Many of the structural forces shaping the new financial landscape in the past fifteen years – securitization, the use of derivatives, the growth of equities markets, highly-leveraged corporate restructuring – developed in large measure in response to the demands of the institutional investor community.[31]

The emergence of institutional investors as major market players in the new financial landscape has exerted a major influence on patterns of corporate control and governance. There is growing evidence that in OECD countries, the expansion of the institutional sector has had (and is having) a growing influence on financial governance channels, including the market for corporate control.

It can be expected that the determinants of the growth of the institutional sector (financial deregulation, liberalization of the investment activities of the institutional sector, an aging of the population, privatization of social security, the growth of the money management industry) will continue to affect both the structure and *modus operandi* of financial markets and corporate governance.

Appendix A:
Securities Holdings by Institutional Investors in a Sample of OECD Countries

PORTFOLIO COMPOSITION OF INSTITUTIONAL INVESTORS IN G-7 COUNTRIES
(in US$ billion and per cent)

	1990	1991	1992	1993	1994	1995
Insurance companies						
Assets	4548.8	5089.0	5314.3	6047.2	6688.0	7464.5
of which:						
– Shares	18%	19%	19%	20%	20%	21%
– Fixed income securities	41%	41%	42%	42%	42%	44%
– Other	41%	40%	39%	38%	38%	35%
Pension funds						
Assets	3348.1	3706.2	3908.4	4319.8	4478.5	5233.5
of which:						
– Shares	40%	44%	47%	49%	48%	52%
– Fixed income securities	33%	30%	30%	29%	30%	28%
– Other	27%	26%	23%	22%	22%	20%
Investment companies						
Assets[1]	2285.1	2611.2	2912.5	3639.6	3913.6	4632.6
of which:						
– Shares	27%	27%	26%	30%	32%	35%
– Fixed income securities	56%	57%	57%	55%	53%	50%
– Other	17%	16%	17%	15%	15%	15%
Other forms of institutional saving						
Assets[1]	2202.4	2419.4	2533.0	2798.0	3137.0	3310.5
of which:						
– Shares	20%	21%	21%	21%	20%	23%
– Fixed income securities	18%	17%	17%	18%	18%	18%
– Other	62%	62%	62%	61%	62%	59%

[1] Financial assets for Japan.
Source: OECD/DAFFE.

Notes

1. E. P. Davis, 1996, The Role of Institutional Investors in the Evolution of Financial Structure and Behaviour, Paper prepared for the Reserve Bank of Australia's Conference on 'The Future of the Financial System', 8–9 July 1996, Sydney, Australia.

2. H. J. Blommestein, Structural changes in Financial Markets: Overview of Trends and Prospects, in: H. J. Blommestein and K. Biltoft, eds., *The New Financial Landscape*, OECD, Paris, 1995.
3. A statistical survey was conducted for supporting this study by the CMF Group of Financial Statisticians, encompassing as categories of institutional investors: insurance companies, pension funds, investment companies, and other forms of institutional savings [DAFFE/CMF/RD(97)1]. The latter category was introduced in order to allow for problems in giving a precise definition of 'institutional investors' and complications in demarcation of different categories of institutional investors. These complications should be kept in mind when interpreting the figures from the statistical survey, as well as data from other sources.
4. Efficiency in terms of costs and processing time. See for details H. J. Blommestein and B. J. Summers, Banking and the Payment System, in: Bruce J. Summers, ed., *The Payment System – Design, Management and Supervision*, IMF, 1994; and I. Sendrovic, Technology and the Payment System, in: Bruce J. Summers, ed., *The Payment System – Design, Management and Supervision*, IMF, 1994.
5. H. J. Blommestein, Comment on 'Building Stability in Latin American Financial Markets' by L. Rojas-Suarez and S. R. Weisbrod, in: R. Hausmann and H. Reisen, eds., *Securing Stability and Growth in Latin America*, OECD, 1996.
6. H. J. Blommestein and M. G. Spencer, 'Sound Finance and the Wealth of Nations', North American Journal of Economics and Finance, 1996.
7. E. P. Davis, 1995, 'Pension Funds', Clarendon Press, Oxford, reports the following average transaction sizes: $275,000 (London), $50,000 (Frankfurt), $25,000 (Paris).
8. Lower transaction costs boost liquidity because it enables more frequent trade transactions and it increases the number of potential market participants.
9. A Revolution in Securities Markets' Structures?, Financial Market Trends No. 65, November 1996.
10. However, experience in countries such as the Netherlands suggest that there is no one to one relation between pension funds and equity market development, even with a favourable regulatory framework (Davis, 1995, p. 176).
11. D. Blake, 1990, *Financial Market Analysis*, McGraw Hill, London; M. Tamura, 1992, Improving Japan's Employee Pension Fund System, Nomura Research Institute Quarterly, summer, pp. 66–83; Davis, 1995, p. 154.
12. See for details, OECD Financial Market Trends, No. 63, February 1996.
13. R. Comment and G. W. Schwert, 1993, Poison or Placebo? Evidence on the Deterrent and Wealth Effects of Modern Anti-take-over Measures, NBER Working Paper No. 4316, April 1993.
14. M. P. Smith, 1996, Shareholder Activism by Institutional Investors: Evidence from CalPERS, the Journal of Finance, Vol. LI, No. 1, March.
15. 'Activism' refers to the involvement in monitoring the management of portfolio firms as opposed to active selection of private securities (e.g. stock picking) without taking an active role in monitoring.
16. See for details OECD Financial Market Trends, No. 63, February 1996 and E. P. Davis, 1995, 'Pension Funds', Claredon Press, Oxford.
17. C. Mayer, 1996, Corporate Governance, Competition and Performance, Economics Department Working Paper, No. 164, OCDE/(96)99.
18. R. J. Gilson, 1994, in: M. Isaksson and R. Skog, eds., Aspects of Corporate Governance, Juristfoerlaget, Stockholm, 1994.
19. R. J. Gilson, 1994, in: M. Isaksson and R. Skog, eds., Aspects of Corporate Governance, Juristfoerlaget, Stockholm, 1994.
20. In the United States, pension funds were historically passive. This attitude started to change in the 1980s during the takeover boom. The shift to a more active stance was stimulated by three

major events of developments: first, the United States Department of labor (the supervisor of the pension funds) stated in a 1988 ruling that decisions on voting were fiduciary acts of plan asset management under ERISA; second, shareholder initiatives on social issues (e.g. environment, South Africa) in the late 1980s, stimulated increased interest by public pension funds in the importance of proxy issues generally; third, the collapse of the take-over movement helped to boost shareholder activism as an alternative mechanism of corporate control.

21. R. H. Koppes and M. L. Reilly, An Ounce of prevention: meeting the Fiduciary Duty to Monitor an Index Fund, Journal of Corporate Law, University of Iowa, Summer, 1995.
22. The US Private Litigation Reform Act of 1995 provides for a court-appointed lead plaintiff. It stipulates that the most adequate plaintiff is the person with the largest financial interest in class-action shareholder suits.
23. For example, the UK Report of the Pension Law Review Committee argued that the average period that a pension fund held a share in the period 1983–1987 declined from 7 years to 2.5 years; see The Pension Law Reform Committee, Pension Law Reform, Volume I, 1993.
24. Institute of Directors, Short-termism and the State We're In, August 1996; Jeremy Monk, The Dynamics of Institutional Share Ownership in Major Quoted UK Companies, The Investor Relations Society, 1995.
25. Council of Institutional Investors, Does Ownership Add Value? Washington D.C.; S. Nesbitt, Long-term Rewards from Corporate Governance, Wilshire Associates, November 1993; Gordon Group, Active Investing in the US Equity Market: Past Performance and Future Prospects, 1993.
26. See reference in footnote 1.
27. *Financial Times*, An extremely Anglo-Saxon takeover bid, 10 March 1997.
28. Handelsblatt, Krupp continues to pursue full merger with rival Thyssen, 21/March/1997 (English Internet version).
29. *International Herald Tribune*. The Hostile Takeover Gets Civilized, March 30th, 1997.
30. *International Herald Tribune*. The Hostile Takeover Gets Civilized, March 30th, 1997.
31. H. J. Blommestein, Structural changes in Financial Markets: Overview of Trends and Prospects, in: H. J. Blommestein and K. Biltoft, eds., *The New Financial Landscape*, OECD, Paris, 1995.

Privatization and Corporate Governance

ABSTRACT

This paper examines different privatization methods and their implications in terms of corporate governance, focusing on the experiences of the Czech Republic and Poland. The paper's main conclusion is that it is important that the right set of incentives be in place to guarantee an efficient allocation of resources. Speed may be deemed less important than the search for an effective governance structure, but only if there is a well-defined and credible privatization strategy binding the management to *immediately* adopt practices consistent with profit maximization in the presence of hard budget constraints while authorities keep pursuing sound macroeconomic policies and creating a regulatory framework that will allow resources to be allocated efficiently.

Tito Boeri has worked for ten years at the OECD and is now professor of economics at Bocconi University in Milan.

Giancarlo Perasso is an economist in the Country Study Branch of the Economics Department of the OECD.

IV. Privatization and Corporate Governance: Some Lessons from the Experience of Transitional Economies*

TITO BOERI AND GIANCARLO PERASSO

1. INTRODUCTION

All former planned economies have started privatization programmes: some (Central and Eastern European Countries) are more advanced in transferring property from the state to individuals, others (mostly former Soviet Republics other than Russia) are just starting. Different methods of privatization have been implemented, ranging from mass privatization through voucher schemes to direct sales of enterprises (often to foreigners), and from spontaneous privatization to well-organised transfers of property rights to employees. These different methods have brought about different models, or structures, of corporate governance that affect the way enterprises are responding to market signals, and, more broadly, to the stimuli of the emerging market environment.

This paper will review evidence from two countries that have followed very different routes and methods in privatizing their productive assets: the Czech Republic and Poland. In the Czech Republic, voucher privatization accounted for the transfer of property rights of a fairly large share of the country's assets; in Poland, insider-privatization – ranging from management and employee (mostly leveraged) buyouts to the so-called privatization through 'liquidation' – has been the dominant privatization method. The private sector is now contributing to economic growth decisively. Yet, the different nature of the privatization process has resulted in a very different structure of ownership and control, which, by affecting firms' investment decisions, may increase asymmetries in the performance of private enterprises in the two countries in the years to come.

The plan of the paper is as follows. First, main privatization methods followed in central and eastern Europe and Russia are outlined and assessed in the light

---

* The authors would like to thank Rauf Gonenc, Vincent Koen and Silvana Malle for valuable comments on an initial draft. The views expressed in the paper are those of the authors and do not reflect those of the OECD nor of its member countries.

of commonly accepted normative criteria. Second, evidence on the performance of privatized enterprises in the two countries is reviewed by highlighting the effects of corporate governance on the behaviour of firms. The final section draws some tentative conclusions.

2. Privatization Methods

Three main routes have been used to privatize former large and medium-sized state enterprises in Central and Eastern Europe and Russia. The first privatization mechanism is *capital privatization*, i.e., the sale of enterprise assets to strategic investors via tenders, public auctions, and public offerings (usually, but not always, involving only minority stakes) and debt-equity swaps. The second privatization method is the so-called *mass privatization*, that is, the free (or at a symbolic price) distribution of certificates to the population, which are generally freely marketable. Such vouchers can be either sold or converted into company shares and/or participation in mutual funds set up at the start of the process. Finally, the third privatization route is *insider privatization*, that is, the creation of a holding through equity issues subscribed mainly by managers and workers. This scheme usually involves the concession of preferential credits, if not the free distribution of shares to workers. Insider privatization can be an alternative to the liquidation of a state enterprise, but can also be achieved *de facto* via the liquidation of firms in poor financial condition, and the sale or lease of their assets to managers and (less frequently) to workers.[1]

There is extensive literature weighing the pros and cons of privatization methods. Such an assessment is usually carried out merely on the basis of theoretical considerations concerning the design features of the various schemes, the incentives they have on managers' and workers' performance, their social acceptability, etc. Six to seven years after the start of privatization processes in Central and Eastern Europe it is possible to complement these subjective (and rather speculative) evaluations with preliminary evidence on the outcomes of the different privatization methods. Table 1 summarizes available information on the privatization strategies followed in the Czech Republic, Hungary, Poland and Russia – the four countries in the region for which most detailed information on privatization methods and performance is nowadays available – and on their outcomes.

In particular, three performance indicators are used, namely the *speed* of privatization, that is, the proportion of former state enterprises which has changed ownership within the first four years of the privatization process, the relevance of *outside ownership* (percentage of privatized enterprises with dominant outside ownership) in the resulting ownership structure of firms, and finally, the degree of *control* exerted over managerial decisions by the owners

TABLE 1
Methods of privatization of large and medium-sized enterprises

Country	Privatization method (weights)[a]			Outcomes			Overall country ratings[e]
	Capital privatization	Mass privatization	Management/employee buyout and liquidation	Speed[b]	Outside ownership[c]	Control[d]	
Czech Republic	17.8	74.2	7.7	99.0	58.3	33.0	9
Hungary	93.2	0.0	6.8	66.9	73.9	60.9	10
Poland	6.8	13.9	79.8	25.6	48.4	34.6	6
Russia	0.0	19.5	80.5	81.7	16.3	8.1	5
Method range[f]	11.3	8.5	10.2				

Notes:

[a] Value of films privatized with this method (as a % estimated value of privatized SOEs). Czech Republic: book value; Hungary: transaction value; Poland: nr. of firms privatized with this method as % of total nr. of privatized enterprises; Russia: book value.
[b] Number of firms being privatized in the country within the first four years of privatizations (as % of former SOEs targeted for privat).
[c] Percentage of privatized firms with dominant outsider ownership (EBRD).
[d] Percentage of firms with dominant either foreign or domestic outside ownership by companies (EBRD).
[e] Average of the rank of the country (increasing in country's performance) according to the three criteria listed before.
[f] Weighted average (weights are given by the share of privatizations achieved with the method at issue) of the overall country rating.

of the firm. The latter indicator is proxied by the involvement in privatization of foreign and domestic companies, which are better equipped than investment funds – usually lacking skilled staff and having to manage a vast array of shareholdings – to exert effective supervision over the management of firms.

As shown by the first three columns of the Table, the four countries have so far followed quite different privatization strategies: in the Czech Republic ownership changes were mainly achieved via a mass privatization scheme, while in Hungary capital privatization was the dominant route and in Poland and Russia a strong involvement of insiders was pursued. Given such wide differences in privatization strategies, the four countries' experience offers a natural comparison of the various privatization methods. In Table 1 we use the cross-country variation not only to obtain a ranking of the various countries and overall privatization strategies, but also to provide a rating of the various ownership change mechanisms. As can be grasped by reading the Table horizontally, the privatization strategy followed by the Czech Republic was extremely rapid (with over 99 per cent of state enterprise assets slated for privatization being transferred within a very short time frame), achieved a significant degree of outside ownership, but has resulted so far in a rather weak control structure. Hungary's strategy was somewhat less rapid, but achieved better results in terms of both relevance of outside ownership and control. Poland was slow to privatize (as discussed in Section 3 below, mass privatization was started only in 1995), achieved a rather low degree of outside ownership, but it resulted in a good control structure within the set of firms dominated by outsiders. Finally, Russia is another success story in terms of the speed of privatization, but this performance has been achieved at high costs in terms of the resulting ownership and control structure insofar as mostly insiders have been the key players in the privatization process.

Overall, each method involves a trade-off between different objectives. By assigning the same weight to the different criteria listed in Table 1, one reaches the conclusion that capital privatization is the single most successful method. However, there may be cases where some criteria are more important than others, and, in the early stages of transition, common wisdom deemed speed the most relevant. The key issue is: How closely do the three criteria listed in Table 1 correspond to the performance of firms? This question will be addressed in the next two sections which cover the rather extreme experiences of the Czech Republic and Poland, respectively.

3. THE CASE OF THE CZECH REPUBLIC

A fairly common misconception is that the Czech economy was fully and rapidly privatized thanks to the use of vouchers. A speedy transfer of property

TABLE 2

Estimated ownership structure in non-financial corporate sector (Czech Republic, 1994, percentage shares)

	Employment	Output
Total	100	100
of which:		
Voucher privatized	27	30
Co-operative (including agriculture)	8	9
Residual state ownership[1]	5	3
Other private	15	13
'Strategic' holdings of the state	20	21
For privatization but not yet privatized	25	24

[1] What was left from companies that were split and privatized by segments.
Source: OECD (1996a).

rights was indeed the rationale for implementing the voucher scheme, and great success was achieved in this effort.[2] About half of state holdings slated for privatization in the non financial corporate sector were privatized via voucher privatization very rapidly, both in terms of employment or output,[3] but – as Table 2 shows – state shareholdings in privatized enterprises, which are all practically vested in the National Property Fund (NPF), remain substantial.[4] here

These holdings can be divided into two groups: 'residual' holdings, i.e., what could not be sold so far and which the NPF is trying to sell, and 'strategic' companies,[5] that will also be privatized 'in the future'. The NPF may not hold a majority shareholding in these enterprises – hence some of them are correctly, from a purely statistical point of view, classified as 'private enterprises' – however it exerts control over the enterprises since the other shareholders are either small investors or are investment privatization funds (IPFs), which acquired vouchers from individual holders. The largest IPFs are controlled by banks, especially the big four banks, whose main shareholder, but not majority except in one case, is the state, via the NPF.[6]

This state influence in the Czech enterprise sector – which cannot be revealed by looking at official statistics – may manifest itself in many forms: as a direct shareholder, as a shareholder in banks, as a tax collector, and, in some cases, as a regulator. This happens in other countries as well, but the important point is whether the involvement of the state brings about managerial, and public policy, decisions that are different from those that would be taken in a fully privatized enterprise. Although in the Czech Republic there seems to be rather little direct state intervention in the economy, some indirect influence, may be likely, through some 'concerted action' or 'co-operation' between the state and/or its agencies and the management of the companies.

A very important case of this 'moral suasion' exerted by the state on enterprises is the Banking Council. Members of the Banking Council are the Governor of the Central Bank, the Minister of Finance, the Chairman of the National Property Fund and, occasionally, the chairmen of the largest four banks. Although there is no indication of government intervention in determining the allocation of credit, the potential for state 'suggestions' concerning banks' strategic options is very high.[7]

It is important to stress that the ownership structure of banks and enterprises is far from being settled. The NPF is still actively trying to sell its residual holdings, and recent indications show that it is ready to dispose of its holding in one of the major banks.

Ultimately, what is important is that the right set of incentives is present for the development of a genuinely market-oriented economy. The lower limit on the level of efficiency in an enterprise is given by the credible threat of bankruptcy. Some bankruptcies have taken place in the Czech Republic but banks, via their IPFs, appear to be reluctant to take large enterprises to court. It follows that the discipline provided by the hard budget constraint is not yet fully and extensively enforced in the Czech Republic.[8]

A semi-hard budget constraint may well be the byproduct of voucher privatization. Bank-owned IPFs play a large role in the exertion of corporate governance and, at this stage of the transition, are more concerned to 'preserve the life' of the enterprise that has borrowed from the parent bank than to liquidate it.[9] If this is the case, as it appears to be quite frequently, the question is whether the right incentives for enterprise restructuring are, and will be, present.

Looking at macroeconomic data, there appears to have been, so far, little incentive to restructure enterprises. Despite double digit investment growth rates in recent years, productivity has increased only slightly; exports are not growing as rapidly as in the past, while imports are booming. Finally the Czech Republic is the only country in the region currently experiencing an increase in unemployment (although from one of the lowest levels in the OECD area[10]). At the microeconomic level, a survey conducted by Coopers & Lybrand, quoted in OECD (1996), indicated that the managing boards of only 1 in 6 enterprises surveyed had their salary linked to enterprise performance; in almost as many cases (1 in 8) the supervisory board's reward was linked to performance. There was no case of reward linked to the share price. Among managing directors, only half felt that profit maximization was a 'very important' goal (less than half of board members shared this view). Supervising assets and supervising management were the two other important goals identified by board members.

The picture presented so far is that of a system of incentives geared to achieving restructuring gradually and avoiding sharp shocks to the enterprises, most notably hostile take-overs and/or changes in management. The issue is whether this process is being undertaken at too slow a pace.[11] Time will tell, although the deteriorating trade performance does not bode well[12] and may even be an indication of the slowness of restructuring due to the present structure of corporate governance.

Corporate governance in the Czech Republic is evolving neither along the lines of the 'bank-based' model, nor according to the 'stock exchange-based' model.[13] Directly, or via their IPFs, banks are the predominant players but their strategy of nurturing enterprise growth, and hence of not concentrating on (short-term) profit maximisation, could endanger the stability of the financial system, if it is not carefully followed. The return on average assets of Czech banks is lower than those of Hungarian and Polish banks, and the share of their non-performing loans in total loans is twice that of Hungarian banks and much higher than that of Polish banks.[14] There have been cases of closure of small banks, but this process is strengthening the position of the big NPF-controlled banks which, as we saw earlier, are reluctant to take enterprises to court. Such a 'relaxed' attitude concerning the enforcement of the hard budget constraint on the part of banks could, however, cause more damage than good to the Czech economy.

4. THE POLISH EXPERIENCE

The privatization process in Poland has been much slower than in the Czech lands. By June 1996, privatization had been completed in 2624 enterprises[15] out of the 8853 state enterprises existing in 1990, when the process was started. As in the case of the Czech Republic, these numbers should be interpreted with caution, as the state has in some cases retained substantial participation in privatized units, remaining *de facto*, the controlling shareholder (OECD, 1996b). The size of the residual state sector may provide a better measure of the extent of privatization than the number of privatized units *per se*: the total book value of the state shares in the business sector was estimated in November 1995 to amount to about 140 billion zlotys. This compares with a book value of about 8 billion zlotys for all firms quoted on the Warsaw Stock Exchange and revenues from the sale of state assets of the order of 2.6 billion in 1996.

Large and medium-sized state enterprises scheduled for privatization in Poland have first to be transformed into a joint stock company under the jurisdiction of the Treasury. Although this so-called 'commercialization' stage does not alter the ownership of firms, it modifies their control structure by phasing out the Workers' Councils and establishing a Board of Directors composed of up to seven top managers and two representatives of workers. This transformation is supposed to break the so-called 'Bermuda triangle' (Belka et al., 1995) control structure of former Polish state enterprises, which apparently involved paralysing negotiations among the Directors, the trade unions and the Workers' Council. Furthermore, the dismantling of the Workers' Council significantly reduces the power of workers in affecting firm's strategies. Far from being a consultative body (like the German Workers' Councils), the Polish Workers' Council has, in principle, most of the powers typically held by governing bodies in a corporation, including the possibility to appoint and lay-off the managers of the firm. The commercialized unit is therefore still a self-governed state firm dominated by insiders – as most Polish state enterprises are, at least since the 1980s – but one where workers have lost most of their power *vis-à-vis* the management.

Within two years of being 'commercialized', procedures for the actual sale of the enterprise should start along one of the possible routes envisaged by the 1990 Privatization Law.[16] As shown in Table 1, the dominant privatization track for large and medium-sized enterprises in Poland has been so far the so-called 'liquidation' route. This method involves the sale or lease of state enterprise assets to other private firms or – as in most cases – to the insiders.[17] The sale or lease can either involve the enterprise as a whole or parts of its assets, as in the case of enterprises in poor financial condition.[18] Several concessions have been granted to the insiders, including the lowering of interest rates used to compute the repayments and the postponement of the capital contributions. While these concessions have accelerated the privatization process, they have nonetheless reduced even further the resources of the firm undergoing privatization as well as its capacity to raise loans.

While capital privatization has involved only about 7 per cent of former state enterprises (first column of Table 1) it has been the main source of revenues from privatization: for instance, in the first six months of 1996, revenues from capital privatization accounted for almost 80 per cent of the total funds raised from privatization. Capital privatization typically involves the largest state enterprises and is achieved mainly via tenders and the search for strategic investors, who are for the most part foreign or foreign/domestic partnerships. The main problem is the slow pace of this process, which has been further reduced by increasingly complex deals concerning the fate and wages of the enterprises' employees as well as investment commitments by the new owner. While these commitments are requested to seek support for privatization, they may make the search for strategic investors more difficult, leaving the commercialized unit in limbo just when it would require strategic decisions and deeper restructuring.

Although plans for mass privatization date back to late 1990, concrete arrangements to start the process were only made at the end of 1994. An important characteristic of the Polish mass privatization scheme – and one that makes it quite different from the Czech vouchers scheme – is that it ensures that each firm has a strategic investor. Shares of the firms included in the programme are allocated to the 15 National Investment Funds (NIFs) set up in 1995 in such a way that each NIF has shares in all firms, but also a strategic 33 per cent stake in some (randomly selected) units. This design feature of the Polish scheme should result in a better governance structure than that currently prevailing in the Czech Republic. However, the late start of the process and the fact that some of the best performing state enterprises targeted for privatization have displayed some reluctance in being involved in this scheme (because they feared losing potential foreign investors) seem to have negatively affected the quality of the firms involved in the scheme. This will certainly make the task of the NIF managers more difficult, as they are called to supervise a relatively large number of former state enterprises requiring significant restructuring. Moreover, the state retains a significant minority stake (25 per cent) in firms being privatized and another 15 per cent is allotted, free of charge, to the workers. This does not fully rule out the possibility that political pressures may result in supervisory boards postponing the needed deep restructuring of the firms rather than pushing it through. Indeed, there have been a few cases where important conflicts have arisen between the NIF management and the supervisory board of the firm in which the investment fund had a strategic stake. Given the very recent start of the scheme, it is premature to draw any definite conclusion about its effectiveness. History will tell whether or not the present difficulties and tensions between NIFs and the supervisory boards of some firms undergoing privatization are just a byproduct of a physiological learning process which ultimately generates an effective supervision of firms.

Pending the evaluation of the outcome of the mass privatization process, the Polish experience offers a good case-study on the pros and cons of the insiders versus the outsiders privatization route. Comparisons of the performance of commercialized units, firms being privatized via management/employee buyouts and capital privatization are problematic due to substantial differences in the composition of the various privatization pools prior to the actual sale and on the timing of restructuring (e.g., enterprises sold to outsiders have generally undergone considerable pre-privatization restructuring). The fact that governing bodies of commercialized units can choose among the various privatization methods makes such comparisons even more difficult because self-selection is likely to increase even further the asymmetries among the various privatization pools.

Bearing the above caveats in mind, Table 3 offers some information on the control structure and performance of firms of different ownership type. In particular, the first four rows of the table report findings from a survey of about 200 Polish firms carried out at the end of 1993 (Pinto et al., 1994).

TABLE 3

Corporate governance and enterprise performance in Poland

	State	Insiders	Domestic outsiders	Foreign
Role of the Board of Directors in the following decisions[a]				
Profit allocation		29		10
Hiring/firing managers		43		10
Managerial compensation		48		20
Major investment		57		30
Performance indicators				
Real wages (% change)	−0.5	0.6	−3.8	14.6
Employment (% change)	−5.5	−0.7	0.8	−5.5
Sales (% change)	5	12.5	10	19.8
Labour productivity (% change)	14.4	28.2		
Films introducing new technology (%)[b]	51.6	75	71.4	87.5

Notes:
[a] Percentage of enterprises within the ownership type reporting that the decisions on the subject matter listed below are made by the Board of Directors.
[b] Percentage of films within the ownership type reporting major investment in new technology in the last two years.
Source: Belka et al. (1995); EBRD (1995).

This suggests that the decision structure of insider-dominated firms is characterised by a very strong position of managers *vis-à-vis* the other organs, notably the Supervisory Board and the shareholders' meetings. In particular, in less than 50 per cent insider-of dominated firms, the Board of Directors can appoint or fire managers and decide upon their compensation. The dominance of managers is reinforced by the limited role assigned to workers in the Board of Directors of firms in the commercialization stage (see above).

The next five rows of the table display results from an enterprise survey carried out by the World Bank in 1993 (World Bank, 1996; Pinto et al., 1994). As argued above, differences in the performance of firms of different ownership type are likely to reflect selection bias. Yet, two facts highlighted by the table would seem to be particularly important. The first is the much better sales and technology performance of enterprises with foreign owners, within the class of outsider-dominated firms. The latter would seem to have shed more labour than domestic-outsiders firms, while granting significant wage increases to the 'surviving' workforce. Another important fact highlighted by the table is the substantial employment reductions and significant gains in productivity taking place in enterprises that are still in state hands. This confirms the picture of Polish state enterprises provided by Pinto and van Wijnbergen (1995). Insofar as incentives for managers of state enterprises to pursue profit-maximizing behaviour come from the aspiration of being confirmed and/or rewarded by the new owners, this result suggests that even a slow, but credible, privatization process may produce immediate results on firm performance.

5. Concluding Remarks

Governments of Central and Eastern European countries that were/are committed to genuine privatization face a formidable task. The sheer size of the assets to be privatized and the lack of established financial markets and intermediaries presented an incredible challenge to the authorities. Privatization strategies had to be devised which would accomplish three main tasks: first, rapidly increase the size of the private sector; second, prevent a decapitalization of the enterprise in the process and possibly inject fresh capital; third, ensure an effective control structure over management. All this while gaining political support for reforms and developing domestic capital markets.

Many assets still remain to be privatized in Central and Eastern Europe – Hungary being the exception since privatization has gone farther than in any other country, including some Western European countries – and authorities should learn from their, and other countries', past experiences. Privatization strategies actually implemented differed quite substantially across countries. This was due partly to exogenous constraints (e.g., the geographical orientation of foreign direct investments), and partly to political considerations inducing public authorities to give priority to one particular objective over others. In this paper, we have exploited these cross-country differences in privatization methods in an attempt to make some inferences on their effects on corporate governance.

In particular, we have considered the two rather extreme routes taken by the Czech and Polish authorities. In the Czech Republic, a decision was made to go ahead rapidly and give priority to speed in the transfer of property rights. In Poland, a more cautious and slow approach to privatization was taken, giving priority to direct sales of large units and insider privatization of small and medium-sized state enterprises.

The Czech experience shows that speed in transferring property rights may not lead to an effective corporate governance structure if institutional investors controlled by domestic banks (largely state-controlled) take the lead in the privatization process. It also shows that dispersing ownership among citizens without adopting appropriate regulations concerning transparency and minority shareholders' rights brings about a concentration of ownership that is harmful to competition, i.e., it hampers an efficient allocation of resources. Mass privatization, perhaps more than capital or insider privatization, can be successful only if a good regulatory framework is in place preventing the violation of minority's rights and lack of transparency in the build-up of control groups. The importance of having credible 'rules of the game' that are conducive to an efficient use of resources is highlighted by the Polish experience. When the right set of incentives was finally introduced, it made managers of state-owned enterprises behave efficiently even before the actual privatization of assets. The experience of Poland also indicates that a prolonged piecemeal approach to privatization may delay the liberalization of markets and not provide adequate information on relative scarcities.

Does this mean that speed should be given less importance than other objectives of privatization? In the end, what is important is that the right set of incentives be in place to guarantee an efficient allocation of resources. In this respect, the enforcement of the hard budget constraint is only a necessary condition – but not a sufficient one – for guaranteeing efficiency. A long-term strategy is also required when restructuring enterprises and this can only be achieved when there is little uncertainty about the evolving corporate governance of the firm.

In a nutshell, speed may be deemed less important than the search for an effective governance structure, but only if there is a well-defined and credible privatization strategy binding the management to *immediately* adopt practices consistent with profit maximisation in the presence of hard budget constraints while authorities keep pursuing sound macroeconomic policies and creating a regulatory framework that will allow resources to be allocated efficiently.

Notes

1. See Johnson and Kroll (1991) for a review of uncontrolled and spontaneous privatisation methods.
2. There is, by now, a vast literature on voucher privatization. For the Czech and Slovak experience, see OECD (1994). See also Shafik (1993) and Anderson (1994) for description and analysis of the role of voucher funds in corporate governance.
3. If one considers the book value of these firms, the share of voucher-privatized firms is higher (see Table 1 and Kotrba, 1995). Book value data, though, especially in the first years of the transition could represent an imprecise picture of the enterprise.
4. This is also the finding of a recent study by Pistor and Turkewitz (1996).
5. Strategic companies include electricity distribution companies, coal mines, petrochemical companies, pharmaceutical companies. At the end of 1995, there were 56 strategic enterprises, including the country's four largest banks.
6. In this case as well, given the dispersion of other shareholders the NPF is *de facto* controlling the four largest banks. For example, at the banks' meeting of shareholders in 1996, the NPF 'suggested' a distribution of dividends below what was proposed by the management and nobody raised any objection.
7. This (in)direct state influence is further reinforced by the web of cross-ownership among banks, see Mejstrik (1994), and financial intermediaries, see Kenway-Klvacova (1996).

8. The case of truck-maker Tatra is a good example of banks' reluctance to take large enterprises to court. In general, it is difficult to assess whether banks do not enforce their creditor's rights because of the length of the bankruptcy procedures or because they are optimistic about the restructuring effort being undertaken by companies.
9. Furthermore, the staff of bank-owned IPFs was initially, and generally still is, dominated by employees whose careers probably depend on their assessment by the bank hierarchy.
10. See OECD (1995) for a discussion of the factors behind the 'Czech employment miracle'.
11. There are many other issues involved, especially that of transparency, the lack of which is a major shortcoming of the Czech capital markets, see OECD (1996a) for a discussion of this issue.
12. Czech authorities are quick to point out that the trade deficit is mainly due to the importation of investment goods, which account for a large share of imports. Leaving aside the doubts about the criteria used by the authorities for classifying what goods are investment goods, the weak increase in productivity despite the growth in investments remains a cause of concern.
13. See Coffee (1996) for a detailed analysis of the present corporate governance system in the Czech Republic.
14. See Deutsche Morgan Grenfell (1997). Although the criteria for loan classification may differ among countries, differences in the share of non-performing loans in banks' portfolio are as marked as to survive to these definitional problems.
15. See EBRD (1996).
16. Delays in the privatization process have extended the duration of the commercialisation phase for a number of enterprises. The new privatization law approved by the Parliament in September 1996 also allows for commercialization without subsequent privatization for enterprises requiring substantial restructuring.
17. According to Earle and Estrin (1996), almost $\frac{3}{4}$ of the firms privatized via liquidation are insider-owned.
18. This is the case of liquidations via article 19 of the 1990 Privatization Law. The possibility offered to 'unbundle' firms in poor financial condition is an innovative characteristic of the Polish privatization route, which has allowed idle capacity to be put back into use (OECD, 1996b).

References

Anderson, R. E. (1994) Voucher Funds in Transitional Economies, the Czech and Slovak Experience, *World Bank Policy Research Working Papers No. 1324*.

Coffee, J. C. Jr. (1996) Institutional Investors in Transitional Economies: Lessons from the Czech Experience, in R. Frydman, C. W. Gray and A. Rapaczynski (eds.), *Corporate Governance in Central Europe and Russia*, Central European University Press.

Deutsche Morgan Grenfell (1997) Emerging Markets. Focus Eastern Europe, January 27.

Earle, J. and S. Estrin (1996) Employee Ownership in Transition, in R. Frydman, C. W. Gray and A. Rapaczynski (eds), *Corporate Governance in Central Europe and Russia*, Central European University Press.

EBRD (1995) Transition Report 1995, European Bank for Reconstruction and Development, London.

EBRD (1996) Transition Report 1996, European Bank for Reconstruction and Development, London.

Johnson, S. and H. Kroll (1991) Managerial Strategies for Spontaneous privatization, *Soviet Economy* 7, 281–316.

Kenway, P. and E. Klvacova (1995) The Web of Cross-ownership among Czech Financial Intermediaries: An Assessment, *Europe-Asia Studies* 48, No. 5, 797–809.

Kotrba, J. (1995) Privatization Process in the Czech Republic: Players and Winners, in J. Svejnar (ed.), *The Czech Republic and Economic Transition in Eastern Europe*, Academic Press.

Mejstrik, M. (1994) Czech Investment Funds as a Part of Financial Sector and their Role in Privatization of the Economy, Institute of Economic Studies, Charles University, *Reform Round Table Working Paper No. 14*.

OECD (1994) Economic Survey of the Czech and Slovak Republics, Paris, OECD.

OECD (1995) Review of the Labour Market in the Czech Republic, Paris, OECD.

OECD (1996a) Economic Survey of the Czech Republic, Paris, OECD.

OECD (1996b) Economic Survey of Poland, Paris, OECD.

Pinto, B., M. Belka and S. Krajewski (1994) Transforming State Enterprises in Poland: Evidence on Adjustment by Manufacturing Firms, *Brookings Papers on Economic Activity*.

Pistor, K. and J. Turkewitz (1996) Coping with Hydra – State Ownership after Privatization: A Comparative Study of the Czech Republic, Hungary and Russia, in R. Frydmanm C. W. Gray and A. Rapaczynski (eds.), *Corporate Governance in Central Europe and Russia*, Central European University Press.

Shafik, N. (1993) Making a Market. Mass Privatization in the Czech and Slovak Republics, *World Bank Policy Research Working Papers No. 1321*.

World Bank (1996) *World Development Report*, Washington.

ABSTRACT

This paper focuses on Dutch shareholders' structures and the participations by funds and banks in particular. Statistics show that foreigners possess the main proportion of Dutch shares, funds a relatively large proportion and banks only a small proportion. In the Netherlands there has been an increasing interest in shares, in general, and funds and banks have tripled their investments in shares as a part of total assets during 1980–1996. Participations of banks in non-financial institutions have also increased considerably lately. The current Dutch debate about a possible move of the Dutch corporate governance model towards a more Anglo-Saxon model is also summarized.

Wilko Bolt and **Marga Peeters** are economists at the Econometric Research and Special Studies Department of De Nederlandsche Bank. Wilko Bolt obtained a MSc degree and a PhD in Econometrics from the Free University of Amsterdam. He wrote a thesis about the theory of negotiation and published in the American Economic Review and Economic Theory. Marga Peeters obtained a MSc degree in Econometrics from the University of Tilburg and a PhD in Econometrics from the University Maastricht. She published at Springer Verlag, in Applied Economics and in Annales d'Economie et de Statistique.

V. Corporate Governance in the Netherlands

WILKO BOLT AND MARGA PEETERS

1. INTRODUCTION

Corporate governance has become a topical issue and a main subject of intense academic and policy debates. It concerns the control of a corporation, in particular the relationship between the owners on the one hand and management and directors on the other hand. In a broader sense corporate governance is defined as the control of a corporation which concerns the interactions between all stakeholders, including employees, clients, local governments, etc.

Especially in the United States and the United Kingdom the owners of companies play an important role today. The influence of shareholders on management and directors is large and poorly performing corporations have clearly felt shareholders' pressure. The debate on governance has also become important in other countries, even in those countries where shareholders do not have a crucial say in a corporation's decision making.

One reason for corporate governance being debated is the strong desire of – among others – the government to know who owns a country's corporations. This is definitely important for countries where shareholders have a decisive say, e.g. in the US. US shareholders are influential, shares are mainly in the hands of households and might be in the possession of a relatively small group of people. In Europe corporate governance has become an issue for another reason, namely as a part of the 'convergence' discussion. Many different systems exist, like the Anglo-Saxon model (UK), the German model (Germany), the Latin model (Spain and Italy) and the structure model (the Netherlands).[1] Discussions today are about the wish to move towards the Anglo-Saxon model, which has as main characteristics transparency and no strict separation between the owners and the management of a corporation.

In the Netherlands this discussion is held also, fed by the discussions abroad. The Dutch situation is special in that Dutch shares are largely held by foreigners, as a consequence of the open character of the Dutch economy. Under a more Anglo-Saxon model of corporate governance more say would therefore be given to non-Dutch citizens. As in many other countries, another reason for the interest in corporate governance concerns the changing shareholding structures. Insurance companies and pension funds collect more and more funds that need to be invested profitably for the aging population. Investments in shares have become very common. Also, banks seem to change their (risky) investments behaviour. Allegedly more investments in shares by funds and banks take place but the reasons behind the specific investments choices and the enforcements of rights associated with shares are difficult to pin down. We do not know yet whether the increase in share investments have entailed ownerships of corporations that are more concentrated, nor do we know to what extent corporate behaviour or performance is influenced by the (new) developments in shareholding structures.

The literature on corporate governance is broad but the majority of studies discuss this issue only in a theoretical way. An empirical exception is Nickell et al. (1996), who investigate whether UK companies' performance is significantly affected by shareholders' governance, measured as a major shareholdership of one person outside a company. Some descriptive studies further exist, though for the Netherlands there is not much evidence. One study focusing on the Netherlands has been carried out by Gelauff and Den Broeder (1997). It is extensive in its presentation and presents some aggregate statistical evidence on corporate governance issues in comparison with Germany. The scarce evidence on Dutch corporate governance probably results from the fact that Dutch corporations do not have to give public notice on many issues.

An aim of this study is to answer first some simple questions about Dutch shareholding structures. For instance, the questions what the situation in the Netherlands is in comparison with other countries, and which investors' groups have changed their interest in shares investments are answered. We then concentrate on banks.[2] Banks have a particular position in that they can be a lender to as well as an investor in a certain company. Their investments' possibilities in risky assets have always been restricted, in order to protect the bank's creditors, though these restrictions have been weakened since the early eighties. The information that we have can provide some insights in their portfolio investments' behaviour. In addition to this statistical evidence, the recent Dutch discussion on corporate governance is summarized. This provides information about the Dutch situation and could encourage an international discussion.

The outline of the paper is as follows. Section 2 presents the background information on corporate governance in a broad sense. Section 3 discusses the Dutch situation on shareholding on the basis of the available data. Section 4 provides more detailed information on shareholding by Dutch banks. Section 5 summarizes the current discussion about a recent proposal to move corporate governance in the Netherlands towards a more Anglo-Saxon model. Section 6 presents the conclusions.

2. BACKGROUND ON CORPORATE GOVERNANCE

Ever since the notion that modern corporations are characterized by the separation of ownership and control (Berle and Means, 1933), the issue of aligning the interests of the owners and managers and other stakeholders – the main problem of corporate governance although the term 'corporate governance' was not coined until two decades ago – has given rise to a large academic literature and has been the subject of intense policy debate for quite some time. However, the discussion on corporate governance has recently attracted increased attention, originating in the US and UK at the end of the 1980s, and which by now has spread all over Europe.

There are several reasons for this. First, increased competitiveness of firms and corporations in a world where financial markets are becoming larger, more complex and more closely integrated than ever before, requires adequate governance structures to provide a proper framework for the exercise and control of power. The focus on the medium and long-term perspective makes good corporate governance vital. Second, the sharp increase in takeovers and management buy-outs in the 1980s in the US and the UK seems to have done more harm than good from an economic performance point of view. Third, a series of corporate failures (IBM, Rolls Royce, Barings, Maxwell, etc.) where the weakness of corporate governance was clearly one of the contributing factors adds to the picture. There is a growing common perception that managers have become insufficiently accountable to shareholders and other individuals or institutions that have stakes in companies (i.e. the stakeholders). It is argued that it is this unaccountability which provides the wrong incentives for managers, leading to short-term decision-making, and to a lack of long-run investing in physical and human capital and innovating businesses, which may ultimately have a negative impact on economic performance. In fact, we may say that corporate governance is foremost a matter of *performance accountability* (Demb and Neubauer, 1992).

These events and the widespread belief that corporate governance affects economic performance have spurred a public policy agenda and a variety of reforms. A good example is the so-called Cadbury Code in 1992 on corporate governance in the UK. Similarly, in the Netherlands we have had the Peters' Committee 1996 which has put forward a number of recommendations and suggestions for changing Dutch corporate governance structures (see also Section 5). These recommendations concern questions such as: how should directors of companies be selected, reappointed or disqualified; what should they be paid; what is the relationship between investors (stakeholders) and management; what are the rules in times of financial distress; how important are auditors and what responsibility do they have; what is the exact role of the

Board of Directors and shareholders, etc. All these questions deserve attention in order to safeguard a proper framework of governance structures.

Basically, corporate governance can be described as the complete system of institutional arrangements and relations through which companies and financial institutions are directed and controlled. It presents the framework that governs the ability of economic agents (i.e. groups of persons or institutions) to manage corporate resources and it focuses on the crucial relationship between ownership, control and economic performance. The central problem of governance is to come up with an optimal system of relations which enhances the continuity of efficient business relationships in the presence of self-interested opportunistic agents, the stakeholders, by means of appropriate incentive schemes, safeguards and dispute resolution procedures (Kester, 1992). But who are the stakeholders in a company? Well-known categories of stakeholders are shareholders, creditors and managers, yet employees, suppliers and consumers are stakeholders as well.[3]

Research concerning corporate governance issues has developed along two lines. One line concerns the empirical content of the effects of corporate governance on economic performance. In such studies, corporate governance is for example measured by a degree of dominance of shareholders, or the size and/or composition (executive vs. non-executive members) of the Board of Directors, or the payment structure of management (e.g. stock option plans to link managerial effort to performance), or the frequency of proxy voting, etc. One is ultimately interested in the question whether different governance structures imply differences in corporate performance (see e.g. Nickell et al., 1996).

The other line concentrates on the theoretic modelling of corporate governance, especially on the application of principal-agent models. A first question which immediately comes to mind is why corporate governance issues should arise in the first place. In this context, Hart (1995) argues that corporate governance does matter in an organization whenever two conditions are present: an agency problem which concerns a conflict of interest among the stakeholders, and transaction costs such that this agency problem cannot be dealt with through a comprehensive contract. Hart claims that corporate governance plays an active role only when some future actions have not been specified in the initial contract: governance provides a way for deciding on these actions. However, in a complete comprehensive contracting world there are no 'residual' decisions, since everything has been specified in advance in the initial contract. In particular, corporate governance is concerned with the proper allocation of residual rights over the company's assets.

In general the goal of a company's management is to maximize the value of its financial assets. In order to carry out this task properly, management control of assets is separated from ownership of these assets. This separation enables the management to spread the risks over a large group of shareholders in attracting equity capital, and it facilitates the hiring of professional managers with more knowledge and expertise on management issues than the owners of assets in a company. However, too much separation and managerial discretion may induce the wrong incentives that underlie the basic principal-agent problem. Management might invest too much capital in projects that require little managerial effort or in projects that increase private gains, such as salaries, power and status. Hence, management must be monitored and be given the proper incentives in order to align management and investors' objectives. A major part of corporate governance is concerned with the design of checks and balances on managerial behaviour. Several mechanisms for controlling the management can be distinguished.

A first mechanism is provided by the *Board of Directors* which monitors the management and ratifies major decisions. In principle, the board plays a key role in monitoring; however, in practice its effectiveness may be limited due to all kinds of cross-relationships with the company itself. In this context, the Cadbury Committee recommends an independent member as chairman of the board and a formal selection procedure for non-executive directors. A second mechanism is presented by the *shareholders* themselves. They own the company in terms of the residual control rights, but they may have little or no incentive to monitor management. This is typically the case in the UK and the US where shareholders are numerous but not sufficiently influential to exert pressure individually. They face a significant *free-rider* problem: an individual shareholder can incur the cost of monitoring, while the benefits of the improved company performance accrue to all shareholders. So, almost no monitoring takes place. This problem is also present in the third mechanism device, namely *proxy voting*. Nobody wants to bear the cost of initially investigating the company's underperformance and launching the proxy fight, since the benefits from a better management are divided under all shareholders in the form of a higher share price.

As a fourth mechanism, given this free-rider problem associated with highly dispersed shareholders, one may argue that in order to improve corporate governance a company must have one or more *dominant* shareholders. Obviously, this reduces the free-rider problem but can create other difficulties at the same time. For instance, a company cannot enjoy the risk reduction benefits from portfolio diversification any longer and may also be subjected to costly trades with the large shareholder. Also, other agency problems may be introduced if the large shareholder is an institution itself with its own shareholders. Empirical evidence also confirms that large stakeholders play a mixed role in a company's performance (see e.g. Morck, Schleifer and Vishny (1988)).

To alleviate all these incentive and free-rider problems, one may take the view that *hostile takeovers* provide, in principle, a much more powerful mechanism to align the interests of the management and the other stakeholders in a company. It allows the individual who identifies an underperforming company to obtain a large reward, so there is basically no free-rider problem present. Therefore, one may argue that regulations which protect managers from hostile takeovers lower the disciplinary role of takeovers and may in the end be counterproductive. On the other hand, the enormous rise in the numbers of hostile takeovers in the UK and US in 1980s raised serious doubts as to whether it really improved economic performance in the long run. Further, increased competition between bidders in hostile takeovers may raise the price and lower profits from a takeover. Also the use of debt by the management as a way of committing itself not to 'empire-build' in the future raises the price of the company, which makes a takeover less likely. This last point makes it clear that the *corporate financial structure* also acts as a source of discipline on management.

The existence of debt in a company forces the management to use part of the revenues to make repayments. These debt obligations constrain the management's opportunities to invest in the wrong projects in terms of economic performance. So, debt finance acts as a *discipline device*. This reflects the important role of banks and other financial institutions in financing the business sector. It is often the case that banks, because of close relationships with companies, may be better informed than other providers of capital. Obviously, it is in their own interest that banks signal financial and economic crises at a early stage and, in response, enforce harsh restructuring plans in the firm. If management does not comply with their demands, banks can credibly threaten to withdraw their loans and to shut down the credit channel. This credibility depends to a large extent on the priority of debt finance. Without priority of debt finance, restructuring plans would not be carried out as soon as possible, which forces other providers of capital to demand higher rates of return. In this sense debt finance is *complementary,* since it allows the company to attract other sources of capital from financial markets at reasonable costs.

In literature there is some discussion on the combined position of banks as creditors/shareholders in a company. Banks often only worry about the downside risk of a firm, which could lead to too conservative or riskless behaviour and, in contrast, do not focus on the upside potential of a firm, which is usually the drive for the necessary innovations for continuity in the long run. Combining the two positions could lead to a better decision-making process. Moreover, the incentive to take too large risks with borrowed credit to benefit the shareholders is reduced if shareholders have issued debt to the firm at the same time. However, it is also argued that a combined creditor-shareholder position could undermine the discipline mechanism of banks on firms (Boot, 1994). If banks – apart from debt – do also have equity at stake in a firm, it makes it more difficult for them to act credibly in times of financial distress.

TABLE 1

The structure of shareholding in selected countries (percentage of total, as at end of year)

	G 1990	F 1992	I 1993	UK 1993	US 1992	J	NL 1992
1992	1995						
Institutional investors	22	23	11	60	31	47	24
Banks	10		10	1	0	26	2
Pension Funds/Insurers	12		1	52	24	17	22
Others (Unit trusts)			0	7	7	4	
Households	17	34	34	19	48	23	19
Private Companies	42	21	23	4	14	25	19
Public Authorities	5	2	27	1		1	
Foreign Investors	14	20	5	16	7	4	37

Note: The figures do not necessarily add up to 100 because of differences in definitions used by the providers of the data and differences in regulatory structures. A bank is a universal bank in Germany and a high-street bank in the UK.
Sources: Lannoo (1995, see Table 3, data for Germany, France, Italy, UK, US and Japan) and Annual Report of De Nederlandsche Bank (data for the Netherlands).

That is, the credibility of the threat to cut off the credit channel is reduced since it would also hurt the bank itself.

3. Shareholding and Other Portfolio Investments in the Netherlands

This section presents some structures and trends in Dutch shareholding by various investors' groups. The main objective is to provide some insights into the changing shareholding structures in comparison with other countries and in comparison with other investment opportunities.

Table 1 shows the shareholding structures in Germany (G), France (F), Italy (I), the UK, the US and Japan (J), as published in Lannoo (1995, Table 3). In addition, data for the Netherlands (NL) are presented in the last column to make a comparison. Some caution is needed in comparing the figures as the year of measurement is not the same for each country and also the definitions of investor groups may slightly differ across countries. For the Netherlands it follows that institutional investors possessed 24 per cent of Dutch shares in 1995, of which 2 per cent by banks and 22 per cent by pension funds and insurance companies. Households and private companies each possessed about 19 per cent and with 37 per cent foreign investors possessed the major part. A comparison with the other countries shows that the Dutch shareholding structure resembles that in France most, although foreigners hold only 20 per cent of all shares in France. In none of the non-Dutch countries foreigners hold the majority of shares, which probably reflects the fact that these economies are less open than the Dutch one. The tiny percentage of shares held by banks in the Netherlands (2 per cent) is comparable with the situation in the UK and the US, but is in glaring contrast to Germany, Italy and in particular Japan. Banks in the latter countries are known to be involved in long- term relationships with companies and for this reason are larger stakeholders. The high share-ownership, i.e. 42 per cent, of private companies in Germany and of households, i.e. 48 per cent, in the US is also striking. For more information about these and other countries, see Lannoo (1995) and Mayer (1996).

We concentrate further on the Dutch situation. Figure 1 shows the development of the shareholders structure during 1980–1996. In this figure, banks, funds (insurance companies and pension funds), households and private companies, and foreigners are represented. The figure shows that banks own a small proportion and funds a large proportion of the total shares of about 2 per cent and 20 per cent, respectively. These shares remain quite constant over the whole sample period. It could be expected that institutional investors invest more in shares due to the fact that they possess more and more funds because of the aging population, as is observed in some other countries. But whereas the total value of shares, i.e. the market capitalization, has been multiplied by as much as five during 1980–1996, funds do not have a strongly growing part of the total share stock. Households and private companies, on the other hand, both have a strongly increasing part over the sample period. This is probably due to the increase in private pension schemes. The increase in shareholdership of households and private investors in the nineties turns out to have been wholly at the expense of foreign investors.

As Figure 1 does not reveal whether investors have shown a growing interest in share investments as such, some more detailed information is given. Figures 2 and 3 show the investments in domestic bonds, domestic shares, foreign shares and real estate by funds and banks, respectively. These investments are all risky and expressed here as a percentage of the total assets. Our main focus is domestic shareholding, although, foreign shareholding is shown to give an indication of the interest of domestic institutions in foreign investments.[4] From Figure 2 it follows that investments in domestic and foreign shares, and domestic bonds are strongly increasing parts of the total assets of funds. For each of these risky assets, the proportion of the total assets in 1996 is even at least four times the proportion in 1980. From Figure 3 it follows that the strongly increasing pattern also holds for investments in all four risky assets by banks. Domestic bonds increased from 1.8 per cent in 1980 to 5.1 per cent in 1996, real estate from 0.1 per cent in 1980 to 0.3 per cent in 1996 and domestic shares from 0.22 per cent in 1980 to 0.75 per cent in 1996. As for funds, banks hold fewer shares than bonds. Investments in risky assets by banks seem

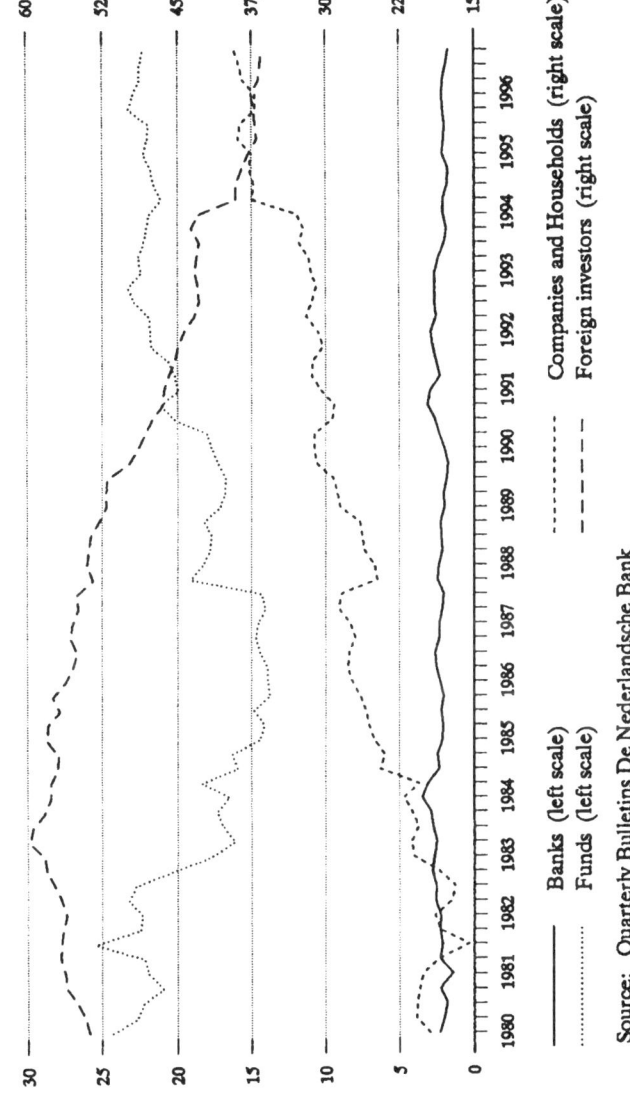

Fig. 1. The structure of shareholding in the Netherlands.

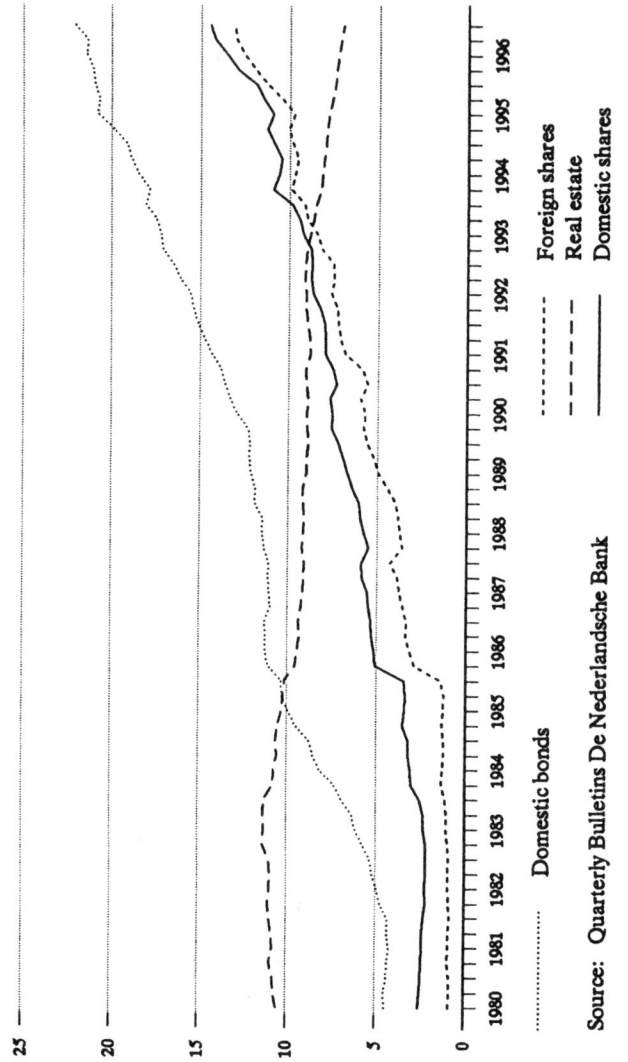

Fig. 2. Shareholding by funds in relation to total assets.

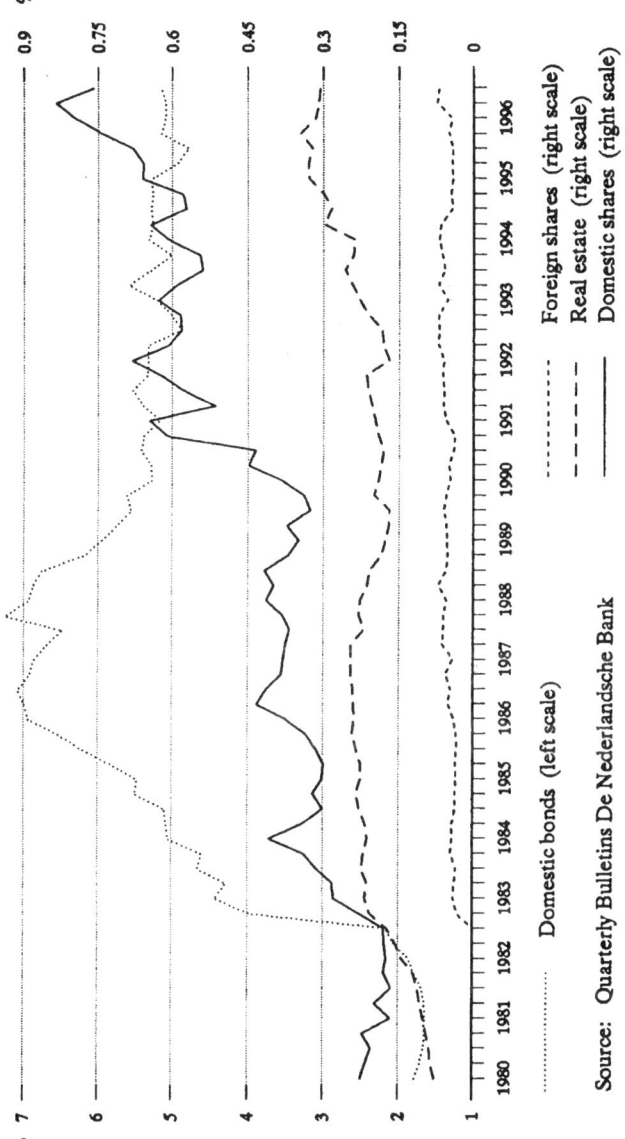

Fig. 3. Shareholding by banks in relation to total assets.

however overall lower than those by funds. This is due to stronger regulations for banks. For instance, banks are not allowed to invest excessively in risky assets. A solvency measure, known as the Cooke ratio, that was included in the 1988 Basle accords,[5] necessitates an $8 coverage of own equity for each $1 investment in a risky asset. For banks foreign shareholding started in 1982 and is nowadays about 0.1 per cent of the total assets, as Figure 3 shows. In comparison with other countries, for instance the US, Dutch banks are large, so that the small percentages of 0.22–0.75 per cent in domestic shares and 0.1 per cent in foreign shares can represent a large amount. It is also typical that, unlike German or Japanese banks, Dutch banks often only take equity positions in non-financial corporations under particular circumstances.[6]

To summarize, Dutch shares are mainly owned by foreigners (about 40 per cent) and funds (about 20 per cent). Only 2 per cent is in the hands of banks. Investments in risky assets by funds and banks relative to total assets have considerably increased during the sample period 1980–1996, among which share investments.

4. INVESTMENTS BY DUTCH BANKS

Dutch banks possess a small percentage of the total Dutch shares but the shares' part of their total assets has grown during 1980–1996, as Figures 1 and 3 show. The deregulation that took place in the early eighties seems to be a main cause here.

Banks are impeded from excessive investment in risky assets to protect banks' creditors. Before 1980 a bank needed permission from the Dutch Central Bank for each participation of more than 5 per cent in a financial corporation. Investments in non-financial corporations were even prohibited until 1980. After 1980 the participation rule was relaxed to a 10 per cent participation. The participation has to be approved by the Ministry of Finance and in case of approval a 'certificate of no objection' ('vvgb' or *verklaring van geen bezwaar* in Dutch) is obtained via the Dutch Central Bank. This certificate is free of charge and – usually – does not expire.

Figure 4 shows the numbers of certificates granted to banks during 1980–1996. A distinction is made between participations in financial and non-financial corporations. The figure shows that banks invest more in financial than non-financial corporations; in 1996 for instance, 500 and 150 certificates were granted for participations in financial corporations (see right scale) and non-financial corporations (left scale), respectively. The obvious reason for the discrepancy between the two types of investments is that linkages with financial corporations are stronger. Moreover, investments in non-financial corporations have only been allowed since 1980. The certificates granted steadily increased

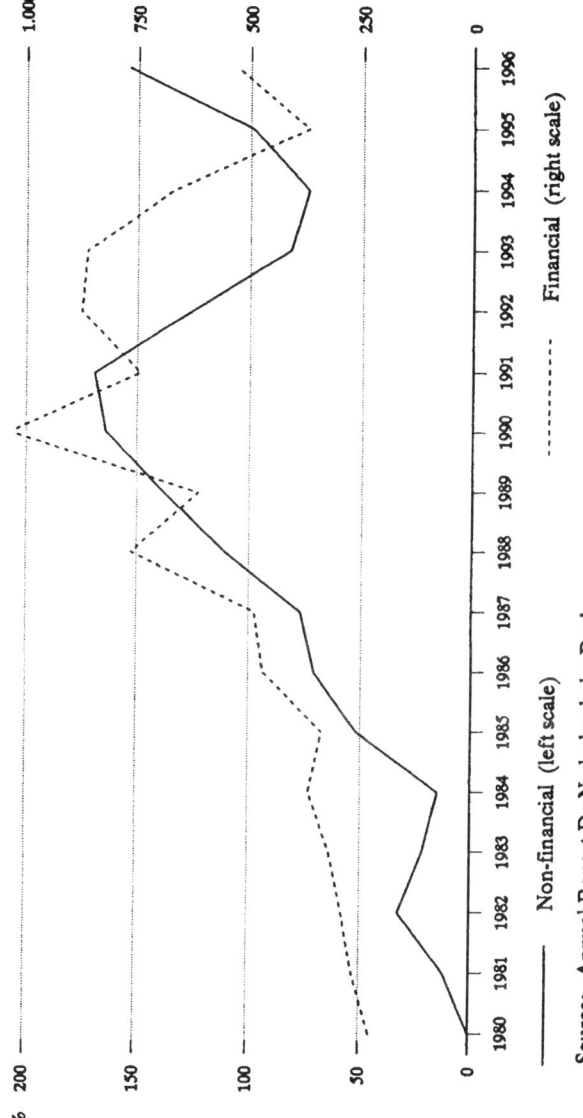

Fig. 4. Number of certificates of no objection ('wgb').

TABLE 2

Investments by Dutch banks in financial institutions (percentages)

Participation (%)	1993	1994	1995	1996
11–20	1	4	4	2
21–30	2	3	4	4
31–40	1	2	3	3
41–50	3	3	8	6
51–60	0	2	6	6
61–70	1	2	5	1
71–80	0	1	3	2
81–90	0	0	2	1
91–100	93	84	66	76

Source: Quarterly reports and internal sources, De Nederlandsche Bank.

TABLE 3

Investments by Dutch banks in non-financial institutions (percentages)

Participation (%)	1993	1994	1995	1996
11–20	12	19	28	13
21–30	19	33	21	16
31–40	27	23	14	11
41–50	23	14	10	15
51–60	4	0	1	5
61–70	8	1	2	2
71–80	0	0	0	1
81–90	0	0	1	1
91–100	8	10	22	35

Source: See Table 2.

until 1990 and slightly fell thereafter. More interesting are the participations in non-financial institutions as they concern investments in activities different from their banking activity. Figure 4 shows that the certificates for investments in non-financial corporations also increased strongly until 1990. So banks seem to have a growing interest in non-financial corporations.[7]

Along with each certificate granted by the Ministry of Finance it is known from 1993 onwards, what percentage of total shares of a corporation is bought by each bank. In Tables 2 and 3 figures are shown for investments in financial and non-financial corporations, respectively.[8] Table 2 shows that only 1 per cent of all certificates concerned a participation between 11 per cent and 20 per cent in 1993. Also participations in the range 21–30 per cent, 31–40 per cent until 81–90 per cent were small.

This holds true for all years, though rather less so for 1995 and 1996. The major part of participations thus concerns majority participations of more than 90 per cent, i.e. 93 per cent of all certificates in 1993, 84 per cent in 1994, 66 per cent in 1995 and 76 per cent in 1996. Table 3 gives a completely different story for investments in non-financial corporations. Only 8 per cent of all certificates concerns participations of more than 90 per cent in 1993, followed by 10 per cent, 22 per cent and 35 per cent in subsequent years. Most participations are small. For instance 12 per cent, 19 per cent, 28 per cent and 13 per cent in 1993 until 1996 concerned participations of only 11 per cent to 20 per cent. A major participation of banks in non-financial institutions, in that more than 50 per cent of the total shares of the corporation under consideration were bought, holds for 20 per cent of the total bank investments in 1993, and 11 per cent, 26 per cent and 44 per cent in subsequent years. Majority participations are hence strongly increasing over time.

From these figures it follows that banks' main share investments concern financial corporations and that the participation is high. Banks' share investments in non-financial corporations are mainly minority. Majority participations however increased from 20 per cent in 1993 to 44 per cent in 1996. Possibly more companies temporarily lodged their shares at a bank (before issue), or otherwise, banks became involved in companies as shareholders when the companies were unable to pay back their loans. Other possible reasons for the increase in non-financial participations are higher returns on these share investments and/or possibilities of management. We can assume that management is more likely to take place in case of majority participations but the data do not reveal whether this has been a motivation for investing in the particular corporation. It is also noticeable that participations are either low or high, and not about 61-90 per cent. This might be explained from the point of view that a participation of more than 60 per cent is a majority and hence almost equal to possessing and/or running the whole corporation.

As said before, the figures in Tables 2 and 3 concern the certificates of no objection for a participation of more than 10 per cent granted to banks during a certain year. These figures provide information neither on the duration nor on the withdrawal of the participation. A participation of 11 per cent in January 1993, for instance, that lasts a couple of months is measured in the same way as a participation of 11 per cent that lasts forever. Moreover, Tables 2 and 3 do not provide information on small participations of less than 10 per cent.

More specific information is given in Table 4. The data presented concern all participations of ten major Dutch banks that cover about 90 per cent of all Dutch banks (in terms of assets). For each bank the participations are subdivided in 10 categories for 1994 and 1995, as in the previous tables. In contrast with the figures in Tables 2 and 3 that concern participations during a whole year, these figures concern stock data measured at the last day of the year.

TABLE 4

Investments by ten Dutch banks (percentages)

Participation (%)	1994	1995
0–10	14	14
11–20	4	5
21–30	3	3
31–40	2	2
41–50	5	5
51–60	1	1
61–70	1	1
71–80	1	1
81–90	0	1
91–100	69	68

Figures reported are the averages of ten large banks in the Netherlands.
Source: Internal sources, De Nederlandsche Bank.

Hence, a participation of more than 10 per cent by one of the ten major banks for which a certificate was granted in 1994 or 1995 is included in Tables 2 or 3, and also in Table 4. Participations in Table 4, though, also cover small ones and can include participations that were granted before 1994.

The figures in Table 4 show that about 70 per cent of all participations exceed 90 per cent in 1994 and 1995. This is a large majority of the total participations and resembles the figure for investments in financial institutions reported in Table 2. Table 4 does (unfortunately) not distinguish between financial and non-financial institutions but probably the major part of the 91–100 per cent participations concerns financial institutions. In only one out of the ten banks under consideration majority participations do not prevail, indicating that the influence of banks in most corporations where it is a shareholder can be large. It is also very clear from Table 4 that mainly small participations occur, as a second choice after majority participations of 91–100 per cent. Participations of 0–10 per cent equal 14 per cent on average, although across the ten banks this percentage varies from 3 per cent to 36 per cent. As in Tables 2 and 3 it thus follows from Table 4 that participations in 1994 and 1995 are either very high, in which case exerting influence seems evident, or very small, in which case managerial intentions seem weak. Between the two years under investigation, not many differences in the distributions exist. The total number of participations, however, clearly changes. Seven banks increase this number, ranging from 3.1 per cent to 46.6 per cent, the other three banks decrease it, ranging from 2 per cent to 21.4 per cent, whereas the overall increase is 5 per cent. The shares investments behaviour in 1994 and 1995 thus clearly differs.

To summarize, banks have mainly majority participations of more than 90 per cent in financial corporations and mainly minority participations in non-financial corporations. From 1993 until 1996, though, majority participations in non-financial corporations have increased from 20 per cent to 44 per cent. Data from ten individual banks for 1994 and 1995 show participations of either 0–50 per cent or 91–100 per cent. These banks have increased their share investments by 5 per cent on average.

5. THE RECENT DISCUSSION ON DUTCH CORPORATE GOVERNANCE

Last year attention was drawn to corporate governance in the Netherlands by a report of a committee chaired by former Aegon chief executive R. F. M. Peters (1996). The committee was set up by the Dutch Association of Stockbroking (*Vereniging van Effectenhandel in Dutch*) and had as its main task to (re-)consider aspects of corporate governance in the Netherlands, i.e. relationships between supervision, management and the providers of financial means of Dutch corporations. Social and environmental aspects were not considered. The advice of the committee on possible future changes in current corporate governance was given in the report whose main intention is to provide some recommendations and initiate a general discussion.

Several reasons underlie the study of Dutch corporate governance. On the one hand are the expanding international character of the Dutch economy and changing international relations. On the other hand are a renewed interest in the value added of corporations and an increasing international attention on the role, position and influence of providers of financial means. The changing structures of the investors in shares in recent years, as shown in Section 3, were also crucial.

A similar study was carried out under the chairmanship of Sir Adrian Cadbury in the United Kingdom in 1992, whose results are given in the Cadbury report. The study was a response to a number of bankruptcies of corporations in the United Kingdom. This is unlike the Peters study although several bankruptcies of companies have also occurred in the Netherlands in recent years. As one of the first in Europe the Cadbury report recommended more transparency in the structure of corporations. Moreover, much more influence can nowadays be exerted by shareholders.

The Peters report gives advice concerning the composition, task, appointment, remuneration and procedure of the Supervisory Board and the Board of Directors. The main finding of the report is that there are reasons to increase the influence of shareholders under normal circumstances, in many cases. There is an appeal for the boards and shareholders of each corporation to reconsider the influence of the shareholders. Some criteria are reported and it is suggested that the corporation's considerations along with these criteria should be discussed at the General Meeting of Shareholders of each corporation in 1998. A report on the compliance with the recommendations, the discussions and the conclusions of the meeting should be made, but which institution will be in charge of this report has not been defined. The report also recommends that buying own shares in the Netherlands should be possible. Currently strong fiscal restrictions exist that should be weakened in view of the treatment of this issue in other countries.

In the report the procedures for the Supervisory Board, Board of Directors and the most important, the General Meeting of Shareholders, are laid out concisely. The recommendations for changes are clear, although in most respects difficult to define precisely. This is in general a problem with corporate governance and as a consequence of this, it is hard to verify whether managers comply with the desires and recommendations of shareholders or not.

The Peters committee, though, states the necessity for the management to give account to shareholders under any circumstances. The report is seen as an appeal for an Anglo-Saxon model instead of the current Dutch 'structure'-system, because in essence more influence for shareholders and transparency are desirable. A first principle is that the adage 'one share, one vote' holds, implying that a shareholder has a say proportional to his number of shares. A second principle is that the management should give a clear and transparent account to shareholders. In some situations, however, exceptions may occur. An example is the case where a only few shareholders attend the meeting of shareholders, which means that they are able to exert an influence that is disproportionally large. In such a case the committee justifies priority shares or certain certificates. A further assumption of the committee is that the more shareholders attend the shareholders' meeting, the higher the 'quality' of decision making is and hence less need for deviating from the 'one share, one vote' rule. In order to achieve continuity of decision making, a representative shareholders' meeting is deemed necessary by the committee. For this reason shareholders, in particular institutional and other large investors, are urged to show up and have a say at the meeting. An efficient proxy soliciting system seems moreover also important. Small shareholders can in this way – without additional costs – be represented at the meeting by a person who votes in their interest.

Six concrete points are mentioned to test the role and influence of shareholders. The first is the strategic policy of the corporation, such as the growth prospects, the risk profile and the desired profit level. The second concerns a major change in the nature and the extent of the corporations. The third is the dividend policy. The fourth is the extent and composition of the total shares, such as forthcoming issues, priority rights, etc. The fifth concerns changes in statutes and the sixth the arrangement and approval of the annual accounts.

The report on corporate governance contains many more points but our summary stops here. Criticisms that have been made, mainly in comments in the press, concern the points mentioned above. Some of them are positive, some (strongly) negative. We briefly outline some here.

The strong preference of the current Dutch model to the Anglo-Saxon model arises from the idea that shareholders have a lasting and quick return as an objective instead of a say in the corporation. The Anglo-Saxon model therefore might only lead to more profitability in the short run. Moreover, institutional investors, such as investment and pension funds, let alone private investors, are not seen as professionals that can manage a corporation. In the Anglo-Saxon model the power rests with the shareholders' meeting that is seen as an anonymous, amorphous group of people. This is in sharp contrast with the Dutch model where the Supervisory Board, characterised as independent and personally responsible, has the main power. Also, the fact that the cooption system of the Supervisory Board will be curtailed, i.e. the Supervisory Board no longer appoints (all) new members, makes it possible for employees to have a say. As such, the Supervisory Board is no longer independent and confidential, and clear separations between boards, employees and shareholders can no longer exist. Another objective against increasing the role of shareholders is the argument that shareholders already have a considerable say in corporations. This is based on findings from a questionnaire among 538 general directors held in 1996 (see NIVE, 1997). It shows that in strategic decision making the wishes and expectations of 65 per cent of the shareholders were taken into account, 2 per cent more than of employees. The opinions of 65 per cent of the representatives of shareholders, hence a large majority, also already contribute to important management decisions. From another survey among Dutch Chief Financial Executives by Cools (1993, Chapter 6) it appears that shareholders are the principal stakeholders in 8 per cent of all cases. No hierarchy has 52 per cent, customers 22 per cent, employees 14 per cent, suppliers 4 per cent and shareholders hence 8 per cent.

The preference of the Anglo-Saxon model to the current Dutch model, on the other hand, is expressed by another group. A bottleneck of the current system is said to be the cooptation-system which hampers shareholders from having a crucial say. The viewpoint of the Peters committee is upheld and by some even not found sufficiently far-reaching. Legal regulations, instead of having corporations making decisions themselves as the Peters report suggests, should force corporations to follow the suggestions made in the report.

To summarize, the recent Dutch report on corporate governance that expresses the wish for a more Anglo-Saxon model where shareholders have more impact, has triggered a lot of discussion. Many people seem to offer resistance because of various reasons, but of course, there are two sides to every coin. In order to reach a solution it seems important to gather more information on the current situation of Dutch firms. This could clarify what the position of stakeholders today is, and what the opinion of all stakeholders is on giving more responsibility to shareholders in the decision making process. It seems moreover important to consider the different types of shareholders. The situation where banks are the main shareholders could be different from the situation where, for instance, households are the main shareholders. The particular position of banks as debtholder and shareholder could play a role in this matter.

6. SUMMARY AND CONCLUSIONS

The focus in this paper has been on the Dutch situation of changing shareholders' structures, participations by banks and the current discussion on a possible move towards a more Anglo-Saxon model where shareholders have an important say. Statistics show that there has been an increasing interest in equity investment, in general probably because shares have been profitable in comparison with other investment possibilities. For funds and banks equity investment as a part of total assets has tripled during 1980–1996. The deregulations in the early eighties and the increasing share values during 1992–1996 can have played a role here. Remarkably, banks have increased their majority participations in non-financial institutions from 20 per cent in 1993 to 44 per cent in 1996, thus showing a strongly growing part in non-banking activities.

The recent Dutch discussion on changing the Dutch structure system of corporate governance is lifely and important. In cases where the main rules of the Anglo-Saxon model are accepted, shareholders will be given a lot of influence, and the Boards of Directors and the Supervisory Boards relatively far less than they have today. This could be far-reaching, in particular in the Netherlands where about 40 per cent of all shares are owned by foreigners who might not have adequate knowledge of the Dutch corporation and its economic environment. Moreover, the (domestic or foreign) investor's interest in equity investment might be more concerned with the high profitability of shares (in comparison with other investments) rather than the possibilities of governance. Under an Anglo-Saxon model an important say would be given to investors with basically short-term profitability objectives instead of a profound knowledge of the corporation and its environment.

Much more information is however needed to investigate the Dutch case. It would be interesting to have more insights in the investors' reasonings behind equity investment. The question whether governing or short-term profitability is the main motivation, could then be answered. In addition, it would be interesting to study the current impact of shareholders on the performance of corporations in much more depth. But in order to do this, (more) information on corporations and their shareholders should become publicly available.

NOTES

1. The list is not complete, one reason being that the distinction between the various models and matching countries is not clear-cut.
2. The choice for banks comes among others from the availability of data.
3. Broadly construed, three types of stakeholder relationships can be distinguished: *corporate governance*, i.e. the relation between shareholders and management, *contractual governance*, i.e. the relation between different companies, and *work governance*, i.e. the relation between employees and management.
4. See also Sparling (1997) on investments in both shares and bonds, Dutch and foreign, by foreign and Dutch investors.
5. See for instance Dewatripont and Tirole (1994) on the precise definition; the background and implications for banking.
6. On the sizes of Dutch banks and their equity positions, see Cools (1993, chapter 5).
7. Some caution is needed here as banks might be involved in share issues by other corporations.
8. For 1993 not all participations are known. We assume here that the restricted sample available is representative for all certificates granted in this year.

REFERENCES

Berle, A. and G. Means (1933) *The Modern Corporation and Private Property*, Macmillan, New York.
Boot, A. W. A. (1994) *De Financiering van het Bedrijfsleven: Tussen Structuurregime en Financiële Sector* (in English: Financing Private Companies: Between Structure Regime and Financial Sector), Amsterdam University Press, University of Amsterdam.
Cools, K. (1993) *Capital Structure Choice*, Unpublished thesis, University of Tilburg.
Cubbin, J. and D. Leech (1983) The Effect of Shareholding Dispersion on the Degree of Control in British Companies: Theory and Measurement, *The Economic Journal* 93, 351–369.
Demb, A. and F. Neubauer (1992) *The Corporate Board: Confronting the Paradoxes*, Oxford University Press, Oxford.
Dewatripont, M. and J. Tirole (1994) *The Prudential Regulation of Banks*, The MIT Press, Cambridge, Massachusetts.
The Economist (1994) A survey of corporate governance.
Gelauff, G. M. M. and C. Den Broeder (1996) Governance of Stakeholder Relationships: The German and Dutch experience, *SUERF Studies No. 1*.
Hart, O. (1995) Corporate Governance: Some Theory and Implications, *The Economic Journal* 105, 678–689.
Kester, W. (1992) Industrial Groups as Systems of Contractual Governance, *Oxford Review of Economic Policy* 6, 24–44.
Lannoo, K. (1995) Corporate Governance in Europe, CEPS Working Party Report No. 12, Centre for European Policy Studies, Brussels.
Mayer, C. (1996) Corporate Governance, Competition and Performance, OECD Economics Department Working Papers, No. 164, Paris.

Morck, R., A. Schleifer and R. Vishny (1988) Management Ownership and Market Valuation: An Empirical Analysis, *Journal of Financial Economics* 20, 293–315.

Nickell, S., D. Nicolitsas and N. Dryden (1996) What Makes Firms Perform Well?, paper presented at the European Economic Association meeting in Istanbul.

NIVE (Nederlandse Vereniging Voor Management) (1997) NIVE-enquête 1996.

Peters, J. F. M. et al. (1996) Corporate Governance in Nederland: Een Aanzet tot Verandering en een Uitnodiging tot Discussie (in English: Corporate Governance in the Netherlands: Initiative to Change and an Invitation for Discussion), report by The Commission Corporate Governance installed by The Association of Stokebroking.

Sparling, R. P. (1997) Beleggen in het Buitenland (in English: Investments in Foreign Countries), *Economische Statistische Berichten*, nr 4093.

Changing Corporate Governance in Japan

ABSTRACT

The paper describes the governance structure which has characterized the Japanese economy until recently. The paper first describes some features of the corporate sector and the stock market and then surveys a number of recent empirical studies of the effects of different ownership structures and financial relationships on the performance of firms. The paper concludes from this survey that the role of large shareholders is important in influencing management of Japanese firms. Managers are not completely insulated from outside pressure and there is some evidence that bank ownership performs differently from ownership by other firms. The paper then looks at the changing financial structure of Japanese firms and examines whether the role of the main bank changed during the 'bubble' years. The paper concludes that changes have been modest and slow so far.

Dr Jenny Corbett has a BA in Japanese and Economics from the Australian National University (1972) and a PhD in Economics from the University of Michigan (1986). Since 1983 she has been the University Lecturer (Nissan) on the Economic and Social Development of Japan at the University of Oxford and a Fellow of St Antony's College. She became a Research Fellow at the Centre for Economic Policy Research (London) in 1989. Since 1992 she has been the convenor of the CEPR European Network on the Japanese Economy. In 1996 she was appointed a Research Associate of the Center on Japanese Economy and Business at Columbia University, New York. Her most recent publication is 'How is Investment Financed? A Study of Germany, Japan, UK and US' with Tim Jenkinson which will appear in *The Manchester School* in 1997.

VI. Changing Corporate Governance in Japan*

JENNY CORBETT

INTRODUCTION

Within the recent debates on corporate governance the Japanese system has drawn attention because it seems to differ significantly from the well-known Anglo-US model, and more subtly from the German model (cf. OECD, 1995a). Within Japan, interest has centred on whether reforms are now needed to a system which served well during a time of less international openness and much faster growth but may now be an impediment to flexible adjustment.

If the problem of corporate governance is the conventional one, i.e. to ensure that firms are efficiently managed to maximize firm value, there are broadly three types of governance mechanism which may solve it.

The first is to motivate managers to carry out efficient management rather than to impose external monitoring on them. Executive compensation plans, or mechanisms which create managerial career concern (such as managerial labour markets in which reputation matters), may induce managers' effort with or without explicit contracts.

The second method is to use external pressures or indirect means of corporate control. The most well-known external mechanism is provided by capital market control either via take-overs or through external debt.

The third mechanism may be described as 'direct control' and gives more power to shareholders, or other stakeholders in the firm, by concentrating shareholdings or by strengthening their ability to monitor or their institutional rights. The first and third mechanism involve internal or direct discipline. The features of the Japanese system of corporate governance involve a different combination of these methods than the systems commonly used in the US and UK which are generally more familiar.

One approach to international comparisons of systems is to consider the variations on these three methods of solving the governance problem which is essentially what this paper does below. Section 2 considers the role of large shareholders while Section 3 examines financial structure and the role of banks.

---

* The author wishes to thank the OECD for permission to publish material in this paper which was originally prepared for the *OECD Country Study, Japan* in 1996.

The paper concludes that
- Large, institutional shareholders with concentrated shareholdings do have a direct effect on the behaviour and performance of Japanese firms.
- Managers are not insulated from outside pressure related to the performance of firms. Their pay and rates of turnover reflect this.
- Among large shareholders, banks, particularly main banks, have an important governance role. Some evidence suggests that the financial institutions' role is more productive than inter-corporate ownership.
- Despite continuing changes in patterns of financing the corporate sector was, until 1994, relatively heavily dependent on bank financing.
- Neither is the pattern of cross-shareholding and corporate grouping changing significantly yet.
- Survey evidence suggests the main bank relationship is not breaking down for many firms, even for those large firms whose financing patterns have changed most.
- Recent public concern about the health of the banking sector and about ethical standards in business will probably increase pressure to allow alternative governance patterns to emerge but the dominant model will be the bank-centred one for some time to come.

1. THE GOVERNANCE PROBLEM IN JAPAN

A more radical approach to international comparison is to question the way the problem is stated. The conventional view is that unless managers maximize profits (shareholder value) the economy will be operating inefficiently. Economies differ however, and it may be that even when managers have other objectives the economy may be efficient and welfare may be maximized (Garvey and Swan, 1996). This is particularly likely if some markets, such as financial and labour markets, are imperfect.

It is arguable that Japanese managers, who regularly claim (see OECD, 1996) not to have only shareholders' interests in mind, are fulfilling some similar function. If not, some of the features of the Japanese governance structure would appear to be economically inefficient.[1] The rest of this paper is restricted to a more narrow view about the nature of the governance problem.

Legal Structure

The legal features of the Japanese corporate system are not so different from other OECD countries as to explain differences in corporate governance. The basis of the corporate law is German commercial law and it permitted the establishment of limited liability companies from 1899 (Fukao, 1995). At

TABLE 1

Number of companies by size and status

	Capitalization		Total number of companies (public, private and other)	Percentage of all companies
	Less than ¥1 billion	More than ¥1 billion		
Public limited				
1975	673,493	1890	1,211,000	55.8
1987	942,153	3203	1,783,434	53.0
1994	1,118,397	5479	2,369,282	47.4
Private limited				
1975	480,389	2	1,211,000	39.7
1987	789,304	12	1,783,434	44.3
1994	1,183,077	53	2,369,282	49.9

Source: 1975 from Ballon, 1988. 1987 and 1994 from National Tax Administration, *Houjin Kigyou no jittai*; OECD, 1996.

TABLE 2

Listed companies and market capitalization (1990)

Country	Listed domestic companies	Average size $ millions	Market capitalization of quoted equity (per cent of GDP)
United States[1]	6342	512	56.5
Japan[2]	2205	1192	88.5
Germany	649	539	23.3
France[3]	443	696	25.8
United Kingdom	2006	394	80.8

[1] Total companies on New/York Exchange, NASDAQ, and American Exchange.
[2] Total companies on all stock exchanges.
[3] Total companies on Paris Stock Exchange.
Source: Mayer (1993); OECD, 1996.

present the majority of large companies are organized as public limited companies (in contrast to Germany, cf. OECD, 1995) although a large number of medium sized firms are private limited companies.

Of the public limited companies in the size category which permits listing (shareholders' equity of ¥1 billion or more), a substantial number are listed on stock exchanges (2263 at the end of 1995) again in contrast to Germany (Table 2). There is a large and active share market (OECD, 1996). Given these forms of corporate organization the classic split of ownership and management applies to a large number of Japanese firms and to the majority of large firms.

How, then, are the three types of control mechanism (managerial incentives, indirect control by external sources and direct control by shareholders or others connected with the firm) deployed in Japan and how do they differ from other countries?

2. SHAREHOLDERS AND MECHANISMS OF GOVERNANCE

Direct Incentives for Managers

The most obvious way for shareholders to motivate managers to act in their interests is to link pay or promotion to the performance of the firm. In many countries high managerial salaries and schemes such as executive share options have been used for this purpose. In Japan executive pay is on average lower than in other OECD countries and stock options have not generally been used because of restrictions on companies' ability to buy back their own shares and because the income tax treatment of such packages has been unfavourable. The dispersion of earnings between the top and bottom of companies is also narrower in Japan.[2]

Nevertheless, recent research suggests that the difference in factors determining pay, promotion and turnover of executives between Japan and elsewhere are not as great as might be expected. Kaplan (1994a) found compensation of top management in the largest Japanese and US companies was responsive to stock performance, sales growth and changes in pre-tax corporate income in remarkably similar ways. In Japan pay was more sensitive to falling earnings than in the US. The Japanese system may be seen as a difference in degree, rather than in kind, although another incentive mechanism, reputation, may work more intensely in Japan. However, despite inconclusive evidence of positive effects of high executive pay and stock options on firm performance in other countries, legal obstacles to the use of stock options were removed in Japan in June 1997.

Takeovers are Limited

As noted below, large shareholders are to some extent locked in to their companies and are expected to exercise voice rather than exit. This has obvious implications for the second method of 'indirect' or external corporate control: takeovers and the related activity of mergers and acquisitions. Takeovers may be the most widely used mechanism for shareholder control in the US and UK, but it is well-known that takeovers are relatively little used in Japan. This is not because there are legal impediments to takeovers. A Ministry of Finance study (MOF, 1996) argues that it may be a result of the attitude of executives who regard their companies as organizations grouping employees and other

TABLE 3

Mergers and acquisitions activity involving Japanese firms

	Value of acquisitions		Completely domestic transactions	Japanese acquisitions abroad	Foreign acquisitions in Japan	Number of cases in Japan	*Memorandum* Number of cases in US
	Million dollars	Billion yen					
1986	54.5	323	226	204	21	451	2521
1987	108.4	750	219	228	22	469	2513
1988	211.7	1652	223	315	17	555	3008
1989	308.0	2232	240	405	15	660	3798
1990	276.3	1908	293	440	18	751	4287
1991	98.5	733	302	294	18	614	3513
1992	55.1	435	260	186	37	483	3678
1993	47.8	430	259	140	32	431	3930
1994	38.3	374	286	175	46	504	–
1995	134.1	1425	301	212	52	565	–
Average	133.3	1026	218	190	21	430	–

Source: Yamaichi Securities and Nomura Research Institute; OECD, 1996.

stakeholders rather than as a system designed to make a profit. In addition, given the prevalence of cross- and stable shareholding described below, it is quite difficult to carry out a purchase of significant portions of shares through the market.

Mergers and acquisitions, however, are increasingly prevalent. International comparisons of M&A activity are difficult but OECD (1996) shows that the US is the prime location for M&As. In Japan, overseas-over-domestic M&As are very small in number compared to domestic-over-overseas.

Table 3 shows a large increase in activity in the late 1980s, which has remained quite steady, but also highlights the increase in purely domestic M&As relative to the wave of domestic-over-overseas (in-out type) during the bubble years.

This makes clear that it is not impossible to reform companies under new management structures in Japan by a form of market activity though, in fact, many of these activities involve the intermediation of a large shareholder in one or other firm. Furthermore, as is argued below, a mechanism rather similar to the take-over market is at work in Japan which may explain why there is, as yet, little evidence of any significant increase in hostile take-overs.

Concentration of Ownership

Given that these hallmarks of Anglo-Saxon governance structures are relatively less used in Japan it is the use of various methods of direct involvement by

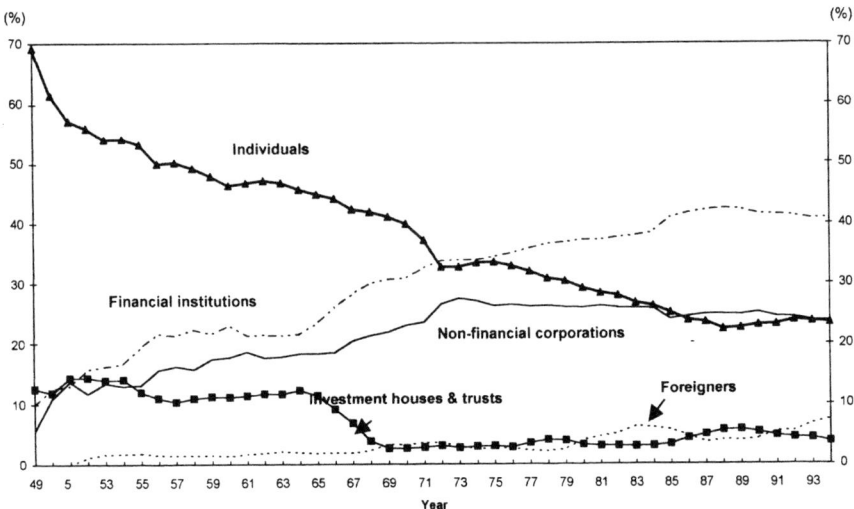

Fig. 1. Transition in share-holding ratio by holder.

shareholders (or, occasionally, more widely defined stakeholders) which differs in Japan. In considering the operation of this method of corporate governance, direct control by shareholders, the extent of ownership concentration, and the identity of large shareholders, can be important determinants of the effectiveness of corporate control. Dispersed shareholders have little or no incentive to monitor management because of the public good problem. Where ownership is sufficiently concentrated in the hands of large shareholders they may have an incentive to do costly monitoring. On the other hand, large, concentrated shareholdings may permit unwarranted interference with management or encourage collusion between some shareholders and management at the expense of other shareholders, creditors, etc.

In Japan, institutions and corporations owned nearly 70 per cent of all outstanding stocks in 1994. Of these, 25 per cent were owned by non-financial corporations and 44 per cent by financial institutions. At the same time the ownership share of domestic individuals has shown a continual decline since the second World War from about 70 per cent to just over 23 per cent.[3] (Figure 1) This ownership structure looks significantly different from most other countries except the UK which has a broadly similar institutional/ individual breakdown although the identity of institutional owners is rather different (see Table 4). Within the financial institutions sector banks and insurance companies dominate in Japan, while pension funds hold rather little.[4]

TABLE 4

Ownership of common stock: an international comparison (per cent of outstanding shares)

	Germany (1993)	United States (1990)	Japan (1990)	France (1993)	Italy (1993)	United Kingdom (1993)
Financial institutions	29.0	30.4	48.0	6.5	11.3	61.8
Banks	14.3	0	18.9	4.3	9.9	0.6
Insurance firms	7.1	4.6	19.6	2.2	0.8	17.3
Pension funds and others	7.7	25.8	9.5	1.9	0.6	43.9
Non-financial institutions	71.0	69.6	52.0	93.5	88.7	38.2
Non-financial enterprises	38.8	14.1	24.9	54.5	23.0	3.1
Households	16.6	50.2	22.4	20.7	33.9	17.7
Public authorities	3.4	0	0.7	4.5	27.0	1.3
Non-residents	12.2	5.4	4.0	11.9	4.8	16.3

Source: Deutsche Bundesbank (1994c); OECD (1995a); Prowse (1994); Central Statistical Office; OECD, 1996.

TABLE 5

Ownership concentration in non-financial corporations[1] (percentage of outstanding shares owned by the largest five shareholders)

	Germany	United States	Japan	Italy	United Kingdom
Mean	41.5	25.4	33.1	86.9	20.9
Median	37.0	20.9	29.7	99.9	15.1
Standard deviation	14.5	16.0	13.8	19.7	16.0
Minimum	15.0	1.3	10.9	n.a.	5.0
Maximum	89.6	87.1	85.0	100.0	87.7

[1] Germany: 41 non-financial corporations in 1990; United States: 457 non-financial corporations in 1980; Japan: 143 mining and manufacturing corporations in 1984; Italy: 734 non-financial corporations in 1993; United Kingdom: 85 manufacturing corporations in 1970.
Source: OECD (1995a) and OECD (1995b).

The identity of owners may be less important than the concentration of their holdings[5] and concentration is significantly higher in Japan than in the US and the UK, though lower than in Germany (Table 5). Furthermore, a variety of evidence indicates that a large part of shares are held in 'stable shareholdings' with an implicit understanding that they will not normally be sold without the agreement of the issuer. Table 6 shows that in large Japanese manufacturing companies the top shareholders will frequently have a business relationship or be parent or group companies. Recent survey evidence (see OECD, 1996) shows that many (63.5 per cent) companies report the share of stable shareholders at

TABLE 6

Categories of large shareholders in US and Japanese companies (1988, per cent)

Category	US companies	Japanese companies
Institutional investors	71.7	12.9
Financial institutions with business relationships	1.9	35.6
Non-financial institutions with business relationships	1.9	9.4
Parent companies or companies in same group (keiretsu)	1.9	30.7
Owner families	15.1	5.4
General investors	5.7	2.5
Other	1.9	3.5

Source: Kigyo Kodo ni Kansuru Chosa Kenkyu Iinkai (1988, p. 20). Data are from responses to a questionnaire sent to large manufacturing companies in Japan and the United States; OECD, 1996.

60 to 70 per cent, roughly corresponding to the share of institutional shareholders.[6]

Cross-Shareholding

Within the general structure of stable shareholding there is a more narrowly defined, and even less volatile, arrangement of 'cross-shareholding'. Stable shareholdings may often be reinforced by mutual holdings: some corporations intentionally hold each other's shares, when they have business relationships or belong to a business group.[7]

The survey data in OECD (1996) show that the share of corporate cross-shareholding is concentrated in a range of 10 to 40 per cent, a much lower proportion than the estimates of stable shareholding.[8]

Following the burst of the bubble, it has often been claimed that cross-shareholding is rapidly collapsing. However the need for cross-holding aimed at strengthening relationships with partner or *keiretsu* companies has not changed much. Despite the anecdotal evidence, there is no firm evidence of a dramatic shift in the nature of stable or cross-shareholding in the period of recent economic slowdown but, rather, a picture of a gradual reduction of the holding built up in circumstances specific to the 1950s and early 1960s (Table 7). The core portion of cross-shareholding will probably remain, although the portion accumulated during the bubble period is dissipating. Kawakita (1994) finds that the ratio of cross-shareholding has not declined very much since the beginning of the 1990s (it was still 21.2 per cent in FY 1993 for a sample covering 68.8 per cent of publicly listed companies).

TABLE 7

The six major business groups: intra-group and reciprocal shareholding

	Average linkage to other members[1]	Average stake size (per cent)	Ratio to total capitalization[2]
Intra-group shareholding			
Mitsui	57.6	1.3	19.3
Mitsubishi	75.3	1.8	38.2
Sumitomo	94.5	1.6	27.8
Average of pre-war *zaibatsu*	75.8	1.6	28.5
Fuji	46.8	1.3	16.9
Sanwa	27.5	1.4	16.7
DKB	29.4	1.0	14.2
Average bank centred groups	34.5	1.2	15.9
Average six major groups	55.2	1.4	22.2
Reciprocal shareholding			
Mitsui	45.8	1.2	13.7
Mitsubishi	61.2	1.3	22.9
Sumitomo	85.3	1.2	20.2
Average pre-war *zaibatsu*	64.1	1.3	18.9
Fuji	36.0	1.2	12.5
Sanwa	18.3	1.0	8.2
DKB	17.3	1.2	9.4
Average bank-centred groups	23.8	1.1	10.0
Average six major groups	44.0	1.2	14.5

[1] Average extent to which any company in the groups holds shares in all other companies in the group.
[2] Shareholding of group members as percentage of total market capitalization of all groups.
Source: FTC (1994); OECD, 1996.

Exit and Voice: Large Shareholders' Influence in Japan

Since institutional shareholders in Japan appear to be a concentrated, and potentially cohesive group, the direct mechanism of corporate governance by shareholders might function fairly well. Further, since institutional shareholders are to some extent locked in by stable relationships (i.e. prevented from 'exit' when the firm performs poorly) they have an incentive to exercise 'voice'.

The conventional view is that shareholders are relatively powerless in the Japanese context. Nevertheless there is some evidence that shareholders have a greater influence than at first appears. Yafeh and Yosha (1995) show that monitoring by large share and debt holders involves a significant reduction of activities with scope for managerial moral hazard. Measures for managerial moral hazard such as advertising, R&D and entertainment expenses are negatively correlated with shareholder concentration and with the fraction of stock held by bank-centred financial corporate groups, but less with the fraction of debt held by these groups. This evidence indicates that monitoring by shareholders, in particular corporate group shareholders, probably takes place continuously even in 'good times' (though debt holders might tend to intervene mainly when firm performance is poor).

Lichtenberg and Pushner (1994) find a significant positive relationship between the ownership by financial institutions and the level of productivity or profitability in 1,241 Japanese manufacturing firms and large negative effects associated with corporate ownership. They also find a positive influence of directors' ownership on corporate performance, much smaller than the positive effects of institutional ownership but still significant. This suggests that intercorporate ownership arrangements can insulate managers from external influence at the expense of firm performance[9] while ownership by financial institutions improves it. Fukao (1995) points out that there are some legal reasons why shareholders may have greater power than at first glance. The nature of insider trading legislation (i.e. explicit but with small penalties) makes it relatively easy for large shareholders and managers to exchange information in advance of annual general meetings. Once agreement is reached, shareholders give proxy votes to the management who, therefore, usually have a majority vote at meetings.

Shareholders and the Board

The other avenue for shareholders to influence management is via the board of directors. As in other countries the Commercial Code gives general shareholders' meetings the highest decision-making powers including the appointment and dismissal of directors and auditors and other important matters. The Commercial Code also stipulates that the representative director, elected by shareholders, should execute business according to the decisions of the board of directors.

In practice, boards of Japanese companies are predominantly composed of directors promoted from within the company itself. Prowse (1994) stresses that in legal terms the board of directors looks remarkably similar to that of US and UK companies and is a unitary board with no formal representation of labour. He notes "Although formally elected by stockholders, the board is typically chosen by the CEO (although perhaps after some consultation with the large shareholders), and consists of both outsiders and members of the management team". ... "large shareholders are not usually represented on boards in Japan unless the firm is in serious distress. Top management and large creditors and shareholders hold regular monthly meetings, which, although not formal governance structures, resemble a second board along the lines of the supervisory board in Germany."

TABLE 8

Origins of company directors of listed companies (per cent)

	1984	1989	1994	Average 1984–1994
Company directors				
Internal	74.2	75.6	73.1	75.1
External	25.8	24.4	26.9	24.9
Other companies	17.1	16.3	18.3	16.7
Banks	5.4	5.4	5.8	5.4
Government	3.3	2.7	2.8	2.8
Senior executives				
Internal				
External	n.a	40.0	33.9	n.a
Other companies	n.a	29.7	22.7	n.a
Banks	7.1	6.3	6.8	6.8
Government	4.7	4.0	4.4	4.5

Source: Toyo Keizai, *Kigyo Keiretsu Soran*, various years; OECD, 1996.

Japanese company boards usually consist of a president (and sometimes a chairman who is nominally above the president in rank but often not in power), senior executive director(s) (*senmu torishimariyaku*) and other executive directors (*jomu torishimariyaku* and *torishimariyaku*). The board is therefore hierarchically ranked rather than functionally divided, although there may also be functional divisions between executive directors.

The most striking difference in Japanese boards is that most of the executive directors will have formerly been middle managers within the company who were promoted from inside so there is much less distinction between the firm's 'managers' and the board. The role of directors from 'outside' the company is legally the same as that of inside directors and they are not regarded as independent of the company. In fact they will mostly come from institutional stakeholders in the company. As Fukao (1995) notes, relatively small shareholders in Japan can, in theory, nominate members of the board and can publicize nominations in the proxy form distributed by the company. In practice this procedure is rarely used in Japan and management usually consults with large shareholders before any changes to the board are made. However, the relative ease of making proposals does mean that large shareholders can change the composition of boards when necessary whereas this may require a takeover in the US or UK.

Table 8 shows that currently outside directors make up 25 per cent in the 2200 odd companies listed on Japanese stock exchanges and that there has been little change since 1985. Banks will play a fairly modest role supplying only around 5.4 per cent of outside directors, while related companies provide the largest number of outside directors. It is striking that the proportion of outside directors generally, and those coming from banks in particular, has remained constant over a long period.[10] There is no evidence either of banks or other shareholders sending more directors during the recent economic slowdown (as would be expected if they were increasing their monitoring of poorly performing firms) nor of them sending fewer (as would be expected if they were severing their ties with firms). An even higher proportion of chairmen, presidents and vice-chairmen and -presidents come from outside than for the board as a whole, but banks account for only a very slightly larger share than for general directors.

If the board is as ineffective as is popularly assumed it is hard to see why large shareholders would want to place directors on firms' boards. In fact, evidence on the placement and effects of outside directors on Japanese firms suggests that there may be benefits to stakeholders and that the mechanism may act as a substitute for the takeover market. Morck and Nakamura (1992) show that the probability of a bank sending a director to a firm's board increases when the firm's stock market performance or its sales, profit or investment performance underperform its industry peers. After the director is sent the performance of firms improves in several respects but, significantly, employment growth and stock market performance do not recover for a considerable period. The evidence is interpreted as consistent with banks supervising restructuring (and 'downsizing') of firms when managers have been unable to achieve this internally. It also suggests that banks do not have general shareholders' interests in mind when the restructuring is carried out and shareholders do not gain value from it. Kang and Shivdasani (1997) confirm that the frequency of downsizing and layoffs in Japanese firms increases with the ownership by the firm's main bank and other blockholders and that operating performance improves following downsizing.

What is not clear is the extent to which the bank's ability to intervene is related to its own shareholding in the firm or to its position as creditor. Sheard (1996) suggests that the higher the leverage of the firm the more likely is the intervention but Morck and Nakamura note that the variable may be picking up other influences (e.g. more highly leveraged firms may be weaker firms in other respects). Horiuchi and Okazaki (1991) suggest that the number of bank directors on boards may be more closely related to the shareholding percentage of banks than to their share in lending. This is important in understanding the likely future power of banks if corporate financing patterns are changing.

Kaplan and Minton (1994b) investigate the determinants of appointment of outsiders (directors previously employed by banks or by other non-financial firms) to the boards of 119 large non-financial Japanese firms. They find that appointments of both bank and outside corporate directors increase significantly with poor stock performance. Appointments of corporate directors increase with more concentrated shareholders and in firms affiliated with a corporate group. They also show that bank directors are appointed in companies that are contracting or financially distressed, while corporate directors are appointed in companies that have temporary problems.

Executive Turnover

A number of studies show that executives of Japanese firms are not insulated from discipline related to the performance of their firms. Kaplan (1994a), Kang and Shivdasani (1995) and Abe (1997) all show that non-standard turnover of chief executives (where presidents leave and do not become chairmen or do not follow the standard post-retirement career of their predecessor president) is related to several measures of firm performance (stock returns, sales growth, change in pre-tax income over assets, negative pre-tax income, employment growth).

Kaplan and Minton (1994b) show that turnover increases substantially in periods when outsiders are appointed even after controlling for company performance. Company performance stabilizes and improves modestly after new appointments. They conclude that banks and corporate shareholders play an important monitoring and disciplinary role.

Kang and Shivdasani (1995) show, in addition to an increasing likelihood of nonroutine turnover in case of poor firm performance, firms with ties to a main bank are more likely to remove top executives for poor earnings performance than are firms without a main bank. At the same time, neither *keiretsu* membership nor the presence of outside directors on the board has any effect on the sensitivity of turnover to either earnings or stock-price performance. Conditional on turnover, they find that new directors are more likely to be appointed from outside the firm when ownership by the top ten shareholders is high or there exists a main bank relation. It is less likely for firms with *keiretsu* membership.

These results further suggest that mechanisms such as bank ownership of shares and other ties with firms, together with concentrated equity ownership, perform an important governance role in Japan. The important result is that direct shareholder intervention may be replacing the role played by the takeover market in more arms' length, Anglo-US type governance systems.

Recent Changes in Shareholder Rights

Despite the fact that large shareholders are able to exert at least as much, if not more, power than in other countries, there have lately been attempts institutionally to strengthen the rights of shareholders. In particular, revisions to the Commercial Code in October 1993 incorporate (1) a revision of the representative shareholder litigation system, (2) a relaxation of the requirements for the right to inspect the financial books, and (3) a revision òf the system of auditors (i.e. mandatory appointment of an outside auditor). Of these, the revision of the representative shareholder litigation system so that the litigation fee is set at 8200 yen, is especially noteworthy. Although the representative shareholder litigation system was introduced in 1950, there had been very few cases of litigation because litigation fees had been computed on the value of the litigation and had to be paid in advance. As a result of the revisions there have been several recent cases of litigation demanding compensation from corporate directors as defendants (OECD, 1997)

3. Financial Structure, Main Banks and the Governance Mechanism

The Main Bank

There has been a considerable literature on the role of debt as a solution to the corporate governance problem (Aghion and Bolton, 1992). It was part of an earlier conventional wisdom that Japan had a high debt structure of corporate finance although that was not associated with particularly high levels of bankruptcy. This was consistent with a view that the debt structure itself and the creditors who provided it might be an important part of the governance structure. Together with the other features of the 'main bank' system much attention has been focused on the role of banks in controlling companies.

The main bank system itself is rather hard to define. Aoki, Patrick and Sheard (1994) note it involves an "informal set of practices, institutional arrangements, and behaviours among industrial and commercial firms, banks of various types, other financial institutions, and the regulatory authorities. At the core is the relationship between the main bank and the firms. This relationship has many aspects which vary considerably both across firms and across time, and depending on circumstance for a given firm ...". Aoki (1994) stresses five functions of the main bank (i) bank loans, (ii) bond issue related service, (iii) shareholding, (iv) payment settlement account, (v) supply of management information and resources and he distinguishes the behaviour of banks towards client firms in good times and bad.

The fundamental role of banks is screening and monitoring and Aoki (1994) describes this in terms of *ex ante* monitoring (basically screening loan applications), interim (gathering information on the ongoing business and affairs of borrowers) and *ex post* monitoring (intervening in the affairs of firms in difficulties (Sheard, 1994)). It is not entirely clear why banks have an incentive to carry out all these functions but it seems to be the case that while they did so in Japan there were a number of advantages for other participants in financial

TABLE 9

Net sources of finance: an international comparison (1970–1994[1]) (percentage of physical investment)

	Germany	Japan	United Kingdom	United States
Internal	80.0	69.9	93.3	96.1
Bank Finance	10.8	26.8	14.6	11.1
Bonds	−1.4	3.9	4.2	15.4
New equity	0.2	3.5	−4.6	−7.6
Trade credit	−1.1	−5.1	−0.9	−2.4
Capital transfers	8.1	–	1.7	–
Other	0.2	1.0	0.0	−4.4
Statistical adj.	3.2	0.0	−8.4	−8.2

[1] Except for Germany where period is 1970 to 1992.
Source: Corbett and Jenkinson (1996); OECD, 1996.

markets. One of the critical questions is whether changes in the financial system have undermined the role of main banks in these areas.

Pattern of Finance

The first part of this package of main bank services, the provision of loans, may have been changing recently. The view that Japan was unusually highly leveraged was first challenged by (Kuroda and Oritani 1980)[11] but has been revisited on a number of occasions since. During the 1980s a number of studies used leverage ratios and similar measures of the outstanding amounts of different types of finance to examine the capital structure of Japanese firms.[12] None of the studies presents systematic comparisons of all these adjustments on data from the same set of firms. As a result, conclusions about the difference between Japan and elsewhere range from Borio (1990) stating "that leverage in Japan remains higher [than the US]" to Frankel (1991) "The debt equity ratio [in Japan] ... has by one measure fallen below the level in the United States" and most recently Rajan and Zingales (1995) which repeats the Frankel result for market value measures of leverage. Much of the discrepancy between studies arises from the use of different samples of firms while most of the rest can be accounted for by the use of ratios of outstanding amounts of finance, such as leverage, which are subject to large valuation effects.

The traditional view of Japan seems less at odds with the figures[13] presented in Table 9. Banks provided 27 per cent of the funds for physical investment in Japan over the period as a whole, although the importance of bank finance has varied in recent years. Equity markets have apparently been small positive providers of finance in Japan (as in Germany), whilst in the UK and US equity

TABLE 10

Net and gross sources of finance in Japan

	1970–74	1975–79	1980–84	1985–89	1990–94
	Per cent of physical investment				
Net sources					
Internal	59.1	70.8	74.6	70.5	71.3
Bank finance	42.7	33.9	31.7	22.9	19.4
Bonds	2.7	2.5	0.6	9.1	2.1
New equity	2.5	3.3	3.6	4.4	3.1
Export credit	−9.9	−12.2	−8.4	−5.7	0.8
Other	2.9	1.7	−2.1	−1.2	3.3
	Per cent of physical and financial investment				
Gross sources					
Internal	31.2	33.6	49.0	43.3	68.4
Bank finance	39.7	31.3	35.2	32.5	18.4
Bonds	1.6	2.8	3.1	5.9	4.5
New equity	3.1	2.9	3.5	5.1	1.4
Export credit	22.2	28.0	10.9	9.2	−0.5
Other	2.3	1.3	−1.8	4.2	7.8

Source: Calculated from EPA, *National Income Accounts*, Corbett and Jenkinson (1996); OECD, 1996.

has actually been a net use, rather than a source, of funds.[14] For Japan then it appears that the view of the whole corporate sector as still relatively dependent on external sources of funding and, particularly, on bank sources is not fundamentally altered. A more detailed look at the changes in financing patterns is however important.

Two features stand out from Table 10. First, the share of bank finance has been very erratic in Japan over the whole period, varying between 67 per cent (1974) and −26 per cent (1978). Second, over the first half of the 1980s (up to 1987) bank finance fell steadily to the extent that, within Japan, discussion began on whether this was the end of the bank based system of finance. The fall in bank finance in part reflected a new phenomenon of bond finance (after market liberalization), especially in 1986 and 1987. However, a good deal of the decline in the net data is due to a surge in firms' holdings of bank deposits as assets (particularly time deposits after market liberalization in the 1980s).[15]

As for the role of market sources of finance: there was a much discussed increase in the issue of various market instruments in the 'bubble years' of the late 1980s which can be seen in the data. Since much of the bond finance was in the form of convertible bonds it is difficult to distinguish accurately between bond and equity finance. Taking the two sources together, the striking feature in comparison to other countries is the relatively large positive contribution of market finance from 1985–89 (13 per cent) together with the fact that the market has never been a net drain of finance as in the UK, US and Germany.

A number of studies, (Gower 1995) (Hoshi, et al. 1993) as well as anecdotal and newspaper comment, suggest that there may have been a major shift in corporate financing patterns following the deregulation of the 1980s.

However a number of subtle but important points emerge from the time trends shown in the aggregate data of Table 10.

- First the difference between Japan's system and those of several other countries persists into the period after deregulation (i.e. in the 1980s). Japanese corporations still have higher internal sources of finance than other major countries and rely on 'negotiated' forms of finance to a greater degree (see EPA, 1992) and Corbett and Jenkinson (1997).
- Second, the shift to market forms of finance is restricted to a particular group of firms. Large firms reduced their dependence on bank debt more than small (EPA, 1992, p. 187). Manufacturing firms reduced bank debt more than all industries. Firms which were eligible to issue bonds reduced debt more than those which were not eligible (Hoshi, 1996) and, importantly, firms with main bank connections reduced their debt by less than those without such connections. Campbell and Hamao (1994) conclude "We have argued that the main bank system continues to have an important role in Japanese corporate finance."

Since the recession of the first half of the 1990s there appeared to be a reversal of the decline in bank borrowing. In the first stage, in fact, bank finance rose after the low of the bubble years as firms moved away from holding financial assets towards physical investment. 1994, however, has shown a dramatic change. In 1994 firms actually repaid loans as well as increasing their cash and deposit holdings. On both a gross and net basis bank borrowing was actually reduced (a negative contribution to fund raising). Furthermore, in total, net sources of financing were negative so that internal sources of finance (retentions and depreciation) had to be used not only to finance new physical investment but also to make net purchases of financial assets and redeem liabilities (as a result in 1994 net retentions were 106.6 per cent of new physical investment).

Therefore, while it is true that for some firms the 1980s, encompassing major liberalizations of access to capital markets for the largest firms, represented a period of significant change in their financial structure, and in the position of their borrowing from banks, this was not true for the majority of firms until 1994. The dramatic changes in that year may reflect the length and severity of the recession rather than a more pervasive change in financial structure but it is still too early to tell. What is clear is that the major change, if it is happening, did not occur during the bubble years but during deep recession. Regardless of the changes in patterns of financing, or rather because they are restricted to

TABLE 11

The evolution of corporate banking relations (companies quoted in the First and Second sections of the Tokyo Stock Exchange by maturity of borrowing)

		1980	1984	1989
Average number of banks				
First section	long term	8.1	7.9	6.6
	short term	7.5	7.4	6.9
Second section	long term	3.5	3.6	3.5
	short term	4.5	4.3	4.2
Proportion of companies that changed main bank				
First section	long term	–	11.7	20.9
	short term	–	8.5	19.1
Second section	long term	–	21.5	30.6
	short term	–	23.2	19.6
Proportion of borrowing from main bank				
First section	long term	9.6	9.3	10.6
	short term	12.4	17.0	19.6
Second section	long term	12.4	17.0	19.6
	short term	15.1	23.6	24.2

Source: Bank of Japan (1992); OECD, 1996.

a very particular group of firms, there is much evidence that important aspects of the main bank relationship remain in place, presumably because they are still advantageous both to the banks and the firms.

Preserving Main Bank Relationships

Table 11 shows that TSE first-section firms concentrated their borrowings on a smaller number of banks between 1980 and 1989 (particularly for long-term borrowing) while second-section firms showed no change. First-section firms also increased the share of their borrowings coming from their main banks on average and the proportion of firms increasing the share rose while the proportion decreasing it fell. For second-section firms there was much less change. Again it seems that the greatest change in financing structure was among those firms which did not have a main bank connection.

On the other hand the proportion of firms on both sections of the TSE which changed their main bank increased quite significantly in the latter half of the 1980s. The Bank of Japan interpreted the data as showing that second-section listed companies (which changed main bank quite frequently although they did not change the number of banks from which they borrowed, nor the concentration of their borrowing) increased their bargaining power with banks.

Overall their study concluded that the main bank framework itself has not been faced with drastic changes even for first-section firms *as evidenced by the increase in proportion of borrowing from main banks* (BoJ, 1992, p. 16). From the banks' standpoint, however, the increased frequency of changes of main bank by second-section firms increased the competition for the position of main bank.

EPA (1992), considering the same question of stability of bank relationships, notes that there is no consistent, time-series data for measuring the stability of main bank relationships and that a number of studies give different results. They conclude that the data show the rate of changes in main bank relationships being higher in the high growth 1960s compared with the stable growth period of the 1970s. Rates of change again increased in the second half of the 1980s (rapid growth) compared with the first half. This suggests that periods of high demand for funds and rapidly developing new business opportunities are the periods when the relationships change most markedly. Periods of slowdown and business slump are associated with greater stability. Thus, although the 'bubble years' may have generated considerable anecdotal evidence about firms breaking off their main bank relationships, there is little evidence that this was true for the majority of firms, nor that it marked a permanent shift in relationship.

Hoshi (1996), who stresses rather more change on the financial side than this report, notes that change is not yet evident in banks' shareholding in firms nor in their seats on boards. He notes that the proportion of city banks among companies' 20 largest shareholder declined from 8.09 per cent in 1980 to 7.46 per cent in 1993 while the number of directors dispatched from city banks to other listed companies has increased from 1167 in 1980 to 1559 in 1993. "Thus as far as the aggregate trend is concerned, no weakening of bank ties is evident". Survey evidence (see OECD, 1996, Figure 51, p. 176) also shows that corporations are not expecting the demise of the main bank system.

PRESSURES FOR CHANGE

The finding may be at odds with the general perception in newspapers where stories of managerial failures have been prominent and where the assumption is that moral hazard and excessive risk-taking with little or not monitoring lay behind the banking crisis of the last few years.

However it is not yet clear which of a number of competing hypotheses explain the banking crisis. At least three possibilities exist.
  (i) The main bank system never did provide monitoring and control of borrowers but it took the 'bubble years' to reveal how easily the system allowed bad management and decisions (Gower, 1996; Horiuchi, 1996).

(ii) The system of main bank and large shareholder monitoring functioned well in the past but broke down, as the result of increased competition and deregulation (Takeda and Turner, 1992) in the 1990s. Banks and shareholders reduced their monitoring in this period (Hoshi, 1995).

(iii) The governance structure has not changed significantly. The crisis is the result of *ex ante* reasonable decisions being confounded by *ex post* results.

It is beyond the scope of this paper to examine these hypotheses although it seems likely that (iii) with some elements of (ii) is probably correct. The survey of evidence in this paper does however permit the following conclusions about the governance structure up to the early 1990s.

- Large, institutional shareholders with concentrated shareholdings do have a direct effect on the behaviour and performance of Japanese firms.
- Managers are not insulated from outside pressure related to the performance of firms. Their pay and rates of turnover reflect this.
- Among large shareholders, banks, particularly main banks, have an important governance role. Some evidence suggests that the financial institutions' role is more productive than inter-corporate ownership.
- Despite continuing changes in patterns of financing the corporate sector is still relatively heavily dependent on bank financing.
- Neither is the pattern of cross-shareholding and corporate grouping changing significantly yet.
- Survey evidence suggests the main bank relationship is not breaking down for many firms, even for those large firms whose financing patterns have changed most.
- Recent public concern about the health of the banking sector and about ethical standards in business will probably increase pressure to allow alternative governance patterns to emerge but the dominant model will be the bank-centred one for some time to come.

NOTES

1. Garvey and Swan argue specifically that many decisions in modern corporations heavily weight the interests of parties other than shareholders, even though it would be relatively easy to give shareholders a greater role. This is not necessarily inefficient in a world of incomplete contracts. In such a world management decisions may be effectively 'filling in' the areas where contracts are incomplete. It may be optimal in a world of incomplete contracts to pre-commit to actions that take account of the interests of other stakeholders in the company. This arises because with incomplete contracts it is not only shareholders who bear risks. Other stakeholders bear risks which cannot be fully specified (or prevented) by contracts and which cannot be fully insured. If this pre-commitment (investment in relationships, etc) has economic value then there is a risk of underinvestment unless there can be a credible promise by management to consider these interests alongside those of shareholders. Fukao (1995) argues slightly differently, that there

may be international differences in the hierarchical importance of different stakeholders in the firm (e.g. whether creditors interests come before shareholders) but that this does not necessarily imply that managers are not profit maximizing. Some survey evidence supports an argument that there is not much difference in this respect between US and Japanese managers (see Table 3-1, Fukao, p. 39). Surveys which find Japanese managers claiming to have different objectives may be reflecting a social milieu in which it is less acceptable to admit to being profit maximizers and which demands the outward appearance of 'caring management'.

2. See Abowd and Bognanno (1995) for multi-country comparisons. Fukao (1995) claims the total compensation (including tax and bonuses) of the top executives of a Japanese company is six to eight times that of the most highly paid blue-collar worker. In US companies the compensation of the top executive is twelve to eighteen times that of the most highly paid blue-collar worker *excluding* bonuses and stock options. He cites figures from Dickson in the *Financial Times*, March 31, 1992 that US chief executives earned 109 times the pay of the average US workers in the late 1980s, while CEOs in Japan earned just 17 times the average and those in the UK about 35 times the average. Kaplan (1994a) indicates that US CEOs receive about twice to three and one half times as much as Japanese managers.
3. The decline seems to have levelled out in the 1990s.
4. Until 1987 banks were permitted to hold 10 per cent of the equity of a single company. That limit was then reduced to 5 per cent.
5. Prowse (1994) notes however, "The identity of a firm's large shareholders may also have implications for governance. Individuals (or families), financial institutions and non-financial corporations may have different monitoring skills, a greater or lesser incentive to monitor and even different objectives" (p. 33).
6. The turnover rates of stock transactions by sector can also be used to see the extent to which shareholders are 'stable'. The turnover rates of business corporations, life insurance companies, and banks are much lower than those of individuals, foreigners, and investment trusts, indicating that these types of share ownership are more 'stable'. In particular, the turnover rate of life insurance companies is extremely low which suggests that they have been playing the role of 'silent partners'. During the second half of the 1980s, when stock prices rose sizeably, the turnover rate also increased for all sectors. Following the collapse of the bubble, it declined, though the turnover rate of banks has not declined as much as in the past, indicating that stock ownership of banks has become slightly more liquid. In addition, shares owned by investment trusts and foreigners, with high turnover rates, increased somewhat during the 1980s.
7. The system originated following the break-up of the *zaibatsu* in the immediate post-war era. Pure holding companies (those whose principal function is to control other companies through stock ownership) were in principle prohibited as a means of eliminating an excessive concentration of economic power. Subsequently, a re-formation of corporate groups took place. In the 1960s a need arose to create stable shareholders as a way to prevent corporate take-overs by foreign capital following the liberalization of international capital transactions. In the bear market conditions of the mid-1960s stocks were purchased by corporations which resulted in the changing ownership pattern demonstrated in Figure 1.
8. A Fair Trade Commission survey and follow-up calculates that in 1992 on average around 22.2 per cent of group shares were held within groups (though groups varied from 14.2 to 38.2 per cent) but only 14.5 per cent were held in bilateral cross-holdings (with a range from 8.2 to 22.9). These ratios rose between 1989 and 1992 but had hardly changed between 1992 and 1993. The trend pattern has been for steady, slow declines in the extent of internal shareholding relationships since the late 1970s (Table 7).
9. They also conclude that equity ownership by financial institutions in Japan may effectively substitute for the missing external take-over market, a point which is elaborated below.
10. In a survey of the top 200 companies in 1966 and 1976 (Mito 1983) found slightly over 30 per cent outside directors. In 1976, in Mito's study, 6 per cent of all directors came from banks

(5.5 per cent in 1966) while 9.0 per cent came from related companies (7.9 per cent). 90 per cent of the directors coming from banks came from banks which held shares in the company. Of the total number of directors, 14.3 per cent in 1976 were from institutional shareholders and 4.2 per cent from individual shareholders (in 1966 12.8 per cent and 4.7 per cent).

11. Who claimed that once accounting differences and off balance sheet sources were taken into account there was no significant difference in leverage between large US and Japanese firms. The case was argued by analogy and the data were limited to a very few firms.
12. The difficulty of adequately accounting for valuation changes during the stock market boom together with international differences in company accounting practices led to a number of adjustments to Japanese accounting data in these studies. Ando (1988) and Ando (1990) removes the effect of special reserves while Prowse (1990) uses consolidated accounts.
13. See Corbett and Jenkinson (1996) and Mayer (1990) for a discussion of the relative merits of stock and flow approaches to measuring corporate financial structure and a description of the netting method used.
14. The negative figures reflect, in the main, the vigorous mergers and acquisition process in the UK and US: a firm that uses its cash flow to buy the equity of another company (from the household or financial sector), and issues no additional equity, will produce a negative net source of finance figure for equity.
15. The share of bank finance in gross sources has fallen much less than the share in net sources.

References

Abe, Y. (1997) Chief Executive Turnover and Firm Performance in Japan. *Journal of the Japanese and International Economies* 11(1).

Abowd, J. and M. Bognanno (1995) International Differences in Executive and Managerial Compensation in Freeman, R. and L. Katz (ed.) *Differences and Changes in Wage Structure*, Chicago: Chicago University Press.

Ando, A. and A. Auerbach (1988) The Cost of Capital in the US and Japan: A Comparison. *JJIE* 2, 134–58.

Ando, A. and A. Auerbach (1990) The Cost of Capital in Japan: Recent Evidence and Further Results. *JJIE* 4, 323–50.

Aghion, P. and P. Bolton (1992) An incomplete contracts approach to financial contracting, *Review of Economic Studies* 59, 473–94.

Aoki, M. (1994) Monitoring Characteristics of the Main Bank System: an Analytical and Developmental View, in M. Aoki and H. Patrick (eds.), op cit, pp. 109–142.

Aoki, M. and H. Patrick (1994) *The Japanese Main Bank System: Its Relevance for Developing and Transforming Economies.* Oxford: Oxford University Press.

Aoki, M., H. Patrick and P. Sheard (1994) The Japanese Main Bank System: An Introductory Overview, in M. Aoki and H. Patrick (eds.), op cit, pp. 3–50.

Bank of Japan (1992) Analysis of recent changes in the relationship between banks and corporations based on financial data of corporations, *BoJ Special Paper No. 217*. Tokyo: Bank of Japan.

Borio, C. (1990) Patterns of corporate finance, BIS Economic Papers 27.

Campbell, J. and Y. Hamao (1994) Changing patterns of corporate financing and the main bank system in Japan, in M. Aoki and R. Dore (eds.), *The Japanese Firm: Sources of Competitive Strength.* Oxford: OUP.

Corbett, J. (1994) Japan's financial system: an overview, in N. Dimsdale and M. Preveser (eds.), *Corporate Governance and Financial Markets.* Oxford: OUP.

Corbett, J. and T. Jenkinson (1996) The financing of industry 1970–1989: an international comparison, *Journal of the Japanese and International Economies* 10(1), 71–96.

Corbett, J. and T. Jenkinson (1997 forthcoming) How is Investment Financed? *Manchester School*.
EPA (1992) Economic Survey of Japan 1991–92, Economic Planning Agency of Japan.
EPA (1993) Economic Survey of Japan 1992–93, Economic Planning Agency of Japan.
Frankel, J. (1991) Japanese finance in the 1980s: a survey, in P. Krugman (ed.), *Trade with Japan: Has the Door Opened Wider?* Chicago: University of Chicago Press.
Fukao, M. (1995) *Financial Integration, Corporate Governance, and the Performance of Multinational Companies*. Washington, D.C.: The Brookings Institution.
Garvey, G. and P. Swan (1996) Corporate governance and employment incentives: is the Japanese system really different?, in P. Sheard (ed.), *Japanese Firms, Finance and Markets*. Canberra: Harper for Australia Japan Research Centre, ANU.
Gower, L. (1995) *Corporate Monitoring and the Japanese Main Bank System*, PhD thesis, ANU.
Gower, L. (1996) Moral hazard and main bank monitoring, in P. Sheard (ed.). *Japanese Firms, Finance and Markets*. Canberra: ANU.
Horiuchi, A. (1996) Financial liberalisation and the safety net, in P. Sheard (ed.), *Japanese Firms, Finance and Markets*. Canberra: Harper for Australia Japan Research Centre, ANU.
Horiuchi, A. and A. Okazaki (1991) Kigyou no setsubi toushi to meinbank kankei (Corporate investment and main bank relationships, in Japanese), *Bank of Japan Working Papers*.
Hoshi, T. (1995) Bank organization and screening performance, *Center on Japanese Economy and Business Working Paper Series*, 110.
Hoshi, T. (1996) Financial deregulation and corporate financing in Japan, in P. Sheard (ed.), *Japanese Firms, Finance and Markets*. Canberra: Harper for Australia Japan Research Centre, ANU.
Hoshi, T., A. Kashyap and D. Scharfstein (1990b) The role of banks in reducing the costs of financial distress in Japan, *Journal of Financial Economics* 27, 67–88.
Kang, J.-K. and A. Shivdasani (1995a) Firm performance, corporate governance, and top executive turnover in Japan, *Journal of Financial Economics* 38, 29–58.
Kang, J.-K. and A. Shivdasani (1997) Corporate restructuring during performance declines in Japan, *Journal of Financial Economics* forthcoming.
Kaplan, S. N. (1994a) Top executive rewards and firm performance: a comparison of Japan and the US, *Journal of Political Economy* 102, 510–46.
Kaplan, S. N. and B. A. Minton (1994b) Appointment of outsiders to Japanese boards: determinants and implications for managers, *Journal of Financial Economics* 36, 225–58.
Kawakita, H. (1994), The collapse of Japan's cross-shareholding system, *JCR Financial Digest* 44, 1–6.
Kuroda, I. and Y. Oritani. (1980) A reexamination of the unique features of Japan's corporate financial structure: a comparison of corporate balance sheets in Japan and the United States, *Japanese Economic Studies* 8, 82–117.
Lichtenberg, F. and G. Pushner (1994) Ownership Structure and Corporate Performance in Japan, *Japan and the World Economy* 6, 239–261.
Mayer, C. (1990) Financial systems, corporate finance, and economic development, in R. G. Hubbard (ed,), *Asymmetric Information, Corporate Finance and Investment*. Chicago: University of Chicago Press.
Mito, H. (1983) *Nihon Daikigyou no Shoyuukouzou* (The Ownership Structure of Japanese Large Enterprises, in Japanese). Tokyo: Bunshindoo.
MOF (1996) Socio-Economic Systems of Japan, the United States, the United Kingdom, Germany and France, Study Group of the Institute of Fiscal and Monetary Policy, Ministry of Finance.
Morck, R. and M. Nakamura (1992) Banks and corporate control in Japan, *mimeo*. Vancouver: University of British Columbia.
OECD (1995a) *Economic Surveys: Germany*. Paris: Organization for Economic Cooperation and Development.

OECD (1995b) *Economic Surveys: Italy, Paris.* Organization for Economic Cooperation and Development.
OECD (1996) *Economic Surveys: Japan.* Paris: OECD.
Prowse, S. (1994) Corporate governance in international perspective: a survey of corporate control mechanisms among large firms in the United States, the United Kingdom, Japan and Germany, BIS Economic Papers 41.
Rajan, R. and L. Zingales (1995) What do we know about capital structure? Some evidence from international data, *Journal of Finance* 50, 1421–1460.
Sheard, P. (1994) Main banks and the governance of financial distress, in M. Aoki and H. Patrick (eds.), *The Japanese Main Bank System: Its Relevance for Developing and Transforming Economies.* Oxford: Oxford University Press.
Sheard, P. (1996) *Japanese Firms, Finance and Markets.* Canberra: Harper for Australia Japan Research Centre, ANU.
Suzuki, S. and R. Wright (1985) Financial structure and bankruptcy risk in Japan, *Journal of International Business Studies* 16, 97–100.
Takeda, M. and P. Turner (1992) The liberalisation of Japan's financial markets: some major themes, *BIS Economic Papers* 34.
Yafeh, Y. and O. Yosha (1995) Large shareholders and banks: who monitors and how?, CEPR Discussion Paper No. 1178. London: Centre for Economic Policy Research.

Stock Exchange Governance in the European Union

ABSTRACT

In this paper I examine some of the issues posed by the treatment of exchanges as firms. After briefly considering the types of services offered by an exchange and the transformation of European practices and regulations in this respect, I deal with some of the main features of exchange governance. I analyse, in particular, the issue of exchange ownership from the point of view of the choice between member or investor ownership. I then move on to examine exchange self-regulation, in the light both of the preceding study on exchange ownership and of recent research. I finally consider some aspects of the governance structures of exchanges with reference to the allocation of policy and executive powers and of those relating to regulation and market surveillance. In the last paragraph I draw some general conclusions.

Guido Ferrarini, LL.M. (Yale), is a Professor of Law at the University of Genoa. His fields of specialization include banking and financial law and corporate law. He has been in practice as a business lawyer for about fifteen years. He now works as a legal consultant in fields relating to his research interests. He is a member of the Italian Securities Commission's Advisory Committee (Rome). He is also an advisor to the Italian Stock Exchange on its privatization and new market rules. He is the editor of two volumes published by Kluwer Law International: *Prudential Regulation of Banks and Securities Firms. European and International Aspects* (1995) and *European Securities Markets. The Investment Services Directive and Beyond* (forthcoming).

VII. Stock Exchange Governance in the European Union

GUIDO FERRARINI

1. EXCHANGES AS FIRMS

Types of Services

Stock exchanges are generally viewed as a type of firm that produces 'transaction services'. They facilitate transactions between buyers and sellers of securities by providing either a centralized location for trades to take place or an electronic system to perform the same function.[1] Thus, the primary benefit of exchanges is that they save traders the cost of independently searching for someone on the other side of the transaction.[2] Another benefit is that exchanges produce information, as reflected in the prices of the instruments traded on them.[3]

Exchanges provide other important services, such as the monitoring of the listed companies and of the market in which their financial instruments trade (Macey-Kanda (1990)). In so doing they protect their reputation as places where transactions will be executed fairly and efficiently. Fischel-Grossman (1984, at 291) state that: "The exchange faces the same incentives to produce quality products (i.e. transactions services) as any other business. The incentives of an exchange are not very different from those of a producer of electric equipment. The latter attempts to produce high quality items because this will maximize the profit it can achieve from their sale ... The desire to achieve a good reputation leads the exchange to prevent member abuses to the extent it is economically possible and worthwhile to do so."

Among the 'ancillary' services offered by stock exchanges are those relating to clearing and settlement. However, most frequently such services are performed by entities different from the exchange where the transactions have occurred. In fact, vertical integration between exchanges and clearance and settlement providers often does not make sense on cost grounds (see Giddy-Saunders-Walter (1996), who add that vertical integration is easier in derivatives markets, which only require simple cash settlement). Moreover, increasing competition pushes exchanges to divest themselves of ancillary services, in order to reduce costs and increase efficiency (*ibidem*).

Competition

Although exchanges can be non-profit organizations, their objective is to succeed by generating volume (Carlton (1984)). In pursuing this objective they operate in an increasingly competitive environment (Lehn (1995); Pagano–Steil (1996)). Not only do they compete amongst themselves, but also against other enterprises that offer transaction services, such as the proprietary trading systems (PTS) (Schwartz (1995)). Such a structural change in capital markets, with respect to past structures, has been mainly caused by two factors. First, the advances in information technology have reduced the costs of 'producing' trading services. Second, the growing importance of institutional investors has affected the demand for trading services. For example, index funds may be less interested in transacting immediately than other investors and consequently be reluctant to pay for the 'immediacy' provided in a continuous auction market (Lehn (1995)).

Competition takes place on several grounds, such as the provision of immediacy, price discovery, low price volatility, liquidity, transparency, and transaction costs (Bronfman–Lehn–Schwartz (1994)). Moreover, competition is a substitute for regulation. Indeed, the more competition there is, the more likely it is that exchanges themselves will adopt rules that benefit and protect customers (Carlton (1984)).

2. RECENT DEVELOPMENTS

The treatment of exchanges as firms has recently obtained recognition in the laws of some Member States of the EU. For some time, solely the U.K. represented the view that investment exchanges must be regulated not only as markets but also as undertakings which provide dealing services to investment firms and investors (Securities and Investments Board (1994)). Gradually such a view has been shared by other Member States and the implementation of the ISD has accelerated the convergence of national laws towards the UK model; such a model is, however, often substantially adapted to fit the legal traditions and the political preferences of the individual Member States (see Wymeersch (1997)).

In this paragraph I shall briefly analyse how the exchange as a firm view influenced exchange law and organization in some Member States. Firstly, I shall examine the transformation which took place in Germany and the Netherlands, in the absence of radical changes of the law, under the stimulus of international competition. Secondly, I shall consider the new legal regimes adopted in France, Belgium and Italy for regulated markets. Thirdly, I shall refer to Sweden and Denmark for examples of exchange privatization.

Germany and the Netherlands

German stock exchanges are defined as public law institutions (Kümpel (1995); Schwark (1994)). Their formation must be approved by the competent State authority, which is also in charge of the exchange supervision (para. 1 (1) and (2) *Börsengesetz*). Each exchange has a supporting body (*Träger*) which provides trading and ancillary services. This body can be either the local chamber of industry and commerce (i.e. a public law entity: see para. 4 (1) *Börsengesetz*) or a private law association (Siebel (1995)). However, the supporting body of the Frankfurt Stock Exchange (FWB), is *Deutsche Börse AG* (DB), a joint-stock company the capital of which belongs to banks (80%), regional bourses (10%) and stockbrokers (10%).

DB was formed in 1993 and is also the holding company of the German Securities Deposit (*Deutscher Kassenverein AG*) and of the supporting body (Deutsche Terminbörse GmbH) of the German Options and Futures Exchange (DTB) (Francioni (1995)). The creation of DB reflects the exchange as a firm concept. Although exchanges are regulated as public markets, the managing entities of the main stock exchange (FWB) and the only derivatives exchange (DTB) are private corporations belonging to the market participants (Rudolph (1992); similar developments are taking place in Austria, where the newly formed *Wiener Börse AG* will conduct all the operations relating to the cash and derivatives markets; the Council of the Vienna Stock Exchange will retain all its regulatory powers over these markets). Moreover, DB runs IBIS, the integrated exchange traded and information system which is operated in tandem with the floors of the FWB and the other seven German stock exchanges (Pagano–Steil (1996)).

In addition, DB promotes cooperation between the various exchanges. Four of them (Berlin, Düsseldorf, Frankfurt and Munich) resolved at the end of 1995 to initiate closer cooperation, aimed at achieving higher-quality price formation and lower costs for participants. Their action extends to cooperation between the market supervisory offices and the establishment of a central office for listing. This responds to the objective of "... standardizing the central functions used by the exchange operating companies and bringing them all together in the medium term in one operating company" (Deutsche Börse (1995), at 29).

As to the Netherlands, two years ago the Amsterdam Stock Exchange (ASE) resolved to undergo a fundamental restructuring in order to maintain its position as a medium size stock market in the face of increasing competition in Europe (see Amsterdam Stock Exchange (1995)). The ASE and the European Options Exchange (EOE) were incorporated as subsidiaries of a newly created holding company, Amsterdam Exchanges (AEX). The clearing and settlement entities were incorporated as another subsidiary of AEX, named Amsterdam Securities Depository (ASD). The ASE and EOE Associations kept regulatory and monitoring functions as to the exchanges' members, whereas the regulation and supervision of trading and listing became AEX responsibilities. The property of AEX shares was recently sold to the exchanges' members, listed companies and pension funds (see para. 3 below).

France, Belgium and Italy

French Law accepted the idea that exchanges must be run by private companies before the enactment of the ISD.[4] However, the Law n. 96-597 of 2nd July 1996 concerning the modernization of financial activities – which implemented the Directive in France – introduced the new concept of 'regulated markets' and stated new rules concerning such markets. Briefly, *marchés reglementés* are operated by business companies, defined as *entreprises de marché*, whose object is to provide for the functioning of a regulated market of financial instruments and can be extended to cover the offer of clearing and settlement services. The regulated markets are recognized by an order of the Minister of Economy and Finance,[5] following a proposal of the *Conseil des Marchés Financiers* and on the advice of the *Commission des operations de bourse* and the *Banque de France*. According to Art. 97, VII, those securities and futures markets already existing and regularly functioning on the date of enactment of the new law are recognized as regulated markets.[6]

Similarly, in Belgium the Law of 6 April 1995 implementing the ISD and CAD reformed the regulation of financial exchanges by amending the relevant rules of the Law of 4 December 1990 on financial transactions and financial markets. The 1995 Law distinguishes between *bourses de valeurs mobilières* (Art. 7-29) and *autres marchés* which may be established and organized by Royal Decree whenever the King considers it necessary for the further development of Belgium as a financial centre or for the protection of persons admitted to these markets (Art. 30-35). The bourses must be managed by legal entities constituted under public law in a co-operative form, which are subject to company law rules except as provided in the 1995 Law. As to the 'other markets', the rules are less detailed than those applicable to the bourses and more room is left to government regulations.

In Italy, the implementation of the ISD was also accompanied by a reform of the law concerning regulated markets. The Legislative Decree 12th July 1996, N.415, defines the organization and management of regulated markets as a business and states that it must be exercized by share companies, not necessarily for a profit (Art. 46, para. 1). The Decree also provides that the management company's activities will include the organization of, and the services to, the relevant market; the surveillance of market transactions and regulatory compliance; decisions as to the access of traders and admission of financial instruments to the market; cooperation with the Securities Commission (Consob) in case of breaches in market rules (Art. 49, para. 1).[7] Art. 48, para. 1, states that regulated markets shall be authorized by Consob, provided that the management company complies with the requirements fixed by a Consob regulation (as to minimum capital and ancillary services) and that the market rules comply with EU Law and enable the transparency of the market, the orderly performance of transactions and the protection of investors.[8]

From the perspective of the stock exchange as a firm, one of the main differences between the new Italian law with respect to the relevant French and Belgian legislation is represented by the fact that in Italy private parties can take the initiative to create an exchange, subject to an authorization by public bodies, whereas in Belgium and France the initiative is taken by public bodies, possibly following a demand by the relevant interest groups.

Sweden and Denmark

The Stockholm Stock Exchange was the first in Europe to be privatized. Until 1992 it was a public institution and had a legal monopoly in share trading. In that year, a law was approved providing for the transformation of the Stockholm Stock Exchange into a limited company by shares and for the ending of its monopoly rights. In 1993 Stockholms Fondbors AB was in business, owned in equal parts by the exchange members and listed companies. From 1994, its shares became freely transferable, meaning that other institutions may buy them and even acquire control of the company (Pagano–Steil 1996). At the end of 1996, the ten major shareholders owned 72.9% of the share capital: nine of them were banks, listed companies and institutional investors; OM Group (which owns OM, the derivatives exchange) was the largest shareholder with 20.7% of the shares.

Similar developments recently occurred in Denmark. A securities trading law was passed in 1995 abolishing the Copenhagen Stock Exchange monopoly and providing for the transformation of the exchange into a limited company. In 1996, Københavns Fondsbørs A/S (Copenhagen Stock Exchange Limited) started operations. Its shares were subscribed by securities dealers (60%), bond issuers (20%) and listed companies (20%). Also the Danish derivatives exchange (FUTOP Clearing Centre) was converted into a limited company, which became a wholly owned subsidiary of the Copenhagen Stock Exchange Company. The acquisition was justified with reference to the competition resulting from implementation of the ISD.

3. OWNERSHIP

Most of the major stock exchanges are organized as companies owned by their members, i.e. the brokers and dealers transacting on the exchange: the London Stock Exchange Ltd and Société de la Bourse de Luxembourg S.A. are good examples in Europe (other cases were mentioned in para. 2 above). Some economists define member-owned exchanges in general as co-operatives (see Hart–Moore (1995)). For present purposes, it is convenient to avoid definitions which could vary across different legal systems, and the terms 'member owned exchange' or 'members' ownership' will be used in the discussion (another term which is sometimes used is that of 'membership organization': see Bronfman–Lehn–Schwartz (1994)).

Other exchanges are organized as companies owned exclusively or predominantly by third-party investors: OM in Stockholm, Tradepoint and OMLX in London belong to this category. They will be indicated hereafter as 'investor-owned exchanges' and the term 'outside ownership' will be used to express the idea that "the assets of the exchange are controlled by an outside owner (who maximizes profit)" (Hart–Moore (1995), at 7).

The theoretical issues relating to exchange ownership are more economic than legal. Firstly, it is interesting to ask why 'members' ownership' has prevailed. Secondly, it is important to consider whether the present features of financial markets suggest that 'outside ownership' will be more frequently adopted. Thirdly, attention should be paid to some recent cases which share elements of the members' and outside ownership models.

Members' Ownership

As to the first question, an answer can be found in Hansmann (1996). His starting point is that ownership is commonly assigned to persons who transact with a firm, either as purchasers of the firm's products or as sellers to the firm of some factor of production, including capital (such persons are defined as 'patrons'). The reason for this is that market contracting can be especially costly in the presence of 'market failures', such as limited competition or asymmetric information: "in such circumstances, the total costs of transacting can sometimes be reduced by merging the purchasing and the selling party in an ownership relationship, hence eliminating the conflict of interest between buyer and seller that underlies or aggravates many of the avoidable costs of market contracting" (Hansmann (1990), at 287).

With respect to customer-owned retail, wholesale, and supply firms, Hansmann notes that market power appears to provide an incentive for customer ownership, at least in cases where economies of scale leave room for only a few firms (e.g. at the wholesale level). If such firms have market power *vis-à-vis* their patrons (e.g. wholesale firms having market power *vis-à-vis* retailers), the latter have an incentive to avoid price exploitation by owning the firms that serve them.

In addition, the analysis of 'ownership costs' is conducive to customer ownership in the situations examined by Hansmann (1996, 1990). Firstly, the customer is in a position to oversee the affairs of the firm without incurring substantial costs. Secondly, the supply business does not require large amounts of organization-specific capital. Thirdly, the customers' interests with respect to the firm are reasonably homogeneous, so that collective decisions can be taken at a low cost.

A similar reasoning can explain the origins of most member-owned exchanges. When they were set up, exchanges were often in a monopolistic or similar position in their geographic area. In fact, economies of scale have always been substantial for financial exchanges. Moreover, their members represented rather close and homogeneous groups, and the capital required to run an exchange was not too high. Exchanges were organized by intermediaries so as to prevent the exploitation by others who, as a result, could gain monopolistic profits from exchange transactions. Furthermore, intermediaries had the information needed to organize and manage the relevant markets.

Investor Ownership

The situation is different today. As Hart–Moore (1995) suggest exchanges in all countries face a number of important new challenges. Two of them have already been mentioned here. Firstly, there is increasing direct competition between exchanges. Secondly, exchanges no longer need to be vertically integrated, as many of their traditional services are offered by specialist service providers. Thus, competition occurs both 'horizontally' (between exchanges) and 'vertically' (between exchanges and service providers). The third challenge lies in the fact that exchanges have become more capital intensive and periodically need to finance substantial investment projects. The fourth relates to membership, which has become more open and as a result more diverse: "... members not only perform different functions within the exchange but they may have other activities outside the exchange (such as over-the-counter business) which make them competitors of the exchange" (Hart–Moore, 1995, at 1).

Hart–Moore compare the exchanges' current structures in the light of such developments. They distinguish between members' co-operatives (where the assets of the exchange are controlled by the members, who take decisions on a one member, one vote basis) and outside ownership (which ranges from owner-managed business to widely-held public corporations). As to co-operatives, they make use of ideas developed by political scientists in the context of voting theory, with particular regard to the Median Voter Theorem (they refer particularly to Roberts (1977)). In a democracy, real decision-making power rests with the pivotal voter, who may not represent average opinion. "The discrepancy between the pivotal voter's preferences and average preferences can be explained by the fact that the distribution of opinion is skewed ... This is a subtle but crucial idea: the shape of distribution of opinion matters."[9]

The outcome of Hart–Moore's analysis is that two factors critically determine the relative performance of a members' co-operative and outside ownership. These are the variation in membership of the exchange in terms of the size or nature of the members' business and the degree of competition the exchange faces either from other exchanges, or from off-board trading. In particular they make two claims. The first is that outside ownership becomes relatively more efficient than a member's cooperative as the variation across the membership becomes more skewed. The second is that outside ownership becomes relatively more efficient than a members' cooperative as the exchange faces more competition.

These authors' 'overall message' to an exchange currently operating as a members' co-operative is that "as the population of traders becomes more uneven (which is what has happened in many cases) and/or as the environment becomes more competitive (which it certainly has done recently), so, on efficiency grounds, there may be more of a case for selling off the exchange to an outside owner" (Hart–Moore, at 14). Moreover, an outside owner could have fewer difficulties than a members' co-operative in raising the capital needed to finance the investments often required by modern financial exchanges (id., at 33).

Mixed Models

However, a direct transition from members' to investors' ownership is unlikely to occur in practice. Recent experiences in Europe show that a first likely step is the offer of minority shareholdings in the exchange management company to the listed companies and to (institutional) investors.

The Swedish and Danish cases are good examples (see para. 2 above). The main shareholder (with 20.7% of capital) of the Stockholm Stock Exchange is OM Group, specializing in exchange management and owned by investors; other shareholders are banks, investment firms, listed companies and institutional investors. Similarly, the majority of the Copenhagen Stock Exchange's shares are owned by its members, whilst the remainder belongs to the issuers of securities listed on the exchange (see para. 2 above).

With regards to Amsterdam Exchanges (holding company of ASE and EOE), the members own all the 'A' shares; 'B' shares, of equal size and nominal value, were offered also to Dutch pension funds and listed companies. As a result, the members now own 60 per cent of AEX share capital, and about 25 shareholders own the remaining 40 per cent. For a period of five years, there will be a market of AEX shares limited to exchange members, pension funds and listed companies. Afterwards, trading will be free and AEX shares will be listed at the ASE; however, no shareholder shall be entitled to own more than 10% of the share capital (see *The Financial Times*, 28.02.1997).

Similarly in Italy, according to Art. 56 of the Legislative Decree 12th July 1996, N. 415 (providing for the privatization of the Italian Stock Exchange), the shares of the newly created Borsa Italiana S.p.A. will be offered to the exchange members (51%) and to other investors (49%), including the listed companies. Once the shares have been allotted, their market will be free. However, the shareholders will have to comply with the fitness requirements fixed by a Treasury regulation.

4. Regulation and Surveillance

Self-regulation

The regulation of stock exchanges should comprise at least three types of rules: (i) market rules; (ii) membership rules; (iii) listing requirements. In theory, all such rules could be adopted exclusively by exchanges through self-regulation. In practice, exchanges are also subject to state laws and regulations.

The distribution of the relevant powers between the public and the private domains reflects each country's degree of financial liberalization. Pure self-regulation is rare in stock markets. Examples can be found in the UK with respect to corporate governance (the Cadbury Committee's *Code of Best Practice*) and take-overs and mergers (*City Code*). Co-regulation is preferably adopted as a strategy of market governance which combines private and government regulation, generally in so called 'two-tier systems' (see Ayres–Braithwaite (1992)). Public regulation is common in fields such as insider trading and manipulation (Goode (1990)).

The case for self-regulation is that exchanges face the same incentives to produce quality services as any other business (Fischel–Grossman (1984)). The analogy with an industrial corporation is helpful. Such a corporation will find it profit-maximizing to produce items of high quality relative to cost. To the extent that there is competition, it will be forced to produce the best price-quality-quantity combination feasible. Similarly, an exchange will use self-regulation and surveillance to produce the highest quality-quantity combination possible at a given cost, and competition will lead to prices which induce the socially optimal purchases by customers (Fischel–Grossman (1984); Miller (1991)).

Moreover, exchanges are better positioned than outside regulators to draw up detailed rules for trading, clearing and settlement. Public regulators do not have the right incentives to make business tradeoffs.[10] Except for problems such as price manipulation or insider trading, where (as shown below) private regulations must be supplemented by public ones, a broader scope should be recognized to exchange self-regulation than is usually the case.[11]

In sum, from the exchange as a firm perspective, self-regulation is nothing but an aspect of the exchange business. The organization and policy of an exchange are reflected by its rules, and the market surveillance can be analysed as an aspect of the exchange management. Moreover, as competition increases, a clearer trend towards exchange deregulation can be detected. I shall examine hereafter some of the problems concerning the transition to exchange self-regulation, taking into account the two main ownership structures.

Member-Owned Exchanges

The self-regulation of member-owned exchanges presents problems of conflict of interest. These may arise either among members of the exchange or between some members and the exchange. A simple case of conflict is that of a broker's fraudulent act, which causes harm, if detected, to all other members of the exchange, as it discourages customer participation to trade. According to Fischel–Grossman (1984) this type of problem will be resolved by the members' bargaining among themselves until a strategy which maximizes the sum of their wealth is achieved. In particular, the exchange will vote to put procedures in place which prevent frauds, as the wealth gained by one member in a fraudulent act is more than offset by the wealth lost by the other members.

Recent research has cast some doubt on the general validity of this assumption. Pirrong (1995) in a study on the self-regulation of commodities exchanges has criticized the traditional literature for not recognizing that exchanges are coalitions of individual members with divergent interests, and transactions costs are positive. In the case of manipulation, an exchange may take few precautions against it because transactions costs preclude the negotiation of an agreement that makes all parties better off. The affected parties will opportunistically attempt to influence the exchange's decision makers in order to obtain a larger share of rents and the costs of influence activities may be large. Exchange rule enforcers may not use their discretionary authority to stop manipulations because their decisions are intended to balance the interests of parties contending for rents, rather than to maximize efficiency. This would be especially true if the exchange membership were large.

These arguments are similar to those traditionally advanced by public choice theory to criticize regulation (for a summary of the latter arguments, see Ogus (1995)). Such a theory treats legislation as a response to the competing demands of interest groups and suggests that regulation serves mainly to confer rents on the regulated firms. In the words of one author: "with self-regulation regulatory capture is there from the outset".[12]

Looking at the trends prevailing in Europe, the problem of conflicts of interest in self-regulation is partly dealt with by introducing some form of public regulation.[13] Briefly, either a two-tier system of regulation is created, where the exchange as a regulator is under the control of a public body (examples are given at para. 2 above) or some form of state regulation and surveillance of the exchange markets is adopted (see para. 5 and 6 below, where other forms of reaction to the conflicts of interest problem are explored).

Investor-Owned Exchanges

Investor-owned exchanges should be considered as less exposed to capture and thus better equipped to regulate the activities of the intermediaries operating on their markets. A preference for outside ownership from a regulatory perspective can also be grounded on the arguments used in the previous discussion. Self-regulation affects the quality of the transactions services offered by an exchange. Hart–Moore's theory of exchange ownership illustrated above covers both the choice of price and quality. Therefore, their claims concerning the efficient ownership structure of exchanges also apply to self-regulation. As already mentioned, they suggest that – as the membership becomes more 'skewed' and the exchange faces more competition – outside ownership exhibits greater efficiency over the members' ownership model. With respect to self-regulation, this implies that outside ownership secures better investor protection if, as frequently happens, membership is diverse and competition is effective.

However, as noted above, the investor-ownership model is still less frequent than the mixed model, in which ownership belongs to exchange members and other investors, such as the listed companies and institutional investors. In the mixed model, the conflicts of interest may be aggravated by the presence of the listed companies in the ownership and governance structures and by the fact that not all members are at the same time owners of the exchange.

5. Delegating Management and Supervision

The problems inherent in exchange self-regulation are also dealt with through the design of appropriate governance structures. In any case, such structures should respond to the requirements of an efficient organization and management of exchanges, and prevent conflicts of interest in general (e.g. between brokers and market makers in the choice of an exchange trading system). Of course, the design of governance structures also depends on the choices made as to exchange ownership.

In order to focus the problems at issue and some of their possible solutions, I shall now examine a few recent situations where the exchange governance structures have been either voluntarily reviewed or publicly regulated in order to diminish the potential for conflicts of interest and assure an efficient management and supervision.

The London Experience

The Stock Exchange carried out a review of its own governance arrangements (London Stock Exchange (1996)). Such a review was conducted over a period of six months through interviews and written submissions from a number of firms and individuals. This exercise was undertaken in response to the profound dissatisfaction which had been caused by recent conflicts in the LSE governance (which led, *inter alia*, to the dismissal of the exchange general manager).[14] The purpose of the review was to consider how the LSE decision-making processes might be improved and due weight be given to the views of members and other constituencies.

Some aspects of the report may be of interest to present purposes. First of all, it reaffirms the soundness of a board of directors comprising a number of members (21) which is greater than the current norm among commercial companies. The argument is that the board is deliberately structured to give all 'constituencies' representation on it. From a comparative perspective, most governing bodies of similar organizations have an equivalent number of members. The constituencies now represented on the LSE board are the securities houses (five members), private client firms (three), listed companies (three), institutional investors (two) and government brokers (one). The remaining members are the chairman, the deputy chairman and five executive directors. The benefit of such a structure is that the board fulfils a 'quasi parliamentary role'. The disadvantage is that a large and diverse board may encounter difficulties in taking key policy decisions.

However, the LSE is also governed by an executive committee, appointed by the board of directors and comprising the executive directors and three senior staff members. Such a committee is responsible for the day-to-day management and regulation of the exchange, and is accountable to the board. The report proposes to maintain this governance structure with the argument that the exchange is a business and should be run by a capable executive which is free to manage.

In addition, both the LSE board and the executive committee are assisted by several 'practitioners' committees' which provide input from the market into the exchange's policies. A similar committee structure is common to other exchanges in the U.K. and in other countries. The LSE report reaffirms the validity of such a structure and makes proposals to improve it. As a result, the exchange advisory committees have been reorganized in a two-tier structure, with a primary markets committee and a secondary markets committee in the top tier. Furthermore, the advisory committees report to the executive committee, but their views on policy issues must be made available to the board. Importance is also attached to the fact that key firms can serve on a committee on a regular basis and cross-memberships exist between the board and the committees.

Another report which is of interest to the present analysis, though referring to a commodity market, was published by SIB following a review of the London Metal Exchange (Securities and Investments Board (1996)). This review was conducted by SIB at the request of the LME in the wake of the Sumitomo affair[15] and touched upon various matters including the LME's governance arrangements. As to the composition of the board of directors, many regarded the existing arrangements as unduly favouring one category of members (the 'ring members'). SIB recommended that "the LME should review the composition and practices of its Board to ensure that potential conflicts of interest between the LME's regulatory duties and its commercial interests are avoided". As to the role of the board, SIB suggested that "the LME should review the Board's relationship with its committees and with the Chief Executive and his staff with a view to much greater delegation to both of matters concerning the running of the Exchange and market supervision and surveillance". In order to avoid conflicts of interest in supervision and surveillance, SIB's recommendation was that "the LME Board should formally delegate responsibility for monitoring market trading and for intervening where necessary to maintain a proper market".

The Belgian Experience

As anticipated (para. 2 above), Belgium implemented the ISD through the Law 6 April 1995 including new rules on *bourses de valeurs mobilières* and *autres marchés*. The bourses are managed by co-operative companies, the governance structure of which consists of a board of directors and a management committee. The board of directors is appointed by the company's general meeting, but its chairman and deputy-chairman are appointed by the Minister of Finance subsequent to a proposal by the board. The board of directors has three main tasks: (i) to define the general policy of the company; (ii) to supervise the company's management committee; (iii) to propose amendments to the exchange's rules and regulations (Art. 14).

The management committee is appointed by the Minister of Finance on the basis of a list of names proposed by the board of directors. The committee sees to the management of the stock exchange company according to the general policy defined by the board (Art. 15). Furthermore, it serves as a market authority (*autorité de marché*) which is completely independent from all other company bodies or third parties. The committee's members are forbidden to undertake any professional activity which could impair their autonomy (Art. 16). The main tasks of the committee as a market authority relate to the (i) admission to listing; (ii) access to membership; (iii) organization and functioning of the exchange markets; (iv) supervision of intermediaries and listed companies; (v) market surveillance.

As to the 'other markets', their governance structure is determined, from time to time, by royal decrees (Art. 31). An example is offered by the governance rules stated by the Royal Decree of 10 June 1996 concerning the formation and organisation of EASDAQ. The general policy of EASDAQ S.A. is determined by the company's board of directors. In addition, the board issues the EASDAQ Regulation (which includes the admission requirements, membership requirements, procedural rules and trading rules) and, in certain circumstances, the EASDAQ Rules. The board is appointed by the shareholders' meeting, which selects one third of the directors from a list submitted by EASD (the association which promoted the market), one third from a list submitted by the shareholders and the remaining third from a list jointly proposed by EASD and the shareholders.[16] A management committee may be established for the daily management of the company.

Furthermore, the EASDAQ market authority is entrusted with the daily operation and supervision of the market. It is a fully independent body consisting of at least four members appointed by the board of directors subject to the approval of the Minister of Finance. Such an authority has similar powers to those entrusted to the exchanges' market authorities by the 1995 Law.

To conclude on the Belgian experience, the supervision of exchanges and other markets is arranged in a two-tier structure. The first tier is constituted by the market authorities which have a self-regulatory nature, whereas the second tier is represented by a public regulator such as the BFC.

Comparison

The London and Belgian models share common elements, while at the same time showing substantial differences. Both models separate policy from management and supervision with varying degrees of exchange policy being entrusted to the board of directors. In London, regulation falls within the board of directors' terms of reference, whereas in Belgium the board of directors can only make regulatory proposals.

Management and supervision are delegated to executive bodies in order to assure that exchanges are run as businesses and that conflicts of interest are limited. However, in the case of London exchanges, such a delegation of powers is deliberated by the board of directors under company law rules. In Belgium, the powers and role of the management committee are regulated by the law which defines the same as a market authority.

Furthermore, the independence of the management committee is sanctioned by Belgian law and is reinforced by the fact that the committee's members are appointed by the government. All this reflects the public law nature of Belgian stock exchanges, but appears in contrast with the exchange as a firm conception which is clearly followed by the UK regulation and practice.

In more general terms, the benefit of total management independence should be compared with the costs of a clear-cut separation between the exchange board of directors and the exchange executive body, such as that implemented in Belgium. From the exchange as a firm perspective adopted throughout this paper, if the owners lose control of exchange management and supervision, the incentives to invest money in the exchange are greatly reduced.

6. Separating Management from Supervision

I shall now move on to consider two models, one European and the other American, where exchange management has been separated from supervision so as to minimize conflicts of interests among members.

The French Model

In France the 1996 Law mentioned above (para. 2) gives the market-enterprises regulatory powers that encompass the conditions for the access to the market and listing requirements, the rules on the organization of transactions, the conditions for suspension in trading of one or more instruments, and the rules on registration and publicity of transactions.

Such enterprises must submit the market rules for approval to the *Conseil de Marchés Financiers* (CMF), a newly formed self-regulatory body that replaces the suppressed *Conseil de Bourse de Valeurs* and *Conseil de Marché à terme*. As its predecessors, the CMF is defined as a professional authority provided with *personnalité morale* (Art. 27 of the 1996 Law) and consists of representatives of the various professionial sectors who are appointed by the Minister of the Economy and Finance after consultation with the relevant professional bodies. Of the sixteen CMF members, six represent the financial market intermediaries, one the commodities markets, three the listed companies, three the investors, one the investment services providers' employees, and two are financial experts.

The CMF issues its rules through a general regulation which must be approved by the Minister of the Economy and Finance following the opinion of the *Commission des operations de bourse* and *Banque de France*. Such regulation concerns both the investment services (with the exception of prudential controls on intermediaries) and the regulated markets. As to the latter, the CMF states, *inter alia*, the general criteria to be complied with respect to their organization and functioning, and the rules concerning the execution, reporting and transparency of market transactions. Furthermore, the CMF takes the initiative for the creation of new markets (para. 2 above). In addition, the CMF has supervisory powers concerning the investment services providers, market-enterprises, clearing houses and regulated markets. With respect to the latter, the supervision concerns the regularity of transactions and can be delegated to market enterprises.

To summarize, French law provides for a two-tier system of self-regulation. Firstly, the market enterprises adopt the market rules, which must comply with the criteria fixed by CMF and be approved by the latter. Secondly, CMF has regulatory powers concerning both the markets and the investment services providers, and supervisory powers relating to regulated markets and market-enterprises. Therefore, market surveillance is separated from the management of regulated markets and only the latter is performed by the market-enterprises.

NASDAQ

The French model of market governance is, to some extent, similar to that of the American Nasdaq which has recently separated the market's management from its supervision.

Nasdaq is a stock market (not an exchange) belonging to the National Association of Securities Dealers (NASD). A restructuring of NASD and Nasdaq followed heavy public criticism of the Association's governance and performance. This included "charges that large member firms, particularly Nasdaq market makers, control(led) the NASD for their own benefit, and conversely, that small NASD member firms, and issuers, investors and other members of the public, (had) scant voice in NASD or Nasdaq market governance" (see the Rudman Report (1995), at 2). Critics also contended that "the NASD's regulation of the Nasdaq stock market (had) been flawed and uneven and the NASD's policing of its member firms (had) been ineffective and unfair" (*ibidem*). The SEC conducted an investigation of the operations and activities of NASD and of market making activities in the Nasdaq stock market and published a report on its findings (Securities and Exchange Commission (1996)). The investigation identified a number of serious deficiencies in the NASD's performance of its duties as a self-regulatory organization, especially as they concern the Nasdaq market. Consequently, the SEC instituted proceedings against the NASD pursuant to section 19(h) of the Exchange Act.

In the meantime, the NASD had taken significant steps to reform its governance and regulatory structure after a review of the same conducted by an NASD select committee chaired by Senator Rudman. As the committee stated: "Congress and the SEC have acknowledged that self-regulation has certain limitations, deriving primarily from the 'inherent conflict' between the self-regulators' commercial interests and their regulatory obligations" (Rudman Report (1995), at 5). However, the SEC and Congress have not imposed any standard governance format on the self-regulatory organizations, but have established certain guiding principles: "Central among these, in addition to fair representation of the SROs' members, is representation of the public on the SROs' governing bodies. The 'public' means individuals or institutions not affiliated with the SROs' members ... Public representation reflects the quasi-governmental status of the SROs. It also ensures a balanced perspective and diversity of informed viewpoints on the SROs' governing bodies, thereby enhancing both the system of self-regulation and the vitality and competitiveness of the nation's securities markets". As to the "fair representation" principle, it "keeps the 'self' in self-regulation and also provides an important check against any one segment of the SROs' membership dominating their governance" (*ibidem*).

The Rudman Report includes recommendations as to NASD's governance structure. In the committee's view, the NASD and the Nasdaq market should not be divorced, because "this would sacrifice a key benefit of the self-regulatory system, which links industry expertise with industry regulation ..." (*ibidem*, at 9 ff.). However, regulation of the broker-dealer profession should be separated from regulation of the Nasdaq and other OTC markets: "to this end, the governing board charged with regulating the NASD's member firms should be separate and independent from the governing board overseeing the Nasdaq market. So, too, should their respective professional staffs".

The select committee's recommendations have been implemented through a deep restructuring of the NASD. Firstly, NASD Regulation, Inc. (NASDR) was established as a separate, independent subsidiary of the Association. Its mission is to regulate the securities markets for the ultimate benefit and protection of the investor. In addition to being the securities industry's primary self-regulator, NASDR regulates the markets operated by its sister subsidiary, The Nasdaq Stock Market, Inc.. The latter corporation must develop, operate, and maintain systems, services and products for a number of securities markets. The NASD has also delegated to it responsibility for the formulation of regulatory policies and listing criteria applicable to the markets it operates.

Both NASDR and The Nasdaq Stock Market, Inc. are governed by a board of directors whose composition consists of at least 50 per cent representation from outside the securities industry. The parent association has a board of governors consisting of the chief executive officer, three representatives of the NASD membership and five non-industry governors representing investors, issuers and other constituencies.

Comparison

Clearly, the French and Nasdaq models show substantial differences. The former relates to regulated markets in general, the latter to a stock market which is not regulated as an exchange under US law. The French model is directly defined by the law, whereas the Nasdaq restructuring was effected by NASD, albeit under the pressure of public criticism and investigations. Also the ownership structures are different. The Nasdaq market belongs to an association of all the securities dealers, even those who do not operate in the Nasdaq market. In France the 'market-enterprises' are owned by their members, but members need not be shareholders and shareholders need not be members.

The similarities between the two models lie in the separation between management and supervision. In the case of Nasdaq, this separation was accomplished by creating two distinct entities, one for the management and regulation of the stock market, the other for all NASD's regulatory tasks, including the supervision of the Nasdaq market. In France, the 'market-enterprises' have management and regulatory tasks, but the CMF has a general regulatory power and supervises directly the regulated markets. Therefore, in both cases market surveillance is effected by distinct self-regulatory bodies.

From the exchange as a firm perspective, the separation of management from supervision is open to criticism, as it deprives the exchange executives of quality control on trading services. In the French case, a situation could arise in which a regulated market is owned by third-party investors, despite being subject to exclusive CMF surveillance. Of course, from a purely regulatory perspective, a benefit is represented by the fact that market surveillance is carried out by a self-regulatory body which is fairly representative of the various constituencies and is formed by members who are knowledgeable about the markets that they regulate.

7. CONCLUSIONS

The exchange as a firm view is gaining ground in Europe despite being enforced with varying degrees of conviction in the different Member States. Where stock exchanges are defined and regulated as enterprises, they are most frequently owned by their members although there are some cases of investor owned exchanges. In other cases, ownership of an exchange belongs to its various constituencies and this may represent a step towards more investor ownership. This would be preferable in the light of strong competition and diversification of membership.

Competition among stock exchanges has also determined deregulation in some Member States. Self-regulation is expanding and the exchange-management companies subsequently gain regulatory and supervisory powers. However, conflicts of interest may arise, especially in the case of member-owned exchanges. These conflicts, which could be limited by investor ownership, must necessarily be considered by exchange governance structures.

One remedy, in the case of member-owned exchanges, is to ensure that the governing bodies are representative of all their constituencies, so that the exchange policy and regulation reflect a fair balance of interests. An additional remedy is to create independent executive bodies which take care of market management and supervision and are, to some extent, separated from those in charge of the exchange policy.

A different course of action is to separate market surveillance from exchange governance and to assign the former to distinct self-regulatory bodies. This solution seems adequate to respond also to cases where the exchange is owned either by investors or by a mixture of members, listed companies and investors. A weakness of the separation between governance and surveillance, however, is represented by the circumstance that the quality of trading services is not controlled by the enterprise running the exchange.

NOTES

* Parts of this paper will appear in a volume, edited by the author, on *European Securities Markets. The Investment Services Directive and Beyond* (Kluwer Law International, 1997).
1. For similar statements as to futures markets see Fischel–Grossman (1984); Carlton (1984).
2. See Fischel (1987) who thinks that there is little fundamental difference between the economic role of a stock exchange and that of an ordinary shopping centre or flea market. All facilitate trading by bringing together buyers and sellers in a known location and thereby reducing search costs.
3. See Mulherin–Netter–Overdahl (1991). In their opinion, a financial exchange is a firm that creates a market in financial instruments; its product is accurate information as reflected in prices.
4. *Société des Bourses Françaises* and *MATIF SA* were set up, in conformity with the laws then in force, as private companies whose object was to run securities and derivatives markets and to provide the clearing and settlement services required by such markets. They were originally conceived as 'specialised financial institutions' with a 'mission of public interest'. Such a mission covered not only the organization and management of the relevant markets but also the surveillance of the activities taking place in the same. See de Vauplanne–Bornet (1994); de Juglart-Ippolito (1991).
5. In order for the recognition to be granted, the regular functioning of the market must be secured. To that effect, the market enterprise must adopt market rules which have to be approved by the

Conseil des Marchés Financiers. These rules cover the following areas: the conditions for access to the market and listing requirements, the rules on the organization of transactions, the conditions for the suspension of the trading of one or more instruments, and the rules on registration and publicity of transactions. The market enterprise is also entitled to admit financial instruments to the transactions on a regulated market, but the *Commission des opérations de bourse* can object to such an admission.

6. Therefore, the securities markets presently operated by *Société des Bourses Françaises* and *Société du Nouveau Marché* along with the futures markets operated by MATIF SA have been automatically recognized as regulated markets under the new law. Indeed, even before the passing of the new law, on the 14th February 1996 a law was passed by the French Parliament which granted the status of 'regulated market' to the existing securities and futures markets and gave them the right to extend their activities throughout Europe (see *Paris Bourse News*, No.9, April 1996).
7. Under Art. 46, para. 2, of the 1996 Decree, the Securities Commission (Consob) must state the minimum capital requirement of such management companies, the ancillary services that they can offer as well as those services relating to the organization and management of regulated markets. Under Art. 46, para. 3, the Treasury Minister must set the reputation and experience requirements applicable to the persons who have executive, management and control functions in the management companies, as well as the reputation requirements applicable to the shareholders of the same companies.
8. Art. 50 states that Consob will provide surveillance of the regulated markets so as to assure their transparency, the orderly performance of transactions and the protection of investors. Management companies are also subject to Consob's surveillance (Art. 53).
9. Hart–Moore (1995), at 12; these authors specify that by 'skewed' they mean that "the distribution is more to one side than the other ... To put the same idea formally: the median is not equal to the mean" (at 8, note 12).
10. See Miller (1991) who states: "self-regulatory structures have the very great advantage that the detailed rules are made by those with both the greatest long-run interest in maintaining reliability and the greatest store of specialised technical knowledge about the market and its real vulnerabilities."
11. On the balancing between centralization and decentralization see Bronfman–Lehn–Schwartz (1994).
12. See Ogus (1995) quoting Kay, 'The forms of Regulation', in Seldon (Ed.), *Financial Regulation – or Over-Regulation* (1988), p. 34.
13. According to Pirrong (1995), at 196, in the case of manipulation there is an alternative between 'ex ante regulation' (which consists e.g. of position limits and entry barriers) and 'ex post regulation' (through the judicial enforcement of civil or criminal rules proscribing manipulation). The former is act-based or preventative, whereas the latter is harm-based (see Shavell (1993)). Despite the weaknesses of self-regulation, ex ante regulation is not necessarily superior; in contrast, the nature of manipulation is well suited to harm-based sanctions: Pirrong (1995), at 197.
14. See 'Stock Exchange faces fresh crisis as chief is dismissed', *Financial Times*, January 5, 1996.
15. The review was announced on 19 June 1996 after the Sumitomo Corporation's disclosure that it had lost $1.8 billion due to the alleged unauthorized trading activities of its employee, Mr. Hamanaka.
16. See Art. 14 of EASDAQ S.A.'s memorandum of association which was approved by a Royal Decree of 27 September 1996.

References

Amsterdam Stock Exchange (1995) Annual Report.
Ayres, I. and J. Braithwaite (1992) *Responsive Regulation. Transcending the Deregulation Debate*, Oxford University Press, New York–Oxford.
Bronfman, C., K. Lehn and R. Schwartz (1994) 'US Securities Markets Regulation: Regulatory Structure', in B. Steil (ed.), *International Financial Market Regulation*, J. Wiley, Chichester–New York, 37–73.
Carlton, D. W. (1984) 'Futures Markets: Their Purpose, Their History, Their Growth, Their Successes and Failures', *Journal of Futures Markets* 4(3), 237–271.
de Juglart-Ippolito (1991) *Traité de Droit Commercial, 7, Banques et Bourses*, 3rd ed. by Martin, Paris.
Deutsche Börse (1995) Annual Report.
de Vauplane, H. and J. P. Bornet (1994) *Droit de la Bourse*, Litec, Paris.
Fischel, D. R. (1987) 'Organized Exchanges and the Regulation of Dual Class Common Stock', *University of Chicago Law Review* 54, 119 et seq.
Fischel, D. R. and S. J. Grossman (1984) 'Customer Protection in Futures and Securities Markets', *Journal of Futures Markets* 4(3), 273–295.
Francioni, R. (1995) 'The German Equities Market', in R. A. Schwartz (ed.), *Global Equity Markets. Technological, Competitive, and Regulatory Challenges*, Irwin, Chicago, 473–484.
Giddy, I., A. Saunders and I. Walter (1996) 'Clearance and Settlement', in B. Steil (ed.), *The European Equity Markets. The State of the Union and an Agenda for the Millennium*, The Royal Institute of International Affairs, London, 321–354.
Goode, R. (1990) 'The Concept and Implications of a Market in Commercial Law', *Israel Law Review* 24, 185–210.
Hansmann, H. (1990) 'Ownership of the Firm', in Bebchuck (ed.) *Corporate Law and Economic Analysis*, Cambridge University Press, 281–313.
Hansmann, H. (1996) *The Ownership of Enterprise*, The Belknap Press of Harvard University Press, Cambridge, Mass.–London, England.
Hart, O. and J. Moore (1995) *The Governance of Exchanges: Members' Co-operatives versus Outside Ownership*, Discussion Paper No. 229, LSE Financial Markets Group, December.
Kümpel, S. (1995) *Bank- und Kapitalmarktrecht*, O. Schmidt, Koln.
Lehn, K. (1995) 'The Market for Marketplaces: Reflections on Market 2000', in R. A. Schwartz (ed.), *Global Equity Markets. Technological, Competitive, and Regulatory Challenges*, Irwin, Chicago, 206–217.
London Stock Exchange (1996) Governance of the London Stock Exchange, August.
Macey, J. and H. Kanda (1990) 'The Stock Exchange as a Firm: the Emergence of Close Substitutes for the New York and Tokyo Stock Exchanges', *Cornell Law Review* 75, 1007–1052.
Merkin-de Saint Mars (1996) 'Projet de Loi de Modernisation des Activités Financières', Revue de Droit Bancaire et de la Bourse 53, 4.
Miller, M. H. (1991) *Financial Innovations and Market Volatility*, Blackwell, Cambridge, Mass.–Oxford, UK.
Mulherin, J. H., J. M. Netter and J. A. Overdahl (1991) 'Prices are Property: the Organization of Financial Exchanges from a Transaction Cost Perspective', *Journal of Law and Economics* 34, 591 et seq.
Pagano, M. and B. Steil (1996) 'Equity Trading I: The Evolution of European Trading Systems', in B. Steil (ed.), *The European Equity Markets. The State of the Union and an Agenda for the Millennium*, The Royal Institute of International Affairs, London, 1–58.
Pirrong, S. C. (1995) 'The Self-Regulation of Commodity Exchanges: the Case of Market Manipulation', *Journal of Law and Economics* 38, April, 141–206.

Roberts, K. (1977) 'Voting over Income Tax Schedules', *Journal of Public Economics* 8, 329–340.

Rudman Report (1995) Report by the NASD Select Committee on Structure and Governance chaired by Senator W. B. Rudman, dated September 15.

Rudolph, B. (1992) 'Effekten- und Wertpapierbörsen, Finanztermin- und Devisenbörsen seit 1945', in G. Jachmich (ed.), *Deutsche Börsengeschichte*, Frankfurt a. M., 291–440.

Schwark, E. (1994) *Börsengesetz. Kommentar*, 2nd ed., C. H. Beck'sche Verlagsbuchhandlung, Munchen.

Schwartz, R. A. (1995) 'Introduction', in ID. (ed.), *Global Equity Markets. Technological, Competitive, and Regulatory Challenges*, Irwin, Chicago, 1–16.

Securities and Exchange Commission (1996) Report Pursuant to Section 21(a) of the Securities Exchange Act of 1934 Regarding the NASD and the Nasdaq Market, August 8.

Securities and Investments Board (1994) Regulation of the United Kingdom Equity Markets. Discussion Paper, February.

Securities and Investments Board (1996) A Review of the London Metal Exchange. Summary and Conclusions, December.

Shavell, S. (1993) 'The Optimal Structure of Law Enforcement', *Journal of Law and Economics* 36, April, 255–287.

Siebel, U. R. (1995) 'The German Capital Market and the Law', in Siebel-Lowenstein-Finney (ed.), *German Capital Market Law*, New York–Munich, 1–35.

Steil, B. (ed.) (1996) *The European Equity Markets. The State of the Union and an Agenda for the Millennium*, London, 1

Wymeersch, E. (1997) 'The Implementation of the ISD and CAD in National Legal Systems', in G. Ferrarini (ed.), *European Securities Markets. The Investment Services Directive and Beyond*, London (forthcoming).

Should We Trust Banks?

ABSTRACT

When financial markets are not fully developed large shareholders are an important feature of an efficient corporate governance system. Thanks to their (relative) financial strength, banks are good candidates to perform this leading role in the governance of firms. However, in the type of monitoring provided and in the strategies that they may choose, banks are affected by significant conflicts of interests: expecially when they exert power through proxy votes and they are important lenders of the firm.

Francesco Giavazzi is professor of economics at Bocconi University in Milan, a co-director of CEPR's International Macroeconomics Programme, and a Research Associate of the National Bureau of Economic Research. From 1992 to 1994 he served as director general of the Italian Treasury, where he was responsible for the management of the public debt and for privatizations. Since 1992 he has been member of the board and executive committee of I.N.A. spa, Italy's largest life insurance company. He is an editor of the *European Economic Review*, the official journal of the European economic association, and has written extensively of European monetary issues. His joint book with professor Alberto Giovannini *Limiting Exchange Rate Flexibility: the European Monetary System*, was published by MIT Press in 1990.

Marco Battaglini is a Ph.D. candidate at Northwestern University. In 1997 he received the 'Arturo Osio, Imbriani Longo, Guido Carli' fellowship from *Banca Nazionale del Lavoro*.

VIII. Should We Trust Banks When They Sit On the Board of Directors?

FRANCESCO GIAVAZZI AND MARCO BATTAGLINI

A. 'I Wear The Morgan Collar, But I Am Proud Of It'[1]

In the twenties, when the president of New York, New Haven and Hartford Railroad Charles Mellen said he was proud of his 'Morgan Collar', his company was only one of the many controlled by investment banks such as the House of Morgan. As J. Bredford De Long (1991) reports, in 1910–1920 these institutions were influential in corporations that capitalized nearly one and a half years' national product: the companies where the partners of J. P. Morgan and Company sat on the board of directors alone amounted to 30 per cent of the listed equity value. Banks such as the National City Bank, Kidder, Peabody and Company, Kuhn, Loeb and Company, First National Bank and J. P. Morgan and Company were quite different from today's US commercial banks. Until the Glass Steagal Act, these large investors played a very active role in industrial organization and development: monitoring the firms in which they sat, but also fostering and financing mergers or acquisitions.[2] In this sense, their activity was similar to that of the German *Grossbanken*[3] which were, in the early years of the century, the channel through which German industrialization was financed.

The German and American historic experiences seem to be direct evidence in favour of financial systems where large financial investors like banks have a relevant role in firms' governance: both these countries in that period not only had double digit growth rates but also build up the basis of their industrial strength. However whether the beginning of the century in the USA was a golden era and the German financial system is an advisable option are still open questions.

When financial markets are not fully developed, large shareholders are an important feature of an efficient corporate governance system. Thanks to their (relative) financial strength, banks are good candidates to perform this leading role in the governance of firms. This is what happened in the examples cited above and what still happens today in Germany: where, for example, Deutsche Bank A.G. owns 28.5 per cent of the Daimler Benz A.G.[4] However, in the type of monitoring provided and in the strategies that they may choose, banks are affected by significant conflicts of interests: especially when they exert power through proxy votes and they are important lenders of the firm.

The question of the role of banks in corporate governance is particularly topical, because many countries have still to choose the corporate governance system. This is obviously true for the former socialist countries, where the collapse of the central states has left a real vacuum in the control of economic activity and asset stripping has become the norm. In Russia, as Aoki[5] notes:

> "... the director of a State owned enterprise, who had already built a virtually autonomous empire in the communist regime, became almost invincible after the dismantling of the party and its planning apparatus ..."

Clearly, if these countries have to attract investments from foreign countries the vacuum should be filled by some sort of corporate control and banks may be a solution.

But it is also true for western countries – such as Italy – where (hopefully) privatizations will question the corporate governance *status quo*.

In this paper we examine the pros and cons of the presence of a bank on the board of directors of a firm. We will first study the activity of large shareholders in the governance of firms and then discuss whether banks can play this role. Since reality is much less clear-cut than theory, in order to draw some lessons for policy-makers, we 'test' the theoretical results trying to analyze and to interpret the cases of Japan and Italy.

B. OWNERSHIP STRUCTURES, LARGE SHAREHOLDERS AND THE EFFICIENT MANAGEMENT OF THE FIRM: WHAT DOES THEORY SAY?

Out of the 'Black Box': The Benefits from the Presence of a Large Shareholder

Since the work by Berle and Means (1932) and Coase (1937), the traditional view of the firm as a profit maximizing entity has been questioned, and the emphasis has shifted to the contrasting interests of the different stakeholders. Economists have recognized that the hypothesis of profit maximization is somewhat arbitrary, and not necessarily supported by the empirical evidence: a more solid theory of the firm, founded on the study of the interaction among stakeholders, was thus needed. As Jensen and Mackling put it:

> "The firm is not an individual. It is a legal fiction which serves as a focus for a complex process in which the conflicting objectives of individuals (some of whom may 'represent' other organizations) are brought into equilibrium within a framework of contractual relations. In this sense the behavior of

the firm is like the behavior of the market; i.e., the outcome of a complex equilibrium process."[6]

With respect to this view, the distribution of ownership rights seemed a crucial element in order to understand what lies inside the 'black box'. In the thirties Berle and Means argued that due to the dispersion of ownership rights that characterizes the modern corporation, shareholders' control over managers is relaxed, and managers are free to pursue their own interests, which often are in contrast with those of the shareholders. Dispersed ownership rights have thus been associated with managerial discretion and with divergence from profit maximization. The work of Berle and Means started a long debate over the desirability of concentrated ownership structures as a solution to many corporate governance problems.

An assessment of the pros and cons of concentrated ownership structures – i.e. of the presence of a large shareholder – needs, however, an analysis of a wide range of variables that influence the performance of corporations. To understand the role played by a large shareholder (LSH) it is necessary to distinguish two cases: (a) when the LSH directly manages the firm (*inside shareholder*); (b) when, on the contrary, the LSH is an *outsider*: he does not manage the firm directly, and does not enjoy private benefits of control (see Figure 1). In the first case there is an obvious advantage from the presence of an insider-manager with a large stake in the firm: the alignment of interests between insiders and outsiders that derives from it. When an insider owns 100 per cent of the firm he fully enjoys all the benefits that derive from his efforts: he would enjoy 100 per cent of any increase in profits and in firm value. On the contrary, if the insider-manager owns, say, 30 per cent of the firm he would enjoy only 30 per cent of the increase in profits that would follow from higher personal effort in the management of the firm: he would, however, bear the full costs of this increased level of effort. Therefore, the lower is the fraction of the firm owned by insiders-managers, the lower are the marginal benefits that the insider enjoys from an improved management. When the stake of insiders-managers is negligible we are back to the case described by Berle and Means: the interests of insiders may differ considerably from those of shareholders.

In the second case, the role of a large shareholder who is not an insider is much less intuitive since outsiders do not manage the firm directly: however, this case is important because typically, and not only in the US,[7] managers own small fractions of a firm's capital. The relevance of the presence of an outside LSH is indirect: it may foster (or hinder as we shall see in the next paragraph) the disciplinary devices that limit managerial discretion, such as take-overs and internal monitoring by outside shareholders. In general, any disciplinary device suffers from a free-rider problem. The efficient management

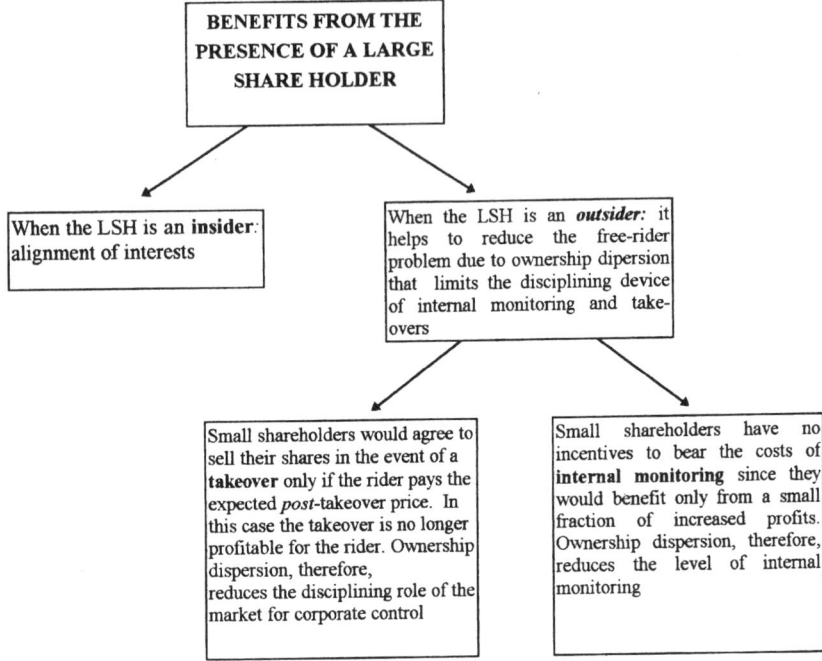

Fig. 1. Benefits from the presence of a large shareholder.

of firms is a public good: a small shareholder who wanted to increase his monitoring effort would bear the full cost of this activity, but would gain only a fraction of the benefit. Improvements in firm management are reflected in higher profits; however, a small shareholder would receive only the small fraction that is proportional to his share of ownership rights – and co-ordination of small shareholders in order to redistribute the costs of a managerial improvement would be prohibitively expensive since a very large number of shareholders would have to be involved.

It is useful to make a distinction between the types of free-rider problem that may arise as the results differ from one case to the other and, in particular, a different role for the LSH emerges in the two cases. A first type of free-rider problem arises when takeovers are the relevant disciplinary device. As argued by Grossman and Hart (1980), any profit a raider can make from the increase in share price after a takeover, it is a profit that other outside shareholders could have made had they not tendered their shares to the raider. If an outsider holds very few shares and, therefore, thinks that, even if he does not tender, the take-over will be successful, his rational choice would be to wait and sell after the expected improvement, or to sell at a price equal to the expected post-takeover value. But in this case the raider would not have enough incentives to launch the takeover. Yet, Shleifer and Vishny (1986) point out that a large shareholder would still benefit from launching a takeover. Suppose he owns 49 per cent of the firm and needs 51 per cent to seize control: in this case he would need to buy only 2 per cent of the firm and, even if he paid the full post-takeover value, he would enjoy the increase in value over the 49 per cent. However, a shareholder who owned only 2 per cent would need to buy 49 per cent of the firm and would therefore profit only over his initial tiny stake.

A different type of free-rider problem arises when 'Barbarians are not at the gate' and the only disciplinary device is direct monitoring of outside shareholders over managers. In many legal systems even small shareholders can sue managers who breach their fiduciary duty: it could thus be argued that ownership concentration is no longer relevant. However, a free-rider problem is present here too: since monitoring is a public good, small shareholders would try to enjoy other shareholders' monitoring, thus producing a sub-optimal level of control. Obviously, the presence of a LSH overcomes this inefficiency, since a LSH internalizes enough benefits to bear the costs of monitoring.

This distinction is not only academic: on the contrary, it is very useful to interpret different corporate governance structures. In particular the 'function' that a large shareholder performs is in these two situations – monitoring through the threat of takeovers, as opposed to direct monitoring – is very different, and suggests that the characteristics of a large shareholder that could improve corporate governance depend on the features of the financial system, and will therefore differ from country to country.

In the presence of an active market for corporate control, the large shareholder does not need to belong to a board of directors that performs a day-to-day monitoring activity: discipline is exercised through the threat of a takeover. In particular, as Shleifer and Vishny (1986) demonstrate, there are situations in which the LSH should undertake not to talk to the incumbent management. The reasoning runs as follows: large improvements in firm value require a change of the incumbent management through a takeover; only smaller improvements could be realized at a lower cost with informal negotiations ('jawboning'). Hence, when the large shareholder decides to launch a takeover, the other shareholders interpret this as a signal that there will be a large improvement in the value of the firm: thus they tender only for large premia. For these reasons, the LSH may be worse off with the option to jawbone: if he undertakes not to negotiate with the incumbent management, in the case of a takeover he would face smaller expected premia and, thus, higher expected profits.

On the contrary, when the market for corporate control is dormant, and only internal monitoring can affect managers' behaviour, the role of a LSH is considerably different: he is directly involved in day-to-day monitoring and is an active member of the board of directors. Casual evidence seems to confirm this distinction. In Germany, where take-overs are not frequent, large shareholders take an active part in the *Aufsichtsrat*, the firm's supervisory board, and control managers directly: this function is normally performed by non-financial institutions and by banks – since mutual funds in Germany are not much developed. In the Anglo-Saxon financial systems, on the other hand, where the typical LSH is a mutual fund or a pension fund, these investors play a much more passive role, but their role is often crucial in the event of a takeover.[8]

It is often argued, in this respect, that continental European countries should actively develop institutional investors other than banks – such as mutual and pension funds – since their presence would improve corporate governance. However, since these types of large shareholders are not generally involved in day-to-day monitoring, and do not play an active role on the board of directors – often their statutes prevent them from sitting on the board of directors – they are probably not very useful (at least as far as corporate governance is concerned) in countries where an efficient market for corporate control does not exist and takeovers are rare.

Large shareholders are often associated with financial systems where takeovers are not frequent, as a substitute for market discipline (for example in Germany and Japan), while dispersed ownership is associated with an Anglo-Saxon type financial system. However, a scope for concentrated ownership is theoretically justified also in market-based financial systems. As reported by Shleifer and Vishny (1986), more than half of the Fortune 500 firms have at least one large shareholder holding a block of shares that exceeds 5 per cent of the firm's capital. The fact that ownership concentration is lower than in Germany is not only a consequence of economic incentives: it is also the result of a legal system that strongly discourages shareholders from being actively involved in control (see, for example, Prowse 1995) because of antitrust and fiscal regulations, and of stricter disclosure requirements.

The Flip-Side of the Coin: The Costs of the Presence of a Large Shareholder

In the previous paragraph we stressed the benefits that can derive from the presence of a LSH: we now turn to the costs and inefficiencies that a concentrated ownership structure could generate. The empirical evidence suggest that there is a trade-off in the choice of the best ownership structure. In particular, it seems that the relationship between ownership concentration and the value of the firm is not monotone. Morck, Shleifer and Vishny (1988), for example, estimate the relation between Tobin's q and the fraction of shares owned by insiders in a sample of 371 large US firms: ownership concentration seems to improve the ratio of firm market value to the replacement costs of its assets (Tobin's q) significantly only if the share owned by insiders is below 5 per cent; between 5 and 25 per cent the relationship is, on the contrary, negative; only a weakly positive relationship is found for concentration levels higher than 25 per cent. Similar results are found by other studies.[9] The study by Slovin and Sushka (1993) is noteworthy since it employs a different methodology, trying to solve the potential causality problem that affects other studies.[10] They analyze the impact on the firm's value of an exogenous event that affects the ownership structure of the firm: the death of a large inside blockholder. Here too the relation between the death of the insider (which causes ownership dispersion) and firm value does not seems to be monotone, and does not support the 'alignment of interest hypothesis', which would suggest the optimality of the presence of a large shareholder: they find that the response of the share price to the death of an inside blockholder is significantly positive when the share controlled by the deceased exceeds 10 per cent.

Theoretically, there could many reasons for the presence of a trade off in the choice of the optimal ownership concentration. First of all, and most obviously, the concentration of ownership rights limits the opportunities to diversify risk and, therefore, reduces the expected utility of risk-averse agents. However, what is most relevant for our discussion are the drawbacks that are directly related to the corporate governance of the firm: the undesired effects on managers' incentives. Here it is useful to return to the distinction between an *insider* and an *outsider* LSH.

In the first case we could have the so-called 'entrenchment effect': when insiders own a large fraction of equity, the probability that a hostile take-over succeeds is reduced, and the incumbent management is sheltered from outside discipline.[11] In this case a LSH would be sheltered from the threat of a takeover and could thus try to exploit the private benefits of control. These could be so large that the LSH could be better off maximizing them rather than the value of the firm, even if he owns a large fraction of it. Private benefits can be of many types. A famous historical example is provided by the Italian Banca di Sconto in the first half of the century: the owners (the Perrone family) used the bank's funds to finance their own non-financial activities (Ansaldo, a manufacturing firm) leading the bank into bankruptcy. The trade-off here is between the 'alignment of interests hypothesis', which we discussed above, and the 'entrenchment effect'.

When the LSH is an *outsider*, the case is different, but there are drawbacks here too. Burkart, Gromb and Panunzi (1995) point out that the presence of a LSH could hinder managers' discretion and therefore depress their initiative. A large shareholder has the power to turn down the management's plans, thus limiting their discretion, authority and initiative: the outcome can be that managers have weaker incentives to 'work hard'. If managers' initiative is valuable, it may be optimal to limit monitoring, leaving them enough authority. A dispersed ownership structure may work as a commitment device to delegate authority from shareholders to self-interested managers.

Hölmstrom and Tirole (1993) point to yet another trade-off. The presence of a LSH (who typically is a long term-investor) reduces the liquidity of the market (see also Bhushan, 1989): this reduction in liquidity limits the ability of speculators to disguise themselves as prices become more sensitive. Since speculators can use their information less effectively, they will have less incentives to monitor and gather information: the market thus becomes less informative, resulting in a less efficient allocation of resources.

It follows that information plays very different roles in markets characterized by the presence of a LSH, compared with situations where ownership is dispersed. In the Shleifer–Vishny case we have 'strategic information': the large shareholder is interested in information about potential value under a new management and a new strategy. In the other case (the one analyzed by Hölmstrom and Tirole) we have the production of 'speculative information': there is no expected change in management and strategy, and speculators try to forecast the consequences of past managerial actions.

The bottom line of this brief review of the literature is that there is a direct relation between the market for corporate control (its liquidity and efficiency), the allocation of voting rights, and the type of incentives and information that it is produced by the system in equilibrium.

Conclusions and Further Questions

From our discussion so far it appears that the choice of an optimal concentration of ownership is not a trivial question. Table 1, which summarizes the main theoretical results, shows that at least two dimensions are relevant to assess the *pros* and *cons* of the presence of a large shareholder: (1) the degree of collusion between the LSH and the management; and (2) the context in which the LSH operates, whether or not the market for corporate control is efficient. It is quite meaningless to discuss the benefits of a LSH without simultaneous reference to these two features: a LSH-insider in an environment that does not allow for takeovers – and therefore for the correction of adverse-selection problems – could be very harmful in the absence of adequate large outside shareholders who act as watchdogs. On the contrary, when LSHs do not collude with management, they may effectively limit managers' moral hazards, both because they foster market discipline and, when markets are particularly under-developed, they may monitor the management directly.

TABLE 1

What theory suggests

Characteristics of the financial market	The large shareholder is an	
	insider	outsider
Takeovers are the norm	*LSH profile:* active investor who joins the board of directors and manages the firm directly. *Benefits:* the interests of shareholders and of managers are aligned. *Costs:* (1) 'entrenchment effect' (2) reduction in the informational role of prices.	*LSH profile:* passive investor who votes with his feet and does not share managerial responsibilities. *Benefits:* higher discipline from the market for corporate governance. *Costs:* it reduces the informational role of prices.
Takeovers are rare	*LSH profile:* active investor who joins the board of directors and manages the firm directly. *Benefits:* the interests of shareholders and of managers are aligned. *Costs:* the LSH could have no counterbalance, and could thus maximize private benefits, if these are high enough.	*LSH profile:* active investor who joins the board of directors and strictly controls management. *Benefits:* more incentives to monitor since it internalizes the benefits. *Costs:* LSH tends to monitor too much, reducing managers' incentives.

In conclusion, two points should be remembered, and will be further analyzed in the pages that follow:
1. it is widely held that the presence of LSH is particularly beneficial in financial systems that are not fully developed. It is in fact argued that in countries with a developed market for corporate control takeovers may be sufficient to limit managerial discretion. However, a role for LSHs is present also in countries with efficient financial markets: where ownership dispersion creates a free-rider problem, a LSH can facilitate a takeover, thus strengthening market discipline;
2. it is important to study the incentives that the LSH has to monitor. The size of his stake is an important variable, but other elements should be considered. For example, the activity of the LSH: as we shall further explain below (whether it is a bank, a mutual fund, or a private non-financial investor) and therefore the other business relations that it may entertain with the firm.

C. Does It Make a Difference Who Is The Large Shareholder? The Role of Banks

In the previous paragraphs we argued that one of the main benefits from the presence of a LSH is the fact that it provides a monitoring activity over incumbent managers: because of a free-rider problem, only a LSH can enjoy sufficient benefits from monitoring to find it profitable to bear the cost.

In making this point, we assumed that the goal of an outside LSH was simply the maximization of the value of its share of ownership rights. Although we already mentioned private benefits, we have not yet studied the possibility that a LSH, in its monitoring activity, may be subject to incentives and conflicts. LSHs, typically, are institutional investors – such as banks, pension funds or insurance companies – which often have important business relations with the firms in which they own large blocks of shares. Banks, for example, will want to sell loans; insurance companies and mutual funds manage pension plans, and so on. The monitoring activity performed by these types of shareholders will thus be influenced by their overall relations with the firm. Institutional ownership of common stock has substantially increased since the seventies. In the United States it increased from approximately 17 per cent in 1970, to more than 30 per cent in the mid-eighties. This calls for an analysis of how institutional voting power is exercised, and to what extent it depends on the other business relations that institutional investors entertain with the firm.

The available evidence points to well established patterns of behavior. Brickley, Lease and Smith (1988), in particular – who study the voting behavior of different classes of institutional investors – confirm this point. They divide investors in three groups: *pressure-sensitive institutions*, that is institutions with relevant business relations with the firm in which they have shareholdings, such as insurance companies, banks, and non-bank trusts owing at least one percent of the firm's stock; *pressure-resistant institutions*, such as public pension funds, endowments, and foundations; and institutions that they call *pressure indeterminate*, in particular mutual funds. They find that the stance toward the incumbent management is quite different for these classes of investors: *pressure resistant institutions* are more likely to oppose management, and that the hypothesis that *pressure sensitive institutions* and *pressure resistant institutions* have the same voting behavior can be statistically rejected. In this paragraph we shall describe the potential conflicts of interest that may interfere with the monitoring activity that a bank-LSH is supposed to perform.

Banks are, perhaps, the most relevant case to study: both because of the degree of the potential conflict of interest, and because of the important role that they play, as institutional investors, in continental Europe and in Japan. There may be significant conflicts of interests between of a bank as lender and as shareholder of a firm: banks may use their shareholdings to enforce their rights 'as lenders' rather than 'as shareholders'. In Germany and Japan, banks are, at the same time, important share-holders and debt-holders. As noted by Sheard (1989), in 1980, the 'main bank' of a Japanese listed company – that is the bank which provides and guarantees most of the firm's debt finance – had the largest, or second-largest, shareholding in 39 per cent of the cases; in 72 per cent of cases it was among the first five shareholders (see Table 3).

Prowse (1995), among the 133 Japanese firms that he analyses,[12] finds that in 57 cases the largest debt-holder is also the largest shareholder, and in 124 cases the largest shareholder and debt-holder are members of the same *keiretsu*.

The situation in Germany is similar. Even if the importance of bank finance – both through debt and equity – is less relevant what is generally believed,[13] German banks play a crucial role in the financing of industry: 20 per cent of gross finance for investment on average, between 1970 and 1985.

The fact that a bank is at the same time an equity holder and (the main) lender is important because a shareholder and a debt-holder have different and possibly contrasting incentives to monitor the firm. As debt-holder the bank is not interested in boosting firm profits: what matters for a lender is that profits are large enough to service the debt. The pay-off of a lender is concave in the pay-off of the firm: it could be very low if the firm goes bankrupt, but it is limited if profits are high. Therefore, the lender will tend to limit investments in projects with risky payoffs – because he would bear the risks but not the benefits. Monitoring by a lender focuses on the minimization of the probability of bankruptcy: there are no incentives for a lender to monitor a firm in good states of the world, since the benefits from this activity only accrue to shareholders. Clearly, this type of 'debt-driven' monitoring leads to socially inefficient outcomes; a lender will try to block projects with a relatively high probability to fail, but also with very high expected pay-offs: the bank's risk aversion will cause the loss of good investment opportunities, or produce a downward bias in R&D expenses.

When the bank also owns equity in the firm, this problem is alleviated, because the pay-off function becomes a weighted average of that of a debt-holder and that of an equity-holder. However, the bias toward a sub-optimal risk configuration remains. Yet, in many cases, banks control voting rights without directly owning the underlying equity: thus, in taking decisions, only the incentives that derive from their provision of debt finance are relevant. This is certainly the case of Germany, where the proxy market is dominated by banks. As can be seen from Table 4, the voting power of German banks derives more from proxy votes than from direct shareholdings. For instance, in the ten largest AGs, in 1974, banks' combined votes amounted to 67.03 per cent of the total, but only 3.56 per cent was related to direct equity-holdings.

The empirical literature has begun to study the monitoring activities of banks, investigating to what extent they depend on the incentives that derive from debt

TABLE 2
Who is 'the best' LSH?

		Do they have incentives to own big blocks of shares?	Is there conflict of interests?	Who controls the controller?
Mutual funds	Closed-end	Yes: closed-end funds are used to finance venture capital investments; but they are not common in the US.	No, since they generally have no other business relations with the firms in which they invest their portfolio.	Discipline over closed-end mutual fund managers is not as high as in the case of open-end funds. However, a strict regulation limits managerial discretion.
	Open-end	No: they must be liquid since they must be ready to turn shares into cash to face redemptions. In the US, Section 16.b of the SEA strongly discourages short-term swing trading.	No, since they generally have no other business relations with the firms in which they invest their portfolio.	There is a high level of control. Liquid open-end funds that redeem overnight provide excellent discipline over fund managers.
Banks		In countries where banks are allowed to acquire blocks of shares, they tend to do it. See, for example, France after the 1984 bank reform act.	Banks as lenders tend to be more concerned with the bottom part of the tail of the distribution of returns.	It depends on the ownership of the bank. In Germany, banks are manager-controlled. Even if banks are subject to strict prudential regulation, this does not mean that banks are necessarily good shareholders. The regulator is concerned with bank solvency, and not with the role of the bank 'as shareholder', making the bank even more risk averse.

Continued

TABLE 2 (Continued)

		Do they have incentives to own big blocks of shares?	Is there conflict of interests?	Who controls the controller?
Pension funds	Fixed payments	They tend to invest in more liquid securities, and avoid large blocks.	At least in the US there is a potentially large conflict of interest since, in the private sector, pension funds are typically controlled by the management of the firm. Public pension funds act in a much more independent way.	Except in the case of public pension funds, managers control the pension fund of their own firm.
	Fixed contribution	They could be assimilated to mutual funds that are not subject to overnight redemptions; thus, they could own large equity blocks.	At least in the US there is a potentially large conflict of interest since, in the private sector, pension funds are typically controlled by the management of the firm. Public pension funds act in a much more independent way.	Except in the case of public pension funds, managers control the pension fund of their own firm. This can be a problem if the amount invested in their own firm is small, because casual evidence shows that there may be collusion between managers of different firms.
Insurance companies		Yes: since they can forecast their capital outflows, they do not suffer the overnight redemption problem of open-end mutual funds.	Since they are large holders of corporate bonds, like banks they may be more interested in the service of their debt rather than in firm profitability.	It depends on who owns the insurance company.

TABLE 3

Listed Japanese firms according to rank of main bank as shareholder in 1980, and source of borrowing in 1971

Rank	Breakdown of listed firms			
	Rank of main bank as shareholder, 1980		Rank of main bank as debt holder, 1971	
	No. of firms	Relative frequency (%)	No. of firms	Relative frequency (%)
1	124	16.4	469	67.3
2	172	22.7	125	17.2
3	113	14.9	47	6.5
4	84	11.1	17	2.3
5	52	6.9	14	1.9
6	34	4.5	7	1.0
7	20	2.6	10	1.4
8	13	1.7	7	1.0
9	15	2.0	2	0.3
10 or more	131	17.3	9	1.2
Total	758	100	727	100

Source: Sheard (1989).

and equity holdings. Kaplan, in a series of related papers,[15] has studied the relation between management compensation and management turnover, and firm performance in German, Japanese and US companies. Since the relation between the rewards of managers and the performance of the firm reflects the objectives of the board of directors – and therefore those of the shareholders – these findings provide evidence on the behavior and on the type of incentives that a bank-based corporate system and a market-based system exert on managers. Kaplan finds that in Japan and in Germany, like in the US, managers' turnover and compensation are positively correlated with the current performance of the firm, as measured by stock returns and earnings. However, in Japan and in Germany both compensations and turnover are more sensitive to negative earnings. In both countries governance mechanisms seem to become active when the firm faces difficulties in servicing the debt: this triggers the appointment of new executive directors, and a turn-over of management.

Kaplan and Minton (1993) further study the characteristics of the appointments of outside directors in Japan, trying to distinguish between bank appointments and appointments by non-financial firms. Although both types of outside appointments are disciplinary (in the sense that they are followed by a turnover of incumbent managers), they seem to depend upon different circumstances. Bank appointments are strongly correlated with the ratio of total debt to assets and, in particular, to the relative amount of borrowing from the largest

TABLE 4

Banks' voting rights in 56 among the top 100 German AGs in 1974

Rank class of AGs by nominal capital	Number of AGs with combined bank vote >5%	Nominal capital of AGs in column (2) as per cent of nominal capital of rank class	Average percentage of bank vote in AGs in column (2) due to banks' direct holdings of equity	Average percentage of bank vote in AGs in column (2) due to proxy votes	Average combined bank vote in AGs in column (2)
1–10	8	88.2	3.56	63.47	67.03
11–25	6	42.5	6.10	48.19	54.29
26–50	14	51.3	14.65	25.03	39.68
51–100	28	54.4	13.52	29.01	42.53

Source: Edwards and Fischer (1991). Data taken from Monopolkommission, II Hauptgutachten 1976/1977.

lender: a two standard deviation difference (14 per cent) in this variable is accompanied by a 5 per cent increase in the likelihood of a board appointment. But what is particularly noteworthy is the fact that the likelihood of a bank-designated director being appointed to the board does not depend on the bank's shareholdings – thus suggesting that a bank appointment to the board is driven by its lending activity and not by its shareholdings. 'These patterns provide additional support for the view that bank-designated directors are appointed in firms and situations where there is a bank loan to protect'.[16]

Additional evidence on bank behaviour is provided by Weinstein and Yafeh (1994), who study the effects of a bank-centered financial system (Japan, where, as we said, banks are at the same time large equity-holders and debt-holders) on firm performance. Firms with tight financial links with a bank seem to suffer less from credit rationing problems, especially when capital markets are underdeveloped. But the firm pays a cost for this provision of liquidity: the authors find that the 'main bank' extracts relevant rents from its position: the profitability of firms with strong bank relations is significantly lower than that of 'independent firms'; they also tend to grow slower.

An interpretation of these findings could be that the main bank puts its interest as a debt-holder before its interest as an equity-holder. This seems to be confirmed by the fact that firms with close bank ties paid higher interest rates than 'independent' firms: a premium of more than 50 basis points in 1977, and still as large as nearly 30 basis points in 1986. This could appear strange in view of the fact that the main bank was in most cases also the largest shareholder (see Table 3) and therefore had an interest in the firm's profitability.

This observation raises a further question: whether banks buy shares to protect their rights as debt-holders, or to enjoy profits, as any other shareholder. Prowse (1995), who addresses this problem, finds that banks' shareholdings are significantly correlated with their lending to the firm; but, more importantly, the correlation becomes even more significant for those firms that operate in more risky environments, where 'asset substitution'[17] by shareholders is more likely to occur (for instance in firms that have relatively high R&D expenses). To protect their position as lenders from asset substitution policies, banks tend to increase their power in the firm *vis-à-vis* incumbent managers. This is consistent with the view that banks place their interests as lenders before any other business connection. Shareholdings are considered as an instrument to protect their main concern: their credits.

D. The Importance of Informal Relations: The Case of Japan and Italy

The ability of a LSH to control a firm does not depend only on the number of shares it owns directly, but also on the informal relations that are set up

TABLE 5

Ownership of common stock in major industrial countries (percentages)

Type of owner	United States	United Kingdom	Japan	Germany	Italy	
					All listed companies	Listed companies except banks
Financial institutions	30.4	60.8	47.0	22	13.9	6.0
Banks	0	0.9	25.2	10	10.9	2.8
Insurance companies	4.6	18.4	17.3	12	0.8	0.8
Pension funds	20.1	30.4	0.9	–	–	–
Other	5.7	11.1	3.6	–	2.2	2.4
Non-financial institutions	69.7	26.9	48.8	78	81.8	88.7
Corporations	14.1	3.6	25.1	42	21.6	27.3
State	0	2.0	0.6	5	28.0	26.8
Individuals	50.2	21.3	23.1	17	32.2	34.6
Foreign owners	5.4	12.3	4.2	14	4.3	5.3

Sources: for the USA, US Federal Reserve Flow of Funds, 1990; for Germany, Deutsche Bundesbank, Monthly Report, 1990; for Japan and the UK (years 1990–1991), Kester (1992); for Italy, Barca et al. (1994).

among shareholders both through voting agreements and through indirect ownership. In many instances these relations have grown endogenously to address particular corporate governance problems; their presence alters the relative power of shareholders, and thus the benefits and costs of the presence of a LSH. To the extent that it is difficult to have a single LSH that owns the firm and has the right incentives to monitor management, these informal relations are set up to surrogate for a *stable* and *concentrated* ownership structure that could otherwise not be established. These considerations on informal relations are not only important to understand how a bank or another LSH exerts its power in a firm, but also they have deep implications for policy options. We shall discuss two cases where these informal relations are particularly important: Japan and Italy.

We saw above that banks are the largest equityholders in Japan, owning more than 25 per cent of all outstanding shares (see Table 5). The role of banks as shareholders, however, should be understood in the broader perspective of the inter-corporate shareholdings that characterize the ownership structure of Japanese firms. Inter-corporate shareholdings give rise to a particular type of corporate grouping that shapes the relations among most Japanese firms: the

TABLE 6

Japan: six major corporate groups (*keiretsu*) in 1980

	Mitsui	Mitsubishi	Sumitomo	Sanwa	Fuyo	Ikkan	Total
Number of firms in the group	24	28	21	40	29	45	182
Intra-group shareholdings (%)	17.4	29.3	26.8	16.8	16.2	14.7	
Intra-group bank finance (%)	19.1		27.8	27	18.8	13.2	
Intra-group directorate holdings (%)	3.8	24.9	13.4	5.8	4.2	8.2	
Weight of group in the entire non-financial sector							
– in terms of assets (%)	2.47	13.1	1.52	3.01	2.79	4.03	15.34
– in terms of profits (%)	2.54	2.89	1.28	2.22	1.52	3.05	12.84
– in terms of employees (%)	0.75	1.84	0.43	1.24	1.03	1.57	4.91

Source: Aoki (1984a).

so-called *keiretsu* (or *kigyo shudan*). Table 6 shows these relations in six of the major Japanese corporate groups in 1980. There are two distinct features of this type of organization: first, each group includes a major commercial bank (*city bank*) which acts as the major lender for the group's firms, or implicitly guarantees loans for the group's firms from other lenders; second, there are reciprocal shareholdings between firms of the same group, in particular with respect to the *city bank* which is at the same time a shareholder of the group's firms (in most cases the largest, see Table 6), a provider of funds, (in most cases also the largest, see Table 6), and is owned by firms in the group. Therefore, even in cases where a 'main bank' is the largest shareholder of a firm, it would not be correct to define such firms as 'bank-owned': the connection is, in fact, much more intertwined and involves a two-sided relationship. This is confirmed by the fact that the group's policy is not only a matter for the bank: for instance, in the case of *financial keiretsu*, these issues are discussed in the 'Presidents' Clubs', which are composed of the presidents of the major members of the *keiretsu*.

There are many explanations for the existence of *keiretsu* groups. Our interest here is in understanding how such an arrangement could arise endogenously to guarantee *stability* and *ownership concentration*. In the immediate postwar period the US Commander for Allied Powers led a reform of the Japanese corporate structure aimed at dissolving the *zaibatsu* holdings, and at establishing a US-type corporate governance system, where the market for corporate control was to play a major role. A strict regulation of ownership was introduced: the 1947 anti-trust Law prohibited industrial companies from holding stocks, and restricted financial institutions other than banks from holding more than 5 per cent of a given company; the Security Trade Act, also introduced in 1947, prohibited banks from underwriting, holding, or even dealing in corporate securities.[19] After the stock market collapse in 1949, these regulations were loosened, and institutional ownership was allowed in an attempt to stabilize share prices.[20] This, however, was not enough to guarantee stability in the control of firms – as it became clear (see Aoki, 1984a) in 1965, when at the same time there was a stock market plunge and a liberalization of capital inflows, giving rise to the threat of takeovers and thus of a change in established control groups. As a reaction, major corporations started to built up mutual shareholdings in order to insulate themselves from the market for corporate control. These connections produced two results. They fostered co-operation among shareholders, giving them a better opportunity to act as a single LSH (see for instance the Presidents' Clubs); they also secured established control, and thus made insiders able to commit to long term relations.

The second reason why these mutual ownership structures and informal relations among shareholders were established, was to limit the power of banks in the management of firms. As we argued in the previous paragraph, banks, as lenders, are mostly concerned with the bottom tail of the distribution of returns. Since in the *keiretsu* banks have an important, but not exclusive, role in the control of firms, this bias is limited.

In Italy too, special relations among shareholders arose as a 'substitute' for ownership concentration and other corporate governance devices. The case of Italy deserves particular attention also because in recent years the country's privatization program has frequently stumbled on the question of what is the proper ownership structure once control in transferred from the state to private shareholders.

The Italian public enterprise sector has traditionally been larger than in other major OECD countries: the state was not only present in the utility sector; almost all banks, the largest insurance companies and a relevant share of industrial firms were state-owned. Yet, since 1990, the picture has begun to change: between 1992 and 1995, sales of state-owned firms amounted to one half of 1 per cent of 1993 GDP. However, the most ambitious part of the privatization program is still to be implemented: thus Italy will be, in the near future, the European country most involved in privatizations. Corporate governance issues are thus relatively more urgent in Italy than elsewhere – a fact explicitly recognized, for instance, by the Banca d'Italia:

"... the [privatization] program places special emphasis on the need to attain stable configurations for the property structure of privatized companies, so as to ensure efficient mechanisms of corporate governance. Such objective is to be achieved by carefully identifying, on a case by case basis, the most suitable form of property structure for the enterprises to be privatized ..."[21]

As in the case of Japan, the statistical indicators that were presented above, do not provide a truthful picture of the ownership structure of Italian firms, because of the presence of indirect relations among shareholders that influence the way in which corporate control is exercised. Yet, the relations among firms are different from those that occur in the *keiretsu* groups: most Italian listed companies are linked through so-called *pyramidal groups*.

A *pyramidal group* is a situation in which many companies are controlled by the same entrepreneur through a chain of control relations: firm A controls 51 per cent of firm B's outstanding equity, and firm B controls 51 per cent of firm C: therefore firm A controls firm C. This arrangement, that may comprise hundreds of firms, allows an 'artificial' ownership concentration: although the entrepreneur, through his indirect shareholdings, has complete control of all the firms in the group, the amount of equity provided is limited: in the case above, only 26 per cent of C pertains to A. As Barca et al. (1994) and Barca (1995) report, around 35 per cent of Italian small companies (from 50 to 100 employees) and a fraction from 60 to 85 per cent of medium size companies are controlled by a group.[22] It is, however, for very large companies, especially listed ones, that the pyramidal organization is most employed, so that almost all of them are part of a group. The authors were able to map the ownership relations of a vast group of firms: considering the 258 companies listed on the Milan Stock Exchange, and the ownership structure of the firms that own or are owned by them (a total of 6500 firms, of which 4200 Italian), 178 *pyramidal groups* emerged.

Besides direct ownership, it is therefore interesting to see who holds the ultimate control of a firm, and how this power is related to direct or indirect equity holdings in the firm. Barca et al. show that this type of corporate system results in the separation between ownership and control. Table 7 is very clear in this respect: insiders (that is shareholders at the head of the groups) for each unit of capital provided are able to control 2.7 units of the capital of the group; outstanding cases are those of the De Benedetti group where insiders, for each unit of capital, controlled 25 units, and the limited partnership Giovanni Agnelli & C whose control-ownership leverage was 17.[23]

Thanks to pyramidal groups, entrepreneurs, or groups of entrepreneurs, succeed in raising capital in the equity market without losing control of the firm: although this may produce beneficial effects, because it limits free-rider problems, it weakens the incentives of these 'LSHs': they have large voting power, but, paradoxically, they do not enjoy, in proportion, the profits of the firms they control; therefore they run into the same moral hazard problems that a pure non-equity-holder-manager suffers, or even worse. In such *pyramidal groups*, in fact, there are many harmful moral hazard opportunities: for example, in the determination of transfer prices among firms inside the group, or in the setting of other business relations. Thus entrepreneurs – and this is the reason

TABLE 7

Separation between ownership and control through pyramidal groups in Italian companies (weighted percentages)

Characteristics of the company at the head of the group	Control structure			Control-ownership leverage		
	1991	1992	1993	1991	1992	1993
Non-banking private sector	47.6	45.7	43.3	8.4	7.6	7.9
Individuals and partnerships	12.3	12.2	11.2	4.4	4.2	4.0
Limited partnerships and limited liability companies	22.1	20.2	19.4	11.1	9.2	9.7
Other limited companies	1.9	1.9	1.6	2.6	2.1	2.3
Coalitions	12.3	11.4	11.1	–	–	–
State companies other than state-controlled banks	42	41.7	40.5	1.7	1.7	1.9
Banks	6.7	9.1	12.7	1.2	1.3	1.5
of which: state owned	5.4	7.8	11.9	1.1	1.3	1.5
Private	1.3	1.3	0.8	1.4	1.4	1.3
Foreign control	2.7	3.4	3.6	1.9	1.9	2.3
Total	100	100	100	2.7	2.5	2.7

Source: Barca (1994).

why they create 'pyramidal groups' – seek to extend their control over a very wide range of firms: this allows them to enjoy more private benefits. Since control is exercised with a relatively small share of capital of the group, they can extract these private rents at the expense of the profitability of the firm: obviously all of this is at the expense of smaller shareholders, who are excluded from these private benefits and can only enjoy profits.

The Italian experience confirms that it is not sufficient to establish a concentrated ownership structure to solve moral hazard problems: the LSHs, in order to be effective monitors, should have proper incentives. *Pyramidal groups*, while allowing the control of firms to be concentrated, do not provide the ultimate owners with the right incentives: in the example above, firm B could be seen as the LSH of firm C; however, firm B was only an instrument through which firm A could control firm C with relatively limited equity exposure. As a general lesson, we can draw the conclusion that, to understand whether concentrated ownership is beneficial, it is necessary to penetrate the veil between firms and their ultimate owners that is established via indirect equityholdings and other informal arrangements.

The high ownership concentration of Italian firms does not prevent moral hazard problems. Zingales (1994) observes that while in other markets voting shares trade at a premium of 10 to 20 per cent above non-voting shares, in Italy such a premium is as high as 85 percent: this can be interpreted as

TABLE 8

The control of industrial companies in Italy (1993) (percentages)

Models of control	Industrial companies with more than 50 employees (stratified random sample)		Industrial companies with 20 to 500 employees (300 selected companies)	
	According to models employed in each individual company		According to models employed in each individual company	According to models employed in the 'head' of group (if any)
	Unweighted	Weighted	Unweighted	
Absolute control	13.8	8.8	18.5	19.9
Family control	32.1	16.6	53.5	60.1
Coalition control	13.7	9.9	10.5	14
Financial supervision control	0.2	0.2	0.7	0.7
State ownership	6.9	15.9	2.1	2.1
Group control	33.3	49.0	14.7	–
Not identified	–	–	–	3.2
Total	100	100	100	100

Source: Barca (1995).

evidence that who controls a firm has more opportunities to seize the private benefits of control. Nicodano (1993) finds that the ownership structure of Italian companies helps to explain these high voting premia: when a firm belongs to a *pyramidal group* expected premia are higher.

To understand the behaviour of such LSH – that is the heads of the *pyramidal groups* – it is necessary to look inside them and to analyze who controls them, and how such control is exercised. Barca (1995) reports that 41 per cent of the companies at the head of a *pyramidal group* are under 'family control', that is an arrangement in which the 'owners belong to the same family as the entrepreneur',[24] and 19 per cent of the firms are controlled through 'coalition control', that is through binding voting agreements, *patti di sindacato* (see Table 8). Therefore, behind the pattern of direct ownership concentration, there is a complex nexus of relations among shareholders that significantly alters the picture. First of all, the chains of control, which allow some entrepreneurs to control firms with very limited provision of equity finance; second, the fact that in many instances, especially at the top of these chains of indirect shareholdings, control takes place through informal relations among shareholders: mostly, insiders are linked by family bonds.

E. Privatization and Ownership Structure: Lessons and Policy Implications

The Role of the Government when the Ownership Structure is Endogenous. Lessons from the Japanese Post-War Experience

From the examples of Japan and Italy we can draw two lessons. First, when the presence of a LSH or of direct ownership concentration cannot be established, it does not necessarily follow that a market for corporate control will automatically arise, as an alternative corporate governance device. The two cases analyzed above show that ownership concentration may be mimicked through informal relations among shareholders, leading to the concentration of control. Such concentration, however, does not provide proper incentives to the agents that are responsible for exercising control. Usually these informal relations are not visible at first sight: this is, for example, the case of Italy, where statistical indicators show very high ownership concentration levels, but behind the legal 'veil' of *pyramidal groups* lies a substantial separation between ownership and ultimate control. Thus, when the choice of the best ownership structure in a privatization process is at stake, governments should carefully consider the possibility that such informal relations may arise, and their consequences on the corporate governance structure of the privatized company.

The second lesson follows as a consequence of the first: it is very difficult 'to lean against the wind'. The ownership structure that characterizes the firms of a particular country is often an endogenous variable; attempts to establish exogenously a different equilibrium may fail, or produce undesired outcomes. Japan provides an extraordinary example: contrary to the intentions of the US administrators, who tried to set up a US-type, market-based, corporate system, and strongly opposed an active role of institutional investors, the final outcome was the so called 'main bank system'.

Up to 1949, as we have seen, a series of attempts were put in place to establish a US-type corporate system. This was to be realized not only through straightforward limitations on the maximum share of ownership rights that any single investor could hold, but also through an educational campaign aimed at channelling small savers' investments in the stock market, and through financial support to employee ownership. The peak of this process was reached in 1949. Apparently, the reform was successful, since in a few years a widespread ownership structure was established: 13 per cent of the shares of listed companies was owned by securities companies, 70 per cent by individuals; in a single month, September 1949, 27 per cent of total disposed stocks was sold to employees. This result was particularly noteworthy, since in 1945 individuals held only 53 per cent of total outstanding stocks and securities, and corporations 2.8 per cent (see Table 9).

TABLE 9

Ownership structure of postwar Japanese listed companies (percentage of companies' capital)

Category of investor	1945	1949	1951	1953	1955	1960
Government	8.3	2.8	1.8	0.7	0.4	0.2
Financial institutions	11.2	9.9	18.2	22.9	23.6	30.6
Trust banks	–	–	5.2	6.7	4.1	7.5
Securities companies	2.8	12.6	9.2	7.3	7.9	3.7
Other companies	24.6	5.6	13.8	13.5	13.2	17.8
Foreign	–	–	1.8	1.7	1.7	1.3
Individuals	53.1	69.1	57.0	53.8	53.2	46.3

Source: Bank of Japan (1970), as reported in Miyajima (1994).

Behind the surface, however, the reform did not succeeded in establishing an efficient corporate governance system. In 1949, for example, only 250 of the 453 listed companies paid dividends. When a fiscal stabilization program was introduced, in August 1949, and the soft budget constraint of firms was tightened (reduction of subsidies, higher interests rates, curbs on controlled prices) the stock market collapsed. This was the turning point: in order to support stock prices, the rules were relaxed, and more freedom to buy shares allowed to financial institutions: in 1953 the Antitrust Law was changed, raising the limit to which financial institutions were subject in the amount of equity of a single company that they could own, from 5 to 10 per cent. As can be seen from Table 9, this implied an abrupt change in the ownership structure of Japanese firms. In 1949, financial institutions held only 9.9 per cent of listed companies' capital; in 1960 they held more than 30 per cent; on the contrary, individuals' shareholdings fell from 70 to 46.3 per cent. Moreover, small shareholders, frightened by the stock market collapse, did not prove to be long-run investors: only 50 per cent of the employees that had bought shares the year before the market crash held their shares for more than two years. The assumption that, once ownership rights were adequately dispersed and ownership concentration forbidden, a market for corporate control would naturally develop proved wrong.

Italy provides another example of an endogenous ownership structure. In the recent privatization of two of the main Italian banks (Banca Commerciale Italiana and Credito Italiano) the government attempted to establish a dispersed ownership structure. However, immediately after the privatization, a small group of shareholders seized control of the banks through informal voting agreements, establishing a control structure which is much more consistent with the Italian corporate environment. Table 10 shows some data from the Italian firms so far privatized through a public offer:[25] the numbers show that, in all instances, the number of shareholders rapidly shrunk; and, more

TABLE 10

The Italian Privatizion Programme 1993–95: Companies sold through a public offer

Company	Credit	Comit	IMI	INA
Number of purchasers	190,000	297,527	355,000	417,720
Number of shareholders after three months	112,000	232,000	217,000	403,000
Number of shareholders	176,866[1]	175,981[2]	n.a	170,000[3]
Number of shareholders at the first shareholders' meeting	329	1839	74	2238
As % of outstanding equity	23.1	28.8	60.2	57
The ten largest shareholders: as % of equity	16.9	16.1	59.9	58
as % of equity represented at the first shareholders' meeting	73.2	55.8	99.5	n.a
Last shareholders' meeting (date)	29/4/1995	29/4/1995	24/7/1995	11/1/1996
Number of shareholders at the last shareholders' meeting:				
Present	356			644
Postal votes	139			4
Total	495	659	371	648
As % of outstanding ordinary shares	17.21	25.51	66.6	51.52
The ten largest shareholders present at the meeting				
As % of total equity (ordinary shares)	8.01[4]	8.94[5]	45.57[6]	49.39
As % of equity represented at the last shareholders' meeting	46.54	35.28	68.42	95.87

[1] As of 29/4/1995.
[2] As of 29/4/1995. It includes:
        175,000 double votes (par value Lire 1000)
           376 single vote (par value Lire 500)
        175,981 Total.
[3] As of 30/1/1996.
[4] Includes shareholders with more than 2% (that is 3 shareholders: Commercial Union 2.02%, Franco Tosi 3.00%, Allianz 2.99%).
[5] Includes shareholders with more than 2% (that is 3 shareholders: Generali, Commerz Bank, Paribas with approximately 2.98% each). I.R.I. (2.1%) did not exercise its voting rights.
[6] Includes 7 shareholders.
[7] The four largest shareholders as of 10/03/1996, are: Ministero del Tesoro 34.38%, CARIPLO 3%, Gruppo S. Paolo 3%, IMI 3%.
Source: INA Investors Relations.

importantly, that only a very small fraction of them voted in shareholders' meetings. The concentration of control in the hands of a small group of pooled investors emerged endogenously due to the passive role of individual shareholders.

Banks and Policy Options

Given this evidence, many recent papers have focused on the endogeneity of the ownership structure of firms. This stream of research is yielding new insights into the effectiveness of government intervention in corporate governance matters. According to what Oliver Hart (1995) calls the 'Chicago view', the market should reach the first best ownership distribution regardless of initial allocations. At the time of listing a company, its original owners should have incentives to choose the best allocation of ownership rights, i.e. the one that maximizes the value of the firm, since this also maximizes the price at which they can sell their shares. Any mistake, however, will be corrected by the market because a rider would find it profitable to seize control of the firm and change its ownership structure: as Shleifer and Vishny (1995) point out 'takeovers can be viewed as a rapid-fire mechanism for ownership concentration.' This is true for ownership rights, but also, at least in principle, for all the other variables that affect the value of the firm, such as statutory procedures for the resolution of conflicts among shareholders, the choice of managers, etc.

This view does not deny the relevance that government intervention may have: however it suggests that only policies that affect the structure of financial markets are effective. For example, in the attempt to establish a US-type financial system, the government can not choose directly the ownership structure of a firm (the cases of Comit and Credit are instructive); but it can establish the conditions in which such a system may emerge.

In this sense reforms for the development of the financial institutions that can play the role of efficient LSH. As we discussed in the previous sections, the characteristics of LSHs are a critical variable for the success of a privatization program. The reality of continental Europe is that the financial systems are dominated by banks: yet, these institutions are ill-suited to act as 'virtuous controlling shareholders' because of the conflict of interest that may arise with their lending activity. For this reason it is often argued that continental European governments should foster the development of new types of financial investors – pension funds in particular, but also mutual funds. However, the experience so far has been that setting up these institutions requires time – often a lot of time (this for example has been the recent experience of mutual funds and pensions funds in Italy). If privatizations had to wait until these new creations were strong enough to take up a relevant position in the financial system, they might be delayed for years. In the short run, there may be no better alternative to working with what already exists: banks.

Banks play a double role during a privatizations process. They are one of the objects of the process, since in many countries – Spain, France and Italy in particular – a significant fraction (about two-thirds in Spain and Italy) of the banking industry is public. But banks could also be important buyers of the equity of industrial firms sold by the government, since in continental Europe they manage the largest part of private savings. Clearly these two sides of the coin are intimately related: a good bank privatization should also aim to create a potentially good buyer for other privatizations.

The French experience is particularly interesting in this respect, since while privatizing the state-owned banks the government also engaged in a reform of the banking industry. The 1984 bank law allowed French banks to buy equity of industrial firms, and authorized them to act as merchant banks. In 1986, when the privatisation process began, banks were the first asset on sale: Paribas and Indosuez, two of the banks nationalized by Mitterand in 1982, and also the three large banks nationalized by De Gaulle in 1945, BNP, Crédit Lyonnais, and Societé Générale. The newly privatized banks engaged in two types of activity.[26] Some large commercial banks, through their investment banking branches, acquired relevant stakes – 20 to 40 per cent – in listed companies, and began to exert a substantial influence in the firms' board of directors. This is the case, for instance, of the Banque Indosuez which is known to act as a very active shareholder, and took part in important financial operations such as the takeover of Societé Générale de Belgique in 1988. Other banks developed a different approach: they targeted medium and small non-listed companies. Crédit Agricole, for example, exploited its vast branch network to offer corporate governance services to local firms. The Franch experience thus seems to show that the privatisations of banks may generate positive spill-offs which extend beyond their direct role in other privatizations.

Italy, on the contrary, seems to be following quite a different path. Even though two among the country's largest banks were recently privatized, the large majority of remains public – either directly owned by the Treasury (such as Banca Nazionale del Lavoro), or controlled by public foundations (such as San Paolo di Torino, Italy's largest bank in terms of deposits). Three facts are particularly worrying. First, the political will to sell these banks is simply not there – and the Bank of Italy seems not to dislike the presence of banks that are not driven by the need to maximize shareholder equity, and can thus be instrumental in the solution of banking crises (see for instance the recent acquisition by CARIPLO of the largest saving bank in Calabria). Second, these banks are very far from being efficient. Third, they have become active players in other privatizations, while still being public themselves (see for instance the controlling position that CARIPLO and San Paolo have taken up in INA, the recently privatized insurance company, and in IMI, a large investment bank). Moreover, these banks seem not to care particularly about small shareholders, as recently demonstrated by the behaviour of Banca di Roma in the acquisition of the Banca Nazionale dell'Agricoltura: even though the target firm was listed, by virtue of a controversial legal arrangement the buyer avoided launching a public offer, and thus excluded outside shareholders from the offer, limiting the negotiation to the insider. The question naturally arises: are these banks good candidates to play the role of LSH?

Privatizations are a very good opportunity to set up the right environment for the development of new financial intermediaries and in general for a sound corporate governance system. Here too, the sale of companies to the market should not aim to establish directly the 'best' ownership structure: first because nobody can say which structure is best; secondly because the market could reverse the government choice if this were not consistent with the environment. On the contrary, the government should pay attention to establish the best 'rules of the game' and give to the market the right incentives: or, more realistically, avoid giving the wrong incentives.

The introduction of the so-called 'golden share' is a good example in this sense. In many recent privatizations, the government has kept the power to intervene directly in the corporate governance of firms, even after the privatization had been completed. In France, for instance, the government has retained special rights to influence shareholders' deliberations through the so called *action spécifique*, which, *for five years* after the sale of the shares, guarantees a veto power on the sale of a block larger than 10 per cent of the firm's capital.[27] A similar instrument was introduced in the UK ('golden share') in many important sales of public firms,[28] reserving similar rights to the government.

At first sight, the rational for these provisions seems clear: they guarantee the seller that, at least for a certain period of time, it can control the outcome of the privatization. This may be particularly valuable in the privatization of firms with social importance: utilities for example, which often operate in a monopolistic regime. However, the policy-maker should compare the benefits with the costs of these instruments – and if the costs are relevant, ask whether other instruments could be used. We will not go in deep into the problem, except for mentioning that governments often privatize in order to reduce the power of politicians over the economy: it would therefore be nonsense to sell shares to private agents, leaving the ultimate power of decision over the control of the firm to public agents. This is especially because:

1. a veto power over block transfers undermines the development of a genuine market for corporate control;
2. if investors are rational, they will anticipate these moral hazard problems and agree to buy shares only at a discount. More importantly, investors would certainly refrain from buying large blocks of shares, since these may become illiquid, if the government were to veto their sale to a third party, or prevent them for exercising effective control, if the golden share also (as it does in some cases) gives the government the power to intervene in company matters.

The argument against golden shares may be strengthened in the light of the recent British experience. In the UK golden shares played an important role

TABLE 11

Takeovers against electricity distribution companies in the UK

Raider	Target company	Type of takeover	Date	Type of the Raider
Trafalgar House	Northern Electric	Hostile	19/12/95	Holding company
Southern Power	SWEB	Hostile	10/07/95	Electric utility (production and distribution)
Scottish Power	Main Web	Hostile	24/07/95	Electric utility (production and distribution)
Hanson	Eastern Group	Friendly	31/07/95	Electric utility (production)
North West Water	Norweb	Friendly	8/09/95	Electric utility (distribution)
PowerGen	Midlands	Friendly	18/09/95	Electric utility (distribution)

Source: F. Lo Passo and A. Macchiati (1996).

in the privatization of public utilities, proving, up to now, to be an effective instrument: the government wished to keep a fairly dispersed ownership structure of these companies, and has so far succeeded. Golden shares enabled the government to exercise a veto power on the acquisition of blocks of shares by private investors, and in many instances it kept the right to appoint the managers of these firms.[29] These rights, however, did not solve the corporate governance problems of these companies: they merely served as an 'aspirin' as long as the special rights were in place – as became clear in the case of the 12 electricity distribution companies when the special powers granted by golden shares elapsed, on the 31st of March 1996: since then we have witnessed a surge of takeovers, in most instances hostile (see Table 11) organized by electricity generating companies. Golden shares were used as a surrogate for antitrust regulation, and proved to be only a temporary solution for the underlying problems. The government wanted to limit vertical integration in the electricity industry – and therefore too much concentration of market power – but it failed as soon as the golden shares elapsed. After the recent wave of takeovers, the government had to resort to anti-trust regulations, and asked the Monopoly and Merger Commission to intervene. Probably it should have done this from the beginning, avoiding the temporary 'aspirin' solution.

The British experience should be carefully considered by those governments that are currently considering the introduction of golden shares in the statutes of the telephone companies that will be privatized in the near future: STET, in Italy, Deutsche Telekom in Germany, France Telecom in France. The British outcome could be avoided by making such special rights permanent (as the Italian government, for instance is considering), but this may wipe out most of the institutional demand for the shares of these companies, and, more importantly, it would make it virtually impossible to find a group of LSH with the right incentives. This experience also confirms the point made above about ownership structures being endogenous in the long run. In the British utilities case the driving force behind the establishment of an ownership structure was the search for monopolistic rents; in order to avoid them, and reach the first best equilibrium, it was not enough to set up temporary external barriers: it was necessary to act on the underlying forces through effective anti-trust regulations.

F. Conclusions

At the beginning of this paper we posed a question: 'should we trust banks when they sit on the board of directors?'. As we saw, the answer is not unambiguous. The type and degree of a bank's monitoring activity is deeply influenced by its lending activity. A bank tends to protect its credits and thus to minimize the probability of default; a lender derives no benefits from extra profits since its payoff is limited in good states of nature. This is not to say bank monitoring cannot be useful. In a mature industry, say the steel industry, a bank could do a very good job, and the side effects would be limited since extra profits are in any case very small. But many entrepreneurial activities will not take off – for example when new technologies are at stake – if financiers are not ready to take risks. In such cases an efficient market for corporate control is the best mechanism to allocate resources: it would not only serve as a market for equity stakes, but also as a market for entrepreneurial ideas since financial projects would be evaluated by many independent analysts. A too close firm-bank relationship hinders the development of such a market because the bank may use its lending power to entrench its control. This is the reason for keeping a wary eye on 'banks on the board of directors'.

In this context, what is the role of government? We saw that the ownership structure of a firm is an endogenous variable, which cannot, especially in the long run, be determined by the government. The endogenous equilibrium of an ownership structure, however, may be socially inefficient in the absence of perfect information, and in the presence of unforseable contingencies: for this reason there remains scope for government intervention, particularly at the time of a privatization. The government, however, should aim not at determining directly the ownership structure of firms: it should rather aim at creating the best environment in which the market equilibrium can coincide with the socially optimal equilibrium. It thus is important to establish appropriate 'rules of the game', especially in the privatization of public utilities. Financial market reforms should aim at establishing an environment in which market forces contribute to reach the socially efficient equilibrium.

We have used the example of Italy to illustrate some of these issues. The privatization of banks in Italy is the first step in the construction of a sound corporate environment. However, it will not be sufficient. The Italian banking sector is heavily regulated. Up until now the role of regulator has been performed by the central bank which has very strong powers: since, for example, it approves bank mergers and acquisitions and it can influence the behaviour of banks. But in this supervisory activity the Bank of Italy has proved to be more interested in the stability of the banking system than in its efficiency. The problem is not the quality of the supervisory authority, but a conflict of interest between the stability of the system and its efficiency.[30] We can conclude that the sale of bank shares to private investors is insufficient to shape efficient banks and more effective corporate governance structures.

Notes

1. Quoted from J. Bredford De Long (1991), page 215.
2. See A. D. Chandler (1990).
3. It should be stressed that US investment banks and German *Grossbanken* financed their activity in a very different way.
4. It should also be noted that 50 per cent of the Merceders Holding A.G. is owned by Stella and Stern Automobil beteilingungs gesellshaften mbH and Commerzbank, Dresdner bank and the Bayerishe Landesbank Girozentrale own 25 per cent each of these two companies (these data refer to 1991).
5. Aoki (1996), page 9.
6. Jensen and Mackling (1976), page 311.
7. As reported by Kaplan (1993), the typical top Japanese executive holds half of the ownership stake of the typical U.S. top executive, when only shares are considered, and one quarter when options are included.
8. See for example the role performed by institutional investors in the recent Granada-Forte case in the UK.
9. See for example McConnel and Servaes (1990) for a paper which employs a similar methodology (it studies the relation between the Tobin's q and insiders' equity). Contrasting results are shown by Demsetz and Lehn (1985): they find no significant relation between firm profitability and ownership concentration. However contrary to almost all other empirical studies, they postulate a *li near* relation which is ill-suited to capture the non-linear, non-monotone relation found in the other studies. A different methodology is used by Slovin and Sushka (1993): see the text above.
10. Since both Tobin's q and the ownership structure are endogenous variables, there is a problem as to whether ownership concentration affects firm value, or firm value affects the equilibrium ownership structure.
11. See Stulz (1988).
12. Prowse's sample consists of the firms that Nakatani (1984) defines as members of a *keiretsu*, for which both share and debt holdings are available.
13. See Edwards and Fisher (1994).
14. See Edwards and Fisher (1991).
15. See Kaplan (1993a), Kaplan (1993b), and Kaplan and Minton (1994).

16. Kaplan and Minton (1993), page 14.
17. Shareholders, once they are granted a bank credit, and given the expected value of potential investments, tend to invest in projects with high pay-offs and high probability of default. This happens because of the structure of their pay-offs: if the outcome of the investment is good, they gain most of the profits since they are the residual claimant; if instead the outcome is bad, because of limited liability, they suffer only part of the losses. This phenomenon is generally referred to as 'asset substitution'.
18. See for instance Nakatani (1984).
19. For details see Miyajima (1995).
20. However, a bias against ownership concentration remained, and still in today's Japan there are limits in this sense: because of the Anti-Monopoly Act, banks cannot hold more than 5 per cent of any single company – up to 1987 the limit was 10 per cent; for insurance companies it is still 10 per cent).
21. Banca d'Italia (1994), page 16.
22. The authors do not consider the entire population of firms but a large sample.
23. These data come from Barca (1995).
24. Barca (1995) page 16.
25. The public sale of shares of IMI and INA was only partial: privatization was subsequently completed through a private placement.
26. The following information on French banks is from Cardilli, Pinzani and Signorini (1994).
27. The *action spécifique* was introduced in the privatization of Matra, Havas, Elf-Aquitaine and Bull.
28. Britoil, British Telecom, British Gas, Enterprise Oil.
29. A veto power on sales of blocks of shares was introduced in the statutes of British Telecom, Cable and Wireless, National power, and PowerGen; the right to nominate managers, for example, in the cases of British Telecom, and Cable and Wireless.
30. Battaglini (1996) studies the relation between prudential regulation and ownership structure of banks.

References

Aghion, P. and J. Tirole (1994) 'Formal and real authority in organisations', M.I.T working paper, No. 94-13.
Aoki, M. (1984) *The economic analysis of the Japanese firm*, Elsevier Science Publishers.
Aoki, Masahico (1996) 'Controlling Insider control: issues of Corporate Governance in Transition Economies', in M. Aoki (ed.), *Corporate Governance in Transition Economies: Insider Control and the role of Bank*, The World Bank.
Banca d'Italia (1994) Foreign Department, 'Report on Italy's privatisations program', mimeo.
Banca d'Italia (1994) *Il mercato della proprietà e del controllo delle imprese: aspetti teorici e istituzionali*, numero speciale dei 'Contributi all'analisi economica'.
Bank of Japan (1970) *Economic statistics since the Meiji Era*. Tokio.
Barca, F. (1995) 'On corporate governance in Italy: issues, facts and agenda', mimeo.
Barca, F., M. Bianchi, F. Brioschi, L. Buzzacchi, P. Casavola, L. Filippa and M. Pagnini (1994) *Assetti proprietari e mercato delle imprese. Gruppo, proprietà e controllo nelle imprese italiane medio grandi*, Vol. II, Bologna, Il Mulino.
Battaglini, M. (1996) 'Assetti proprietari e regolamentazione delle banche', *Ricerca di Base*, No. 19, Università Bocconi.
Berle, A. A. and G. C. Means (1932) *The modern corporation and private property*, New York, Macmillan.

Bhagat, S. and J. Brickley (1984) 'Cumulative voting: the value of minority shareholder voting rights', *Journal of Law and Economics* 27, 339–365.
Bhushan, R. (1989) 'Firm Characteristics and Analyst Following', *J. Accounting and Econ.* 11, 255–74
Brickley J.A., R. C. Lease and C. W. Smith (1988) 'Ownership structure and voting on anti-takeover amendments', *Journal of Financial Economics* 20, 267–291.
Burkart, M., D. Gromb and F. Panunzi (1994) 'Large shareholders, monitoring and fiduciary duty', mimeo, IGIER.
Cardilli, D., L. Pinzani and P. E. Signorini (1994) 'Mercato e istituzioni della riallocazione proprietaria in Germania, Regno Unito e Francia', in numero speciale dei Contributi all'analisi economica, Il mercato della proprietà e del controllo delle imprese: aspetti teorici e istituzionali, Banca d'Italia.
Coase, R. H. (1937) 'The Nature of the Firm'. *Economica* 4, 386–485.
Cornelli, F. and D. D. Li (1994) 'Large shareholders, private benefits of control and optimal schemes for privatisation', *LSE Financial Markets Group*, Discussion Paper Series, No. 185.
Crémer, J. (1993) 'Arms' length relationships', mimeo, IDEI, Tolosa.
De long, J. Breadford (1991) 'Did Morgan's Men Add Value? An Economist Perspective on Financial Capitalism', in Peter Temin (ed.), *Inside the Business Enterprise: Historical Perspectives on the Use of Information*, Chicago: University Press.
Demsetz, H. and K. Lehn (1985) 'The structure of corporate ownership: causes and consequences', *Journal of Political Economy* 93, 1155–1177.
Edwards, J. and K. Fisher (1991) 'Banks, finance and investment in West Germany', CEPR Discussion Paper, No. 497.
Edwards, J. and K. Fisher (1994) 'Banks, Finance and Investment in Germany', Cambridge, Cambridge University Press.
Franks, J. and C. Mayer (1990) 'Capital markets and corporate control: a study of France, Germany and the UK', *Economic Policy* 11, 191–231.
Fulghieri, P. and L. Zingales (1994) 'Privatizzazioni e struttura del controllo societario: il ruolo della public company', mimeo.
Grossman, S. J. and O. D. Hart (1980) 'Take-over bids, the free rider problem, and the theory of the corporation, *Bell Journal of Economics* 11, 42–64.
Harris, M. and A. Raviv (1988) 'Corporate control contests and capital structure', *Journal of Financial Economics* 20, 55–86.
Hölmstrom and Tirole (1993) 'Market Liquidity and Performance Monitoring', *Journal of Political Economy* Vol. 101, No. 4, 678–709.
Jensen, M. C. and W. H. Meckling (1976) 'Theory of the firm: managerial behaviour, agency costs and ownership structure', *Journal of Financial Economics* 11, 5–50.
Kaplan, S. (1993a) 'Top executive rewards and firm performance. A comparison of Japan and the U.S.'. University of Chicago Working Paper.
Kaplan, S. (1993b) 'Top executives, management turnover and firm performance in Germany', University of Chicago Working Paper.
Kaplan, S and B. Minton (1993) 'Outside Intervention in Japanese Companies: Its Determinants and Its Implications for Managers', NBER Working Paper No. 4276.
Lo Passo, F. and A. Macchiati (1995) 'Gli assetti proprietari nella privatizzazione delle imprese di pubblica utilità', *Rivista di Politica Economica*, forthcoming.
McConnell, J. J. and H. Servaes (1990) 'Additional evidence on equity ownership and corporate value', *Journal of Financial Economics* 27, 595–612.
Miyajima, H. (1994) 'The privatisation of ex-zaibatsu holding stocks and the emergence of bank centered corporate groups in Japan', mimeo.
Modigliani, F. and M. H. Miller (1958) 'The cost of capital, corporate finance and the theory of investment', *American Economic Review* 48, 261–297.

Mork, R., A. Shleifer and R. Vishny (1988) 'Management ownership and market valuation. An empirical analysis', *Journal of Financial Economics* 20, 293–315.
Nakatani, I. (1984) 'The role of financial corporate grouping', in M. Aoki, (ed.), *Economic analisis of the Japanese firm*, North Holland, New York.
Nicodano, G. (1993) 'The value of non-voting shares and pyramidal groups', Università L. Bocconi, Paolo Baffi Centre, Working Paper, No. 77.
OECD (1989) 'Disclosure of information by Multinational enterprises', Working Document by the Working Group on Accounting Standards, No. 6.
Prowse, S. (1995) 'Corporate governance in an international perspective: A survey of corporate control mechanisms among large firms in the U.S., U.K., Japan and Germany', *Financial Markets, Institutions & Instruments* Vol. 4, No. 1.
Roe, M. J. (1990) 'Political and legal restraint on ownership and control of public companies', *Journal of Financial Economics* 27, 7–41.
Roe, M. J. (1994) *Strong managers, weak owners. The political roots of American corporate finance*, Princeton, NJ: Princeton University Press.
Schleifer, A. and R. W. Vishny (1986) 'Large shareholders and corporate control', *Journal of Political Economy* Vol. 94, No. 3.
Sheard, P. (1989) 'The main bank system and corporate monitoring and control in Japan', *Journal of Economic Behavior and Organisation* 11, 399–422.
Shleifer, A. and R. W. Vishny (1995) 'A survey of corporate governance', mimeo.
Slovin, M. B. and M. E. Sushka (1993) 'Ownership concentration, corporate control activity, and firm value: evidence from the death of inside blockholders', *Journal of Finance* XLVIII, No. 4, 1293–1321.
Stulz, R. M. (1988) 'Management control of voting rights. Financing policies and the market for corporate control', *Journal of Financial Economics* 20, 25–53.
Weinstein, D. E. and Y. Yafeh (1994) 'On the costs of a Bank Centered Financial System: evidence from the changing main bank relations in Japan', Paper presented at the CEPR|ECARE Workshop, Brussels 28/29 October 1994.
Wruck, K. H. (1989) 'Equity ownership concentration and firm value', *Journal of Financial Economics* 23, 3–28.

Abstract

This paper reviews the corporate governance debate in Europe in the perspective of enlargement of the EU. It notices in this respect an important ambiguity in the EU framework, which is almost complete for financial services, but still very incomplete in the area of company law. There is freedom to trade in stocks in the EU, but the control rights connected to shares differ widely. It basically allows the CEECs to adopt the corporate governance framework they want, as could already be observed in the first years of the transition. Since significant progress in EU harmonization in this area is unlikely in the coming years, and because of the growing role of the market in corporate control, this paper argues in favour of self-regulation to achieve more convergence in practices.

Karel Lannoo is Head of EU Policies and Business Strategies Unit and Senior Research Fellow at the Centre for European Policy Studies (CEPS), an independent European affairs research institute based in Brussels.

IX. Corporate Governance, West and East: A Synthesis of the EU Framework in the Perspective of Enlargement

KAREL LANNOO

In the framework of preparing for EU membership and the approximation of laws, the Central and Eastern-European countries (CEECs) are confronted with an ambiguous situation in the achievement of the single market as far as corporate governance is concerned. On the one hand, there are the liberalizing effects of a whole series of financial market measures which have radically increased competition, so that institutional investors can with a single licence provide services in another member state. On the other hand, there are some key company law harmonization proposals, such as on the European Company Statute or take-over bids directive, which have been on the Council table for many years and on which no agreement will probably be reached in the foreseeable future. The differences in corporate governance systems in the EU and in the candidate countries can thus be kept, but financial markets' integration will increasingly bring the specificities of national systems under pressure.

Something needs to be done, however, to bring a European approach to the corporate governance discussions. The three semi-official committees which discussed changes to the local corporate governance systems in the UK, France and the Netherlands did not raise the European dimension of the debate at all. This is surprising, since the brief of each group was to examine the appropriateness of the national corporate governance system in an increasingly globalizing economy. Their discussions did, however, not reach further than the national borders. This attitude was confirmed in a recent survey by CEPS on 'Shareholder Voting in Europe', which found that European institutional investors did not exercise their voting rights in other member states. The investors accepted that voting could have an influence on the performance of their investments, but this was only applied, be it to varying degrees, in the home market. A single market in the area of corporate governance clearly does not exist.

The purpose of this paper is to discuss the consequences of this situation for the EU and the candidate states, and to make some policy recommendations.

It is not our intention to review the discussion on corporate governance in transition economies. We will limit ourselves, in a first chapter, to describe which 'systems' have been put in place in some transition economies, and put it in the perspective of the EU legislative framework. A second chapter describes the differences in corporate governance, as we can perceive it in the market. Unfortunately, the discussions each time have to distinguish between the EU and the CEECs, since the issues are different in both cases. In the EU, it concerns the vast differences in corporate governance structures, in the CEECs it regards the progress in the transition to market economies. We will however draw some common policy implications and conclusions at the end.

For sake of clarity, we will in this paper use the more restricted definition of corporate governance as the organization of the relationship between shareholders and managers in the control of a corporation. This does not mean however that we will only examine the company law framework. National corporate governance systems are strongly influenced by financial market developments, which have to be taken into consideration as well.

THE REGULATORY FRAMEWORK

The EU

The EU regulatory framework for a single financial services market is almost in place. Firms can provide banking, insurance or stockbroking services across borders subject to a single authorization and to respecting basic prudential rules on minimum own funds, investment of assets, shareholdings in industry, etc. The notable exception is pension funds, on which a draft directive was withdrawn by the European Commission, as a result of broad disagreements among the member states.

By contrast, the harmonization of company law structures in the EU, be it to ease cross-border mergers and level take-over bid procedures, or to allow for a single European-wide incorporation, has been blocked for some time, and no immediate breakthrough is expected.[1] The reasons for this deadlock are manifold, and cannot just be reduced, as it is often done, to the issue of worker participation in corporate control. Workers' representatives are entitled to have seats on the boards of corporations in Denmark, Germany and the Netherlands, and a lighter structure at European level could bring these national system under pressure. Other sensitive issues are the powers and responsibilities of shareholders and boards, the existence of barriers to take-overs, the discretionary powers of governments, taxation, or more generally, whether further statutory harmonization is desirable in an area where, already at national level, change is very difficult to implement.

TABLE 1

Dominant form of shares and voting rights

Shares	Dominant form	Multiple voting rights	Non-voting shares	Capped voting
A	bearer	no	yes	yes
B	bearer	no	yes	dep. on by-laws (<20%)
D	bearer	uncommon	yes	dep. on by-laws
DK	registered	yes	no	yes
E	bearer	no	yes	yes
F	bearer	yes	yes	yes
FIN	registered	yes (<20×)	no	yes
GR	registered	no	yes	no
IRL	registered	no	no	no
I	registered	no	yes (<50%)	yes
L	bearer	no	yes	no
NL	bearer	yes	yes	yes, see by-laws
P	bearer	no	yes	no
SW	registered	yes (<10×)	no	yes (<20%)
UK	registered	uncommon	uncommon	uncommon
CH	registered	yes	yes	yes, see by-laws
US	registered	uncommon	uncommon	no

Source: Davis and Lannoo (1997).
Note: Voting rights are not only a matter of company law, they can also be set in the by-laws of companies. It is thus very difficult to generalize the situation for a certain country.

Take the issue of control rights. The draft EU directives incorporate language providing for equal treatment of shareholders and the 'one share–one vote' principle. It is clear that this is not the general rule in the EU member states. Voting rights can also be double or multiple; they can be limited under a certain ceiling (capped); or shares might have no voting rights at all. Table 1 gives a general overview of voting rights in the EU and, for purposes of comparison, Switzerland and the US. This is an assessment of the most common situation, which is not only a matter of company law, but also of practice within companies. In the UK, for example, exceptions to the 'one share–one vote' principle are allowed by law, but they have become uncommon.

Double or multiple voting rights are common in all Scandinavian countries, in France and in the Netherlands. In France, double voting rights can be authorized as part of clauses in the articles of incorporation or in the by-laws, under certain conditions. They cease automatically in case of a share transfer, by which they are a form of anti-takeover device. French management is said to be strongly in favour of keeping this option.[2] Multiple voting rights in Finland can be granted for a maximum of twenty votes per share; in Sweden, they must not exceed ten times the right of ordinary shares. The circulation of double or multiple voting shares has an impact on trading and the liquidity of the stock market, since they are generally not traded. They also could depress prices for ordinary shares if investors view these as having inferior voting value. Non-voting shares exist in most EU countries, where such securities may get a higher dividend in return for lesser ownership rights. They are not allowed in Denmark, Ireland and Sweden.

Harmonizing EU legislation in the area of control rights could thus eliminate some forms of barriers to takeovers which exist in EU member states. This would be opposed by employers, or even governments, which would prefer to keep the 'national champions' free from take-over threats.

In 1995, the European Commission launched a modest initiative to overcome this deadlock in harmonizing corporate governance standards by ordering a study on the subject. The EC wanted to examine to what extent a simplification in the national provisions on the governance of public limited companies would be beneficial and feasible. It requested that the report should include:

1. an overview of internal and external controls over management, the rights and obligations of shareholders, voting rights and the principle of proportionality between voting rights and subscribed capital, the protection of minority shareholders, and management liability;
2. solutions for simplifying national requirements, without reducing shareholder and third-party protections, and examining the possibility of different rules between quoted and non-quoted companies; and
3. an examination of the corresponding rules in the draft 5th company law directive and suggestions for revisions.

In the end, the study failed to offer a one-off solution that could break the impasse on the 5th directive. Instead, the authors recommended that EU rules form a flexible framework, which can be implemented in each member state's legal system under a law or a self-regulating national code of best practice. The study saw no way of drafting different rules for 'open' (that is, quoted) as compared to 'closed' companies, because of the protection of third-party interests. It argued that cross-border operations in the EU should be facilitated and simplified in the best interests of all types of companies. The study also called on public authorities and firms to take steps aimed at improving shareholder access to, and quality of, corporate financial information.

Regarding voting rights in listed companies, the study noticed "a certain consensus within the member states in favour of their proportionality to the subscribed capital, and, thus, of the elimination of any measures allowing a minority, by controlling the voting rights, to circumvent any control of such minority by the general meeting of shareholders".[3] It was therefore suggested that ceilings, shares with multiple voting rights and special majorities for the removal of corporate bodies should be abolished.

The forgoing should not give the impression that nothing has been done in the area of company law. The EU has enacted harmonizing legislation regarding the establishment of companies and the reporting procedures. They are however of minor importance compared to the drafts which are still under discussion, or the harmonizing effects were limited due to the existence of many options, as is the case with the accounting directives.[4]

Nevertheless, the achievement of a single market in other sectors will not only highlight these shortcomings, but it will also have a strong impact on the convergence of corporate governance standards, most importantly through financial-market integration. The EU measures in the areas of banking, insurance and capital movements have radically increased competition in the provision of financial services in the EU. This process will be further strengthened in the years to come with the realization of economic and monetary union (EMU), which will lead to the disappearance of the currency bias. EMU will allow institutional investors to have more balanced portfolios, since the national currency will be replaced by the euro in currency matching rules, and will over time bring more convergence in portfolio distribution. Institutional investors in continental Europe have traditionally over-invested in bonds, whereas equity holdings are under-represented. The latter form a much more important part of the portfolio of British and US firms. They are more volatile but give a better return in the long run.

As part of the growing demand for equity in investment portfolios, the capacities of the board in setting the strategy of a firm, ensuring adequate returns and executing effective control will be closely examined. Shareholders will increasingly use their rights at the AGM or on the stock exchange to penalize badly performing firms. The existence of barriers to shareholder accountability are being questioned.

The harmonizing effects of the EU's single market legislation are only starting to emerge, which is probably one of the reasons why the debate on corporate governance is still so much confined to national borders. Corporate governance committees in the UK, France and the Netherlands have published their findings on the adaptation of their systems to globalization and the growing role of the market in corporate control. Only the UK's Cadbury Committee took the most advanced positions, in a system which was already very open and market-oriented. But the French Viénot and Dutch Peters Committees did not basically touch on their national system. The recommendations of the three groups converge regarding board structure, the separation of chairman and CEO (not in Viénot), the need for well qualified independent directors and limitation of the number of directorships, the need for adequate reporting and control, and the method of implementation, i.e. self-regulation (see Table 2). But the discussion of the role of shareholders and the annual general meeting was rather disappointing, certainly in the case of the Viénot and Peters reports.

TABLE 2
A brief comparison of the Cadbury, Viénot and Peters Reports

	Cadbury (UK)	Viénot (France)	Peters (The Netherlands)
Publication	December 1992	July 1995	October 1996 (draft)
Initiative	London Stock Exchange (LSE)	French employers' federation (CNPF)	Listed corporations, Dutch stock exchange
Board structure	• CEO≠Chairman • truly independent directors • executive pay to be disclosed, subject to remuneration committee	• CEO=Chairman • at least two independent directors • number of directorships should be limited • create remuneration and selection committees • Directors' Charter on ethical standards for board members	• CEO≠Chairman • Supervisory board to be independent from management board • number of directorships should be limited • remuneration and selection committees to be considered • co-optation of supervisory board can be maintained
AGM	• institutional investors should exercise their voting rights	• (not discussed)	• limitations on voting rights can, for the time being, be kept in place
Reporting	• need for audit committee • directors to state that business is a going concern	• need for audit committee • directors to state that internal control procedures are going on	• need for audit committee • management board must inform supervisory board of internal control procedures
Result	'Cadbury Code'	?	'Peters Code'
Enforcement	LSE, part of listing rules	not discussed: securities commission (COB)?	to be determined, possibly stock exchange
Method	self-regulation	self-regulation	self-regulation

Both countries employ a system of multiple, respectively capped voting rights, which was not questioned. Even the unique Dutch system of co-optation of the supervisory board in *structuurvennootschappen*, independent from shareholder scrutiny, was kept intact.[5]

This closed attitude in Europe as regards corporate governance was confirmed in a recent CEPS survey on shareholder voting in Europe (Davis and Lannoo, 1997). The survey was intended to compare voting behaviour of European institutional investors in the EU and to examine the virtuality of national borders in this respect. It revealed large differences between countries and a very low incidence of cross-border voting. Although the single market has existed since 1993, national frontiers still form real barriers. Financial market liberalization allowed institutional investors to spread their investments across the EU, a process that will be accelerated by EMU, but the same care is not given to cross-border as compared to national investments. The reasons given for this attitude were a lack of information, high costs, cumbersome procedures and voting structures. US pension funds, on the other hand, do not experience frontiers as barriers for exercising their voting rights, and are increasingly voting abroad. Although they are required by law, it is likely that they vote more in Europe than their Europeans counterparts do across borders.

The CEECs

Central and Eastern European countries did not only have to respond to increasing globalization. They first and foremost needed to create effective corporate governance structures from scratch, or to transform a system where governance was at its worst, where the state exercised both ownership and control. Not only did they need to create a basic company law and financial sector framework, they also had to implement structures to allow for good corporate governance. Only the former is part of the approximation of laws programme to prepare for EU membership, the latter of more country typical privatization or industrial policy, whereby different approaches were followed.

Five main types of ownership structures can be distinguished in transition economies (EBRD, 1995):
1. State ownership with control exercised by insiders;
2. Inside ownership with control exercised by employees;
3. Inside ownership with control exercised by managers;
4. Domestic outside ownership (e.g. voucher holders);
5. Foreign investor ownership (individual or institutional investors).

They have resulted in different forms of governance. The picture which has emerged after six years of transition is that state ownership has remained important in most countries. The second most important group is management and employee ownership. The former has become common in the Czech and

Slovak Republic, while employee ownership has been applied to a certain extent in Poland. Domestic outside ownership through investment funds has emerged as a third widely used form of ownership. It was applied on a large scale in the Czech Republic, but also recently in Poland, and initially, in the Slovak Republic. Hungary is the only country where foreign ownership has been introduced on a large scale. However, the ownership structure is far from final. Some privatizations have been held up by government out of strategic and industrial policy considerations, and shifts have occurred in shareholdings by households (as a result of voucher privatization) to investment funds.

This diverse cross-country ownership picture can also be noticed in banking. Hungary is at the top for having liberalized its banking market, with 60 per cent of the sector controlled by foreign banks. Under Hungarian law, state ownership should fall to less than 25 per cent by the end of 1998. In Poland, only 25 per cent of the banking sector is in foreign hands, but the country is under pressure from the OECD to fully liberalize its banking sector by 1999. Also the Czech and Slovak Republic are pressed to step up reforms.

First indications on enterprise performance in the Visegrad countries show that the best scores were obtained in new (*de novo*) enterprises and firms with dominant foreign ownership. In the former, there is generally no corporate governance problem, since the owner will in most cases also be the manager, in the latter case, the new owner is free to make the necessary management changes. Other firm structures, in contrast, gave mixed results, indicating that there is a governance problem. Insiders have often retained too much influence, at the expense of performance. A survey on the Czech Republic (OECD, 1996a) found that few management changes have taken place in companies since their privatization and that there was only rarely a link between enterprise performance and executive pay. It also revealed a conflict of interest problem with the banks, which, as managers of the investment funds, prefer to further their banking business rather than to promote the interests of shareholders.

In the area of financial market regulation, Eastern European countries have started to model EU directives. However, there remain in some of these countries significant differences from the EU standards in the definition of regulatory capital, as well as in the scope for discretion in the application of rules. Important in the context of this paper are the limits on equity investments for banks and insurance companies. The second banking directive allows banks to possess equity holdings in non-financial undertakings of up to 60 per cent of their own funds, single holdings must not exceed 15 per cent. These rules have been interpreted fairly similarly in the EU.[6] As can be seen from Table 3, comparable rules in selected CEECs are tighter. Also life insurance portfolio regulations do differ substantially across the CEECs and apply tighter restrictions than in most advanced market economies. The rules under the EU insurance directives allow member states to set quantitative (maximum 10 per

TABLE 3

Prudential rules on equity participations by financial institutions

	Bank equity holdings in non-financial undertakings (in % of a bank's own funds)	Life insurance company investment restrictions in listed (unlisted) shares	Pension funds investment restrictions in listed (unlisted) shares
EU rule	<60% (<15% for single holding)	<20%, or qualitative restrictions	n.a.
Czech Republic	qualitative restrictions	<10%	qualitative restrictions
Hungary	<40%	<10% (5%)	<60% (30%)
Poland	<25%	<30% (15%)	<30% (10%)
Slovak Republic	<25%	<15%	<20%
Slovenia	<15%	<10%	n.a.

Sources: EBRD (1995), EBRD (1996), European Commission.

cent of technical reserves in listed and 10 per cent in unlisted shares) or qualitative (prudent man rule) restrictions.

By contrast, comparable rules for pension fund investments are more liberal. As part of the efforts to reform the public pay-as-you-go (PAYG) financed pension system, proposals are gaining increasing support in the Baltics, Hungary and Poland to change the basic nature of mandatory pension provision by placing a larger share in fully-funded systems, possibly privately managed. These funds could become big investors on the stock market and important actors in the corporate governance debate. The future will have to show whether these countries will be faster in overcoming political impediments to reform than some Western-European countries, which have so far unsuccessfully struggled to diminish the overdependence on their PAYG system. This was reflected in the failure to adopt an EU directive on the freedom of investment and management of pension funds.

A third element in financial market regulation are securities markets regulations, that are crucial in determining the attractiveness of shares as a financing instrument. Rules on reporting, the protection of investors and the prohibition of insider trading are a pre-condition to create a stable environment for stock markets. CEECs have to different extents put in place the necessary rules to ensure a stable environment for the use of shares, but some notorious gaps still exist, such as on protection of minority shareholders, insider trading or market transparency. A survey by the *Central and Eastern European Review* with brokers and fund managers gave Poland the highest mark in a corporate governance scorecard on market disclosure, transparency, shareholder protection and insider trading, even beating many established markets.[7]

MARKET INDICATORS

The Importance of Stock Markets

Differences in corporate governance can be 'measured' by the ratio of stock market capitalization to GDP. It indicates the extent to which securities markets are used to mobilize capital and to diversify risks, and thus, the extent to which corporate governance problems are common in a certain economy. Low market capitalization to GDP ratios indicate that the market is not widely used as a financing instrument, and that the market does not play a major role in the transfer of control rights in a company. Corporate governance conflicts will in the latter case be less frequent or apparent, since shareholdings might be rather concentrated in the hands of families or firms. Governance problems will then be settled by other means than by share transfers on the stock market or active shareholder involvement in the annual general meeting.

A comparison of these data for the EU member states shows great differences (Table 4). By the end of 1995, market capitalization of domestic stock as a percentage of GDP ranged from 123per cent in the UK and 74 per cent in the Netherlands to 24 per cent in Germany and 20 per cent in Italy. The number of domestic listed companies ranged from 1971 in the UK to 678 in Germany, 710 in France and 250 in Italy. The average stock market capitalization of the EU as a whole falls far below the levels registered in Japan and the US. By the end of 1995, the 15 member states of the EU had a domestic stock market capitalization of only 43 per cent of GDP, in contrast to 73 per cent in Japan and 98 per cent in the US (NYSE and NASDAQ). Excluding the UK, the average stock market capitalization in the EU amounts to 31 per cent of GDP.

Member countries such as Sweden and the Netherlands are notable exceptions. Neither is known to have especially transparent or open corporate governance mechanisms, but their stock market capitalization is much higher than that of other continental European countries. This is even more the case in Switzerland. Moreover, a marked increase of market capitalization as a percentage of GDP can be observed in the former two countries over the last years, from 62 per cent in 1993 to 74 per cent in 1995 in the Netherlands and from 57 per cent to 77 per cent in Sweden. Meanwhile, the EU figure remained stable.

The number of domestic listed companies in the EU, especially when those of the new member states are added, comes closer to the figure for the US, NYSE and NASDAQ taken jointly. The difference within the EU, however, between the UK on the one hand and the other member states on the other is great.

In the CEECs, the level of stock market capitalization is still influenced by the chosen method of privatization, with the level of capitalization relatively

TABLE 4

Domestic listed companies by country and their total market value (at the end of 1995)

Country	Capitalization (bn ECU)	% GDP	Domestic listed companies
AUS	23920.5	13.4	95
B	79115.2	38.5	150
DK	43816.89	33.1	242
D	438638.7	23.8	678
E	148678.5	34.8	362
GR	12867.13	14.7	186
F	389389	33.2	710
FIN	34138.55	35.3	73
IRL	19954.14	42.6	53
I	163701.6	19.7	250
L	23138.24	176.6	55
NL	223779.4	73.9	217
P	14138.37	17.7	89
SWE	134220.6	76.7	212
UK	1038318	123.2	1971
EU15	2787815	43.3	5343
CH	310784.5	131.1	216
N	34752.64	39.0	151
CZ	7894	22.8	68
H	2891	9.6	42
PL	4907	3.6	53
SLK	1082	8.1	19
SLV		4.6	36
JAPAN	2790428	72.8	1714
US-NYSE	4302727	81.7	1996
US-NASDAQ	882593.6	16.7	4717

Sources: FIBV, FESE, EBRD.

high in countries such as the Czech and Slovak Republic. It should be recalled that the stock exchanges of Hungary, Poland and Slovenia were only established in 1991, those in the Czech and Slovak Republic reopened in 1993.

These data suggest that in addition to the differences in the stock market capitalization, ownership changes in companies will also differ across countries. If there is an open stock market where many companies are quoted and shares are traded, the level of take-overs will also be high. In open markets, the threat of takeovers ensures that shareholders' and managers' interests converge. If shares perform badly, shareholders will sell thereby increasing the risk of a takeover, in which the old management would most likely be replaced. In more

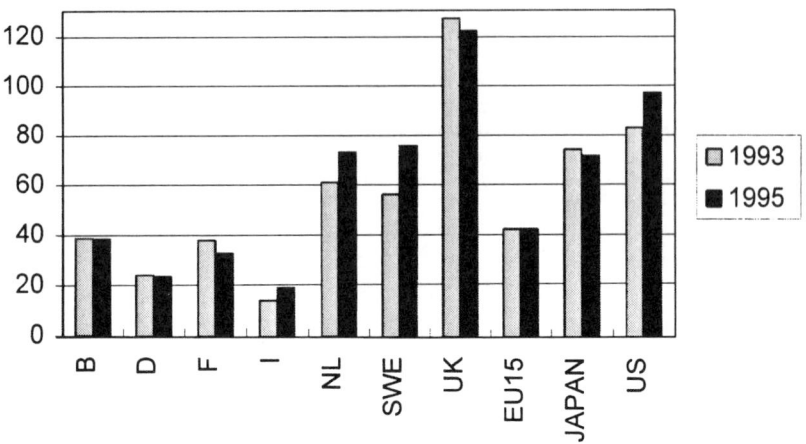

Fig. 1. Stock market capitalization as percentage of GDP.

TABLE 5

The structure of shareholding in selected countries (percentage of total)

(as at end of year)	D 1990	F 1992	I 1993	UK 1993	US 1992	JPN 1992
Institutional investors	22	23	11.3	59.3	31.2	48
of which: Banks	10		9.9	0.6	0.3	26.7
Pension funds/insurers	12		0.8	51.5	23.9	17.2
Others (Unit trusts)			0.6	7.2	7	4.1
Households	17	34	33.9	19.3	48.1	22.6
Private companies	42	21	23	4	14.1	24.8
Public authorities	5	2	27	1.3		0.7
Foreign investors	14	20	4.8	16.3	6.6	3.9

Sources: See Lannoo (1995).

closed markets, takeover activity should be lower and ownership change more limited. Correction of managerial failure happens differently.

The Structure of Shareholding

Fundamental differences in the shareholding structure in European countries are the key to explaining the variations in the importance of their stock markets. Table 5 shows that the largest share owners of quoted companies in the UK are the institutional investors (pension funds, insurance companies, banks and unit trusts), which possess an average equity of 59 per cent. Households are the second largest group in the UK with 19 per cent, and industry (including investment trusts) owns 4 per cent. In Germany, on the other hand, the situation is rather the reverse: industry is the largest owner of quoted companies with 42 per cent, institutional investors possess a much smaller part with only 15 per cent (of which banks hold 10 per cent) and households possess 17 per cent. Households – in this case, families – are the most important owners of quoted stock in France and Italy, and in the US. Government is the second most important shareholder of quoted companies in Italy with 27 per cent. No reliable data exist for the other EU member states not shown in the table. Only Sweden has a system in which ownership data are constantly followed by the stock exchange authorities.

Seen in comparison with the US and Japan, the dominating role of institutional investors in the UK is fairly exceptional. Foreign investors, on the other hand, are of minor importance in the US and Japan.

Over time, a strong growth can be noticed in the shareholding by institutional and foreign investors in several European countries. In Germany, the share of institutional investors rose from 9 per cent in 1960 to 22 per cent in 1990; foreign investors' share increased in the same period from 6 per cent to 14 per cent. In the UK, the institutionals' share rose from 19 per cent in 1963 to 59 per cent in 1993, while foreign investors increased their share from 7 per cent to 16 per cent in the same period. In France, only the share of foreign investors rose between 1977 and 1993 from 12 per cent to 20 per cent; institutional investors' shareholding remained stable. In Sweden, foreign investors share went up from 8 per cent in 1983 to 30 per cent in 1995.[8]

The structure of shareholding has to be seen in conjunction with differences in the concentration of ownership in the EU. Single majority stakes account for about 60 per cent of total stock market capitalization in Italy, compared to about 5 per cent in the UK, the US and Japan. The largest five shareholders own on average 87 per cent of outstanding shares of listed companies in Italy, compared to 41 per cent in Germany, 33 per cent in Japan, 25 per cent in the US and 21 per cent in the UK.[9]

In the CEECs, the structure of shareholding will more be an indication of the method of or the progress towards privatization. As far as all corporations are concerned, the state will still be the major shareholder, with institutional investors coming in second place and households third. As far as quoted companies are concerned (which are still limited in number), a large share are controlled by investment funds, or indirectly by banks, where the concentration will be fairly high. Czech banks control at least 40 per cent of quoted firms directly or indirectly. In Hungary, substantial bank ownership is the result of the conversion of old loans into equity holdings.

POLICY CONCLUSIONS

Western European countries have to adapt their corporate governance structures to take the shifts in shareholding structures into account. Whereas before, shareholding was concentrated in the state, firms or families, an evolution is underway whereby the market is getting a bigger role in the financing of firms. This has in some European countries led to the creation of committees to discuss the adequacy of their corporate control procedures.

So far the results of three local working groups surveyed in this paper were disparate. With the exception of the Cadbury group, the Viénot and Peters groups were disappointing in the results, and one could speak about some form of window-dressing. The basic features of the French and Dutch corporate governance system were not questioned and kept in place. The Viénot report for example stressed the collective responsibility of the board and retained the sharp hierarchy in the French system, symbolized in the combination of the positions chairman and chief executive, Peters did not alter two controversial features of the Dutch system, capped voting and the co-optation of the supervisory board.

The problem in the Central and Eastern European transition economies is to implement effective corporate governance mechanisms. As part of the privatization processes followed, these countries have generally gone immediately towards an extensive level of institutional shareholding, with, in the case of successful firms, a strong wealth maximizing behaviour on the part of managers. The institutional investors often lack the expertise, or have conflicts of interest, to adequately exercise corporate governance and to ensure profit maximization. Or they are not properly governed themselves.

The common observation for Continental Europe is thus that there is still too much insider control, in Eastern Europe as a result of privatizations whereby outside control is too weak, and insiders exploit their position, in Western Europe as the result of economic traditions, where stock markets and institutional investors have traditionally not played an important role in corporate control. A common recommendation could thus be to enforce ways which allow stronger outside control, such as through the separation of chairman and CEO, well-qualified outside directors on the board, one share-one vote structures, effective board control procedures, transparent and broad reporting. There is of course a large difference in degree between both regions, and Eastern Europe still has a much longer way to go.

Since the statutory change at EU or national level is difficult to achieve, the lead to set common rules on corporate governance should be taken by market players. A recent CEPS Working Party Report on 'Corporate Governance in Europe' suggested that, as a way out of the regulatory deadlock at European level, European industry should take the initiative and adopt a European-wide Code of Good Practice in corporate control. This code should set minimum standards for the direction and control of corporations in the EU. Observance of the guidelines should be monitored by an independent body, such as the stock exchange authorities or the chartered auditors of the company.

This is not an unrealistic approach, and has already been applied in practice by one association, the new screen-based European stock exchange EASDAQ, which started trading on 28 November 1996. EASDAQ, which wants to become the exchange for emerging companies following the example of NASDAQ, requires listed companies to appoint two independent directors, a remuneration committee and an audit committee.

Such a self-regulatory method would serve as an intermediate and probably faster way to reach convergence in corporate governance standards in Europe. Due to the complexities of governance mechanisms in the member states and the present difficulties in adopting far-reaching harmonizing legislation in that area, this proposed form of self-regulation appears to offer a more appropriate and faster way forward. It could also function as a benchmark for CEEC in the transition to market economies and the development of performing corporate governance standards.

NOTES

1. It concerns the draft 5th, 10th and 13th company law directives and the draft regulation for a European company statute. The draft 5th directive would harmonize the operational structures of PLCs. The 10th concerns cross-border mergers, the 13th would create a level playing field for take-over bids. The company regulation would create an optional structure for European corporations to operate EU-wide under a single legal entity.
2. European Commission (1995), p. 51.
3. Ibid., p. x.
4. See Lannoo (1995) for a more detailed overview.
5. In the Netherlands, a company becomes a *structuurvennootschap* when it fulfills two of the following criteria: minimum capital of 25 million guilders, at least 100 employees, and the existence of a workers' council.
6. Member states are allowed to set stricter standards for their country, but cannot prohibit banks from other member states which employ lower standards to provide services on their territory; see Lannoo (1993) for an overview of the implementation of the EU's second banking directive.
7. Who's Steering, *Central and Eastern European Review*, March 1996.
8. See Lannoo (1995), pp. 14–15.
9. See OECD (1995), pp. 60–61.

REFERENCES

Berglöf, E. (1994) Corporate Governance in Transition Economies, Brussels, mimeo.
Cadbury Report (1992) *Report of the Committee on the Financial Aspects of Corporate Governance*.
Davis, S. and K. Lannoo (1997) Shareholder Voting in Europe, in *Shareholder Value: Quantité Négligéable*, Centre for European Policy Studies, Research Report, forthcoming.
EBRD (1995) *Transition Report*.
EBRD (1996) *Transition Report*.
European Commission (1995) The Simplification of the Operating Regulations for Public Limited Companies in the EU, December.

Federation of European Stock Exchanges (FESE) (1996) European Stock Exchange Statistics, Annual Report 1995.
Fédération Internationale des Bourses de Valeurs (FIBV) (1996). Annual Report 1995.
Lannoo, K. and J. Mortensen (1993) Towards a European Financial Area: Achievements, Implementation and Remaining Hurdles, CEPS Research Report No. 13.
Lannoo, K. (1995) *Corporate Governance in Europe*, CEPS Working Party Report No. 12
OECD (1996) Corporate Governance in Transition Economies, Lessons from recent developments in OECD member countries, mimeo.
OECD (1996a) The Czech Republic, *Economic Surveys*.
OECD (1996b) Poland, *Economic Surveys*.
Peters Report (1996) Corporate Governance in Nederland: Een aanzet tot verandering en een uitnodiging tot discussie, Commissie Corporate Governance, October.
Viénot Report (1995) Le Conseil d'Administration des Sociétés Cotées, CNPF.

Abstract

In this chapter the extent of institutional share ownership in UK financial institutions has been identified, with a special emphasis on the retail banking sector. A detailed analysis of the annual reports of the UK financial sector shows that best practice in corporate governance is generally being followed. Interviews carried out with retail banks and institutional investors highlight the usefulness of one-to-one meetings between banks and their largest institutional investors. The meetings are seen as essential for maintaining a good relationship, for obtaining input and feedback on strategies, and for highlighting any concerns, for example in the corporate governance arena.

Chris Mallin, BSc PhD FCA, is Professor of Finance at Nottingham Business School, the Nottingham Trent University, and Associate Fellow of the Centre for Corporate Strategy and Change, Warwick Business School. She has published widely on corporate governance issues in both academic and professional journals, and has presented research papers at many conferences in the UK and overseas, including Australia, the USA, Norway, and Hungary.

X. The Role of Institutional Investors in the Corporate Governance of Financial Institutions: the UK Case

CHRIS MALLIN

1. INTRODUCTION

Back in the 1930s, Berle and Means (1932) highlighted the impact of the separation of ownership and control in corporations. Over sixty years later institutional investors own large portions of equity in many companies across the world, and the key role played by institutional investors in corporate governance cannot be underestimated. The Cadbury Committee (1992) viewed institutional investors as having a special responsibility to try to ensure that its recommendations were adopted by companies, stating that 'we look to the institutions in particular ... to use their influence as owners to ensure that the companies in which they have invested comply with the Code'. A similar view was expressed in the more recently published Greenbury Report (1995) as one of the main action points is 'the investor institutions should use their power and influence to ensure the implementation of best practice as set out in the Code'. Therefore the two most influential committees which have reported on corporate governance in the UK clearly emphasize the role of institutional investors. The institutional investors' potential to exert significant influence on companies has clear implications for corporate governance, especially in terms of the standards of corporate governance and issues concerned with enforcement.

This perception of the key role to be played by institutional investors is not purely a UK phenomenon. In his seminal work, Useem (1996), details the rise of 'investor capitalism' in the US and describes how the concentration of shares, and hence power, into a relatively small number of hands, has enabled institutional investors to directly challenge management on issues of concern. Similarly in the context of the Australian market, Bosch (1993) states 'institutional shareholders because of their increasing influence, by virtue of their size, should take an active interest in the governance of the Company and develop their own principles of good practice'.

This emphasis is to be expected from countries such as the US, UK, and Australia which all have a significant concentration of share ownership in the hands of institutional investors. However the Centre for European Policy Studies (CEPS) reporting in 1995, stated 'in any attempt to understand the control of corporations, the role of insurance companies, pension funds, and other institutional investors, and other actors, such as employees or banks, has to be taken into account to different extents in European countries'. The report goes on to state 'international diversification and increasing cross-border activity or institutional investors will accelerate this process. American and British pension funds, in particular, which represent about 72 per cent of total pension fund assets in the western world, can be instrumental in changing corporate governance standards as a result of the active stance towards investment that is required by local laws and codes'. There is then, it seems, a clear and unambiguous global view that institutional investors have a key role to play in corporate governance. In this paper, the role of institutional investors in corporate governance is examined, with a special emphasis on their influence in financial institutions, especially banks.

2. Institutional Investment

The structure of share ownership varies considerably across European countries. The Oslo Stock Exchange (1995) published a report on the share ownership structure in Europe which showed that 'private financial enterprises [defined as insurance companies, pension funds, banks, mortgage companies, unit trusts/collective savings schemes and investment companies] do, with one exception, own between 31 per cent and 15 per cent of the listed shares in Europe. The striking exception is London where this group, dominated by insurance companies and pension funds, owns 62 per cent'. The other European markets where private financial enterprises have significant shareholdings are Stockholm and Copenhagen, 31 per cent and 30 per cent respectively; whilst Oslo is at the other extreme with only 15 per cent. The report also highlights a trend of increasing ownership of shares by foreign investors and a decline in ownership by individual investors.

As mentioned earlier the CEPS Working Party recognized the growing influence of institutional investors and foreign investment in Europe. The aspect of foreign share ownership should not be underestimated as these 'new' investors in Europe will tend to be institutional investors from the US, the UK, and other countries. The large proportion of institutional share ownership in both the US, where over 50 per cent of US equities are owned by institutional investors and 80 per cent of all share trades are made by institutional investors, and the UK, where institutional ownership is around 65 per cent–75 per cent, mean that the voice of the institutional investor cannot go unheard. The extent of institutional ownership in the UK is now discussed in detail.

TABLE 1

Institutional Investment in the UK (summary balance sheet values, £ billion)

Year	IT	UT	LTIC	GIC	SAPF	Total
1990	20.6	46.1	234.0	42.7	303.1	646.5
1991	23.7	54.9	279.2	45.5	343.5	746.8
1992	29.9	64.2	328.0	51.8	382.1	855.9
1993	37.2	94.8	435.6	62.5	480.0	1109.2
1994	41.1	91.9	406.2	62.9	442.7	1044.8
1995	45.3	111.3	485.4	70.8	519.0	1231.8

Source: ABI Insurance Trends Jan 1997.
Note: IT = investment trusts; UT = unit trusts; LTIC = long-term insurance companies; GIC = general insurance companies; SAPF = self-administered pension funds.

The UK has a complex array of financial institutions which over the years have become major investors. From Table 1 it can be seen that the total amount of institutional investment (measured by summary balance sheet values) in the UK has risen from £646.5 billion in 1990 to £1231.8 billion in 1995, almost doubling in size over the six year period. The split between investment trusts, unit trusts, long-term insurance companies, general insurance companies and self-administered pension funds is also shown. Whilst the absolute level of investment by all categories has increased, there is a trend over time for the relative share of investment by long-term insurance companies to be increasing, whilst that of the self-administered pension funds is on the decline. Comparing the make-up of the total institutional investment in 1990 to 1995, it can be seen that investment by long-term insurance companies accounted for 36 per cent of the total in 1990 compared to over 39 per cent in 1995, whilst investment by self-administered pension funds has declined from just under 47 per cent of the total to 42 per cent over the same period.

A particularly interesting aspect is that financial institutions are often both institutional investors in other financial institutions, and, on the opposite side of the coin, are subject themselves to the influence of institutional investors who hold shares in their businesses. This could pose a possible conflict of interest and raise questions regarding competition, but what it should mean is that there are certain standards of corporate governance which are common to financial institutions – it would, for example, be difficult for an institutional investor to criticize a business' corporate governance structures as inadequate, and remain credible, if the institution's own corporate governance structures were not better than the ones which, as institutional investors, they were criticizing. In the following section the extent of institutional investor ownership in UK financial institutions is examined.

3. INSTITUTIONAL INVESTORS OWNERSHIP OF FINANCIAL INSTITUTIONS

Banks and other financial institutions are represented in the Financial Times All-Share Banking and Insurance sector index (hereafter FTAllB&I). The index comprises 8 retail banks, 7 merchant banks, 24 insurance companies, and 6 life assurance companies.

The share ownership structure of the companies in this index was examined to determine the level of institutional ownership. Raad and Ryan (1995) discuss the extent to which disclosure about shareholder composition in financial institutions should be made public. In the UK there is a legal obligation to disclose shareholdings of 3 per cent or more in the company's annual report (usually in the directors' report). However, particularly for FTSE 100 companies, institutional investors may own large shareholdings which nonetheless are less than 3 per cent of the issued share capital and hence do not have to be disclosed, or they may not be the beneficial owners in which case a 10 per cent threshold may be applied. In order to determine as much information as possible about the shareholdings, a Citywatch analysis was obtained of the shareholdings of companies in the FTALLB&I index. This analysis enables even comparatively small shareholdings to be identified; Table 2 shows the holdings of the largest institutional investors in the sector, down to holdings of 0.5 per cent of the sector as a whole (although the full analysis extends to much smaller holdings). This analysis makes clear two facts: (i) that there is significant ownership of these companies by institutional investors and (ii) the same institutional investor names appear again and again as major shareholders.

The largest institutional investor is Mercury Asset Management (MAM) which owns 3.50 per cent of the sector (defined by the FTALLB&I) and 3.96 per cent of the total UK market. Schroder Investment Management is the second largest investor in the sector with 3.01 per cent (and 2.81 per cent of the total UK market). There are four other institutional investors which each own more than 2 per cent of the sector, these are Prudential Portfolio Managers 2.87 per cent, Standard Life Investment Management 2.16 per cent, Barclays Global Investors 2.14 per cent, and Legal and General Investment Management 2.07 per cent (they own 3.05, 1.98, 1.98, and 1.89 per cent respectively of the total UK market). These are just the very largest holdings, and the table details those holdings down to 0.5 per cent of the sector; even these are quite large in monetary terms (as an example, a 0.5 per cent holding in Barclays Bank alone represents over 7.7 million £1 nominal shares). The power of these institutional

TABLE 2

Institutional Investment in UK Financial Institutions

Manager	Market	Sector
Mercury Asset Mgmt	3.96	3.50
Schroder Inv Mgmt	2.81	3.01
Prudential Port Mgrs	3.05	2.87
Standard Life Inv Mgmt	1.98	2.16
Barclays Global Investors	1.98	2.14
Legal & General Inv Mgmt	1.89	2.07
Fleming Inv Mgmt	1.03	1.32
Hill Samuel Asset Mgmt	1.34	1.32
Royal & Sun Alliance	1.28	1.31
Chase (Cust)	1.07	1.30
Hermes PF Mgmt	1.36	1.28
Threadneedle Asset Mgmt	1.14	1.22
Sepon	0.75	1.20
Gartmore Inv Mgmt	1.57	1.19
Citicorp (Cust)	0.92	1.19
Morgan Grenfell Asset Mgmt	1.20	1.16
PDFM	2.05	1.08
M&G Inv Mgmt	0.99	1.08
Foreign & Colonial	0.95	0.92
Goldman Sachs Asset Mgmt	0.87	0.91
GAIMS	0.82	0.88
Sun Life Inv Mgmt	0.74	0.82
AMP Asset Mgmt	0.75	0.80
Equitable	0.69	0.77
Britannic Assurance	0.51	0.77
Bank of Scotland (Cust)	0.68	0.75
Scottish Widows Inv Mgmt	0.85	0.75
Scottish Amicable Inv Mgrs	0.65	0.69
Tan Sri Khoo Teck Paut	0.11	0.68
Guardian Asset Mgmt	0.50	0.66
Bankers Trust (Cust)	0.70	0.63
Universities SS	0.57	0.60
Co-operative Ins Soc	0.77	0.60
FP Asset Mgmt	0.60	0.57
BP Pension Fund	0.46	0.54
British Gas PF Mgmt	0.49	0.52
Commercial Union	0.54	0.51
HSBC Asset Mgmt	0.49	0.50
Northern Trust Co (Cust)	0.37	0.50

TABLE 3

Structure of Shareholdings in UK Retail Banks

Company	5 largest shareholders %	10 largest shareholders %
Abbey National	13.12 (10.8)	21.32 (18.34)
Bank of Scotland	26.12 (5.21)	36.43 (13.91)
Barclays	22.8 (12.13)	34.28 (19.51)
HSBC (75p shares)	19.52 (11.71)	31.92 (18.63)
Lloyds TSB	13.73 (11.95)	23.77 (19.16)
National Westminster	17.09 (10.77)	26.17 (18.81)
Royal Bank of Scotland	28.73 (6.62)	37.53 (15.8)
Standard Chartered	33.86 (8.23)	46.56 (12.52)

Note: The figures in parentheses are the percentages owned by the same five/ten investors in the FTALLB&I sector as a whole.

investors clearly cannot be underestimated, and the influence which they can wield is enormous.

The analysis in Table 3 details the shareholding structure in the retail banks in the FTALLB&I.

In all of the retail banks, the five largest investors own more than 10 per cent of the shares. A few unusually large holdings deserve special mention: PDFM (11.99 per cent in Bank of Scotland), MAM (10.61 per cent in Royal Bank of Scotland) and Tan Sri Khoo Teck Paut (14.96 per cent in Standard Chartered Bank). However in the majority of the retail banks the large shareholdings are typically held by Prudential, MAM, Standard Life, Legal and General, Britannic Assurance, Norwich Union, Citicorp, Chase, Threadneedle Asset Management, Morgan Grenfell, and Fleming Investment Management.

From Table 3 it can be seen that the five/ten largest shareholders in each bank are all overweight in retail bank stocks when compared to the FTALLB&I sector as a whole. This is not surprising given the larger market capitalisation of the companies in the retail bank sector compared to the sector as a whole.

It is evident that the institutional investors can influence companies in which they invest by virtue of the size of their holdings. It is interesting to note that the large institutional investors usually belong to one of two representative bodies which act as a professional group 'voice' for their views. These two bodies are the Association of British Insurers (ABI) and the National Association of Pension Funds (NAPF). Both the ABI and the NAPF have best practice corporate governance guidelines based on the recommendations of the Cadbury and Greenbury committees, they monitor the corporate governance activities of companies and will provide advice to members. Institutional investors will generally consult ABI and/or NAPF reports on whether particular companies are complying with 'good' corporate governance practice, as well as undertaking their own research and analysis. In the following section, a detailed analysis is made of the annual reports of all the companies in the FTALLB&I sector to determine their overall level of compliance with corporate governance best practice.

4. CORPORATE GOVERNANCE STRUCTURES OF FINANCIAL INSTITUTIONS

To determine the corporate governance structures of each company, a detailed analysis was carried out of the most recent two years annual reports for all companies in the FTALLB&I index. The analysis identified whether the roles of Chair and CEO were separate; the total number of directors, split between executive and non-executive; the presence and composition of audit committees, nominations committees, and remuneration (compensation) committees; whether a separate remuneration committee report was given in the annual report; and whether 12 month service contracts were in operation. The analysis therefore covered the main points of corporate governance best practice in the UK.

The first and last of these points, relating to splitting the roles of Chair and CEO, and 12 month service contracts, are dealt with separately at this point and the structural details of key board committees are then dealt with in some detail below. In relation to the separation of the roles of Chair and CEO, all of the companies separated out these roles, although in some companies both roles did not seem to formally exist. In relation to adoption of a 12 month service contract, the majority of retail banks have moved towards this model, otherwise it has not been taken up to any great extent.

For the purposes of this paper, we will concentrate in this section on the retail banks' corporate governance structures, but provide a comparison by benchmarking their corporate governance structures with those of the merchant banks, insurance companies, and life assurance companies which also form part of the FTALLB&I index.

In Table 4 the corporate governance structures of the retail banks are analysed. It can be seen that the boards tend to be quite large: ranging from 13 to 25 directors. All of the banks have at least half and in some cases two-thirds or more, of non-executive directors amongst the total board membership. The average board size is 18, with nearly two-thirds made up of non-executive directors. All of the retail banks are also FTSE 100 companies and an interesting comparison can be drawn with the composition of FTSE 100 boards generally. Conyon and Mallin (1997) found that the average board size for all FTSE 100 companies was 12.31 with half of the board comprising non-executive directors.

TABLE 4
Retail Banks

Ref.	Company	YE	Year	Board of Directors			Audit Committee			Nominations Comm.			Remuneration Comm.			RC Report	12 mth SC
				Exec.	Non-Exec.	Total	Exec.	Non-Exec.	Total	Exec.	Non-Exec.	Total	Exec.	Non-Exec.	Total		
1	ABBEY NATIONAL	Dec	1994	7	9	16	0	4	4	N/A	N/A	N/A	0	4	4	0	?
		Dec	1995	7	8	15	0	4	4	N/A	N/A	N/A	0	3	3	1	1
2	BK OF SCOTLAND	Feb	1995	1	15	16	0	4	4	N/A	N/A	N/A	0	4	4	0	1
		Feb	1996	2	16	18	0	4	4	N/A	N/A	N/A	0	4	4	1	1
3	BARCLAYS	Dec	1994	6	8	14	0	4	4	N/A	N/A	N/A	0	5	5	0	1
		Dec	1995	7	8	15	0	4	4	0	5	5	0	5	5	1	1
4	HSBC HOLDINGS	Dec	1994	7	12	19	0	3	3	1	3	4	0	3	3	0	?
		Dec	1995	7	14	21	0	3	3	1	3	4	0	3	3	1	1
5	LLOYDS TSB GP.	Dec	1995	6	16	22	0	5	5	N/A	N/A	N/A	0	5	5	1	1
		Dec	1996	9	16	25	0	5	5	N/A	N/A	N/A	0	5	5	1	1
6	NAT. WSTM. BANK	Dec	1994	7	12	19	0	7	7	2	3	5	0	4	4	1	0
		Dec	1995	6	14	20	0	6	6	1	5	6	0	4	4	1	0
7	RYL. BK. OF SCTL.	Sept	1995	7	12	19	0	6	6	N/A	N/A	N/A	0	5	5	1	0
		Sept	1996	7	13	20	0	6	6	N/A	N/A	N/A	0	4	4	1	0
8	STD. CHARTERED	Dec	1994	7	6	13	0	3	3	N/A	N/A	N/A	0	4	4	0	?
		Dec	1995	8	8	16	0	4	4	N/A	N/A	N/A	0	4	4	1	0
Average				6.31	11.69	18.00	0.00	4.50	4.50	0.83	4.00	4.83	0.00	4.13	4.13	0.63	0.62

	Year 1	Year 2
No. of companies	8	8
No. with AC	8	8
No. with RC	8	8
No. with NC	3	3
RC Report	2	8
12 mth SC	5*	5

Boards (8)
	Year 1	Year 2
Average No. of EO	6.0	6.6
Average No. of NEO	11.3	12.1
Average Total No.	17.3	18.8

Audit Committees (8)
	Year 1	Year 2
Average No. of EO	0.0	0.0
Average No. of NEO	4.5	4.5
Average Total No.	4.5	4.5

Remuneration Committees (8)
	Year 1	Year 2
Average No. of EO	0.0	0.0
Average No. of NEO	4.3	4.0
Average Total No.	4.3	4.0

Nominations Committees (3)
	Year 1	Year 2
Average No. of EO	1.0	0.7
Average No. of NEO	3.7	4.3
Average Total No.	4.7	5.0

*Assuming Abbey National's and HSBC's SC were in place in year 1.

Clearly the boards of the retail banks are generally much larger, and have a higher proportion of non-executive directors.

As far as key board committees are concerned, all of the retail banks have adopted both an audit committee and a remuneration committee comprised totally of non-executive directors, with the average size being 4.5 and 4.13 respectively. Following the publication of the Greenbury recommendations in July 1995, all of the retail banks now publish a separate Remuneration Committee Report (prior to its publication only two of the eight produced such a report).

A less commonly adopted committee is the nominations committee which although not a requirement of the Cadbury Code, was nonetheless advocated by the Cadbury Committee 'as a means of clarifying the board appointments process'. The Cadbury compliance report (1995) found that 69 of the top 100 companies had introduced a nominations committee–the retail banking sector is therefore unfavourably out-of-line in this respect, with only 37.5 per cent having adopted a nominations committee.

A comparison with the other financial institutions in the FTALLB&I index is appropriate at this point. From Table 5 it can be seen that the merchant banks' board size ranges from 5 to 26, with an average of 13.7. In contrast to the retail banks, executive directors generally outnumber non-executive directors, often by as much as two to one. All of the merchant banks have adopted audit and remuneration committees, though in two companies even by 1996 there is still executive director representation on the audit committee and one company retains executive director representation on the remuneration committee in 1996. All produce a separate report of the remuneration committee. Only one has a nominations committee. As might be expected, given the generally smaller board size, the audit and remuneration committees tend to be slightly smaller in the merchant banks.

The general insurance companies are the largest group within the index, comprising 24 companies and including large companies such as Commercial Union, General Accident and Guardian Royal Exchange, as shown in Table 6. Board size ranges from 4 to 16, with an average of 10.6, and considerable variation in the proportions of executive and non-executive directors, with half the companies having a larger number of executives than non-executives, and half having more non-executive than executives. All companies had adopted audit and remuneration committees (Masthead being the exception for which data was not available), though a couple of companies still retained executive director representation on the audit and remuneration committees. Once more the incidence of nominations committee adoption was rather patchy, with 11 of the 24 companies having adopted such a committee, and where a nominations committee had been established, there was often executive director representation.

226   Chris Mallin

TABLE 5
Merchant Banks

Ref.	Company	YE	Year	Board of Directors			Audit Committee			Nominations Comm.			Remuneration Comm.			RC Report	12 mth SC
				Exec.	Non-Exec.	Total	Exec.	Non-Exec.	Total	Exec.	Non-Exec.	Total	Exec.	Non-Exec.	Total		
9	CATER ALLEN HDG.	Apr	1995	11	1	12	3	1	4	N/A	N/A	N/A	2	1	3	0	0
		Apr	1996	9	2	11	3	2	5	N/A	N/A	N/A	1	2	3	1	0
10	CLOSE BROTHERS	July	1995	8	4	12	0	4	4	1	2	3	0	4	4	0	0
		July	1996	8	5	13	0	5	5	1	2	3	0	5	5	1	0
11	GERRARD GROUP	Mar	1995	9	2	11	0	2	2	N/A	N/A	N/A	0	2	2	0	0
		Mar	1996	8	3	11	0	3	3	N/A	N/A	N/A	0	3	3	1	0
12	HAMBROS	Mar	1995	12	5	17	1	3	4	N/A	N/A	N/A	1	3	4	0	0
		Mar	1996	12	6	18	0	3	3	N/A	N/A	N/A	0	3	3	1	0
13	SCHRODERS	Dec	1994	8	6	14	0	4	4	N/A	N/A	N/A	2	3	5	1	0
		Dec	1995	6	6	12	0	4	4	N/A	N/A	N/A	0	3	3	1	0
14	SINGER & FRIED. GP.	Dec	1994	2	3	5	0	3	3	N/A	N/A	N/A	1	2	3	0	?
		Dec	1995	2	3	5	0	3	3	N/A	N/A	N/A	0	2	2	1	0
45	WARBURG (SG)	Mar	1994	16	10	26	1	3	4	N/A	N/A	N/A	0	8	8	0	1
		Mar	1995	13	12	25	?	?	?	N/A	N/A	N/A	0	?	?	0	1
Average (including Warburg)				8.86	4.86	13.71	0.69	3.08	3.77	1.00	2.00	3.00	0.50	3.15	3.69	0.50	0.15

	Year 1	Year 2
No. of companies	7	7
No. with AC	7	7*
No. with RC	7	7*
No. with NC	1	1
RC Report	1	6
12 mth SC	1	1

Boards (7)	Year 1	Year 2
Average No. of EO	9.4	8.3
Average No. of NEO	4.4	5.3
Average Total No.	13.9	13.6
Audit Committees (7)		
Average No. of EO*	0.7	0.7
Average No. of NEO*	2.9	3.3
Average Total No.*	3.6	4.0
Remuneration Committees (7)		
Average No. of EO	0.9	0.1
Average No. of NEO*	3.3	3.7
Average Total No.*	4.1	3.9
Nominations Committees (1)		
Average No. of EO	1.0	1.0
Average No. of NEO	2.0	2.0
Average Total No.	3.0	3.0

* Assuming committees at Warburg remain unchanged.

TABLE 6
Insurance

Ref.	Company	YE	Year	Board of Directors			Audit Committee			Nominations Comm.			Remuneration Comm.			RC Report	12 mth SC
				Exec.	Non-Exec.	Total	Exec.	Non-Exec.	Total	Exec.	Non-Exec.	Total	Exec.	Non-Exec.	Total		
15	ANGE. UNDWRT. TST.	May	1995	0	5	5	0	4	4	0	4	4	0	4	4	0	0
		May	1996	0	10	10	0	3	3	0	?	?	0	?	?	0	0
16	BRADSTOCK GROUP	Sept	1995	6	2	8	1	2	3	N/A	N/A	N/A	1	2	3	0	0
		Sept	1996	7	2	9	1	2	3	N/A	N/A	N/A	1	2	3	1	0
17	CLM IN. FUND	Dec	1994	1	8	9	0	3	3	N/A	N/A	N/A	0	8	8	0	0
		Dec	1995	1	8	9	0	3	3	N/A	N/A	N/A	0	8	8	1	0
18	COMMERCIAL UNION	Dec	1994	4	7	11	0	4	4	N/A	N/A	N/A	0	4	4	0	0
		Dec	1995	4	6	10	0	5	5	2	3	5	0	4	4	1	0
19	DOMESTIC & GENERAL G	Jun	1995	6	3	9	1	3	4	2	3	5	1	3	4	0	0
		Jun	1996	6	3	9	1	3	4	N/A	N/A	N/A	0	3	3	0	1
20	FENCHURCH	Sept	1995	8	3	11	0	3	3	N/A	N/A	N/A	0	3	3	1	1
		Sept	1996	8	3	11	0	3	3	N/A	N/A	N/A	0	3	3	1	1
21	GENERAL ACCIDENT	Dec	1994	4	12	16	0	4	4	1	5	6	0	6	6	0	0
		Dec	1995	2	10	12	0	4	4	—	5	5	0	6	6	1	0
22	GUARDIAN RYL. EX.	Dec	1994	5	9	14	0	3	3	0	4	4	0	4	4	0	1
		Dec	1995	6	9	15	0	4	4	0	5	5	0	5	5	1	—
23	HEATH (CE)	Mar	1995	8	4	12	0	4	4	1	4	5	0	4	4	0	?
		Mar	1996	8	4	12	0	4	4	—	3	4	0	4	4	1	0
24	INDE. INSURANCE GP.	Dec	1994	4	5	9	0	3	3	0	5	5	0	2	2	0	0
		Dec	1995	4	7	11	0	4	4	0	7	7	0	3	3	1	?
25	JIB GROUP	Dec	1994	8	6	14	0	6	6	N/A	N/A	N/A	0	3	3	0	?
		Dec	1995	8	6	14	0	6	6	N/A	N/A	N/A	0	3	3	0	?
26	JARDINE LLOYD THOMP.	Jun	1995	6	1	7	1	1	2	N/A	N/A	N/A	2	1	3	0	?
		Jun	1996	5	2	7	0	2	2	N/A	N/A	N/A	0	2	2	0	1
27	LONDON INS. MKTS.	Mar	1995	4	3	7	0	3	3	2	3	5	1	3	4	0	0
		Mar	1996	3	4	7	0	3	3	—	4	5	0	4	4	1	0
28	LOWNDES LAMBERT	Mar	1995	11	5	16	1	2	3	N/A	N/A	N/A	1	2	3	0	0
		Mar	1996	10	4	14	0	3	3	N/A	N/A	N/A	0	2	2	1	0
29	MASTHEAD	Dec	1994	0	5	5	N/A	N/A	N/A	N/A	N/A	N/A	N/A	N/A	N/A	0	0
		Dec	1995	0	5	5	N/A	N/A	N/A	N/A	N/A	N/A	N/A	N/A	N/A	0	0

TABLE 6 (Continued)

Ref.	Company	YE	Year	Board of Directors			Audit Committee			Nominations Comm.			Remuneration Comm.			RC Report	12 mth SC
				Exec.	Non-Exec.	Total	Exec.	Non-Exec.	Total	Exec.	Non-Exec.	Total	Exec.	Non-Exec.	Total		
30	NELSON HURST	Dec	1994	6	4	10	0	3	3	N/A	N/A	N/A	1	3	4	0	0
		Dec	1995	5	4	9	0	4	4	N/A	N/A	N/A	0	4	4	1	0
31	NEW LONDON CAP.	Mar	1995	0	5	5	0	5	5	N/A	N/A	N/A	0	5	5	0	?
		Mar	1996	0	5	5	0	3	3	N/A	N/A	N/A	?	?	?	0	?
32	ROYAL IN. HDG. (DEAD)	Dec	1994	5	8	13	0	4	4	0	3	3	0	3	3	0	0
		Dec	1995	5	6	11	0	3	3	0	4	4	0	4	4	0	0
33	SEDGWICK GROUP	Dec	1994	7	4	11	0	4	4	2	1	3	0	4	4	0	1
		Dec	1995	6	5	11	0	4	4	2	1	3	0	4	4	1	1
34	STEEL BURRILL	Dec	1994	10	3	13	1	2	3	N/A	N/A	N/A	1	2	3	0	?
		Dec	1995	5	4	9	0	3	3	N/A	N/A	N/A	0	3	3	1	1
35	SUN ALLIANCE (DEAD)	Dec	1994	6	9	15	0	4	4	N/A	N/A	N/A	0	4	4	0	?
		Dec	1995	6	9	15	0	3	3	N/A	N/A	N/A	0	4	4	1	?
36	SYNDICATE CAP. TST.	Jun	1995	0	4	4	0	4	4	0	4	4	N/A	N/A	N/A	0	0
		Jun	1996	1	4	5	0	4	4	1	4	5	0	4	4	1	1
37	WILLIS CORROON	Dec	1994	7	5	12	5	3	8	0	5	5	0	4	4	1	1
		Dec	1995	6	5	11	5	3	8	0	5	5	0	4	4	0	1
44	TRADE INDEMNITY	Dec	1994	4	7	11	0	3	3	N/A	N/A	N/A	0	2	2	0	1
		Dec	1995	3	7	10	0	3	3	N/A	N/A	N/A	0	3	3	0	1
Average (including Trade Indemnity)				4.98	5.63	10.61	0.37	3.39	3.76	0.73	3.90	4.67	0.20	3.52	3.73	0.41	0.32

	Year 1	Year 2
Boards (24)		
Average No. of EO	5.0	4.5
Average No. of NEO	5.3	5.5
Average Total No.	10.3	10.0
Audit Committees (23)		
Average No. of EO	0.4	0.3
Average No. of NEO	3.3	3.4
Average Total No.	3.8	3.7

	Year 1	Year 2
Remuneration Committees (6)		
Average No. of EO	0.4	0.3
Average No. of NEO	1.9	2.0
Average Total No.	2.2	2.3
Nominations Committees (11)		
Average No. of EO	0.7	0.1
Average No. of NEO	6.9	7.2
Average Total No.	7.6	7.3

	Year 1	Year 2
No. of companies	24	24
No. with AC	23	23
No. with RC	22	23
No. with NC	11	11
RC Report	0	19
12 mth SC*	7	7

*Assuming entries marked ? were as year before (or after).

The life assurance companies' corporate governance structures are analysed in Table 7. This group includes some of the largest institutional investors in the UK: Prudential, Legal and General, and Britannic Assurance. Board sizes are generally smaller ranging from 6 to 13, with an average of 9. In general non-executive directors tend to be in the same proportion as executive directors. Audit and remuneration committees have been adopted by all companies and, without exception, are comprised solely of non-executive directors. All of the life assurance companies have adopted a nominations committee, with varying proportions of executive and non-executive director representation. The life assurance group has therefore complied with more of the Cadbury prescripts than any of the other groups within the FTALLB&I index.

The clear leaders in terms of adoption of key board committees are therefore the life assurance companies, whilst the retail banks stand out as having the highest proportion of non-executive to executive directors. Many companies which have not adopted a separate nominations committee seem to roll this up with the remuneration committee function, in such cases the company has not been shown as having a separate nominations committee.

5. INSTITUTIONAL INVESTORS' RELATIONSHIP WITH COMPANIES IN WHICH THEY INVEST

Given the size of their shareholdings the power of the institutional investors cannot be doubted. In his seminal work, Hirschman (1970) identified the exercise of institutional power within an 'exit and voice' framework, arguing that 'dissatisfaction [may be expressed] directly to management', the *voice* option, or by selling the shareholding, the *exit* option. The latter choice is not viable for many institutional investors given the size of their holdings or a policy of holding a balanced portfolio. The meetings between institutional investors and companies are therefore extremely important as a means of communication between the two parties.

In the previous section we saw that, in general, the companies in the FTALLB&I sector are complying well with corporate governance best practice, with life assurance companies being leaders in terms of adoption of key board committees, and the retail banks having the highest proportions of non-executive to executive directors. In this section the results of interviews carried out with a number of financial institutions (to date three large retail banks and two institutional investors) are reported, and in particular the ways in which institutional investors are perceived to influence retail banks are noted. In addition, the author is able to draw on the findings of her earlier research on institutional investors (Mallin 1994, 1996).

TABLE 7

Life Assurance

Ref.	Company	YE	Year	Board of Directors			Audit Committee			Nominations Comm.			Remuneration Comm.			RC Report	12 mth SC
				Exec.	Non-Exec.	Total	Exec.	Non-Exec.	Total	Exec.	Non-Exec.	Total	Exec.	Non-Exec.	Total		
38	BRITANNIC ASSURANCE	Dec	1994	3	3	6	0	3	3	0	3	3	0	3	3	0	0
		Dec	1995	3	3	6	0	3	3	0	3	3	0	3	3	1	0
39	LEGAL & GENERAL	Dec	1994	3	7	10	0	3	3	0	7	7	0	7	7	0	0
		Dec	1995	5	8	13	0	3	3	0	3	3	0	8	8	1	0
40	LDN. & MANC. GP.	Dec	1994	4	5	9	0	4	4	1	2	3	0	5	5	0	0
		Dec	1995	4	4	8	0	3	3	1	2	3	0	4	4	1	0
41	PRUDENTIAL CORP.	Dec	1994	6	7	13	0	4	4	0	3	3	0	4	4	0	0
		Dec	1995	6	6	12	0	4	4	0	2	2	0	5	5	1	0
42	UNITED ASSURANCE GP	Dec	1994	5	4	9	0	4	4	N/A	N/A	N/A	0	4	4	0	0
		Dec	1995	5	4	9	0	4	4	N/A	N/A	N/A	0	4	4	1	0
43	UTD. FRIENDLY GP	Dec	1994	4	4	8	0	3	3	4	4	8	0	4	4	0	0
		Dec	1995	3	3	6	0	3	3	3	3	6	0	3	3	1	0
Average				4.25	4.83	9.08	0.00	3.42	3.42	0.91	2.91	3.82	0.00	4.50	4.50	0.50	0.00

	Year 1	Year 2
No. of companies	6	6
No. with AC	6	6
No. with RC	6	6
No. with NC	5	6
RC Report	0	6
12 mth SC	0	0

	Year 1	Year 2
Boards (6)		
Average No. of EO	4.2	4.3
Average No. of NEO	5.0	4.7
Average Total No.	9.2	9.0
Audit Committees (6)		
Average No. of EO	0.0	0.0
Average No. of NEO	3.5	3.3
Average Total No.	3.5	3.3
Remuneration Committees (6)		
Average No. of EO	0.0	0.0
Average No. of NEO	4.5	4.5
Average Total No.	4.5	4.5
Nominations Committees (5/6)		
Average No. of EO	1.0	2.0
Average No. of NEO	3.8	3.4
Average Total No.	4.8	5.4

The interviews were face-to face and lasted between an hour and an hour and a half. The areas discussed centred around the relationship between the board and institutional investors and the influence exerted by the institutional investors, particularly in corporate governance matters; and how active the institutional investors are in terms of attanding annual general meetings (AGMs) and voting.

The interviews with the banks showed that the banks have a close relationship with their institutional investors in terms of monitoring very closely the shareholdings of their institutional investors, and in particular identifying any institutional investors who may be underweight in their shares compared to other banks, or who may be starting to sell their shares in the bank. Meetings would then be arranged with the institutional investor identified to try to ascertain why the institutional investor was underweight in the shares, or why they were selling. Shares may be held in nominee account names in which case the bank can pursue a Sec 212 enquiry which helps them to identify the names behind the nominee account.

The banks may draw up their meeting programs at the start of the year, planning to meet with institutional investors on a one-to-one basis during the course of the year (this may amount to 100 or more one-to-one meetings). The meetings tend to be at the highest level and usually involve individual key members of the board in a meeting once, or maybe twice, a week. Their 'target' institutional investor audience would include large shareholders (say the top 30) and brokers' analysts (say the top 10), and any investors who are underweight or selling their shares. In addition, they would tend to ring up an institutional investor if they hadn't seen them in the last year to eighteen months. Meetings are often followed up with 'phone calls by the bank to the institutional investor to ensure that everything has been discussed.

The issues which are most discussed at these meetings between banks and their large institutional investors are areas of the bank's strategy and how the bank is planning to achieve its objectives, whether objectives are being met, the quality of the management, etc. Institutional investors are seen as 'important for the way the business is managed', and their views may be fed back to the board in the planning process, and incorporated, as appropriate, in an annual strategy paper. They are seen as having a collective infuence, with management paying most attention to the commonality of institutional investors' views in meetings over time. The banks want to try to ensure that institutional investors understand the business and its strategy so that the value of the business is fully recognized.

Several of the institutional investors have terms of reference which incorporate corporate governance aspects, or have issued separate corporate governance guidelines. These guidelines are generally based around the Cadbury and Greenbury recommendations, and further guidance that may have been issued by the NAPF or ABI (particularly for the performance criteria for executive share option schemes). Companies would try to ensure that they met these guidelines.

Institutional investors and analysts are invited to a results presentation day (generally twice a year) for the interim and final results, and tend not to attend the AGM; partly because they already know what will be said at the AGM but also because AGMs have unfortunately become a target for disruptive shareholder agitation by a minority of shareholders. The institutional investors can register their views by postal voting, and most of the large institutional investors now have a policy of trying to vote on all issues which may be raised at their investee company's AGM. Some may vote directly on all resolutions, others may appoint a proxy (which may be a board member). Generally an institutional investor will try to sort out any contentious issues with management 'behind the scenes', however if this fails, then they may abstain from voting on a particular issue (rather than voting with incumbent management as they generally would) or they may actually vote against a resolution. In this case they would generally inform the bank of their intention to vote against. It tends to be corporate governance issues which are the most contentious, particularly directors' remuneration and length of contracts.

From the interviews a general consensus emerged that institutional investors act as a beneficial and healthy infuence and keep the banks 'on their toes'. It is seen as a 'must do' to communicate about the business and as long as the bank is performing well, the institutional investors will give them a relatively easy time – however the banks are fully aware that any decline in performance, any inconsistent strategy, or any major problems in the corporate governance arena will lead the institutional investors to act quickly and firmly.

6. Conclusions

In this paper the extent of institutional share ownership in UK financial institutions has been identified. We have seen how emphasis has been placed on the role of institutional investors in corporate governance in a global context. A detailed analysis of the annual reports of the UK financial sector has shown that best practice in corporate governance is generally being followed, with most companies having established audit and remuneration committees, although the incidence of nominations committees is still lower than might be desired. The life assurance companies have the highest adoption of key board committees, whilst the retail bank sector has the highest proportion of non-executive directors.

Interviews carried out with retail banks and institutional investors highlight the usefulness of one-to-one meetings between banks and their largest institutional investors. The meetings are seen as essential for maintaining a good relationship, for obtaining input/feedback on strategies, and for highlighting any concerns, for example in the corporate governance arena.

Acknowledgements

I would like to express my thanks to the individuals representing the financial institutions who took part in the interviews, and to Graham Sadler for his help with data collection.

References

Association of British Insurers (1997) *Insurance Trends*, January 1997, ABI, London.
Berle A. A. and G. C. Means (1932) *The Modern Corporation and Private Property*, MaxMillan, New York.
Bosch H. (1993) *Corporate Practices and Conduct*, Business Council of Australia, Melbourne.
Cadbury Sir Adrian (1992) *Report of the Committee on the Financial Aspects of Corporate Governance*, Gee & Co. Ltd, London.
Cadbury Sir Adrian (1995) *Report of the Committee on the Financial Aspects of Corporate Governance: Compliance with the Code of Best Practice*, Gee & Co. Ltd, London.
Centre for European Policy Studies (1995) *Corporate Governance in Europe*, Brussels.
Conyon M. J. and C. A. Mallin (1997) 'A Review of Compliance with Cadbury', forthcoming *Journal of General Management*, March 1997.
Greenbury, Sir Richard (1995) *Directors' Remuneration*, Gee & Co. Ltd, London.
Hirschman A. (1972) *Exit, Voice, and Loyalty: Responses to Decline in Firms, Organizations, and States*, Harvard University Press, Harvard, M.A.
Mallin C. A. (1994) *The Role of Institutional Investors in Corporate Governance*, ICAEW Research Board Monograph, Institute of Chartered Accountants in England & Wales, London.
Mallin C. A. (1996) 'The Voting Framework: A Comparative Study of Voting Behaviour of Institutional Investors in the US and the UK', *Corporate Governance: An International Review*, Vol. 4, No.2, April 1996.
Oslo Stock Exchange (1995) *Share Ownership Structure in Europe*, Federation of European Stock Exchanges, Oslo.
Raad E. and R. Ryan (1995) 'Capital Structure and Ownership Distribution of Tender Offer Targets: an Empirical Study', *Financial Management*, Vol. 24, Issue 1.
Sametz A. (1995) 'An Expanded Role for Private Institutions in US Corporate Governance', *BankAmerica Journal of Applied Corporate Finance*, Vol. 8, No.2.
Useem M. (1996) *Investor Capitalism – How Money Managers Are Changing the Face of Corporate America*, BasicBooks, Harper Collins Publishers Inc., New York.

ABSTRACT

The paper is an overview of the interrelation between corporate governance, competition and performance. Traditional theories of the firm emphasize the importance of managerial incentives and disciplining in corporate governance. There has also been much discussion of how institutional arrangements affect the financing of firms. The paper argues that incentives, disciplining and corporate finance are not the fundamental distinguishing features of different financial systems. Instead, ownership and control emerge as displaying more substantial variations across countries. These differences are associated with the formulation, implementation and adaptation of corporate strategy. The insider systems of Continental Europe and Japan may be superior at implementing policies which involve relations with stakeholders. Outsider, Anglo-American, systems may be more responsive to change. Ownership and control structures are interrelated with competition in product markets: concentration of ownership may be required to establish relations between stakeholders and may impede product market competition.

Colin Mayer is Professor of Management Studies and Deputy Director (Academic) of the School of Management Studies at the University of Oxford.

XI. Corporate Governance, Competition and Performance*

COLIN MAYER

INTRODUCTION

Corporate governance has become a subject of active academic and policy debate throughout the world. In the UK and US, there is much discussion of the deficiencies of the market system in delivering effective governance. In continental Europe, there is a concern that existing systems of governance are stifling innovation and growth. In Eastern Europe, privatization has given way to questions about the way in which private enterprises should be governed. China is experimenting with forms of corporate governance which attempt to blend some of the features of market systems with state ownership of enterprises.

Despite the intense debate, evidence on the effects of different governance systems is still sparse. Corporate governance has become a subject on which opinion has drowned fact. The purpose of this paper is to review what is known about the relation of corporate governance and corporate performance.

Policy formulation would be most readily assisted by evidence on the direct relation between governance and performance. The equivalent of a reduced form relation which identifies the effect of changing governance on performance is what is generally regarded as the bottom line of the governance debate. However, such a relation is extremely difficult to uncover. The range of factors which bear on cross-firm or cross-country variations in performance is considerable. This does not stop many from equating differences in economic performance between, for example, Germany and the UK to their different forms of corporate governance. Indeed, the origins of the long-standing debate on governance can be attributed to associations of this sort.

What is more realistic than trying to provide a 'macro' answer is to consider the way in which governance can bear on performance. There are five channels

---

* This paper was originally written for the Economics Department of the OECD as part of its study of product market competition and is to be published in OECD Economic Studies. I am very grateful to Simon Deakin, Jorgen Elmeskov, Rauf Gonenc, Alan Hughes, Nick Vanston and two anonymous referees for helpful comments on earlier versions of this paper. The author is solely responsible for any errors.

through which such a relation might emerge – incentives, disciplining, restructuring, finance/investment, and commitment/trust. This paper will consider the evidence on the influence of corporate governance on each of these in turn. It will draw on the academic literature available on corporate governance systems in several different countries.

A particular focus with which this analysis is concerned is the interaction between competition, governance and performance. The interaction is important for several reasons. Firstly, the effectiveness of different types of governance systems may be influenced by the degree of product market competition. For example, competition in product markets may be particularly needed to encourage good corporate performance where there is limited competition in capital markets for the ownership of firms.

Secondly, forms of corporate governance may be affected by degrees of product market competition. It has been suggested (see Mayer, 1988; Petersen and Rajan, 1995) that competition in financial markets may undermine the ability of firms and financial institutions to establish long-term relations. Attempts therefore to extend competition, through for example deregulation of markets, may have significant effects on the way in which corporate governance functions.

The view that there are important interactions between governance and competition leads to the systems approach to governance as advanced most forcibly by Aoki (1994a). According to this, the governance of companies must be considered in the context of the overall structure of economies. Differences across countries in the structure of capital markets, labour markets and product markets are all closely interlinked. "The main bank system and the imperfect labour market situations do not exist independently, but together form a cluster of complementary institutions" (Aoki, 1994b, p. 19). It is not therefore possible to consider significant changes in one independent of the others. In particular, policies which promote the adoption of specific forms of governance have to take account of the product and labour markets context within which they are being contemplated.

This is not unrelated to the view that proposals to alter corporate governance systems ignore the cultural context within which such systems have emerged. The advantage of Aoki's approach is that it allows analysis to be performed of the interactions between different parts of an economy. The drawback of the cultural assertions is that they are difficult to formulate in a precise way.

The paper begins by providing a framework for the analysis. It discusses the meaning of corporate governance and its relation to the structure of firms. It identifies the criteria by which the performance of governance systems should be judged.

It then discusses the first way in which differences in corporate governance systems may manifest themselves, namely in regard to managerial incentives.

It presents evidence on the relation of different forms of governance to incentives. The following section examines the role of governance systems in disciplining management and restructuring poorly performing companies. Disillusionment with forms of governance rapidly emerges when they fail to restructure or save ailing companies.

Next, the paper considers finance and investment. Do different governance systems elicit different levels of investment and forms in which investment is undertaken? The paper then turns to the relation between corporate governance, commitment and trust. The role of stakeholders (such as creditors, suppliers, purchasers and employees) in addition to shareholders in corporate policy has been the subject of much recent discussion.

The paper then discusses the relation between the structure of product markets and governance. As noted above, competition may affect and be affected by governance systems. In considering policy towards corporate governance, the influence of competition is a particularly important element. The last section concludes and summarizes the paper.

A FRAMEWORK

Corporate governance has been traditionally associated with a principal–agent relationship problem. Investors (the principals) employ managers (the agents) to run firms on their behalf. The interests and objectives of investors and managers differ. Corporate governance is concerned with ways of bringing the interests of the two parties into line and ensuring that firms are run for the benefit of investors. For example, Demb and Neubauer (1992) state that "corporate governance is a question of performance accountability".

The exercise of corporate governance is frequently associated with the structure and function of boards of companies. There has been much discussion of the role of non-executives, separate chairmen and chief executives, and remuneration, audit and nominating committees. The fiduciary duties of directors in representing the interests of shareholders has received much emphasis.

The role of shareholders in exercising good governance has also been a theme. Institutional investors, which are the largest group of shareholders in the UK and have a substantial presence in the US, have been exhorted to play a more active role in the monitoring and control of firms. It has been suggested that the duties of investors in overseeing the functioning of companies extends beyond that of their own financial interests to the stewardship of firms. According to this view, large shareholders have an implicit obligation to other shareholders in ensuring that firms are run in the interests of all shareholders.

Recently the debate has been extended to the notion that firms have responsibilities to parties other than shareholders. At one level, it has been proposed that it is in the interests of shareholders to take account of a broader constituency including employees, suppliers and purchasers from the firm. This view regards the development of long-term relations, trust and commitment as part of the successful development of firms. The best firms, according to this line of argument, are the ones with committed suppliers, customers and employees.

However, there is a broader concept that firms should not simply be run in the interests of their shareholders. They have responsibilities to other stakeholders which may on occasion conflict with their objective of wealth maximization for shareholders. This line of argument sees the firm as an entity which is distinct from its shareholders, where ownership and control is spread amongst a number of parties. Kester (1992), for example, states that "the central problem of governance is to devise specialized systems of incentives, safeguards, and dispute resolution processes that will promote the continuity of business relationships that are efficient in the presence of self-interested opportunism".

The criteria by which performance is judged differ between the two concepts of the firm. According to the shareholder model, the objective of the firm is to maximize its market value through allocative, productive and dynamic efficiency. According to the stakeholder approach, performance is judged by a wider constituency interested in employment, market share and growth in trading relations with suppliers and purchasers as well as financial performance.

Differences in participation in corporate control in large part reflect different patterns of ownership. In the UK and US, ownership is primarily associated with institutional investors. Individual ownership is greater in the US than in the UK. In both countries, the control of firms is dominated by institutional investors – they are generally regarded as the marginal investor. However, that is not true of most countries. As will be discussed further below, ownership in most countries is in the hands of either other corporations or individual investors. Cross-ownership of shares by one firm in another is commonplace and large family holdings frequently dominate institutional investments. This gives rise to a system of ownership which has been described as an 'insider system' (Franks and Mayer, 1994) to distinguish it from the 'outsider system' of the UK and US where ownership and control rests with outside, usually institutional, investors.[1] Inter-corporate shareholdings often give rise to associated positions on the boards of firms. The principal–agent view of corporate governance does not make sense in the context of corporate systems in which companies are owned and controlled by each other. Instead, as Kester suggests, firms are more appropriately viewed as coordination devices for aligning self-interest with the collective good of several parties.

Ownership and the structure of boards affect the way in which companies are managed and controlled. There are a number of forms which these differences can take. Firstly, the flow of information to investors may differ. Closer relations between investors in companies on continental Europe and in Japan may encourage better informed investors. For example, it is frequently suggested that investors in Germany derive information from their positions on supervisory boards. However, critics point to such obvious failures as Metallgesellschaft as evidence that information flows in the German system can be seriously deficient.[2]

Secondly, investors in different countries may have different incentives to intervene. Dispersed shareholdings in the UK and US systems of corporate governance may provide insufficient incentives for any one investor to monitor and control the performance of firms. Where there are large dominant shareholders, the returns to active governance are greater.

Thirdly, markets for corporate control, in particular hostile takeovers, are less active in most countries than in the UK and US. The market for corporate control is regarded as an important discipline on the behaviour of firms.

These differences in monitoring and control will manifest themselves in several ways. Firstly, according to the principal–agent models of the firm, incentives are a key determinant of performance. Incentive systems are a function of information asymmetries between investors and managers, the relative degree of risk aversion of investors and managers and the influence of incentives on the productivity of managers. If patterns of ownership differ significantly across countries then the information available to investors and the degree of risk sharing between investors and managers may vary. For example, where there are large dominant shareholders then they may be better informed but less able to spread risks than small dispersed shareholders. They may therefore impose high powered incentives on managers which are more directly related to the performance of firms.

Secondly, in addition to carrots, principal–agent models emphasize sticks in bringing the objectives of managers into line with those of investors. Where there are concentrated shareholders then there may be a greater willingness to discipline poorly performing management; there is more incentive to intervene and exercise 'voice' rather than 'exit'. On the other hand, long-term relations may make it hard to take action where investors reputations may suffer as a consequence of attempts to dismiss management. In addition, there may be some substitution between carrots and sticks: systems which encourage the use of high powered incentives schemes may not require such strong sticks.

This is particularly related to the restructuring of poorly performing firms. The role of financial institutions in financing failing companies is regarded as a particularly important distinction between different countries' governance systems. The role of Japanese banks in restructuring poorly performing firms is thought to be an important feature of the country's financial system. In the UK and US, it is sometimes asserted that financial institutions (banks, pension funds and life assurance companies) intervene too late in corporate restructurings. There may be difficulties in organizing restructurings and orderly bankruptcy procedures where there are multiple creditors and incentives for creditors to withdraw finance at the earliest opportunity.

Thirdly, governance systems may differ in the incentives which they provide for finance and investment. Continental European and Japanese systems are thought to be characterized by long-term relations which encourage long-term, primarily bank, finance. On the other hand, the UK and US are regarded as benefiting from high levels of equity risk capital.

In summary, the above suggests a relationship between different patterns of ownership, board representation and forms of monitoring and control which manifest themselves in different types of incentives, disciplining, restructuring of firms, finance and investment.

These relations are affected by the legal and regulatory framework within which companies operate. Regulation impinges on ownership through, for example, stock exchange rules regarding the ability of firms to issue dual class shares, takeover codes which require firms to make full tender offers once they have acquired more than a certain percentage of the shares of a firm, and banking laws on the separation of commercial and investment banking which limit bank equity holdings. Legal forms of companies lay down rules regarding the issuance and transferance of shares, the composition and size of boards, and the duties and responsibilities of board members. Bankruptcy codes influence the claims and control of different investors in the event of insolvency.

Regulation is therefore a crucial influence on governance structures. However, regulation is also a product of different governance systems. More market oriented financial systems systems require greater disclosure of information and insider trading rules to promote liquidity. Takeover codes are introduced to protect minority shareholders. Bankruptcy rules may be more debtor oriented in systems which otherwise provide little protection for wider stakeholder interests, such as those of employees. Regulation is therefore a reflection, as well as a cause, of different governance systems.

INCENTIVES

The first potential effect of governance which will be considered is on incentives. Principal–agent models suggest that to align interests of shareholders and managers, there should be a close relation between executive remuneration and corporate performance measured in particular by the value of a firm. Empirical analysis of the relation between executive pay and corporate performance has a long history. Much of this work has focused on the relative importance of shareholder returns and size of company on managerial remuneration (see Murphy (1985) and the survey by Rosen (1992) in the US and by Conyon, Gregg and Machin (1995) in the UK). These analyses find a weak relation between pay and performance (a $3.25 increase in CEO wealth for every $1000 increase in shareholder wealth according to Jensen and Murphy (1990)) and a stronger relation with the size of the firm.

These results were instrumental in promoting the view that management will be more concerned with the growth than the profitability of firms. However, more recent work has suggested the observed relations between pay and performance may not be out of line with those predicted by principal–agent models. Haubrich (1994) demonstrates that a $10 increase in remuneration for every $1000 increase in shareholder value is quite consistent with certain parameter values regarding risk aversion, effort-leisure trade-offs, etc. Similarly Garen (1994) argues that the Jensen and Murphy results cannot be viewed as inconsistent with the principal–agent theory.

Over the last few years there has been a substantial increase in the use of options as a form of executive remuneration. Options are a method of 'gearing up' the relation between remuneration and performance. Since executive remuneration only rises above the exercise price, powerful relations between pay and performance can be established for given levels of expected remuneration. However, remuneration is also then more directly related to volatility of performance than with share schemes (Main, 1995) since executives do not lose from declines in share prices to the extent that they gain from increases. As a consequence, executives may be encouraged to pursue unduly risky strategies to activate their share options. In addition, option contracts present serious problems of self-dealing by which managers sign contracts from which they anticipate earning substantial returns. For example, Yermack (1995) reports that managers receive stock options shortly before shares appreciate in value.

There has been little analysis of the influence of governance arrangements, in particular board structures, on executive pay. Conyon (1994) finds that the incidence of remuneration committees has increased appreciably in the UK. In a longitudinal analysis of 214 large UK companies, he finds that there were remuneration committees in 94 per cent of companies in 1993 as against 54 per cent in 1988. He estimates that these committees have been associated with a 2 per cent reduction in CEOs' pay. However, Main and Johnston (1993) find that remuneration committees are associated with higher levels of remuneration, of the order of 17 per cent, and remuneration was no more incentive oriented with than without a committee.

It has been suggested that outside of the UK and US, managers are more concerned about the growth than the profitability of firms (see, for example, Blinder (1991)). Milgrom and Roberts (1992) argue that "Japanese firms are not run in the interests of their shareholders" (p. 443). Similar points have been made about Germany (see, for example, Schneider-Lenne (1994)). On the other hand, Grundfest (1990), Hoshi, Kashyap and Scharfstein (1990, 1991) and

Prowse (1990) argue that close relationships reduce agency costs in Japan and allow investors to monitor management more effectively than in the US.

Kaplan (1994) compares the relation between executive remuneration (salary and bonus) and performance as measured by earnings levels, changes in earnings and sales growth in large Japanese and US companies in the 1980s. Kaplan concludes that Japanese "compensation respond to all four performance measures, and the responses are generally similar to those in the United States....Cash compensation is positively related to earnings, stock and sales performance. In most cases, the sensitivities in the two countries are not statistically different." (p. 512)

The relation between corporate governance and executive remuneration is therefore unclear. Superficially, the stock market economies of the UK and US offer the opportunity of providing higher powered incentives in the form of, for example, managerial stock options. Close monitoring and well functioning remuneration committees should promote stronger relations between pay and performance in Germany and Japan. Alternatively, they may reduce the need for performance related incentive contracts. But thus far empirical evidence to support these propositions has not been forthcoming.

Disciplining and the Restructuring of Poorly Performing Firms

The Role of Boards

The exercise of corporate governance is often associated with the replacement of poorly performing management. Several studies report an association of board turnover with poor corporate performance in the US (Coughlan and Schmidt, 1985; Warner, Watts and Wruck, 1988). Weisbach (1988) was one of the first studies to report an association of board turnover, firm performance and the presence of outside directors. Fama (1980) argues that "the viability of the board as a market-induced mechanism for low-cost internal transfer of control might be enhanced by the inclusion of outside directors" (pp. 293–294). Echoing this view, the Cadbury Committee (1992) in the UK has argued for more non-executive director representation on the boards of firms and the separation of the role of chairman and chief executive. Consistent with this, Weisbach finds that "performance measures are more highly correlated with CEO turnover for firms in which outsiders dominate the boards of directors than for firms in which insiders dominate. Outsider-dominated boards tend to add to firm value through CEO changes" (p. 458).[3]

In the UK, Franks, Mayer and Renneboog (1995) also find a relation between board turnover and firm performance and "there is more board turnover in poorly performing companies where there is a high proportion of non-executive directors and where there is separation of chairman and chief executive officers" (p. 1).

The Role of Large Share Stakes

Board composition therefore appears to be an important influence on the exercise of corporate governance. However, a number of additional factors have been suggested. Dating back to the work of Berle and Means (1932) it has been appreciated that there is a potential free-rider problem of corporate control. In the presence of dispersed shareholders, there is little incentive on any one shareholder to exercise corporate control. Exit is in general cheaper than intervention and the revelation of an intervention may convey more unexpected bad news to the stock market about the performance of the firm than good news about the prospect of a recovery thereby depressing the value of the holdings of the active investor. Furthermore, there may be significant impediments to coalition formation amongst shareholders (Black and Coffee, 1993): institutions which are underweight in a particular stock may be made worse off relative to their competitors by a successful reorganization. Where their performance is measured relative to their competitors, they may therefore oppose value enhancing restructurings.

Avoidance of the free rider problem of corporate control may require the presence of large shareholders. Shleifer and Vishny (1986) provide a theoretical demonstration that concentrated shareholdings can mitigate free rider problems of corporate control. Franks, Mayer and Renneboog (1995) examine the relation between board turnover in a sample of poorly performing firms in the UK and concentrations of shareholdings. They find that there is "a strong relation between board turnover and concentration of share ownership in the sample of poorly performing companies" (p. 1).

Morck, Shleifer and Vishny (1988), McConnell and Servaes (1990) and Wruck (1989) examine the relation between ownership concentration and corporate performance in the US. They find that corporate performance as measured by Tobin's Q (the ratio of the market value to replacement cost of a firm) initially rises with low levels of concentration of ownership (for example, up to 5 per cent in Morck, Shleifer and Vishny's study) and then declines. A possible explanation for the subsequent decline has been given by Shleifer and Vishny (1995) who suggest that there may be significant disadvantages as well as advantages to concentrated shareholdings. "The fundamental problem is that the concentrated owners represent their own interests, which need not coincide with the interests of other investors in the firm, or with the interests of employees and managers. In the process of using his control rights to maximize his welfare, the concentrated owner can therefore redistribute wealth – in both efficient and inefficient ways – from others" (p. 31).

Franks, Mayer and Renneboog (1995) provide support for this view. They find that, in the UK, the nature as well as the size of shareholdings is important in determining how corporate control is exercised. Large corporate investors exercise more control than institutional investors and those with private benefits of control, such as directors, appear to impede the exercise of good governance. Managerial entrenchment (the successful resistance of external intervention by incumbent management) is most in evidence where companies have recently come to the stock market and director shareholdings are particularly high.

Consistent with this result, Hermalin and Weisbach (1991) report that, in the US, at low levels of ownership, corporate performance increases with managerial ownership as managers' and shareholders' interests are more closely aligned. However, it decreases above this level as management is able to insulate itself from disciplinary sanctions.

Franks and Mayer (1995a) examine the relation between both management and supervisory board turnover, performance and the size of shareholdings in Germany. They do not find evidence of a stronger relation between either management of supervisory board turnover and performance in firms with concentrated ownership and conclude that concentrations of ownership in Germany are "used to extract private benefits rather than wider shareholder interests" (p. 18).

In summary, the evidence available to date points to benefits in the exercise of corporate governance from modest levels of concentrations of ownership but possible exploitation of private benefits at high levels of concentration.

Markets in Share Stakes

Burkhart, Gromb and Panunzi (1995) argue that the optimal ownership structure of a firm depends on its performance. When it is performing well, diffuse ownership may help to limit the degree of undesirable interference from investors. However, when a firm is performing poorly then concentrations of share ownership may be desirable to encourage active control.

This points to the possibility of a dynamic evolution of patterns of ownership. Ownership may evolve from concentrated to more dispersed forms as the required degree of active corporate control diminishes and then reemerge in a concentrated form when firms encounter problems. Franks, Mayer and Renneboog (1995a) report evolving patterns of ownership in the UK which are quite consistent with this prediction. "Where poor performance is observed, sales of share stakes occur between different investors. In particular, there is a market in shares between new and old non-institutional shareholders and directors. These trades in shares are associated with significant changes in boards of poorly performing companies" (p. 14).

Franks and Mayer (1995a) report a similar result for Germany. Surprisingly, in the light of the supposed stability of the German and Japanese financial systems, they find evidence of a high level of turnover of large shareholdings in Germany. These sales of share stakes appear to be associated with poor performance of firms and changes to the supervisory (but not management) boards of companies. Corporate control is therefore particularly closely associated with sales of share stakes in both Germany and the UK.

Markets for Corporate Control

Following Manne (1965), the market for corporate control, or hostile takeovers, is generally viewed as an important method of correcting managerial failure. As Herzel and Shepro (1990) state "the most compelling argument in favour of hostile takeovers is that they are an important discipline on the managements of likely target companies" (p. 3). However, the evidence is not supportive of this. Franks and Mayer (1996) examine whether hostile takeovers are associated with dismissal of management and prior poor performance. They "find clear evidence of high board turnover and significant levels of restructuring in hostile takeovers. Large gains are anticipated, as reflected in high bid premiums paid to target shareholders. However, using a number of different benchmarks, we find little evidence that hostile takeovers are motivated by poor performance prior to bids. We therefore reject the view that hostile takeovers perform a disciplinary role" (p. 164).[4]

The Role of Banks

Banks are supposed to perform an important function in screening and monitoring firms. According to Diamond (1984), they can overcome the free-rider problem in information gathering which afflicts lending by a large number of dispersed investors. Recently, it has been suggested (Mayer, 1988; Sharpe, 1990; von Thadden, 1995) that there may be advantages to long-term relations between banks and firms. Long-term relations improve banks' evaluations of the quality of firms and allow better lending decisions to be made. According to von Thadden, if banks are better informed than other investors, they may be less inclined to favour investments which generate immediate signals of their performance. Banks may thereby diminish short-term biases which would otherwise afflict lending decisions.

However, banks may exploit their informational advantage by charging high lending rates to borrowers. Information introduces a switching cost into the market for credit which limits the extent to which borrowers are able to seek alternative sources of finance. Von Thadden (1995) argues that long-term contracts may mitigate this problem by reducing the scope for banks to extract rents at future dates at the expense of borrowers. Sharpe (1990) suggests that monopoly exploitation may also be discouraged by the desire of banks to preserve their reputations in lending markets.

Information is particularly important in the refinancing of failing firms. Failure of creditors to be able to distinguish between companies with good or bad prospects during periods of financial difficulties may result in premature liquidations. Furthermore, there may be conflicts between creditors leading to inefficiencies when firms are in financial distress (Bulow and Shoven, 1978; White, 1980). Gertner and Scharfstein (1991) demonstrate that these inefficiencies persist when firms can renegotiate with public debtholders.

Hoshi, Kashyap and Scharfstein (1990 and 1991) examine the role of banks in reducing the costs of financial distress in Japan. They examine whether firms with close financial relationships with banks can more effectively overcome problems of financial distress. Using a sample of 121 firms over the period 1978 to 1985, they find that financially distressed firms invest more and have stronger sales performance than non-group firms in the years following the onset of financial distress. Firms that receive a larger fraction of their debt financing from one lender invest and sell more. These results suggest that financial distress is more costly when financial claims are spread out among many creditors than when they are concentrated in the hands of a few financial institutions. Miyami (1995) finds similar results for ex-zaibatsu companies over the earlier period 1957 to 1964.

There is therefore clear evidence of a role for banks in Japan in organizing and financing the rescue of failing companies. In contrast, there is little evidence of German banks playing a direct role in the rescue of German firms. Surveying available evidence on Germany, Edwards and Fischer (1994) conclude that "the evidence on German bank behaviour when firms are in financial distress does not support the view that banks are able to reduce the costs of financial distress and bankruptcy by close monitoring and control of the actions of managers of firms in financial difficulty" (p. 175). Gorton and Schmid (1994) report an association between board turnover, poor performance and banks' own corporate shareholdings but not with banks' proxy shareholdings.

Corbett (1987) reports that when a company encounters financial difficulty in Japan the main bank will appoint a project team which may dispatch advisory managers to the client company. In contrast, Edwards and Fischer state that "there is no evidence that German banks send managers to work with firms in financial distress which are attempting to reorganize" (p. 176).

There therefore appears to be a difference in the way in which banks operate in the two bank oriented financial systems of Germany and Japan. There is more evidence of active involvement of Japanese than German banks in the rescuing of distressed firms.

The Role of Other Financial Institutions

Between 1970 and 1993, pension funds in the US grew from owning less than 9 per cent of the stock market to nearly one-third of the market. Mutual funds and insurers owned a further 16 per cent, implying that nearly one-half of corporate equity was in institutional hands by 1993. In the UK, institutions hold about two-thirds of equity with more than 80 per cent of this being in the hands of pension funds and life assurance firms.

Despite the high proportion of institution holdings, there is a widely held view that institutions fail to monitor managers. The problem is said to lie in the dispersed nature of their shareholdings. While in aggregate institutions hold a large fraction of corporate equity in the UK and US, this is dispersed amongst a large number of institutions, few of which hold significant fractions of shares in any one firm. There are good portfolio reasons, in addition to regulatory constraints, for why institutions may wish to diversify their holdings across a large number of firms. However, the degree of diversification of institutional investments appears considerably greater than that required to achieve most portfolio benefits and may have come at the expense of good corporate governance.

Evidence in support of this comes from Cosh and Hughes (1997) who find that the presence of institutional shareholdings does not affect either executive remuneration or the likelihood of executive dismissal in the UK. However, Cosh, Hughes, Lee and Singh (1989) report that post-takeover performance is somewhat better where acquiring companies have institutions amongst their shareholders. In addition, there is evidence of increased institutional involvement in both the UK and US. Berkshire Hathaway and Calpers are two well known examples in the US. "Concentrated blocks, frequently of 10 per cent or so of a firm's stock, allow Hathaway's senior executives, usually Warren Buffet or Charles Munger, to sit on the board. In a crisis they intervene, as Salomon Brothers' management found out" (Roe, 1994, p. 224).

In the UK, Stapledon (1996) records that in a stratified sample (10 per cent) of the 695 companies in the UK FT-A All Share Index, the six institutions with the largest shareholdings held on average 31 per cent of the ordinary share capital. In the largest firms, the six largest shareholdings amounted to 19 per cent of issued share capital. Stapledon reports that coalition formation amongst institutions was not uncommon. The coalitions represented between roughly 20 per cent and 40 per cent of the issued share capital. An ideal coalition comprised two or three members and four was thought to be a maximum. Stapledon finds that institutional interventions to change management in the UK have occurred since the 1950s and their prevalence in the 1990s suggests that they may be a substitute for takeovers. Successful interventions are most likely in small and medium sized companies because institutional shareholdings are too small to allow effective coalitions to be formed in the largest companies. However, all institutional shareholdings suffer from the indirect nature of their investments. Institutions themselves are prone to similar agency problems to the firms in which they invest and even concentrated holdings by institutions do not overcome the problem of 'who monitors the monitor'.

FINANCE AND INVESTMENT

There is a great deal of evidence on the way in which companies in different countries finance their investment. Mayer (1990) reports a number of stylized facts about financing patterns. Retained earnings (gross of depreciation) are the dominant source of finance in all OECD countries. Bank finance is the single most important source of external finance. Bonds in general contribute little to the financing of firms in aggregate. New equity issues also only account for a small proportion of corporate finance.

There are, however, some important differences in financing patterns across countries. Bank finance is a much more important source of funding in some countries, most notably France and Japan, than others. Bank finance accounts for a particularly small amount of corporate funding in the UK and, surprisingly in view of its status as a bank oriented financial system, in Germany. Bond finance is a significant source of corporate finance in North America but not elsewhere. New equity issues have accounted for a particularly small (actually negative over the recent past) amount of corporate funding in the UK and US. This is also surprising in the light of the apparently sophisticated equity markets of the UK and US.

McCauley and Zimmer (1989 and 1994) have reported that costs of capital were higher in the UK and US than in Germany and Japan during the 1980s. In Japan this resulted from higher levels of leverage and, during the second half of the 1980s, much lower costs of equity. During the 1990s there has been a marked convergence in costs of capital; in the case of Japan, this reflects the sharp fall in stock prices on the Tokyo exchange. McCauley and Zimmer measure the cost of equity in relation to price earnings ratios. However, international differences in price earnings ratios can reflect different anticipated rates of growth of earnings as well as discount factors, so that high price earnings ratios in Japan may result from high anticipated growth of earnings rather than low costs of capital.

Recently Poterba and Summers (1996) report survey evidence of higher costs of capital in the US than in Japan. They sent a survey to all Fortune 1000 companies in the US and had responses from about a quarter. These firms reported average real hurdle rates of return of just over 12 per cent. This compares with an average real return on equities in the US of around 7 per cent and a long-run real return on bonds of 7 per cent. A similar survey sent to a group of large Japanese firms elicited a target nominal return of 10 per cent. Even allowing for inflation this implies a higher cost of capital in the US than in Japan.

There is little direct evidence of an influence of financial systems on differences in levels of investment across countries. Untangling the numerous factors which may impinge on investment is complex. Mayer and Alexander (1990) report similar investment profits ratios of large firms in Germany and the UK during the 1980s. UK firms had higher dividend pay-out ratios (as a proportion of earnings) than German firms but raised more external finance from banks and bond markets. The higher pay-out ratios may assist in achieving superior resource allocation.

Mayer and Alexander (1995) report evidence of an influence of corporate ownership on finance and investment from a comparison of firms with different ownership structures in the UK. They compare the financing and investment activities of quoted and unquoted (listed and unlisted) companies matched by size and industry over the period 1980 to 1987. They find that quoted firms pay out a significantly higher proportion of their profits as dividends but raise significantly more equity finance than unquoted companies. Overall, unquoted firms invest a significantly higher proportion of their total sources of finance in physical assets than quoted firms.

The main difference which Mayer and Alexander report between quoted and unquoted companies concerns the nature of investment. Quoted firms engage in much more acquisition activity than unquoted firms. Much of the new equity which they raise goes towards the purchase of other firms rather than internal growth. As a consequence, overall quoted firms grow far more rapidly than unquoted firms.

In conclusion, while there are significant differences in the ways in which companies in different countries finance themselves, the implications of these differences is unclear. The higher level of dividend distributions associated with UK than German firms and of quoted than unquoted firms in the UK could be a sign of effectiveness of equity markets in rewarding shareholders. On the other hand, high dividends may reduce the availability of internal finance for investment. Thus, although there are several ways in which equity markets could affect corporate investment, through for example stock market reactions to new capital expenditure programmes, there is little conclusive evidence of an influence from the financing of firms.

Differences in costs of capital across countries have not been firmly established either. Higher target pay-out ratios in the UK than in Germany may reflect differences in the nature of investments undertaken by firms across countries. As the next section suggests, there may be good reasons for anticipating differences in the types of investments associated with different capital markets.

RELATIONSHIPS, COMMITMENT AND TRUST

Over the past decade there has been much discussion of the role of financial systems in promoting relationships between firms. This has been particularly considered in the context of relationships between banks and corporate borrowers. It is believed that there are longer-term relations between banks and borrowers in Germany and Japan than in the UK. Evidence in support of this is sometimes suggested to come from the maturity of bank lending in different countries. The average proportion of bank lending to companies with a maturity in excess of 1 year is around 2/3 in Germany and 1/3 in the UK. However, there are serious problems of measurement associated with these figures (see Edwards and Fischer (1994)) and it is unclear what is the implication of differences in maturity for corporate investment. According to recent incomplete contracts models (see, for example, Hart and Moore (1994)), short-term debt may be used to limit risks of strategic default on the part of borrowers. If that is the case then short-term debt may allow more external finance to be provided than would otherwise be the case.

There may be more significant differences in degrees of commitment associated with equity than debt finance. Franks and Mayer (1995b) record striking variations in patterns of ownership of companies in different countries. In France and Germany, in more than 85 per cent of the largest quoted firms there are single shareholders owning more than 25 per cent of shares. In the UK, the equivalent figure is 16 per cent. In more than half of the largest French and German firms there is a single majority shareholder. The equivalent figure in the UK is 6 per cent.

Still more striking are the differences in the nature of equity investors. Outside of the UK and US, private companies account for a substantial proportion of the largest firms. For example, in Germany joint stock companies only account for 20 per cent of turnover and only a small proportion of these are quoted on stock markets. As noted above, in the UK (and to a slightly lesser extent in the US), a majority of shares are held by financial institutions. In France and Germany the dominant shareholders are families and other companies. Contrary to conventional wisdom, banks do not hold a large proportion of German equity on their own account, although they do hold proxy votes on the bearer shares deposited by private investors for safe keeping.

Two types of firms may be distinguished in continental Europe. Firstly, a majority of companies have large concentrated shareholders (defined as companies with single shareholdings of at least 25 per cent). In these firms, control is exercised directly by these shareholders and bank control is limited. Secondly, there is a small proportion of widely held firms. Franks and Mayer (1995a) conclude that banks do exercise a significant degree of control in companies with dispersed shareholdings, primarily through proxy votes and supervisory board representation.

In addition to concentrated share stakes held by families and companies, Franks and Mayer (1995a) report complex systems of shareholdings. Where the main shareholding in a firm is another corporation then the question arises as to who owns that firm in turn. In some cases, ownership has to be traced back over several levels of a hierarchy before ultimate control can be identified. Secondly, in France and to a lesser extent in Germany, there are interlocking shareholdings which may take the form of direct cross-shareholdings by which companies hold reciprocal shareholdings in each other or more complex webs of holdings.

As Franks and Mayer (1995b) note this gives rise to an 'insider system' of corporate control by which companies are owned and controlled by each other and by families. There is little control exercised externally by outside shareholders. In contrast, the UK and US have 'outsider systems' of corporate control dominated by a large number of small shareholders.

The question that this raises is what differences do these patterns of corporate ownership have for the way in which firms are controlled and their performance. As noted above, one effect of concentrated shareholdings is to encourage more direct corporate governance and control. However, concentrated shareholdings may also encourage more relationships and commitment. Firstly, this may result from concentrated sharestakes being held by owners with which a firm has a trading relationship, eg as suppliers or purchasers. Williamson (1975) emphasizes the importance of transaction costs in encouraging the organization of activities within the firm rather than through markets. Cross-shareholdings between firms may have similar effects.

Secondly, even if ownership is not associated with trading relations, concentrated shareholdings may encourage greater commitment. In a system of dispersed shareholdings, individual shareholders can walk away from relations with other stakeholders (such as employees, suppliers and purchasers) without suffering any costs. However, a concentrated shareholder cannot sell out anonymously and is therefore accountable for the effects of his or her actions. Where stakeholders suffer as a consequence of a large shareholder disposing of his or her shares then the shareholder may incur reputational consequences. The UK and US system of corporate ownership is therefore characterized by dispersed, anonymous shareholders where it is difficult to sustain trust and commitment. The continental European and Japanese systems are characterized by large, identifiable shareholdings where relations can be better sustained.

Commitment and trust are particularly important where productive activities depend on the involvement of and investment by a large number of stakeholders. Complex manufacturing processes which require several different supplier and purchaser arrangements may be particularly dependent on ownership patterns that promote commitment and trust. They are also relevant to activities which require firm specific investments by employees in training and acquisition of skills. Incentives to undertake such investments may require commitments by employers to long-term employment and promotion policies within the firm.

Commitment and trust may be less relevant to productive activities which rely more on innovation and serendipity, for example high technology processes such as biotechnology. Furthermore, complex patterns of ownership and large shareholdings may diminish adaptability to change and be positively disadvantageous for encouraging restructuring of firms and industries. Where for example, technological change demands wholesale rationalization then this may be difficult to negotiate in the presence of large shareholdings. Mergers between firms through tender offers may be a much more effective mechanism for effecting such changes.

In summary, the most striking difference between financial systems does not concern patterns of finance and investment but ownership and control of firms. Differences in concentrations of ownership and the nature of owners are pronounced. Those differences are associated with the degree of monitoring and control which owners exercise. However, in addition they are also associated with differences in the degree of commitment and trust which exist between different stakeholders. While high levels of commitment and trust will be desirable for certain activities, that will not be invariably the case.

COMPETITION AND CORPORATE GOVERNANCE

Competition in product markets is generally associated with allocative and productive efficiency. Competition encourages the supply of goods and services at lowest costs and at prices which reflect the underlying costs of provision. However, in light of the above discussion, as noted by Mayer (1988) and formally set out in a model by Petersen and Rajan (1995), that does not necessarily apply in financial markets. Competition may undermine the development of long-term relations between firms and financial institutions. For example, the willingness of banks to provide rescue finance for companies in financial distress may hinge on the expectation that these investments will yield long-term returns. Where there is competition in financial markets and firms are free to shift to lowest costs suppliers of finance once they are out of financial distress then the provision of rescue funding by banks may be discouraged. On the other hand, limitations on competition in financial markets may result in monopoly exploitation of borrowers as noted by Hellwig (1991) and von Thadden (1995). For example, capital requirements create barriers to entry to new banks and confer monopoly rents on existing banks from the overcharging of corporate borrowers.

Mayer (1994) argues that there may be multi-equilibria in the structure of capital and product markets. He contrasts banking systems in which banks provide finance to firms in the middle stages of their developments (as banks provide finance to the Mittelstand in Germany) with cases of where companies go to stock markets. In the case of economies in which firms seek stock market finance, the resulting dispersed ownership may discourage banks from having long-term relations with firms. Anticipating that firms will have dispersed, anonymous shareholders who will be unable to commit to one lender, banks will not provide finance and firms will be forced to stock markets thereby justifying the unwillingness of banks to provide finance. In contrast, where banks do provide finance then ownership can remain concentrated and firms can provide the degree of commitment to banks which is required to induce them to lend in the first place.

This suggests that there may be key differences in the life-cycle development of firms. In some economies, banks provide finance during the all important middle stage of development when firms elsewhere are seeking stock market funding. In the banking systems, ownership remains concentrated and long-term relations develop. In the stock market economies, there is dispersed ownership and more flexibility than commitment. This suggests an important interrelation between the structure of financial and product markets.

Differences in the life cycle development of firms affect industrial structure. Complex patterns of ownership with cross-shareholdings between firms create large corporate groupings and high product market concentration. Extensive family holdings result in concentration of ownership in the hands of a small number of families. These promote monopoly exploitation and allocative inefficiency.

While there may therefore be corporate governance and relationship benefits associated with insider systems of corporate ownership, there are also potential product market problems. The most successful systems of corporate governance may be those which combine insider systems with product market competition. For example, monopoly abuse by *keiretsu* groups in Japan has been avoided through the establishment of competing industrial groups.

Conversely, the degree of both product and financial market competition will influence the development of governance systems. In the presence of competitive markets, the most efficient forms of governance systems would be expected to emerge of their own accord. However, regulation and restrictions on trade may impede this process. In the absence of international competition, the natural selection of most efficient forms of governance systems may be weak. As noted in the introduction, governance arrangements are crucially influenced by legislation and regulation concerning the ownership and control of firms and financial institutions. For example, in much of continental Europe, the ability of markets for corporate control to emerge has been seriously restricted by rules concerning voting right restrictions, proxy votes and tenure of members of corporate boards. Pressure for change has only come with greater international integration of both product and financial markets.

One of the most controversial aspects of alternative governance arrangements is competition in markets for corporate control, namely hostile takeover markets. Justification for them comes from the view that the desirable properties of product market competition can be extended to markets in ownership. However, it is product market competition which achieves allocative efficiency. Productive efficiency may be achieved through several different forms of corporate governance of which a market for corporate control is only one. Not only may competitive ownership markets be unnecessary where there is product market competition, they may actually undermine the development of long-term relations between stakeholders which are required for dynamic efficiency.

Privatization of utilities has raised the question of whether dispersed ownership and markets for corporate control are desirable where it is difficult to create product market competition. There is only very limited evidence available on this. Until recently, privatized utilities in the UK were protected by golden shares which conferred ultimate control rights on the government to determine whether changes in ownership should be permitted. With the elimination of golden shares, an active market in corporate control for utilities has emerged. This may encourage firms to pursue productive efficiency and act in the interests of their shareholders by, for example, returning surplus cash to shareholders rather than pursuing unprofitable diversification. However, gains to shareholders may come at the expense of customers. In the absence of competitive markets, regulators are required to identify cases of monopoly abuse. But regulators only have limited information with which to do this and the regulator's function is complicated by takeovers which merge utilities with other activities. It is therefore far from evident that natural monopolies benefit from outsider systems and markets for corporate control.

Where outsider systems may be most relevant is in markets for monopoly rights. The main feature of the outsider system is that it provides markets in the rights to determine corporate policy. This encourages corporate policy to react rapidly to new opportunities; failure to respond results in changes in ownership and control. Outsider systems may therefore be particularly well placed to respond to the commercial opportunities created by the emergence of new technologies and new international markets. These require rapid adaptation which may be impeded by the complex webs of interrelations between firms and other stakeholders which exist in insider systems. The new found interest in insider systems in the UK and US may thus be coming at exactly the moment when the information technology revolution and globalisation of markets make outsider systems most appropriate.

CONCLUSION

This paper has provided an overview of the interrelation of corporate governance and corporate performance. This is a subject which is in its infancy and it is unquestionably premature to believe that policy should be directed towards the selection of optimal governance arrangements. Indeed one of the most widely accepted views is that, in the light of our ignorance, competition between rather than harmonization of financial systems is desirable. We simply do not know whether insider dominate outsider systems and we suspect that even if this is true in some markets at some times, it is unlikely to be invariably the case.

The paper has examined the influence of corporate governance systems on managerial incentives and disciplining, the restructuring of firms, finance and investment, commitment and trust. It has noted that the relation between corporate governance systems and both incentives and disciplining is far from clear. Superficially, there would appear to be a difference between the high powered incentive arrangements in the UK and US and those in Germany and Japan. However, the limited evidence available to date does not support that assertion. Likewise, while the disciplining system associated with a market for corporate control in the UK would appear to be quite different from supervisory boards in Germany, the mechanism by which discipline is actually imposed is quite similar in the two countries, namely the emergence of concentrated shareholdings in poorly performing firms and markets in partial share stakes. Neither carrots nor sticks appear to be fundamental differences between financial systems.

Similarly, while conventional wisdom would lead us to believe that there are fundamental differences between the way in which German and UK firms are financed, empirical evidence does not support this proposition. The German banking system is not associated with a high level of bank finance and the UK stock market does not provide much external finance in aggregate for UK industry. Japanese banks are involved in the restructuring of their failing firms but German banks are not to anything like the same extent. There may be differences in costs of capital across countries but these have not been established with any measure of confidence to date.

There are, however, important differences in corporate systems across countries. These relate to the ownership and control of firms. Concentration of ownership is markedly higher on continental Europe and in Japan than it is in the UK and US. While financial institutions are the dominant owners in the UK and US, families and other companies are the most important owners in most other countries. Concentration of ownership encourages more active corporate governance and the development of long-term relations. However, concentrated ownership may be used to extract private benefits from firms rather than to pursue wider corporate interests. In addition, there may be positive advantages in not establishing long-term relations. Where changes in corporate policy are required then the replacement of commitments, vested interests, pressure groups etc by a simple market in corporate control may be beneficial.

One interpretation of the evidence is that the main differences in financial systems may concern the formulation, implementation and adaptation of corporate strategy rather than incentives, disciplining, finance and investment. Insider systems are superior at implementing policies which require the development of relations with several stakeholders. Outsider systems are better at responding to change.

The paper has pointed to important interactions between competition and corporate governance. Firstly, competition in financial markets may affect the development of long-term relations between financial institutions and firms. Secondly, inter-corporate holdings can create large corporate groupings which impede product market competition. Thirdly, competition in product markets may affect the speed with which optimal corporate governance systems emerge.

Avoidance of monopoly abuse in insider systems may require the presence of competing corporate groups. However, the recent literature on corporate governance has suggested that the benefits of product market competition cannot be simply extended to markets for corporate control. Good corporate governance and corporate relations may be undermined by markets for corporate control. Instead, the design of governance systems should be determined by the forms of corporate activities which they are supposed to serve.

Regulation is a key influence on the development of governance systems. It reflects as well as influences national differences in corporate organization. An implication of our limited understanding of governance systems is that regulation should be permissive rather than restrictive. Increasing globalisation of product and capital markets will hasten the emergence of optimal governance arrangements. Regulation which impedes this process will act to the competitive disadvantage of nations. Companies should as far as possible be free to choose their preferred forms of corporate organization and relations with other firms and institutions. The fact that markets in corporate control may weaken corporate relations does not justify regulation to impede takeovers: companies should be allowed to choose forms of corporate governance which discourage them if they so wish. Likewise, potential abuses to minority shareholders and competitive practices require careful monitoring and effective sanctions but do not justify the imposition of regulations which inhibit choice of governance arrangements.

NOTES

1. It should be noted that there are a number of alternative definitions of insider and outsider systems. Inside ownership is sometimes used to refer to ownership by directors of firms to distinguish it from outside ownership by non-directors. In some cases, insider systems relate to the direct exercise of monitoring and control by investors (individual or institutional) as against external mechanisms such as takeovers.
2. For an interesting account of the financial mistakes which occurred in the Metallgesellschaft case see Mello and Parsons (1994).
3. Cosh and Hughes (1987) report that in the UK boards are dominated by insiders who have spent the bulk of their career in the same firm. Non-executive directors are often retired executives of the same firm.
4. It might be argued that the threat of a takeover might act as a disciplinary device even in the absence of poor performance on the part of targets. However, strong performance is not then necessarily the best defence against a takeover threat.

REFERENCES

Aoki, M. (1994a) 'The Japanese firm as a system of attributes: A survey and research agendas', in M. Aoki and R. Dore (eds.), *The Japanese Firm: Sources of Competitive Strength*, Oxford: Oxford University Press.

Aoki, M. (1994b) 'The Gains from Organizational Diversity: An Evolutionary Game Parable', in H. Siebert (ed.), *Trends in Business Organization: Do Participation and Cooperation Increase Competitiveness*, Tubingen: J.C.B. Mohr.

Berle, A. and G. Means (1932) *The Modern Corporation and Private Property*, New York: MacMillan.

Black, B. and J. Coffee (1993) 'Hail Britannia?: Institutional investor behaviour under limited regulation', mimeo.

Blinder, A. (1991) 'Profit maximization and international competition', in R. O'Brien (ed.), *Finance and the International Economy 5: The AMEX Bank Review Prize Essays: In Memory of Robert Marjolin*, Oxford: Oxford University Press.

Bulow, J. and J. Shoven (1978) 'The bankruptcy decision', *Bell Journal of Economics* 9, 437–456.

Burkhart, M., D. Gromb and F. Panunzi (1996) 'Large shareholders, monitoring and the value of the firm', mimeo.

Cadbury, A. (1992) *Report of the Committee on the Financial Aspects of Corporate Governance*, Gee & Co Ltd.

Conyon, M. (1994) 'Corporate governance changes in UK companies between 1988 and 1993', *Corporate Governance* 2, 87–99.

Conyon, M., P. Gregg and S. Machin (1995) 'Taking care of business: Executive compensation in the UK', *Economic Journal* 105, 704–714.

Cosh, A. and A. Hughes (1995) 'The anatomy of corporate control: Directors, shareholders and executive remuneration', *Cambridge Journal of Economics* 11, 285–313.

Cosh, A. and A. Hughes (1997) 'Executive remuneration, executive dismissal and institutional shareholdings', *International Journal of Industrial Organization*, forthcoming.

Coughlan, A. and R. Schmidt (1985) 'Executive compensation, managerial turnover and firm performance', *Journal of Accounting and Economics* 7, 43–66.
Diamond, D. (1984) 'Financial intermediation and delegated monitoring', *Review of Economic Studies* 51, 393–414.
Edwards, J. and K. Fischer (1994) *Banks, Finance and Investment in Germany*, Cambridge: Cambridge University Press.
Fama, E. (1980) 'Agency problems and the theory of the firm', *Journal of Political Economy* 88, 288–307.
Franks, J. and C. Mayer (1995a) 'Ownership, control and the performance of German corporations', mimeo.
Franks, J. and C. Mayer (1995b) 'Ownership and control', in H. Siebert (ed.), *Trends in Business Organization: Do Participation and Cooperation Increase Competitiveness?*, Tubingen: J.C.B. Mohr.
Franks, J. and C. Mayer (1996) 'Hostile takeovers and the correction of managerial failure', *Journal of Financial Economics* 40, 163–181.
Franks, J., C. Mayer and L. Renneboog (1995) 'The role of large share stakes in poorly performing companies', mimeo.
Garen, J. (1994) 'Executive compensation and principal–agent theory', *Journal of Political Economy* 102, 1175–1199.
Gertner, R. and D. Scharfstein (1991) 'A theory of workouts and the effects of reorganization law', *Journal of Finance* 46, 1189–1222.
Gorton, G. and F. Schmid (1994) 'Universal banking and the performance of German firms', mimeo.
Grundfest, J. (1990) 'Subordination of American capital', *Journal of Financial Economics* 27, 89–114.
Hart, O. and J. Moore (1994) 'A theory of debt based on the inalienability of human capital', *Quarterly Journal of Economics* 109, 840–879.
Haubrich, J. (1994) 'Risk aversion, performance pay and the principal–agent problem', *Journal of Political Economy* 102, 258–276.
Hellwig, M. (1991), 'Banking, financial intermediation and corporate finance', in A. Giovannini and C. Mayer (eds.), *European Financial Integration*, Cambridge: Cambridge University Press.
Hermalin, B. and M. Weisbach (1991) 'The effects of board composition and direct incentives on firm performance', *Financial Management*, Winter, 101–112.
Herzel, L. and R. Shepro (1990) *Bidders and Targets: Mergers and Acquisitions in the U.S.*, Oxford: Blackwell.
Hoshi, T., A. Kashyap and D. Scharfstein (1990) 'The role of banks in reducing the costs of financial distress in Japan', *Journal of Financial Economics* 27, 67–88.
Hoshi, T., A. Kashyap and D. Scharfstein (1991) 'Corporate structure, liquidity, and investment: Evidence from Japanese industrial groups', *Quarterly Journal of Economics* 106, 33–60.
Jensen, M. and K. Murphy (1990) 'Performance pay and top-management incentives', *Journal of Political Economy* 98, 225–264.
Kaplan, S. (1994) 'Top executive rewards and firm performance: A comparison of Japan and the United States', *Journal of Political Economy* 102, 510–546.
McCauley, R. and S. Zimmer (1989) 'Explaining international differences in the cost of capital', *Federal Reserve Bank of New York Quarterly Review* 14, 7–28.
McCauley, R. and S. Zimmer (1994) 'Exchange rates and international differences in the cost of capital', in Y. Ahimred and R. Levich (eds.), *Exchange Rates and Corporate Performance*, Burr Ridge, Ill: Irwin.
McConnell, J. and H. Servaes (1990) 'Additional evidence on equity ownership and corporate value', *Journal of Financial Economics* 27, 595–612.
Main, B. (1995) 'The governance of remuneration for senior executives', mimeo, University of Edinburgh.

Main, B. and J. Johnston (1993), 'Remuneration committees and corporate governance', *Accounting and Business Research* 23, 351–362.

Manne, H. (1965) 'Mergers and the market for corporate control', *Journal of Political Economy* 73, 110–120.

Mayer, C. (1988) 'New issues in corporate finance', *European Economic Review* 32, 1167–1189.

Mayer, C. (1990) 'Financial systems, corporate finance and economic development', in R. G. Hubbard (ed.), *Asymmetric Information, Corporate Finance and Investment*, Chicago: University of Chicago Press.

Mayer, C. (1994) 'Money and banking: Theory and evidence', *Oxford Review of Economic Policy* 10, 1–13.

Mayer, C. and I. Alexander (1990) 'Banks and securities markets: Corporate financing in Germany and the United Kingdom', *Journal of the Japanese and International Economies* 4, 450–475.

Mayer, C. and I. Alexander (1994) 'Stock markets and corporate performance: A comparison of publicly listed and private companies', mimeo.

Mello, A. and J. Parsons (1994) 'Maturity structure of a hedge matters: Lessons from the Metallgesellschaft debacle', mimeo.

Milgrom, P. and J. Roberts (1992) *Economics, Organization and Management*, Englewood Cliffs, N.J.: Prentice-Hall.

Miyama, H. (1995) 'Bank centred corporate groups and investment: Evidence from the first phase of high growth era in Japan', mimeo.

Morck, R., A. Shleifer and R. Vishny (1988) 'Management ownership and market valuation: An empirical analysis', *Journal of Financial Economics* 20, 293–315.

Murphy, K. (1994) 'Corporate performance and managerial remuneration: An empirical analysis', *Journal of Accounting and Economics* 7, 11–42.

Petersen, M. and R. Rajan (1995) 'The effect of credit market competition on lending relationships', *Quarterly Journal of Economics* 110, 407–443.

Poterba, J. and L. Summers (1996) 'Time horizons and hurdle rates of American firms', *Sloan Management Review*.

Prowse, S. (1990) 'Institutional investment patterns and corporate financial behaviour in the United States and Japan', *Journal of Financial Economics* 27, 43–66.

Roe, M. (1994) *Strong Managers, Weak Owners: The Political Roots of American Corporate Finance*, Princeton: Princeton University Press.

Rosen, S. (1992) 'Contracts and the market for executives', in L. Werin and H. Wijkander (eds.) *Contract Economics*, Oxford: Blackwell, pp 181–211.

Schneider-Lenne, E. (1994) 'The role of the German capital markets and the universal banks, supervisory boards and interlocking directorships', in N. Dimsdale and M. Prevezer (eds.), *Capital Markets and Corporate Governance*, Oxford: Clarendon Press.

Sharpe, S. (1990) 'Asymmetric information, bank lending and implicit contracts: A stylized model of customer relationships', *Journal of Finance* 45, 1069–1087.

Shleifer, A. and R. Vishny (1986) 'Large shareholders and corporate control', *Journal of Political Economy* 94, 461–488.

Shleifer, A. and R. Vishny (1996) 'A survey of corporate governance', National Bureau of Economic Research working paper.

Stapledon, G. P. (1996) *Institutional Shareholders and Corporate Governance*, Oxford: Clarendon Press.

von Thadden, E. (1995) 'Long-term contracts, short-term investment and monitoring', *Review of Economic Studies* 62, 557–575.

Warner, J., R. Watts and K. Wruck (1988), 'Stock prices, event prediction and event studies: An examination of top management restructurings', *Journal of Financial Economics* 20, 461–492.

Weisbach, M. (1988) 'Outside directors and CEO turnover', *Journal of Financial Economics* 20, 431–460.

White, M. (1980) 'Public policy towards bankruptcy: Me-first and other priority rules', *Bell Journal of Economics* 11, 550–564.
Williamson, O. (1975) *Markets and Hierarchies: Analysis and Antitrust Implications*, The Free Press.
Wruck, K. (1989) 'Equity ownership concentration and firm value', *Journal of Financial Economics* 23, 3–28.
Yermack, D. (1995) 'Good timing: CEO stock option awards and company news announcements', manuscript, New York University.

Abstract

This paper documents the ownership structure of Belgian companies quoted on the Brussels Stock Exchange. The Belgian corporate control system resembles the French-German system as relatively few companies are listed, shareholding concentration is strong, control is levered by pyramidal and complex ownership structures, holding companies, families and industrial companies are the major shareholdings, and there is a market for share stakes. The paper also details the regulation on ownership disclosure, voting-rights and the rights of minority shareholders.

Dr Luc Renneboog is currently Assistant Professor in Finance at the department of Applied Economics of the Catholic University of Leuven. He graduated from Leuven with degrees in Management Engineering and Philosophy, and from the University of Chicago with an MBA. At the London Business School he obtained his PhD in Financial Economics. He worked for P&G as a financial analyst and was Salomon Brothers International Doctoral Fellow in Finance and Marie Curie Fellow of the European Commission.

XII. Shareholding Concentration and Pyramidal Ownership Structures in Belgium

LUC RENNEBOOG

1. INSIDER VERSUS OUTSIDER OWNERSHIP AND CONTROL SYSTEMS

According to Berle and Means (1932), dispersed ownership has given rise to separation of ownership and control. Demsetz and Lehn (1985) argue that ownership patterns reflect a trade- off of the risk to investors of concentrated investments in large firms and the control potential of the firm. Diversified shareholdings are useful from the point of view of risk reduction but discourage active participation of investors. As Franks and Mayer (1995c) point out, it is puzzling that the resolution of this trade off has taken such different forms in different countries. German and French equity markets can be characterized by few listed companies, an illiquid capital market where ownership and control is infrequently traded and complex systems of intercorporate holdings (Mayer 1993, Franks and Mayer 1992). Consequently, these structures are appropriately described as *insider systems* in which the corporate sector has controlling interests in itself; outsider investors, while able to participate in equity returns through the stock market, are not able to exert much control. In contrast, the Anglo-American system is a market oriented or *outsider system* and is characterized by a large number of listed companies, a liquid capital market where ownership and control rights are frequently traded and few intercorporate holdings.[1] There are few large, controlling shareholdings and these are rarely associated with the corporate sector itself.

The main characteristics of the Belgian corporate ownership and equity market can be summarized as follows: (i) few Belgian companies are listed, (ii) there is a high degree of ownership concentration, (iii) holding companies and families, and to a lesser extent industrial companies, are the main investor categories, (iv) control is levered by pyramidal and complex ownership structures and (v) there is a market for share stakes. Properties (i) to (iv) imply that Belgium can be portrayed as a German-French 'insider system' rather than an Anglo-American system. However, typical for Belgium is the importance of holding companies which are often part of pyramidal ownership chains and are used to lever control.[2]

TABLE 1

Number of domestic quoted companies per country and the market capitalization as a percentage of GDP

Country	Number of domestic quoted companies	Equity of quoted co's as % of GDP
US	6342	56%
UK	1878	81%
Japan	1627	89%
France	786	26%
Germany	665	18%
Spain	433	20%
Netherlands	314	44%
Switzerland	180	78%
Belgium	171	31%

The numbers of quoted companies refer to 1992, but to 1991 for the U.S. and Japan. For each country, only domestic companies listed on the main stock exchanges have been considered: New York and NASDAQ combined, London, Tokyo, Paris, Frankfurt, Madrid, Amsterdam, all Swiss exchanges, and Brussels.

Source: Own calculations for Belgium and the UK are based on data from the Brussels Stock Exchange and the Department of Trade and Industry in London, Wymeersch (1994b) for the Netherlands, Germany, France and Switzerland; Goergen (1993) for Spain; Franks and Mayer (1992) for the US and Japan.

Table 1 shows the number of quoted companies per country and the total market capitalization as a percentage of GDP. The UK, US and Japan are characterized by a large number of quoted companies; respectively 1878, 6342 and 1627 in 1992. The market capitalization of companies quoted on the London Stock Exchange is around 81 per cent of the UK GDP. Companies quoted on the Tokyo Stock Exchange have a value of 89 per cent of the Japanese GDP while the value of corporations listed on the New York Stock Exchange and NASDAQ amounts to 56 per cent of US GDP. The capital markets of France, Germany, Belgium and Spain and of most of the remainder of continental Europe, present a different situation: they have many less quoted companies with a market capitalization as a percentage of GDP which is lower than 32 per cent.[3]

Compared to the shareholding structure of Continental European corporations, ownership in the US and the UK is much less concentrated (Franks, Mayer & Renneboog 1996). For the US, the average shareholding of the five largest shareholders in a sample of Fortune 500 companies is 15.4 per cent and

23 per cent of these companies do not have a shareholder with a share stake over more than 5 per cent (Shleifer and Vishny 1986, Demsetz and Lehn 1985). These two percentages compare to respectively 60 per cent and to 1 per cent for Belgium. The large shareholders with a stake of at least 5 per cent in the US are mostly families, pension and profitsharing plans as well as banks, insurance companies and investment funds. About two-thirds of the market capitalization is held by individual and institutional investors on behalf of individuals in US and UK quoted companies, but the US has a far higher proportion of equity owned directly by individuals. However, Davies and Stapledon (1994) report the enormous growth in the percentage (by value) of equity held by institutional investors in the UK and a decline in the percentage held by individuals.

Germany, like Belgium, has few widely held listed companies: only 15 per cent of a German sample of the 171 largest companies do not have any shareholder with an equity stake of 25 per cent or more (Franks and Mayer 1995a and 1995b).[4] Other German companies and families own the largest share stakes. Trusts and institutional investors are sometimes large shareholders but their stakes are rarely majority holdings. The same holds for banks. However, the significance of banks is greater than their direct equity holdings would suggest: as holders of bearer shares they are able to exercise proxy votes on behalf of dispersed shareholders.[5] Control is maintained at low cost via complex and pyramidal structures: the average tier of company holdings is 2.2 compared with 3.1 for families and 4.2 for banks.

In a French sample of the largest 155 quoted companies, almost 89 per cent have a shareholder with an equity stake of 25 per cent or more. The major shareholders in the French sample are predominantly other industrial companies (Goergen 1993). So, in France, like in Germany, the corporate sector is by far the single largest group of shareholders. Foreign companies, families and banks are the other large shareholders. Corporations who hold equity stakes in each other are often in related industries or in the same industry (Franks and Mayer 1995c). Furthermore, in most cases, these companies are not trading partners.

The Italian shareholding structure is characterized by high concentration of ownership, the presence of family owners and the pervasive role of the state (see Bianco, Gola and Signorini 1995). About 95 per cent of the largest 500 non-financial companies are controlled with absolute majority (Bianchi and Casavola 1995). Contrary to what one would expect, the concentration of direct ownership is greater in larger firms. Controlling shareholders hold 88 per cent of the largest companies via pyramids and coalitions.

Japanese ownership is highly concentrated as in continental Europe. Financial and industrial groups (*keiretsu*), represent about 61 per cent of the market capitalization of the Tokyo Stock Exchange (Lichtenberg and Pushner

1992). Average ownership in quoted companies held by financial groups has risen to 30 per cent in 1989, while average corporate ownership remained stable over the period 1975-1989 at 43 per cent.[6]

Franks and Mayer (1995c) argue that the theories of ownership and corporate control[7] do not provide adequate explanations for the organization and operation of Anglo-American, Japanese and Continental European capital markets. They advance the hypothesis that the patterns of ownership are associated with different forms of corporate control that allow for different types of correction. Concentrated ownership allows relations involving commitment on the part of investors to be sustained. Large shareholders who face limited free riding costs of control, can give a long-term commitment to the firm, while allowing a large number of small shareholders to trade in investment opportunities without having any effect on control. Dispersed ownership gives management more discretionary power but permits restructuring of management (e.g. by takeovers or by a market for share stakes) even in the absence of past failure, largely because owners are unable to commit. Consequently, it could be expected that different forms of ownership would be suited to promoting different types of activity. Concentrated ownership is needed where investment by other stakeholders is important and cannot be promoted contractually. When little investment is required by other parties or adequate contracts can be written, dispersed ownership will be advantageous.

2. Concentrated Ownership in Belgium

2.1. Ownership Disclosure Legislation

Up to 1989, little was known about the ownership structure of companies listed on the Belgian stock exchanges, given the general use of bearer shares and the lack of ownership disclosure obligation. Following the takeover battle in 1988 between the French Compagnie Financière de Suez and the de Benedetti group for the largest Belgian holding company, Generale Maatschappij van België (Société Générale de Belgique), new legislation concerning corporate control and ownership was initiated. An Ownership Disclosure Law[8] was introduced in 1989 and amendments to the company law with regard to takeovers[9] were made in 1991.

The Ownership Disclosure Law requires all investors, both individuals and companies, to reveal their share stakes in those companies governed by Belgian law, all or part of whose securities conferring voting rights are officially listed on a stock exchange located in a Member State of the European Union. Notification is obligatory if a shareholding equals or exceeds 5 per cent.[10] Furthermore, shareholders have to declare any increases and decreases in ownership and their new ownership position if their stake exceeds a multiple of 5 per cent of the voting rights or falls below such a threshold. For instance, a company that has revealed that it owns a stake of 11 per cent will have to notify the Banking Commission[11] again once this ownership stake reaches 15 per cent or more, or decreases below the 10 per cent-threshold.

The notification percentages refer to real and potential voting rights. As a result, ownership of securities convertible into shares (convertible bonds, warrants, etc.) is treated in the same way as shares in the company.[12] So, when investors make voting rights declarations, they include: (i) the percentage of the actual total voting rights they own proportional to all the actual voting rights outstanding, (ii) the potential voting rights, as a percentage to the aggregate of all potential voting rights; and (iii) the percentage of cumulative actual and potential voting rights in the company based on the aggregate number of the voting rights associated with all outstanding shares and convertible instruments.[13]

Furthermore, the law applies not only to the direct owners of the voting rights, but also to those investors who control voting rights indirectly via a pyramid structure of intermediate companies.[14] Investors are obliged to reveal whether they are affiliated to a group of companies or whether they act in concert[15] with other investors. If the real or potential voting rights of the individual investor or of the investor group exceed or fall below the notification thresholds, they have to reveal their cumulative and individual direct and indirect ownership positions and changes in shareholdings. The Banking Commission suggests that the ultimate shareholder of an investor group assumes notification responsibility for voting rights of its own direct and indirect holdings and for those share stakes held by investors this 'reference shareholder' is affiliated to or acts in concert with.[16] In addition, once the stake of an investor (or of the investors belonging to the same investor group) reaches 20 per cent of the voting rights of the company, the strategic policy with regard to the target has to be declared to the Banking Commission and the target.[17]

With regard to timing of notification, the investor who purchases or sells shares (voting rights) has to disclose his shareholding and the changes in his position to the target and to the Banking Commission in Brussels at the latest on the second working day after the transaction, if a notification threshold has been passed. The target who has been notified about changes in ownership by substantial investors, has a maximum of one working day after disclosure to pass on this information to the Documentation and Statistics Department of the Brussels Stock Exchange (Maertens 1994). This department updates its on-line ownership database BDPart and makes this information available *ad valvas* on the trading floor (*parquet*).[18] The following day, the Documentation department publishes the information in the Cote de la Bourse,[19] a Stock Exchange publication that is inserted in the two Belgian financial newspapers,

De Financieel Economische Tijd and *L'Echo de la Bourse*. The same notification timing applies to disclosure of investors' policies (20 per cent ownership rule).

An investor's failure to disclose a substantial shareholding may lead to a ban on the investor in question from participation in the annual meeting, to a cancellation of the annual meeting which has been called for, to a suspension of the exercise of all or part of the rights pertaining to the securities for a certain period and to liability to penalties.[20,21] The voting rights of recently acquired major shareholdings (5 per cent and more) can only be exercised 45 days after notification.[22]

2.2. Voting Rights and Restrictions, and the Rights of the Minority Shareholders

In principle, the general assembly takes decisions based on a simple majority of the voting rights. Since 1991, the balance of corporate power has shifted to the controlling shareholders who have been given legal instruments to entrench their position in the company and to protect themselves against undesired takeovers. Anti-takeover instruments, like share repurchase schemes or issuance of warrants, are valid for a maximum of five years but can be reinstated for a similar period by the general assembly (Wymeersch 1994a).[23] Such measures have further reduced the likelihood of hostile takeovers in Belgium.[24]

However, to provide more protection to small shareholders, a supermajority of 75 per cent of the voting rights voted at the general assembly, is needed with regard to decisions about changes in the acts of incorporation, increases of the equity capital, limitations or changes in the preferential rights of existing shareholders to purchase shares in new equity issues, changes in the rights of different classes of shareholders,[25] repurchases of shares and changes in the legal form of the corporation (Lievens 1994).

Since 1991, minority shareholders or a group of minority shareholders owning at least 1 per cent of the equity capital or shares with a value of not less than BEF 50 million, can appoint one or more experts who can scrutinize the company's accounting and its internal operations.[26] The appointment of experts is conditional on indications that the interests of the company are threatened. Shareholders owning at least 1 per cent of the votes can initiate a *minority claim* against the directors for the benefit of the company, if it can be proven that the directors have managed or supervised the company poorly and if the minority shareholders have voted against the directors' *discharge*[27] at the annual meeting. For instance, a minority claim would be justified when directors ensured that the company paid out benefits to large shareholders they represent at the detriment of the company.[28]

Another important change, since the law of 1991, is the abolition of automatic voting-right restrictions.[29] This abolition was motivated by the fact that the restrictions could be easily evaded by redistributing the shares to family members, friends and subsidiaries (Van Nuffel 1994). Still, as in Germany, individual companies can apply voting right restrictions by including such clauses in the acts of incorporation. While automatic voting restrictions are abolished, voting agreements among shareholders for (renewable) periods of five years are allowed since 1991 if these agreements do not limit the responsibilities of the directors or are used to create different classes of voting rights.

3. DATA

3.1. Sample Description

The sample consists of all Belgian companies listed on the Brussels Stock Exchange during July 1989 and August 1994.[30] In total, 192 firms are included in the sample; some of these went bankrupt in the period under consideration, while others were introduced after 1989. In 1989 and 1994, respectively, 186 and 165 companies were listed. Sector codes, dates of introduction and of delisting are provided by the Documentation and Statistics Department of the Brussels Stock Exchange. In the analysis, the sample size was reduced by nine companies in 1989 and by ten in 1994 as these listed firms, all in coal mining and steel production, were involved in a long liquidation process but were still listed. Table 2 shows that 40 per cent of the Belgian listed companies are holding companies with multi-industry investments, 13 per cent are in the financial sector (banking, insurance and real estate) and 47 per cent are industrial and commercial companies.

3.2. Ownership Data

Data on the ownership structure over the period 1989–1994 was collected from the Documentation and Statistics Department of the Brussels Stock Exchange. Ownership data are only available since 1989, following the introduction of the Ownership Disclosure. The Documentation Department maintains a daily updated database BDPart (Bourse Data Participations) of the shareholding structure of Belgian listed companies. BDPart provides data on the first level of shareholding (direct ownership) in all Belgian listed companies, such as the names of the investors, the number of shares declared, number of shares issued and the percentage of ownership. Apart from voting rights linked to the shareholdings, BDPart also displays potential voting rights linked to securities that will represent voting rights when converted or exercised (e.g. convertible bonds, warrants). Previous ownership positions in the BDPart database are overwritten once new ownership information becomes available. To capture a company's ownership position at the end of its fiscal year since 1989 and

TABLE 2

Sample description

	1989	1994
All listed sample companies[1]	177	155
Holdings[2]	71	64
Financial sector	23	19
Industrial and Service companies	83	72
Financial Sector		
Banks	8	7
Insurance	7	5
Real estate	8	7
Industry		
Energy[3]	6	5
Materials[4]	4	26
Capital equipment[5]	13	12
Consumer goods[6]	19	16
Services	11	13

[1] For 1989 and 1994, respectively, nine and ten listed companies that have been in liquidation for years, were not included in the sample. These companies are all in coal mining and steel production. The number of de-listings in the period 1989-1994 surpasses the number of new introductions due to mergers, industry restructurings (e.g. in the energy sector) and the policy of the stock exchange to delist infrequently traded companies with tiny market capitalizations.
[2] The holding companies have multi-industry investments. The categorization is based on the NACE classification of the National Bank and the classification of the Bank Brussels Lambert.
[3] Mainly petrochemical and electricity production.
[4] Ferro, non-ferro, chemicals, building, paper, glass.
[5] Electricals, electronics, construction, machine building.
[6] Mainly food, pharmaceuticals and retail.

changes in shareholdings during each year, about 5,000 hardcopy Notifications of Ownership Change from 1989 till 1994 were consulted. These Notifications were sent by the target to the Brussels Stock Exchange which published this information in the official Stock Exchange newspaper *Cote de la Bourse*. Apart from details on voting rights, the investors' status (independent, affiliated or acting in concert with other investors) was compiled from the Notifications. With this information about major direct shareholdings and indirect control, the multi-layered ownership structure was reconstructed for each company over the period 1989-1994. The shareholding data from BDPart and the

Notifications of Ownership Change was verified with ownership data of the database of the National Bank which is based on annual reports.[31]

The 1988–1994 yearbooks of *Trends 20,000*, which comprise industry sector classification and financial data for most listed and non-listed Belgian companies, were used to classify all Belgian investors into the following categories: (i) holding companies, (ii) banks, (iii) institutional investors, (iv) insurance companies, (v) industrial companies, (vi) families and individual investors, (vii) federal or regional governments and (viii) real estate investors. Foreign companies owning a large share stake in Belgian companies were classified with information from *Kompass*.

4. Ownership Structure in Belgium

4.1. Concentrated Direct and Ultimate Ownership by Shareholder Class

The structure of substantial shareholdings in all Belgian companies listed on the Brussels Stock Exchange in August 1994 is presented in Table 3. On average, the sum of the direct share stakes held by large shareholders (who own at least 5 per cent of the outstanding shares) amounts to more than 65 per cent (panel A). Cumulative direct ownership is higher, almost 70 per cent in the financial sector (panel C), and around 65 per cent for both holding companies (column 1 of panel B) and industrial and commercial companies (panel D). It is clear that the concentrated ownership structure does not facilitate hostile takeovers if the acquirer does not initially have a large toehold. In their analysis of the Belgian market for corporate control over the period 1970–1985, Van Hulle, Vermaelen and de Wouters (1991) confirm that tender offers made directly to the public were characterized by substantial initial toehold interests.[32]

Table 3 also reports the cumulative ownership of the three most important investor classes: holding companies, families and individual investors, and industrial and commercial companies.[33] From panel A can be concluded that holding companies are the largest direct investors;[34] they hold on average 33 per cent of the shares and account for half of the substantial ownership stakes in Belgian companies. Domestic and foreign holding companies have invested more in the Belgian holding companies than in the industrial and in the financial sector. Direct investment of industrial and services companies (panel A) totals almost 15 per cent and is focused on other industrial and commercial companies (panel D). Families' direct investment is of less importance with an average stake of about 4 per cent.

A substantial number of share stakes are held by other companies which in turn are held by other shareholders. Therefore, if we want to answer the question who actually owns and controls a sample company, pyramidal and

TABLE 3

Ownership concentration in all Belgian companies listed on the Brussels Stock Exchange

August 1994	All investors	Holding co's	Families	Industr. co's	Belgian investors	Foreign investors
PANEL A: ALL SAMPLE COMPANIES (N = 155)						
Direct	65.38	32.71	3.90	14.60	49.38	16.00
Ultimate	65.38	26.68	15.59	10.84	39.60	24.35
PANEL B: ALL HOLDING COMPANIES (N = 64)						
Direct	63.92	36.73	5.15	13.11	46.85	17.07
Ultimate	63.92	34.43	14.12	8.33	36.08	27.97
PANEL C: FINANCIAL SECTOR (BANKS, INSURANCE, REAL ESTATE) (N = 19)						
Direct	69.96	26.45	1.18	5.45	55.00	14.96
Ultimate	69.96	26.22	5.31	5.41	38.40	23.63
PANEL D: INDUSTRIAL AND COMMERCIAL COMPANIES (N = 72)						
Direct	65.48	30.80	3.50	18.34	50.16	15.32
Ultimate	65.48	20.02	19.70	14.52	43.01	21.36

This table reports the aggregate of individual shareholdings of 5% and more[1] for the main ownership categories. The shareholder classes (holding companies, industrial and commercial companies, and families) consist of both Belgian and foreign investors. Direct stands for the direct shareholdings. Ultimate refers to the fact that the direct shareholdings were classified according to the shareholder class of the ultimate investor and these direct shareholdings belonging to the same ultimate investor group were subsequently summed. Ultimate control is control based on (i) a majority control (minimal 50% of the voting rights) on every ownership tier of the ownership pyramid or (ii) shareholdings of at least 25% on every tier in the absence of other shareholders holding stakes of 25% or more. A chain of fully owned subsidiaries are considered as one single shareholder.
Source: Own calculations based on information from the BDPart database of the Brussels Stock Exchange and Ownership Notifications of the Documentation Centre of the Brussels Stock Exchange.
[1] In line with the Ownership Disclosure Legislation, substantial shareholdings are defined as share stakes that equal or exceed 5% (of the voting rights), unless investors with smaller shareholdings are affiliated to or act in concert with major shareholders, in which case small stakes ought to be revealed as well. The 5% threshold can be reduced to 3% if the company states this in its acts of constitution.

complex ownership structures should be taken into account. Examples of pyramidal and complex ownership structures are illustrated in Figures 1 and 2. Figure 1 shows part of the ownership structure of Floridienne, a company in the chemical and food industry, at the end of 1994. On the direct investment level, Mosane and its fully owned subsidiary Cippar hold 25 per cent of Floridienne's voting rights. Ultimate minority control lies with the Paribas group which controls its Belgian subsidiary Copeba. Ultimate minority control exists when there is a continuous chain of at least 25 per cent if there are no

Shareholding Concentration 273

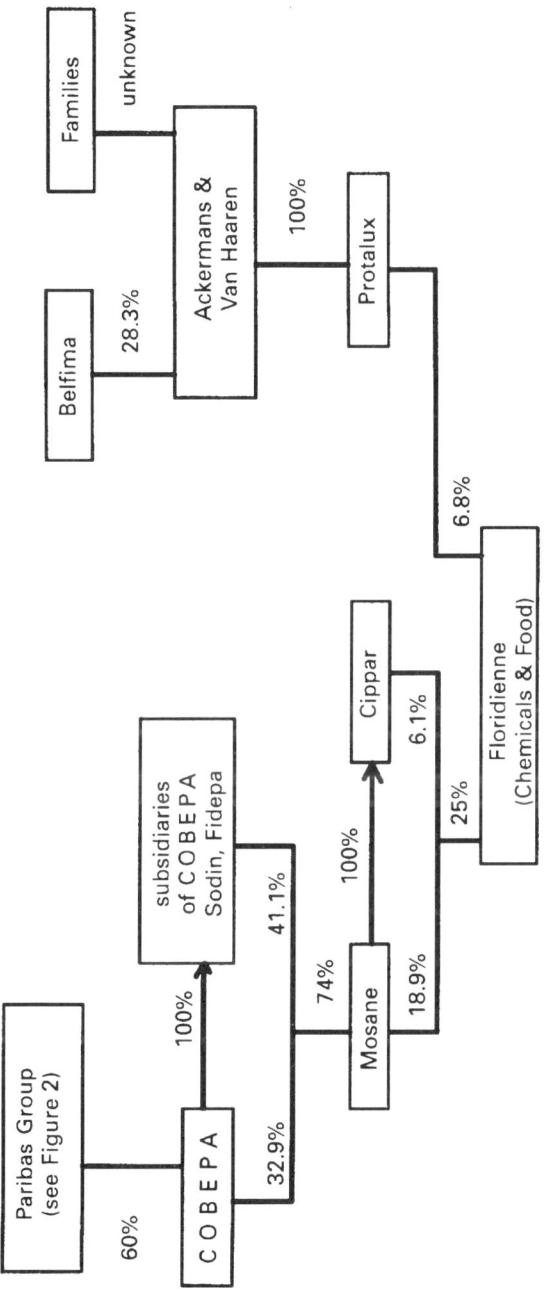

Fig. 1. Pyramidal shareholding structure of Floridienne.

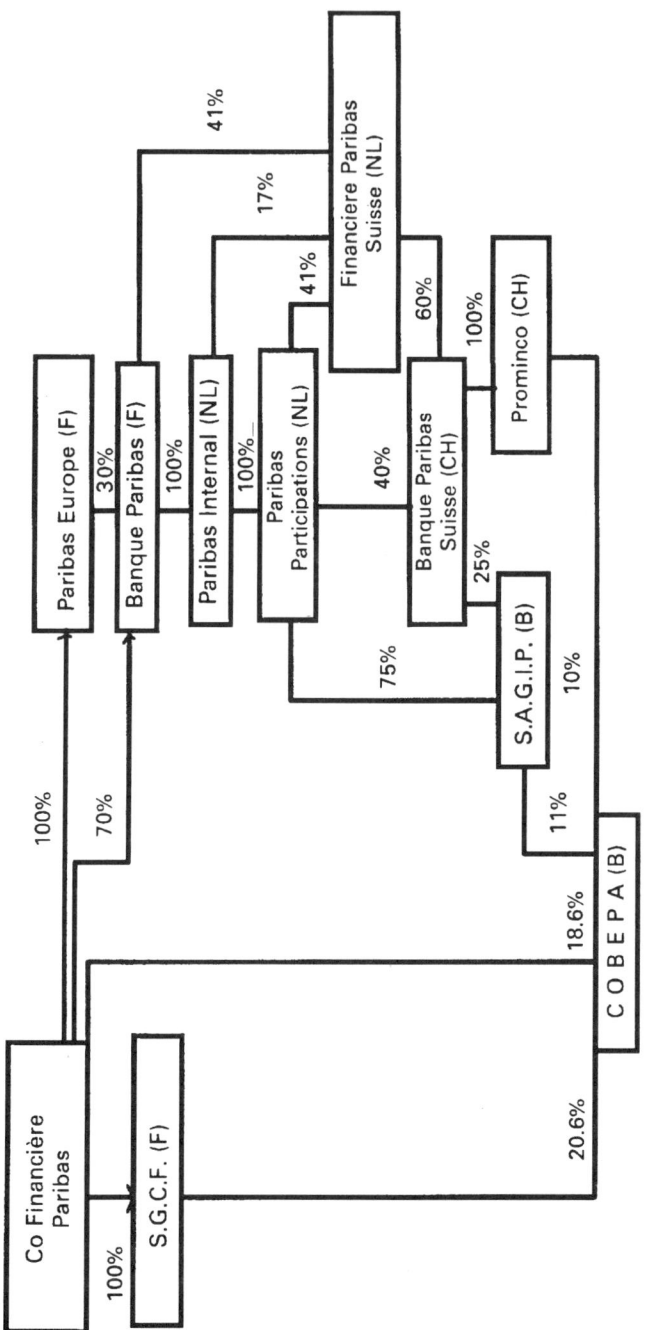

Fig. 2. Shareholder structure of COBEPA.

other shareholders with large stakes available at any ownership tier. A continuous chain of holdings of at least 50 per cent is called ultimate majority control while supermajority control arises when an uninterrupted chain of 75 per cent is in place. The most important reason for the use of pyramids in Belgium is leverage (Wymeersch 1994a): external equity can be raised while retaining control. The Paribas group controls the blocking minority in Floridienne with an interest in cash-flow rights of merely 11 per cent (60% × 74% × 25%). In fact, Paribas exercises *pyramidal* or *levered control* over Mosane. It is clear that, although the one share-one vote rule applies to each individual ownership tier, pyramidal or levered control constitutes a violation of the one-share-one vote rule if control extends throughout multiple ownership tiers (see also Renneboog 1996). Cobepa, a Belgian holding company, is also listed on the Brussels Stock Exchange and its organization chart is exhibited in Figure 2. Within the ownership chain, Swiss, French and Dutch companies and banks belonging to the Paribas group control the underlying levels with almost 100 per cent of the voting rights. This complex ownership structure, however, is not an example of an ownership pyramid, but is a case of majority control where there is hardly any control leverage. Basically, 60 per cent of Cobepa's voting rights are held by one major shareholder, the Compagnie Financière Paribas.

Previous examples clarified that the true owners of the Belgian sample companies are mostly not the direct shareholders (at ownership level 1), but that control is exercised by an ultimate shareholder on a higher ownership tier in the pyramid. It is important to identify these *ultimate shareholders* so that the percentages of voting rights held by direct or first-level shareholders controlled by the same ultimate investor can be aggregated into investor groups. Such investor group is named after and classified according to the identity and shareholder class of the ultimate shareholder.[35] Control exerted by an ultimate shareholder on a sequence of intermediate companies and, ultimately, on the sample company exists if (i) there is a series of uninterrupted majority shareholdings on every ownership tier throughout the pyramid or (ii) if there is a large shareholding of at least 25 per cent on every ownership level in the absence of other shareholders with stakes of blocking minority size or larger. Applying this criterion, henceforth called the *ultimate shareholder criterion*, to the example (Figures 1 and 2), the direct shareholdings of Mosane (18.9%) and Cippar (6.1%) are summed to 25 per cent and classified according to the shareholder category of the ultimate shareholder (Paribas), namely, a holding company.

Table 3 also details the aggregate large-share stakes of the main investor classes after applying the ultimate shareholder criterion.[36] Although holding companies remain the most important shareholder class in Belgian listed companies, their average cumulative shareholding on an ultimate control basis decreases to 26.7 per cent from an average direct shareholding of 32.7 (panel A, Table 3). The differences are explained by the fact that family controlled holding companies are now classified according to the identity of the ultimate investors, namely, families and individuals. The average shareholding held by industrial and commercial companies decreases to 11 per cent for similar reasons. Industrial and commercial companies are more inclined to hold substantial stakes in other industrial firms (panel D). Individual and family investors frequently do not hold shares directly in Belgian companies, but use intermediate companies as their average concentrated ownership amounts to almost 16 per cent, while direct stakes held by individual and family investors average only 4 per cent (panel A). Family shareholdings are most distinctly present in the ownership structure of industrial and commercial companies (panel D) with an average substantial shareholding of nearly 20 per cent.

The relative importance of domestic and foreign investors is examined in the last two columns of Table 3. More than 75 per cent of the direct large shareholdings (or an average of 49.4 per cent of the voting rights) are held by Belgian investors, while foreign investors' direct investments account for an average of 16 per cent. This proportion is similar for holding companies (panel B) and the industrial firms (panel D), but for the financial sector, domestic investments are higher with an average of 55 per cent (panel C). When applying the ultimate shareholder criterion and taking account of the nationality of the ultimate shareholders, columns 5 and 6 show that foreign investors often use Belgian intermediary companies to control Belgian listed companies. Domestic ownership in a Belgian company amounts to nearly 40 per cent; slightly lower (36 per cent) in holding companies, and somewhat higher (43 per cent) in industrial and service companies. Foreign investors hold about 38 per cent of the substantial shareholdings (or an average of 24.3 per cent of the total number of shares) in Belgian listed companies.

A comparison of the size of means and medians of concentrated cumulative ownership in 1994 and 1989 via parametric and non-parametric tests reveals that neither the total ownership concentration nor the average shareholding by shareholder class has changed significantly over time. This suggests that stakes are mostly sold to investors of the same shareholder class with whom the seller has a priority purchase agreement or to investors who belong to the same investor group.

4.2. Pyramiding and the Violation of One Share-One Vote Rule

The ultimate shareholder criterion serves to determine control relations through the pyramidal ownership structures. In the previous section, we aggregated direct shareholdings which belonged to the same investor group and reclassified the aggregate share stake according to the investor class of the ultimate share-

TABLE 4

Largest direct and ultimate levered shareholdings, and the control leverage factor

	1989	1990	1991	1992
Sample size	160	156	156	156
Ultimate ownership level	2.2	2.1	2.1	2.1
	(1.364)	(1.290)	(1.188)	(1.159)
Direct largest shareholding	55.1	56.4	57.2	57.8
	(19.737)	(19.509)	(19.923)	(20.632)
Ultimate levered shareholding	38.0	38.5	40.3	41.7
	(22.524)	(22.906)	(23.988)	(24.600)
Control leverage factor	3.6	3.6	3.0	2.9
(direct/ultimate shareholding)	(8.391)	(8.650)	(6.756)	(6.710)

This table presents the ultimate ownership level, defined as the highest level of ownership in an uninterrupted control chain (direct shareholdings are level 1). Ultimate control is control based on (i) a majority control (minimal 50% of the voting rights) on every ownership tier of the ownership pyramid or (ii) shareholdings of at least 25% on every tier in the absence of other shareholders holding stakes of 25% or more. A chain of fully owned subsidiaries are considered as one single shareholder.

The direct largest shareholding is the average direct largest share stake of at least 25%. The ultimate levered shareholding is calculated by multiplying the share stakes of subsequent ownership tiers. The control leverage factor is the ratio of the direct shareholding divided by the ultimate levered shareholding. For instance, company A, whose shares are widely held, owns 40% of company B which, in turn, owns 40% of company C. The ultimate shareholder level is 2, the direct largest shareholding (of B in C) is 40%, the ultimate shareholding is 16% (40% × 40%), and the leverage factor is 2.5 (40/16).

There was no direct shareholding of at least 25% in 17 sample companies, which were not included in this table. Standard deviation in parentheses.

Source: Own calculations based on data from the BDPart database and the Notifications of Ownership.

holder. In the example of Figure 1, we found that the Paribas controlled 25 per cent of the shares of Floridienne. In this section, we examine pyramiding by estimating deviations from the one share-one vote rule. These deviations have potentially important implications with regard to dilution of control. For instance, it is not certain whether a sequence majority control with e.g. 50 per cent at every ownership tier, yields a determining voice in board decisions of the target sample company (level 0).

Table 4 shows the average ultimate ownership level (ultimate shareholder criterion). Direct share stakes are defined as level 1 shareholdings. The level from which ultimate control is exercised is, on average, 2.2 and only slightly decreases to 2.1 over the four-year period.

As a proxy for the control leverage effect of the pyramid structures, we define the control leverage factor as the ratio of the direct largest shareholding[37] and its ultimate levered shareholding. The average of the largest direct stake per investor group amounts to about 58 per cent in 1992. The ultimate levered shareholding is calculated by multiplying the consecutive controlling shareholdings. For example, the ultimate levered shareholding of Paribas in Floridienne (see Figures 1 and 2) amounts to 11 per cent (60% × 74% × 25%) while the largest direct shareholding of the Paribas group is 25 per cent. Consequently, the control leverage factor is 2.27 (25%/11%). The smaller the shareholdings with which control is maintained throughout intermediate levels and the more intermediate ownership tiers, the higher the control leverage factor or the more considerable the violation of one share-one vote. Table 4 discloses that the control leverage factor in 1989 was 3.6 and decreases to 2.9 in 1992. Since the average ultimate ownership level and the ultimate levered shareholding do not change significantly over time, the decline of the control leverage factor indicates that control on intermediate levels becomes more concentrated. The average direct largest shareholding for companies with a direct share stake of at least 25 per cent amounts to 57 per cent while the ultimate levered shareholding is 41 per cent.

There are substantial differences in pyramiding among the subsamples of the listed Belgian holding companies, financial firms and industrial and commercial companies.[38] In 1992, the ultimate ownership level for financial firms amounted to 2.6 versus 1.9 for industrial companies. Moreover, the control leverage factor for financial firms was 7.1, 3.0 for holding companies and only 1.9 for industrial companies. This reveals that control of holding companies and financial firms is more levered than that of industrial firms.

We also investigate the control leverage established by the different classes of ultimate investors (Table 5). Of the 156 sample companies in 1992, 64 ultimate investors were holding companies, 49 were families and 27 were industrial companies.[39] Both the ultimate ownership level and the control leverage factor point out that holding companies, insurance companies and families use more intermediate companies and smaller intermediate share stakes to ascertain control than industrial companies. Hence, the deviation of the concept of one share-one vote is considerable for investing holding companies and, consequently, the potential for dilution of control increases.

4.3. Blocking Minorities, Majorities and Supermajorities

Table 6 examines control patterns and gives the percentage of Belgian companies with an ownership structure characterized by the presence of blocking minorities, majorities and supermajorities. When a shareholder possesses more than 50 per cent of the voting rights, he can dominate the agenda at the annual meeting and control the selection and hiring process of the board members and the delegated director (CEO). In practice, less than 50 per cent of the voting rights will be needed to have a majority on the annual meeting because

TABLE 5

Largest direct and ultimate levered shareholdings, and the control leverage factor by ultimate investor category

1992	ULTIMATE SHAREHOLDERS					
	Holding co's	Investment co's	Insurance co's	Industrial co's	Families	Government
Sample size	64	5	5	27	49	6
Ultimate ownership level	2.3 (1.270)	1.4 (0.489)	2.4 (1.496)	1.7 (1.116)	2.0 (0.868)	1.7 (1.105)
Direct largest shareholding	57.0 (17.906)	44.6 (12.116)	75.2 (23.961)	60.4 (23.584)	54.6 (20.649)	63.6 (18.607)
Ultimate levered shareholding	35.1 (21.741)	31.2 (12.023)	43.6 (27.659)	50.8 (25.277)	41.5 (23.997)	53.3 (21.116)
Control leverage factor (direct/ultimate shareholding	4.3 (9.959)	1.7 (0.877)	3.0 (3.121)	1.5 (1.387)	2.9 (1.387)	1.1 (1.185)

This table presents the ultimate ownership level, defined as the highest level of ownership in an uninterrupted control chain (direct shareholdings are level 1). Ultimate control is control based on (i) a majority control (minimal 50% of the voting rights) on every ownership tier of the ownership pyramid or (ii) shareholdings of at least 25% on every tier in the absence of other shareholders holding stakes of 25% or more. A chain of fully owned subsidiaries are considered as one single shareholder.
The direct largest shareholding is the average direct largest share stake of at least 25%. The ultimate levered shareholding is calculated by multiplying the share stakes of subsequent ownership tiers. The control leverage factor is the ratio of the direct shareholding divided by the ultimate levered shareholding. For instance, company A, whose shares are widely held, owns 40% of company B which, in turn, owns 40% of company C. The ultimate shareholder level is 2, the direct largest shareholding (of B in C) is 40%, the ultimate shareholding is 16% (40% × 40%), and the leverage factor is 2.5 (40/16).
There was no direct shareholding of at least 25% in 17 sample companies, which were not included in this table.
Standard deviation in parentheses.
Source: Own calculations based on data from the BDPart database and the notification of ownership disclosure.

some, predominantly the small, investors usually choose not to be involved in active monitoring and will only use their voting rights under special circumstances e.g. in the case of a potential acquisition. Table 6 shows the percentage of sample companies with the critical threshold stakes of 25%, 50% and 75%. Both the direct threshold shareholdings are presented and the threshold shareholdings per investor group.[40] Panel A reveals that a voting rights majority exists in more than half (56 per cent) of the Belgian listed companies based on the ultimate shareholder criterion. In 18 per cent of the Belgian companies, a supermajority gives absolute control to one shareholder or a group of share-

TABLE 6

Blocking minority, majority and supermajority shareholdings

August 1994	All investors			Holding co's			Families			Indus. co's			Belgian investors			Foreign investors		
	MIN	MAJ	SUP	MIN	MAJ	SUP	MIN	MAJ	SUP	MIN	MAJ	SUP	MIN	MAJ	SUP	MIN	MAJ	SUP
PANEL A: ALL SAMPLE COMPANIES (N = 157)																		
Direct	82	45	14	48	23	5	2	1	1	21	12	5	63	36	9	19	9	5
Ultimate	85	56	18	41	26	6	23	14	3	15	8	5	51	33	9	34	23	10
PANEL B: HOLDING COMPANIES (N = 64)																		
Direct	79	39	14	50	23	8	5	2	2	17	9	2	59	31	11	20	8	3
Ultimate	83	59	20	50	36	13	22	13	2	9	6	3	45	30	11	38	30	13
PANEL C: FINANCIAL SECTOR (BANKING, INSURANCE, REAL ESTATE) (N = 20)																		
Direct	75	50	10	35	15	0	0	0	0	5	5	5	62	40	10	13	10	0
Ultimate	80	55	15	40	15	0	5	5	0	5	5	5	48	33	10	32	22	5
PANEL D: INDUSTRIAL AND COMMERCIAL COMPANIES (N = 73)																		
Direct	86	47	15	48	25	4	0	0	0	28	15	8	66	37	7	20	10	8
Ultimate	93	55	16	34	19	3	29	18	4	24	11	7	61	37	8	32	18	8

Percentage of the sample companies with a minority, majority or supermajority shareholdings held by the main shareholder categories.
MIN = % of companies with a stake of 25% or larger
MAJ = % of companies with a stake of 50% or larger
SUP = % of companies with a stake of 75% or larger
Direct stands for the direct shareholdings. Ultimate refers to the fact that the direct shareholdings were classified according to the shareholder class of the ultimate investor and these direct shareholdings belonging to the same ultimate investor group were subsequently summed. Ultimate control is control based on (i) a majority control (minimal 50% of the voting rights) on every ownership tier of the ownership pyramid or (ii) shareholdings of at least 25% on every tier in the absence of other shareholders holding stakes of 25% or more. A chain of fully owned subsidiaries are considered as one single shareholder.

Source: Own calculations based on BDPart and Ownership Notifications.

holders as blocking minorities cannot be formed. Shareholdings of 25 per cent or more are present in 85 per cent of all companies. The concentrated ownership pattern is similar in all subsamples. Share stakes of more than 25 per cent exist in more than 80 per cent of the holding companies (panel B) and the financial firms (panel C) and even in 93 per cent of the industrial and commercial companies (panel D). We find that ownership concentration is very strong in most companies within each subsample. Consequently, as, to a large extent, takeovers have to be ruled out as a corporate control mechanism, large shareholders bear responsibility for monitoring management's performance.

Holding companies, both Belgian and foreign, are the main ultimate investors since they dominate with voting-right majorities 26 per cent of the Belgian firms (panel A). Holding companies invest mainly in other Belgian and foreign holding and companies (see panels B and D). Family and individual investment (panel A) is high (on ultimate control basis) since they hold stakes of at least 25 per cent in almost one fourth of all Belgian listed companies and majorities in 14 per cent. This shareholder class owns large stakes (of over 25 per cent) in 29 per cent of the industrial and commercial sector (panel D) and has absolute control in 18 per cent. The industrial shareholders predominantly hold share stakes of minimum blocking minority size in other industrial companies (panel D).

Total Belgian and foreign ownership concentration based upon direct shareholdings gives a different picture when ultimate control is considered. The proportion of about 75%–25% of the sample companies with direct share stakes of at least blocking minority size held by respectively Belgian and foreign shareholders, changes to a 60%–40% ratio on an ultimate shareholder basis. This fact reconfirms that foreign investors predominantly control stakes in Belgian companies via Belgian intermediaries.

With regard to absolute control in the form of supermajorities, foreign investors control 10 per cent of the companies while Belgian investors only control 9 per cent (panel A). Table 6 also reveals that Belgian and foreign investors each hold majority stakes in 30 per cent of the Belgian listed holding companies. Consequently, the proportion domestic of versus foreign ultimate investors has changed to a 50%–50% ratio. The majority of Belgian industrial and services companies (panel D) is still dominated by Belgian investors.

This section has disclosed that over the period 1989 till 1994, Belgian ownership was highly concentrated with more than half of the listed companies controlled with majority stakes. The average substantial stakes held by the different ownership classes has remained relatively stable.[41]

4.4 *Belgian Shareholder Classes*

Of the Belgian shareholder classes,[42] the dominant stakeholders are families and holding companies. These two shareholder groups hold most of the controlling stakes (in respectively 12 per cent and 11 per cent of all the sample companies) and each shareholder class holds share stakes of more than 25 per cent in about 20 per cent of the sample companies.

Family Shareholders

Belgian families own a voting-right majority in 15 per cent of the industrial and commercial companies and hold 26 per cent of the shareholdings of at least 25 per cent. Families also often use the holding companies as investment vehicles to control indirectly a variety of listed and non-listed companies in different industries.

Holding Companies

Belgian holding companies are substantial investors in all sectors: in other Belgian holding companies, in the financial sector and in industrial and commercial companies. The importance of the Belgian holding companies and the lack of large share stakes held by banks should be understood in its historic framework: banking and investment business had to be separated by law in 1934. This resulted in the creation of large financial holding companies which became the major shareholders in the financial institutions and diversified their investments over a wide gamut of industrial and commercial sectors. As clarified in Figure 1, pyramidal ownership structures allowed holding companies[43] to exercise levered control with relatively small share stakes.

Financial Institutions

As of 1934, 'credit institutions' were prohibited from taking share participations in industrial companies. Only since the 1993 Credit Institutions Act[44] which implemented the Second Banking Directive of the European Union, are credit institutions (banks, savings banks and other financial institutions) entitled to hold shares in industrial corporations and holding companies. Currently, credit institutions are allowed to hold up to 10 per cent of their equity in Belgian shares. There is no limitation with regard to the percentage of the outstanding shares of an individual company a credit institution is allowed to own.

In practice, banks still do not invest much in shares of non-financial companies to avoid conflicts of interest:

- According to Belgian law, banks are held liable towards creditors of bankrupt companies, if the banks granted credit to these companies at times when a reasonably prudent banker should not have granted nor maintained the credit. A substantial shareholding in a financially distressed company by a bank might influence that bank's decision with regard to ceasing additional credit.
- Since most banks are controlled by a holding company which might be a substantial shareholder in a company, it is doubtful whether banks would

be able to make independent decisions with regard to a shareholding in that company or the loans granted to a company (Verwilst 1992).
• Most investment and pension funds are managed by a bank that ensures the distribution of the investment fund's certificates (shares). Legally, investment and pension funds' management should use the voting rights associated with the shares of a company they have invested in, independent of the managing bank.

The Government

In principle, the federal state does invest in listed Belgian companies. But it owns 50 per cent of the shares of the National Bank, of which the shares are listed in the Brussels Stock Exchange, and 50 per cent of the 'public credit institutions'. The role of the public credit institutions has been broadened to that of a bank and they are being privatized. The 'public investment companies' owned by the regional governments hold blocks in shares of a few listed companies. Those investments were made either to save ailing companies or to provide risky companies with growth capital so as to stimulate and support entrepreneurial and industrial expansion activities. In general, in contrast to France, federal and regional governments have not considered their shareholdings in companies as a long term financial investment. Only in two per cent of the listed companies does the state still hold a share stake via the regional investment companies.

Employee Shareholdership

Since 1991, mechanisms of beneficial acquisition of shares by employees have been introduced. In general, employee ownership in most companies remains low. For instance, employees of Petrofina own 5.4 per cent of the shares; in de Bank Brussels Lambert, employees hold 7 per cent; in Creyf's Interim 0.9 per cent; in Desimpel Kortemark 0.5 per cent; in Royale Belge, 0.69 per cent (Wymeersch 1994a).

Institutional Investors

Belgian institutional investors (insurance companies, pension funds, credit institutions, investment funds and investment companies) usually hold small share stakes (of under 5 per cent), but own in aggregate about 22 per cent of the shares in Belgian listed companies.[45] For instance, the average shareholding of all Bevek/Sicav-investment funds[46] in the 60 most traded Belgian companies, amounted to 1.5 per cent in 1994 and the average shareholding of pension funds measures about 4 per cent (B.B.L. 1994).[47] Insurance companies are legally allowed to invest up to 25 per cent of their reserves in shares listed on the Belgian stock exchanges, but owned only about 12 per cent of the Belgian shares over the period 1986–1991. Most institutional investors reinforce the present majority's power by systematically voting in favour of management or, more commonly, by not taking part in the general assembly.

4.5. *Foreign Shareholder Classes*

Of the foreign investors, it is primarily the holding companies that hold large share stakes and control with a majority stake in 15 per cent of all the Belgian listed companies.[48] Foreign holding companies invest predominantly in Belgian holding companies, one fourth of which they control with a majority of the voting rights. This way foreign holding companies also indirectly invest in unlisted Belgian companies with shares held in the investment portfolios of Belgian holding companies. Foreign industrial companies prefer Belgian industrial companies as long-term investments, while foreign banks and insurance companies are substantial shareholders in the Belgian financial and insurance sector. Foreign institutional investors do not rely heavily on the Belgian stock market.

Although shareholders from a wide variety of countries[49] are present in the ownership structure of Belgian listed companies, the main investors are from the neighbouring European countries. Dutch investors own an average direct share stake of 3.8 per cent and invest predominantly in Belgian industrial and commercial companies. German direct average ownership is low. German industrial companies mainly invested in the concrete industry via e.g. Heidelberger Zement. Investors from Luxembourg own, on average, directly 4.1 per cent of Belgian companies, and have invested mainly in industrial and commercial companies. But, companies from Luxembourg are almost never the ultimate investor and are used as intermediary investment vehicles by, for example, French companies. UK and North American shareholders hold large stakes in only 3 companies. Only one large shareholding of a Belgian listed company is Japanese: Ashaki acquired a majority stake in the glass manufacturer Glaverbel. The average French direct average shareholding is higher and close to 4.3 per cent.The single most important foreign ultimate investors are French; their accumulated substantial shareholdings amount on average to almost 13 per cent. They invest mainly in the Belgian holding companies of which they own an average stake of 19 per cent and in the financial sector in which they hold an average of 14 per cent of the voting rights. By way of controlling participations in Belgian large holding companies, French investors control a substantial part, estimated at 30 per cent (Wymeersch 1994a), of all the listed and unlisted industrial companies in Belgium. Columns 2 to 5 of Table 7 reveal that it is the French holding companies, rather than French family investors or industrial companies that have acquired a substantial stake of the Belgian listed companies. French insurance companies own significant shareholdings in the Belgian banks and insurance companies.

TABLE 7

Size of large shareholdings held by a French ultimate investor (group)

August 1994	SHAREHOLDINGS OWNED BY ULTIMATE FRENCH INVESTORS					SHAREHOLDINGS EXCLUDING SUEZ AND PARIBAS	
	All investors	Holding co's	Insurance co's	Indus. co's	Families	All investors	Holding co's
PANEL A: ALL SAMPLE COMPANIES (N = 157)							
MEAN	12.89	9.37	1.05	1.41	0.45	6.32	2.80
STD	25.17	22.27	8.53	8.91	5.67	19.39	13.91
t-stat[3]	−1.775[4]	−1.740[4]	−0.453	0.125	−0.600	−0.670	−0.513
PANEL B: ALL HOLDING COMPANIES (N = 64)							
MEAN	18.82	15.28	0.16	2.28	1.11	9.21	5.67
STD	31.09	29.11	1.25	12.40	8.88	24.30	20.07
t-stat[3]	0.040	−0.015	0.120	0.472	−0.064	0.050	−0.025
PANEL C: FINANCIAL SECTOR (BANKS, INSURANCE, REAL ESTATE) (N = 20)							
MEAN	13.96	5.72	7.76	0.00	0.00	11.61	3.37
STD	25.82	15.04	23.19	0.00	0.00	26.01	13.98
t-stat[3]	−1.253	−0.933	−0.408	0.000	−1.000	−0.729	−0.080
PANEL D: INDUSTRIAL AND COMMERCIAL COMPANIES (N = 73)							
MEAN	7.39	5.19	0.00	1.04	0.00	2.33	0.13
STD	17.00	14.87	0.00	6.00	0.00	9.38	0.84
t-stat[3]	−2.274[5]	−2.484[5]	−0.998	−0.384	0.000	−0.783	−1.511

This table reports the aggregate substantial shareholdings[1] owned by the main French investor groups.

Ultimate refers to the fact that the direct shareholdings were classified according to the shareholder class of the ultimate investor and these direct shareholdings belonging to the same ultimate investor group were subsequently summed. Ultimate control is control based on (i) a majority control (minimal 50% of the voting rights) on every ownership tier of the ownership pyramid or (ii) shareholdings of at least 25% on every tier in the absence of other shareholders holding stakes of 25% or more. A chain of fully owned subsidiaries are considered as one single shareholder.

Source: Own calculations based on BDPart and Ownership Notifications.

[1] In line with the Ownership Disclosure Legislation, substantial shareholdings are defined as share stakes that equal or exceed 5% (of the voting rights), unless investors with smaller shareholdings are affiliated to or act in concert with major shareholders, in which case small stakes ought to be revealed as well. The 5% threshold can be reduced to 3% if the company states this in its acts of constitution.

[2] The direct shareholdings are accumulated if they are directly owned or (indirectly) controlled by a French ultimate investor (group)

[3] The t-stat. tests the difference between the ownership means in 1994 and 1989. Non-parametric tests give similar results.

[4] Statistical significance at 10%.

[5] Statistical significance at 5%.

The French Suez group controls the Generale Maatschappij van België (Société Générale de Belgique) and the Paribas group dominates the Belgian Cobepa holding. To investigate the prominence of these two large French holding companies, the average substantial shareholdings held by French investors excluding the Suez and the Paribas group are presented in columns 6 and 7 of Table 7. A comparison of the aggregate concentrated French ownership including and excluding Suez and Paribas reveals that these holding companies account for more than half of the substantial French investments in Belgian listed companies (holding and industrial companies). The average large share stake held by the French holding companies falls from 9.4 per cent to 2.8 per cent after exclusion of the Suez and Paribas holding companies (columns 2 and 7). The 9.4 per cent average shareholding is equivalent to majority control in 10 companies and the 2.8 per cent represents control in 2 companies. Apart from controlling stakes, Suez and Paribas are present with minority stakes in 45 listed companies. Panel D (column 7) shows that the French holding companies other than Suez and Paribas, control virtually no voting rights directly in the Belgian industry.

The slight decrease in the French average shareholding from 1989 to 1994 is mainly due to a reduction of ownership by the French holding companies.[50] An important reason is the restructuring of the Generale Maatschappij van België (Société Générale de Belgique) after the takeover by Suez. Since then, the Generale focuses on eight core strategic sectors and has reduced its shareholdings in others.

4.6. Changes in large shareholdings

We have shown that the aggregated large shareholdings per shareholder category remained stable over time. As selling activity of stakes within shareholder categories is not reflected in the aggregate ownership data, Table 8 examines these changes in large shareholdings. Over the period 1989–1992, there were 238 shareholding increases of more than 1 per cent, while 247 stakes were sold. Of these changes in ownership, there were 120 increases of a magnitude between 5 and 24.9 per cent, versus 110 decreases of similar size. In 16 cases, majority shareholdings were acquired and 28 blocks of blocking minority size were purchased. Thirty-three blocking minorities were sold, in addition to 28 majority stakes. It should be noted that the changes are corrected for shareholding restructuring within investor groups. For example, a redistribution of share stakes in a sample company held by two companies which are controlled by the same ultimate investor, has a limited impact on control and is consequently not included in the changes of large shareholdings. These observations suggest that this market for share stakes is not insignificant: in one fourth of the sample companies, share stake changes of 5 per cent or more occur in the period

TABLE 8

Increases and decreases of large shareholdings over 1989-1992

1989-1992	Number of increases and decreases stakes (in %)					
	[1-5[	[5-10[	[10-25[	[25-50[	[50-100[	Total
PANEL A: INCREASES FOR ALL SAMPLE COMPANIES (number of observations: 693)						
Increases: all shareholders	74	72	48	28	16	238
Increases: holding companies	34	35	17	16	2	104
Increases: institutional investors	24	17	12	4	5	62
Increases: industr. & commerc. co's	5	9	8	4	5	31
Increases: families	11	11	11	4	4	41
PANEL B: DECREASES FOR ALL SAMPLE COMPANIES (number of observations: 693)						
Decreases: all shareholders	76	51	59	33	28	247
Decreases: holding companies	26	31	34	12	18	121
Decreases: institutional investors	31	8	11	9	2	61
Decreases: industr. & commerc. co's	3	2	6	1	4	16
Decreases: families	16	10	8	11	4	49

This table gives the size distribution of increases and decreases of large shareholdings over the period 1989-1992. Increases and decreases were calculated by comparing the share stakes of a shareholder category of a fiscal year to the shareholdings of previous year.
Source: Own calculations based on BDPart and Ownership Notifications.

1989-1992. The relevance of this market as a an external corporate control mechanism will be investigated in the following chapter. Table 8 discloses that the holding companies are the main sellers and purchasers of share stakes. Institutional investors, mainly banks and insurance companies, acquire 38 shareholdings of more than 5 per cent and sell 30 stakes of similar sizes. Families sell 15 stakes of blocking minority size and more, while 8 such stakes are bought by this shareholder category.[51] Most of the exchanges of blocks of shares are negotiated deals and take place ex exchange.[52]

5. CONCLUSION

We have shown that the Belgian equity market is similar to most Continental European ones as few companies are quoted, ownership concentration is strong, pyramidal ownership structures are used to lever control and there is a market for share stakes. Typical for Belgium is the dominance of holding companies as large shareholders. Pyramiding of shareholding structures violates the one share-one vote rule as ultimate shareholders can exercise control with a low percentage of cash-flow rights. Despite the strong concentration of relatively stable large shareholdings, the existence of a market for small share stakes reveals the importance of reaching critical control levels (blocking minorities, majorities and supermajorities) for the exertion of corporate control.

Renneboog (1996) shows that the ownership structure of Belgian companies quoted on the Brussels Stock Exchange is positively correlated to disciplinary actions when performance is poor. Top management and executive directors will be substituted when the company's short share price performance and accounting performance (earnings after tax, cash-flow margin) are low. The monitoring actions against management will be facilitated when there is strong ownership concentration. However, some shareholder categories holding large ownership stakes seem to be better corporate monitors than others. For example, industrial companies holding at least a blocking minority seem to discipline underperforming management, a relation which is not found amongst institutional shareholders (banks, insurance companies, and investment and pension funds). The corporate control activities of the large holding companies seem to be limited. In the same paper, the importance of a market for share stakes is revealed. Increases in share stakes are usually followed by increased management turnover, which suggests that part of the market for share stakes is a corporate control market.

APPENDIX A: CALCULATION OF CROSS SHAREHOLDINGS

To describe the ownership relation between companies, we can distinguish among affiliation, association and participation. Two companies are affiliated if one owns at least 50 per cent in the other company (the subsidiary).[53] When two companies are associated, one of these companies holds a stake of more than 25 per cent in the other company.[54] Note that 25 per cent is the blocking minority threshold. If a company X owns a stake of less than 25 per cent in company Y, there is a 'participating relationship' between them.[55]

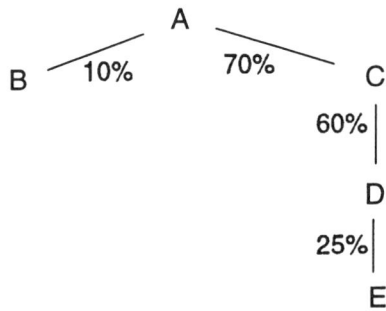

- A, C and D are affiliated. The control percentage of A in D is 60 per cent, while its percentage of interest on a levered basis amounts of 42 per cent (70% × 60%).
- A and E are associated. The control percentage of A in E is 25 per cent, whereas its percentage of interest on a levered basis is only 11 per cent (70% × 60% × 25%).
- A has a participation in B; percentage of control and interest is 10 per cent.

Cross shareholdings
It is possible that there is a reciprocal shareholdership between two companies. For instance, company P (parent) owns 75 per cent of the shares of company S (subsidiary) while company S owns 5 per cent of company P.[56]

$$P \xrightarrow{75\%} S$$
$$P \xleftarrow{5\%} S$$

To calculate the percentage of interest of P in S, let us assume that $a = 75\%$ and $b = 5\%$. P's shareholders own $(1 - b)$ of the share capital of P the remaining $b\%$ is held by S. The direct interest of P's shareholders in S is $[(1 - b) \times a]$. Indirectly – this is via the shareholdings of S in P, they possess:

$$(1 - b) \times a \times b \times a.$$

If this circular reasoning is repeated several times, the total interest of P in S can be expressed as follows:

direct holding of:

$$(1 - b) \times a$$

plus an indirect holding of:

$$(1 - b) \times a + (1 - b) \times a^2 b + \ldots + (1 - b) \times a^{n+1} b^n$$

This sum is a geometrical progression:

$$(1 - b) \times a \times (1 + ab + a^2 b^2 + \ldots + a^n b^n)$$
$$= (1 - b) \times a \times (1 - a^n b^n)/(1 - ab)$$

And since $a^n b^n$ converges to one for a large n, we can write P's interest in S as:

$$(1 - b) \times a/(1 - ab)$$

Applying this result to our example, we conclude that P's ownership in S amounts to 74,03 per cent.

Via a similar reasoning, we find that the percentage of interest of S in P can be formalized (Uytterschaut, 1989):

$$(1 - a)/(1 - ab)$$

Applied to our example, we find that S owns 5.97 per cent of the share capital of P.

Since the shareholdings of the 'subsidiary' are limited to 10 per cent of the share capital of the parent company, the difference between the percentage of interest of the 'parent' company in the subsidiary with and without considering the cross shareholding of the subsidiary will not be substantial.[57]

APPENDIX B

TABLE B1

Largest direct and ultimate shareholdings, and the top level of uninterrupted ownership chains

	1989	1990	1991	1992
Sample size	177	173	173	170
Ultimate ownership level	2.3	2.1	2.1	2.1
	(1.471)	(1.330)	(1.312)	(1.300)
Direct largest shareholding	50.4	51.5	52.6	53.6
	(22.898)	(22.943)	(23.073)	(23.453)
Ultimate levered shareholding	34.8	35.3	37.1	38.6
	(22.131)	(24.544)	(24.544)	(25.222)
Control leverage factor	3.5	3.4	3.0	2.9
(direct/ultimate shareholding)	(7.956)	(8.917)	(6.535)	(6.555)

This table presents ultimate control, defined as control which is uninterrupted throughout the pyramid if there is a majority shareholding or if there is a large shareholder with at least 25% of the voting rights in the absence of other shareholders with stakes of 25% and more.

The ultimate ownership level defined as the highest level of ownership in an uninterrupted control chain, whereby direct shareholdings are at level 1.The direct largest shareholding is the average direct largest share stake. The ultimate levered shareholding is calculated by multiplying subsequent share stakes.

The control leverage factor is the ratio of the direct shareholding divided by the ultimate levered shareholding. For instance, company A, whose shares are widely held, owns 40% of company B which, in turn, owns 40% of company C. The ultimate shareholder level is 2, the direct largest shareholding (of B in C) is 40%, the ultimate shareholding is 16% (40% × 40%), and the leverage factor is 2.5 (40/16).

A chain of fully owned subsidiaries are considered as one single shareholder.

There was no direct shareholding of at least 25% in 17 sample companies, for which the ownership structure of the largest holding was taken into account.

Standard deviations in parentheses.

Source: Own calculations based on data from the BDPart database and the Notifications of Ownership.

TABLE B2

Largest direct and ultimate shareholdings, and the top level of uninterrupted ownership chains

	1989	1990	1991	1992
PANEL A: HOLDING COMPANIES (sample size = 60)				
Ultimate ownership level	2.2	2.2	2.1	2.0
	(1.313)	(1.330)	(1.202)	(1.197)
Direct largest shareholding	51.8	51.7	53.3	55.3
	(16.125)	(16.491)	(16.569)	(18.722)
Ultimate levered shareholding	37.213	37.4	38.4	40.7
	(20.903)	(21.604)	(21.457)	(23.053)
Control leverage factor	3.7	3.8	3.0	3.0
(direct/ultimate shareholding)	(9.253)	(9.498)	(7.107)	(7.150)
PANEL B: FINANCIAL SECTOR (sample size = 20 in 1989 and 17 in other years)				
Ultimate ownership level	2.9	2.6	2.6	2.6
	(2.021)	(1.606)	(1.603)	(1.610)
Direct largest shareholding	55.7	57.8	61.6	61.5
	(19.606)	(19.746)	(20.322)	(20.654)
Ultimate levered shareholding	29.8	32.4	33.8	34.8
	(23.313)	(22.654)	(27.109)	(28.220)
Leverage factor	7.5	6.4	6.9	7.1
(direct/ultimate shareholding)	(13.597)	(13.535)	(13.535)	(13.841)
PANEL C: INDUSTRIAL AND COMMERCIAL COMPANIES (sample size = 78 in 1989 and 76 in other years)				
Ultimate ownership level	2.2	2.1	2.0	1.9
	(1.117)	(1.152)	(1.018)	(0.958)
Direct largest shareholding	57.3	58.9	59.272	59.012
	(21.845)	(21.113)	(21.656)	(21.826)
Ultimate levered shareholding	38.8	40.779	43.2	43.9
	(23.126)	(23.614)	(24.657)	(24.634)
Leverage factor	2.7	2.8	2.1	1.9
(direct/ultimate shareholding)	(4.847)	(5.908)	(2.337)	(1.642)

This table presents ultimate control, defined as control which is uninterrupted throughout the pyramid if there is a majority shareholding or if there is a large shareholder with at least 25% of the voting rights in the absence of other shareholders with stakes of 25% and more.

The ultimate ownership level defined as the highest level of ownership in an uninterrupted control chain, whereby direct shareholdings are at level 1. The direct largest shareholding is the average direct largest share stake of at least 25%. The ultimate shareholding is calculated by multiplying subsequent share stakes. The control leverage factor is the ratio of the direct shareholding divided by the ultimate levered shareholding. For instance, company A, whose shares are widely held, owns 40% of company B which, in turn, owns 40% of company C. The ultimate shareholder level is 2, the direct largest shareholding (of B in C) is 40%, the ultimate shareholding is 16% (40% × 40%), and the leverage factor is 2.5 (40/16). A chain of fully owned subsidiaries are considered as one single shareholder.

There was no direct shareholding of at least 25% in 17 sample companies, which were not included in this table.

Standard deviations in parentheses.

Source: Own calculations based on data from the BDPart database and the Notifications of Ownership.

TABLE B3

Changes in large shareholdings

1989-1992	Number of increases and decreases stakes (in %)					
	[1-5[	[5-10[	[10-25[	[25-50[	[50-100[	Total
PANEL A: CHANGES FOR THE HOLDING COMPANIES (number of observations: 273)						
Decreases: all shareholders	28	35	27	6	1	97
Decreases: holding companies	13	18	14	3	0	48
Decreases: institutional investors	7	6	4	0	0	17
Decreases: industr. & commerc. co's	2	3	2	2	0	9
Decreases: families	6	8	7	1	1	23
Decreases: all shareholders	34	25	29	12	6	106
Decreases: holding companies	9	18	23	4	3	57
Decreases: institutional investors	14	2	4	7	2	29
Decreases: industr. & commerc. co's	1	1	0	0	0	2
Decreases: families	10	4	2	1	1	18
PANEL B: CHANGES FOR THE FINANCIAL SECTOR (number of observations: 91)						
Increases: all shareholders	21	13	2	2	4	42
Increases: holding companies	9	4	0	1	1	15
Increases: institutional investors	10	8	2	1	2	23
Increases: industr. & commerc. co's	2	1	0	0	1	4
Increases: families	0	0	0	0	0	0
Decreases: all shareholders	13	6	9	5	7	40
Decreases: holding companies	6	2	2	0	5	15
Decreases: institutional investors	7	3	6	0	0	16
Decreases: industr. & commerc. co's	0	0	0	0	2	2
Decreases: families	0	1	1	5	0	7
PANEL C: CHANGES FOR THE INDUSTRIAL AND COMMERCIAL COMPANIES (number of observations: 329)						
Increases: all shareholders	25	24	19	21	11	100
Increases: holding companies	12	13	3	12	1	41
Increases: institutional investors	7	3	6	3	3	22
Increases: industr. & commerc. co's	1	5	6	3	4	19
Increases: families	5	3	4	3	3	18
Decreases: all shareholders	29	20	21	16	15	101
Decreases: holding companies	11	11	9	8	10	49
Decreases: institutional investors	10	3	1	2	0	16
Decreases: industr. & commerc. co's	2	1	6	1	2	12
Decreases: families	6	5	5	5	3	24

This table presents the size distribution of increases and decreases of large shareholdings over the period 1989-1992. Increases and decreases were calculated by comparing the share stakes of a shareholder category of a fiscal year to the shareholdings of previous year. The changes in shareholdings per size class over the period 1989-92 are summed.

Source: Own calculations based on BDPart and Ownership Notifications.

NOTES

1. Wymeersch (1994b) makes a distinction similar to Franks and Mayer (1992) between company-oriented and enterprise-oriented systems. A company-oriented system is characterized by the existence of a large number of listed companies. Most of the their shares are effectively traded on the markets. The monitoring function is essentially undertaken by the securities market and active market trading is an essential prerequisite for efficient monitoring. Privileged tools of intervention are the appointment of non executive directors who are chosen on their technical abilities and the designation of special board committees. Ultimately, takeovers drive out inefficient management. The US and the UK fall clearly under the definition of a company-oriented corporate control system. An enterprise-oriented system has a low number of listed companies, control is held by major shareholder so that a limited number of shares are effectively on the market. Monitoring does not take place via the market, but is regulated by group law.
2. In this sense, the Italian equity market is similar to the Belgian one: few companies are quoted, concentration of ownership is high, pyramidal ownership structures with holding companies as intermediate investment vehicles are common (Nikodamo 1995, Bianchi and Casavola 1995). But, whereas the Italian state controls a large number of industrial groups and holding companies, Belgian state ownership is rare.
3. This is also the case for the Netherlands and for Switzerland when the impact of respectively the five Dutch large multinationals and the Swiss financial sector are excluded from the data.
4. For the evolution of German ownership structure: see Baums (1994).
5. Chirinko and Elston (1995) find strong evidence that bank influence and concentrated ownership serve as substitutes for controlling corporations.
6. Miyajima (1995) examines the creation and growth of bank centred corporate groups. For a detailed description of the Japanese ownership structure: see Prowse (1992).
7. There are two strands of the literature on ownership and control. The first focuses on the determinants of ownership while the second concentrates on how corporate control is exercised. With regard to ownership, there are into three classes of models. A first class of the models argues that transaction costs make transactions through markets more costly than internal activities within the firm. In this literature, the firm is considered as a nexus of contracts and it may be costly to write the contracts necessary to undertake transactions between firms through the market place (see, for instance, Coase (1937), Williamson (1975), Aoki, Gustafsson and Williamson (1990)). Secondly, the industrial economics literature emphasizes vertical ownership relations and attempts to explain the reasons why upstream and downstream firms hold stakes in each other (see e.g. Dixit (1983), Salinger (1988)). When upstream firms do not take full account of the interests of downstream firms e.g. with regard to the prices they set, ownership may be required to internalize such externalities in the absence of suitable contractual alternatives. A third series of models concentrate on the effect of incomplete contracts on the ex ante incentive that firms have to make sunk investments. Ownership is here considered as a commitment device with regard to specific investments. Ownership allows parties to avoid decisions being taken in the future that adversely affect the value of past investments (see e.g. Grossman and Hart (1986), Hart and Moore (1990)). The second strand of the literature focuses on corporate control. Manne (1965), Alchian and Demsetz (1972) and Fama and Jensen (1983) state that separation of ownership and control in the outsider system has evoked a number of mechanisms to limit the agency problems that would be expected to arise. Such mechanisms include monitoring and control by non-executive directors, incentive systems and a market in corporate control.
8. Law of 22 March 1989, called *Transparantiewetgeving* (transparency legislation) and Royal Decrees of 10 May 1989 and of 8 November 1989.

9. Law of 18 July 1991.
10. Individual companies can reduce this threshold in the articles of incorporation, but not to less than 3%. Notification of changes in stakes by the shareholders will have to be made if the following thresholds are passed: 3%, 5%, 10%, 15%, and further multiples of 5%. (Law of 22 March 1989, Section 5.) Currently, about 20 companies have adopted the 3% threshold (Wuille 1994).
11. The Commission for Banking and Finance, usually abbreviated to Banking Commission, is the Belgian equivalent of the S.E.C. in the US In a strict legal sense, the authority of the Banking Commission in the area of ownership disclosure supervision and M&A activity is limited, but the Commission has considerable influence on market participants on the basis of its 'moral authority'.
12. Law of 22 March 1989, Section 1, paragraph 3.
13. Banking Commission 1989, pp. 4–6.
14. 'Note on the application of the Law of 22 March 1989' (Banking Commission 1989 p. 2).
15. The definition of 'affiliated investors' is given in Article 5 of the Royal Decree of 10 May 1989 and is based on the Royal Decree of 8 October 1976 on the company's annual accounts and consolidation of accounts. 'Acting in concert' is defined in Articles 7 of the Royal Decree of 10 May 1989. Companies acting in concert have agreements with regard to the possession, the acquisition and the selling of securities.
16. Banking Commission 1989 pp. 8–9.
17. Most 'strategy' statements, however, have a low informational content. For instance, on 14 March 1994, Generale Maatschappij van België (Société Générale de Belgique), the reference shareholder for Union Minière and Naviga, notified that these three shareholders had liquidated their combined shareholdings of 62 per cent in Asturienne because 'the share stake is not considered as strategic'.
18. If a target faxes a ownership notification to the Brussels Stock Exchange in the morning, this information is disclosed to the floor at 11.00 a.m. at the earliest via the bulletin board (*ad valvas*) and via the on-line BDPart database. Important news is via this channel quickly dispersed via Tijd Electronic Services or Reuters.
19. The information in the *Cote de la Bourse* is the full responsibility of the Brussels Stock Exchange. The *Cote de la Bourse* in its current form appeared as of 1 January 1992. Before this date, the Stock Exchange disclosed information via de *Wisselkoerslijst* which was sent to about 1000 subscribers, mostly brokerage houses, banks, institutional investors and news agencies.
20. Penalties are enumerated in Section 204 of the Coordinated Laws on Commercial Companies.
21. Law of 22 March 1989, Sections 7–11. In May 1995, minority shareholders of PB Finance, a listed real estate company, sued the Dutch holding Euver in order to annul Euver's voting rights or to limit them to 5 per cent because Euver had not disclosed the size of its shareholding (of 67 per cent) to the Commission of Banking and Finance and there were suspicions of fraud.
22. Ownership Disclosure Law of 22 March 1989, article 6.
23. The percentage of ownership of the major shareholders is often an underestimation of the real corporate power these shareholders can exercise. The board, nominated by the major shareholders, could interpret a takeover threat as 'grave and imminent danger' which would allow them to repurchase shares. Furthermore, the board can allow share warrants to be exercised or sold to friendly shareholders for a maximum of 10 per cent of equity capital in order to dilute shareholdings of a potential raider. This authority, for a maximum but renewable period of 5 years, has to be granted specifically to the board by the annual general meeting. Autocontrol mechanisms can also be installed whereby the company's shares are held by a subsidiary. However, a subsidiary's stake in the mother company is restricted to 10 per cent.
24. The mandatory bid rule which existed since 1965 on a self-regulatory basis has been incorporated into the amendments of law of 1991. The rule requires the acquirer of shares, in as far as

he obtains control as a consequence of this acquisition, to bid for all remaining shares and the bid price should be set at a premium above the highest market price over the last 12 months. This way, equal treatment of shareholders is ensured since all shareholders are offered the benefit of the control premium. Furthermore, the propensity to trade large blocks, resulting in companies taken over against their will, is diminished. In practice, the proof that (in)direct control is acquired can still be difficult.

25. There are additional conditions for changes in the rights of different classes of shareholders. The board of directors needs to document the reasons for the changes extensively and has to send that report to all shareholders before the annual meeting. On the annual meeting, the proposal is only valid if 50 per cent of the total outstanding voting rights are present and 75 per cent of each category of shareholders votes in favour (Company Law, article 71).
26. Law of 18 June 1991, article 191. This law reduced the threshold from 20 per cent to 1 per cent.
27. At the annual general meeting, the directors are 'discharged' from liabilities that may arise in the future if shareholders present at the annual meeting judge, with information from the external auditors and data in the annual report, that the directors fulfilled their tasks adequately during the fiscal year.
28. Note that the minority claim (Company Law articles 66 bis paragraph 2, article 132 bis and article 158 bis) is for the benefit of the company and not for the benefit of the minority shareholder directly, although the minority shareholders, like all shareholders, might benefit. Consequently, this procedure to appoint experts cannot be used following conflicts between shareholders, but only if the company's economic position and its long-term survival is endangered. Case law is rare, but the appointment of experts was justified in these cases: the stocks were overvalued, a company was badly managed and had negative earnings (Lievens 1994). In addition to lowering the threshold level for the minority claim, the rules of conflicts of interest have been tightened: personal liability cannot be excluded if directors take undue advantage of their position to the detriment of the company (Wymeersch 1994a). An individual liability claim can only be initiated if the shareholder can prove that he has experienced personal damage.
29. Before 1991, no shareholder could participate in the voting at the annual meeting for more than 20 per cent of the voting rights associated with the total shares outstanding or for more than 40 per cent of the voting rights associated with shares represented at the annual meeting. The restriction limiting the exercise of voting rights most had priority.
30. Only two listed companies (Delhaize and An-Hyp) were not included in the sample since ownership information was not available in the Brussels Stock Exchange. These companies should be regarded as widely held (no shareholdings of more than 5 per cent exist). However, the Delhaize family, for instance, is believed to own around 30 per cent of the shares. The non-declaration of these stakes is only legally allowed if several family members own less than 5 per cent (see infra for the Ownership Disclosure Legislation) and if they do not 'act in concert'.
31. The database of the National Bank also comprises data on large shareholdings as reported in the annual reports. However, the data on the Notifications of Ownership Changes are more detailed, often present organization charts of pyramidal ownership structures and give all the ownership changes that took place during the fiscal year rather than the ownership structure at the end of the fiscal year.
32. Legal aspects of the mandatory bid are discussed by Wymeersch (1992).
33. The columns with data on holding companies, families and industrial companies do not add up to the numbers in the all investors column since the total cumulative concentrated ownership of this column is the sum of 8 investor categories. Institutional investors, banks etc. do not hold substantial stakes in the sample companies and are not shown in this table but are available upon request.
34. It was assumed that direct shareholders are not affiliated to any other shareholder; control relations by other shareholders at a higher ownership tier are ignored.

35. To identify and classify investor groups according to the ultimate shareholder criterion, the BDPart database, the Notifications of Ownership Change and annual reports were consulted. If data on the percentage of voting rights held in a part of the control chain were not given and the top company explicitly declared that it controlled a company lower in the control chain, a 51 per cent share stake was assumed and used in the calculations. Our control criterion is closely related to the one used by Bianchi and Casavola (1995). Applying their criterion does not yield significantly different results. They assign a company to an investor group if the voting shares held by the investor group represent a sufficient relative majority. A relative majority in a company i held by the group G (q_{Gi}) is defined as sufficient when it exceeds the sum of the maximum stake held by any other group j ($q_{j,i}$) plus the sum of all the stakes held by the companies not assigned to any other group ($w_{j,i}$). The condition for control to be assigned becomes: $q_{G,i} > \max(q_{j,i} + w_{j,i})$.
36. Note that for Tables 3, 6, 7 and 8, the ultimate shareholder criterion is only used to determine those direct shares that need to be aggregated and reclassified when they belong to the same investor group.
37. Seventeen companies which did not have a large direct shareholder owning at least 25 per cent of the shares were excluded. Table B1 of Appendix B summarizes the data inclusive of companies without a direct shareholding of at least 25 per cent. With regard to these companies the same ultimate control criterion was applied to the largest direct stakeholder.
38. See Table B2 in Appendix B.
39. Only one bank was among ultimate shareholders. The results of this table refer to 1992, but other years in the period 1989–1991 reflect a similar picture.
40. For each direct large shareholding we applied the ultimate shareholder rule: we then aggregated these direct shareholding belonging to the same investor group (ultimate shareholder criterion).
41. Parametric and non-parametric tests on means and medians show that the difference is not statistically significant.
42. Ownership tables about the different Belgian shareholder classes (holding companies, banks, investment and pension funds, insurance co's, industrial co's, families, federal and regional government) are not shown, but are available upon request.
43. Since 1967 (See Article 1 of Royal Decree nr. 64 of 10 November 1967), there is a registration requirement for Belgian holding companies with a portfolio value of over 0.5 billion BEF (£10 million). Company Law does not distinguish between different holding categories and in this paper the NACE classification of the National Bank and of the Bank Brussel Lambert is used. However, as Bodson (1993) points out, the group of holding companies is still rather heterogeneous and includes holdings which are purely financial (e.g. Sofina), a combination of financial and industrial (Generale Maatschappij van België / Société Générale de Belgique) or more like a conglomerate (Tractebel).
44. Law of 22 March 1993. The Royal Decree of 8 May 1990 had already allowed the credit institutions to purchase shares up to 5 per cent of their own funds since 1990.
45. Most share stakes held by institutional investors are under 5 per cent and are as such not included in the analysis. Data about investment funds should be interpreted with caution since some investment funds investing in Belgian shares are domiciled in Luxembourg but managed by subsidiaries of Belgian banks. The Luxembourg authorities do not differentiate according to nationality of the managers of the fund.
46. *Beleggingsfonds met veranderlijk kapitaal (Bevek)/Société d'Investissement à Capital Variable (Sicav)* (mutual fund with variable capital).
47. Until the end of 1990, the investors in investment funds could not be represented by the investment fund on annual general meetings of companies in which the investment fund held shares. In practice, this legal prohibition made it impossible that the voting rights of shares held by investment funds were exercised. The legislation wanted to avoid investment funds becoming

instruments of financial groups which could strengthen their control on quoted companies. However, the result of this legislation was not neutral since the position of controlling shareholders was even reinforced (Cornelis and Peeters 1992). The Law of 4 December 1990, article 112, abolished this prohibition and stated that the acts of incorporation can determine in which cases the investment fund is to exercise the voting rights.

48. Ownership tables with the relative importance of each of the foreign shareholder classes (holding companies, banks, institutional investors, insurance companies, industrial companies, families and the government) are available upon request.
49. Shareholders of almost all the member states of the European Union, Switzerland, US, Canada, Japan, Panama, Zaire, Rwanda, Liberia and the Cayman Islands hold stakes of at least 5 per cent in Belgian listed companies. Details per country are available upon request.
50. Parametric and non-parametric tests on means and medians show that the average investment by French holding companies was significantly reduced (at 1 per cent level).
51. If a firm acquires control of another company through a private transaction, and pays a premium to the selling shareholders, a public tender offer has to be made all the remaining shareholders, under the same terms as the private transaction. Van Hulle, Vermaelen en de Wouters (1991) mention that when the private transaction only involves a fraction of the large shareholder's holding, the offer has to be made for only the same fraction of the remaining shares. For example, if the bidder acquires 60 per cent of the shares of a large shareholder who owns 80 per cent of the outstanding shares, the bidder has to make an offer for 60 per cent of the other 20 per cent of the outstanding shares.
52. Unlike in the US, UK and France, undisclosed accumulation of large shareholdings in Belgium via open market and private transactions was possible until March 1989. Van Hulle, Vermaelen and de Wouters (1991) test, over the period 1970–85, the Schleifer and Vishny (1986) hypothesis which states that bidders in a tender offer would benefit most if they had accumulated large holdings prior to the tender offer. Van Hulle et al. find that, while the targets in tender offers earn significant abnormal returns of 37 per cent, bidders earn abnormal returns or zero. The authors advance as part of the explanation for the bidders' low return, the negotiation process with major shareholders. In most companies it is impossible to build up a large stake via open market transactions. Therefore, private negotiations are almost inevitable for an outsider who wants to enlarge his share stake.
53. Article 4, par. 1 of the Royal Decree of 8 October 1976.
54. Article 3 of the Royal Decree of 9 March 1990 and article 6 of the Royal Decree of 30 December 1991.
55. Participation is the translation of '*deelnemingsverhouding*' (article 67 of Royal Decree of 9 March 1990).
56. Cross participation between two companies, if one of them has the legal form of a '*vennootschap*', is limited to 10% by article 52 5's/6's of the coordinated company laws and by article 11 of the Law of 19 July 1991. For instance, if a company owns 55% in another company, the latter company is not permitted to hold more than 10% of the shares in the former.
57. In our example, the parent's holding of 75.0% (assuming no cross shareholding) would decrease to 74.0% if the subsidiary's cross shareholding of 5% is taken into account. The maximum reduction of the parent's shareholding amounts to 2% (the parent effectively owns 73%) and can be found by considering the maximum allowed cross shareholding of 10%.

References

Alchian, A. A. and H. Demsetz (1972) Production, information costs and economic organization, *American Economic Review* 62, 777–795.

Aoki, M., B. Gustafsson and O. E. Williamson (1990) The Firm as a Nexus of Treaties, London.

Banking Commission (1989) Mise en application du chapitre premier de la loi du 2 mars 1989, relative à la publicité des participations importantes dans les sociétés cotées en bourse et réglementant les offres publiques d'acquisition, May, 1–17.

Baums, T. (1994) Corporate governance in Germany – system and recent developments, published in 'Aspects of Corporate Governance', eds. M. Isaksson and R. Skog, Juristforlaget, 31–54.

Berle, A. and G. Means (1932) The Modern Corporation and Private Property, New York.

Bianchi, M. and P. Casavola (1995) Piercing the corporate veil: truth and appearance in Italian listed pyramidal groups, Working Paper Banca D'Italia, presented at corporate governance and property rights workshop in Milan 16–17 June.

Bianco, M., C. Gola and L. F. Signorini (1995) Dealing with separation between ownership and control: state, family, coalitions and pyramidal groups in Italian corporate governance, Working Paper Banca D'Italia, presented at corporate governance and property rights workshop in Milan 16–17 June.

Bodson, P. (1993) Tractebel: groupe industrielle, Mimeo Tractebel, December, Brussels.

Chirinko, R. S. and J. A. Elston (1995) Finance, control and profitability: an evaluation of German bank influence, Working paper Wissenschafszentrum Berlin Fur Sozialforschung.

Coase, R. (1937) The Nature of the Firm, *Economica* 4, 386–405.

Cornelis, L. and J. Peeters (1992) De gemeenschappelijke beleggingsfondsen en -vennootschappen, published in 'De Nieuwe Beurswetgeving', eds. Cornelis et alii, Jan Ronse Instituut-K.U.Leuven, 302–320.

Davies, P. L. and G. P. Stapledon (1994) Corporate governance in the United Kingdom, published in 'Aspects of Corporate Governance', eds. M. Isaksson and R. Skog, Juristforlaget, pp. 55–81.

Demsetz, H. and K. Lehn (1985) The structure of corporate ownership: causes and consequences, Journal of Political Economy 93, 1155–1177.

Dixit, A. (1983) Vertical integration in a monopolistic competitive industry, *International Journal of Industrial Organization* 1, 63–78.

Fama, E. and M. Jensen (1983) Separation of ownership and control, *Journal of Law and Economics* 26, 301–325.

Franks J. and C. Mayer (1992) Corporate control: a synthesis of the international evidence, Working Paper, London Business School.

Franks, J. and C. Mayer (1996) Hostile takeovers and the correction of managerial failure, *Journal of Financial Economics* 40, 163–181.

Franks, J. and C. Mayer (1995a) Ownership and control of German corporations, Working Paper, London Business School.

Franks, J. and C. Mayer (1995b) Ownership and control, in 'Trends in business organization: do participation and cooperation increase competitiveness?' edited by H. Siebert, published by J. C. B. Mohr (Paul Seibeck) Tuebingen, 171–195.

Franks, J., C. Mayer and L. Renneboog (1996) The role of large share stakes in poorly performing companies in the UK, Working Paper, Catholic University of Leuven.

Goergen, M. (1993) Corporate control in Belgium, Germany, Spain and the U.K., mimeo Warwick Business School.

Grossman, S. J. and O. Hart (1986) The cost and benefits of ownership: a theory of vertical and lateral integration, *Journal of Political Economy* 94, 691–719.

Hart, O. and J. Moore (1990) Property rights and the nature of the firm, *Journal of Political Economy* 98, 1119–1158.

Jensen, M. C. (1986) The takeover controversy: analysis and evidence, *Midland Corporate Finance Journal* 4, 6–32.

Lichtenberg, F. R. and G. M. Pushner (1992) Ownership structure and corporate performance is Japan, NBER Working Paper No. 4092.

Lievens, J. (1994) De rechten van de minderheidsaandeelhouder, Centrum voor fiscale wetenschappen in bedrijfbeleid EHSAL – Fiscale Hogeschool seminaries, seminar on 9 June.

Maertens, M. (1994) Loi sur la transparence du marché – Circulation de l'information, publication of the Brussels Stock Exchange.

Manne, H. G. (1965) Some theoretical aspects of share voting, *Columbia Law Review* 64, 534–554.

Mayer, C. (1993) Ownership, Inaugural Lecture to the University of Warwick, February 1.

Miyajima, H. (1995) Bank centred corporate groups and investment : evidence from the first phase of high growth era in Japan, Working Paper, Waseda University School of Commerce. Presented at the conference on Firm-Bank relations in Wissenschafszentrum Berlin fuer Socialforschung in 4 July 1995.

Plateau, S. and Van Herck, G. (1992) Handboek Consolidatie, Juridische Aspecten en Bedrijfseconomische Toepassingen, ACCO, 21–53.

Prowse, S. (1992) The structure of corporate ownership in Japan, *Journal of Finance* 47, 1121–1140.

Renneboog, L. (1996) Ownership, managerial control and the governance of companies listed on the Brussels stock exchange, Working Paper, Catholic University of Leuven.

Salinger, M. (1988) Vertical merger and market foreclosure, *Quarterly Journal of Economics* 103, 345–356.

Shleifer, A. and R. W. Vishny (1986) Large shareholders and corporate control, *Journal of Political Economy* 95, 461–488.

Uytterschaut, L. (1989) De Geconsolideerde Jaarrekening. Een Handleiding voor het Samenvoegen van Jaarrekeningen, M.I.M., Deurne.

Van Hulle, C., T. Vermaelen and P. de Wouters (1991) Regulation, taxes and the market for corporate control in Belgium, *Journal of Banking and Finance* 15, 1143–1170.

Van Nuffel, M. (1994) Het vragenrecht en de stemming van de algemene vergadering, Centrum voor fiscale wetenschappen in bedrijfbeleid EHSAL – Fiscale Hogeschool seminaries, seminar on 9 June.

Verwilst, H. (1992) Aandelenbezit door banken, *Bank- en Financiewezen*, 367–371.

Weisbach, M. (1988) Outside directors and CEO turnover, *Journal of Financial Economics* 20, 431–460.

Williamson, O. E. (1975) Markets and Hierarchies : Analysis and Anti-trust Implications, New York.

Wuille, S. (1994) Les déclarations de participations publiées dans la Cote de la Bourse de Bruxelles, publication of the Brussels Stock Exchange, July.

Wymeersch, E. (1992) The mandatory takeover bid: a critical view, published in 'Takeovers in Europe, eds. Hopt and Wymeersch, Butterworths London.

Wymeersch, E. (1994a) Aspects of Corporate Governance, *Journal of Corporate Governance* 2, 138–149.

Wymeersch, E. (1994b) Elements of comparative corporate governance in Western Europe, published in 'Aspect of Corporate Governance', eds. M. Isaksson and R. Skog, Juristforlaget, 83–116.

Insurance Company Ownership in the Netherlands

ABSTRACT

In this paper the importance and the developments in the Netherlands in the area of Corporate Governance, in particular on and by insurance companies (and pension funds), are discussed. The element of Financial Governance – in other words, influence by the company's group of capital providers – is of particular importance in this field. In the Netherlands signs have been observed that a considerable increase in Financial Governance is likely. In addition, an analogous influence from the domain of European and national competition policy can be noticed in the insurance industry. These trends require a considerable accommodating behaviour of prudential supervisors.

Dr Arend Jan Vermaat (born 02-11-1939) studied General and Financial Economics during 1957–1962 at Free University Amsterdam; Ph.D in 1966 (The Controversy between the Loanable Funds' Theory and the Liquidity Preference Theory). After an academic career – interrupted by a membership of the Dutch Lower House – he was appointed Chairman of the Verzekeringskamer (the Insurance Supervisory Board in the Netherlands) in 1988.

XIII. Insurance Company Ownership in the Netherlands: Implications for Corporate Governance and Competition

AREND JAN VERMAAT

1. INTRODUCTION: FORMULATION OF THE PROBLEM AND OUTLINE

Corporate Governance[1]

1. It is fashionable to discuss and consider Corporate Governance (CG)!

This was the call by Sir Colin Marshall (CEO of British Airways) at the beginning of 1996 on the occasion of the first annual meeting of the ICGN (International Corporate Governance Network) for a world-wide code of conduct (no laws!) in this area for investors and companies. In part, CG is possibly a hype. Nevertheless at the same time it is a permanent and important topic. It is a new approach to the discussion on the way the market economy works. It is a debate in essence about the direction which should be given to the Western economic order. It is therefore of great structural importance.

This paper will discuss CG within a certain context. In doing so, it is important to mention the following limitations: (i) it deals with the insurance industry in the Netherlands, and (ii) viewed from the perspective – not of the interested citizen, ex-politician or former professor of economics – but of the legal supervisor of insurance companies and pension funds.[2]

2. What do I understand by CG? CG relates to the disciplining of the management of a company-to a greater or lesser degree-by the parties involved.

It relates mainly to larger companies, usually characterized as companies with share capital. Since Berle & Means (1932) the distinction between capital provider/owner as opposed to the management has resulted in the principal agent theory. In the broader sense, CG does not relate to discipline imposed by shareholders (or alternatively the providers of loan capital) only but to the entire group of stakeholders directly or indirectly involved with the company. The diagram overleaf provides an overview of this.

The diagram is largely self-explanatory. I wish to make a number of additional comments, however, for the sake of clarity. A distinction is made between CG with an internal character (i.e. within the circle in the centre of the diagram)

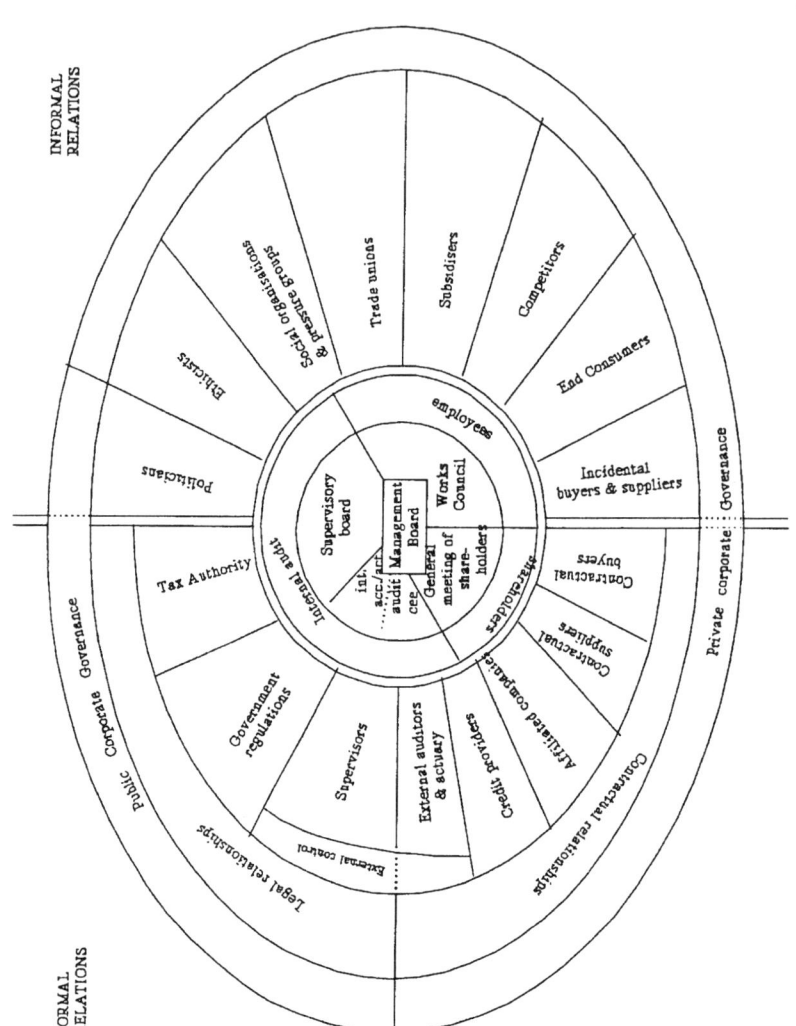

Fig. 1. A topology of Corporate Governance (based on an idea by Wallage, 1975, p. 274).

and CG with an external guise. A further distinction is made with regard to the latter, namely, between (a) (on the left) the formal relationships with the company in question as opposed to (b) (on the right) the informal relationships. Within the formal relationships a further dichotomy is appropriate, namely, that between (a.1) legal relationships (or their equivalents) and (a.2) contractual relationships. The external supervisors are to be found where both components meet. As the legal prudential supervisor of insurance companies, the Dutch Insurance Supervisory Board also falls within this group.

I have summarized the segment of relationships with the company which function on the basis of legal regulations by the term 'public corporate governance'. The remaining segments are collectively referred to as 'private corporate governance'. I wish to reserve the umbrella term CG for the entire group. This deviates from some of the existing literature. Gelauff & Den Broeder (1996), for instance, use the following three terms: Corporate Governance (for influence of finance providers), (ii) Contractual Governance (for inter-firm relationships), and (iii) Work Governance (for the labour factor). In itself it is understandable that these three important parts of CG are referred to by a separate term. I propose adopting this on the understanding that the influence of finance providers (in other words, both equity and loan capital; in this respect suppliers and customers may also be included!) is denoted by the term 'Financial Governance'. Furthermore, the terms 'Public CG' and 'Informal CG' may be used for the other CG forces. Since the term 'stakeholders' is often used in discussions of CG, I would also like to make a distinction between the direct stakeholders (namely, shareholders, employees and contractual relationships) as opposed to indirect stakeholders (in other words, all other parties involved). Finally, it should be noted that in addition to laws and contracts, also codes, customs, social and ethic norms of behaviour etc. exert a considerable influence. In fact, the way in which CG operates is embedded in the entire framework comprising the socio-economic order. It is no longer possible to limit this even to the national economy. The influence of treaties, internationalisation and globalization are now far too intense for this!

A VARIANT OF THE RHINELAND MODEL

3. My discussion in this paper will relate to the Dutch insurance industry. This implies that the context is that of the Dutch economy. In general, this discussion will therefore focus on a specific variant of the so-called Rhineland or German model. An extensive description and analysis of, amongst others, this Dutch variant can be found in Gelauff & Den Broeder (1996). I will limit myself here to two points, namely (i) a brief outline of the major characteristics,

for the foreign reader, and (ii) a comment on the present dynamics in the Dutch economic order.

Firstly, a number of characteristics:
- a relatively small country with a very open economy
- a fairly centralistic structure (in other words, a free market supplemented by agreements between umbrella organizations and the government)
- a labour union committed to consensus (supported by legally regulated influence at the company level through works councils or, alternatively, the phenomenon that the provisions of collective labour agreements are declared to be generally applicable)
- the unique so-called structure regime for large companies in which a dominant role is given to the supervisory board[3]
- considerable influence from constructions which provide protection against hostile takeovers
- a wide distribution of the ownership of the shares, without dominant blocs of shareholders
- little ownership of shares by the management of the company
- limited CG role on the part of banks or institutional investors, and
- a high degree of funded (as opposed to pay-as-you-go) pension arrangements.

The above is a sketch of the situation in recent years (the period of, say, 1970–1990). Certain clear trends in the changes that are occurring are discernible. A number of these are:
- further opening of the Dutch economy (both internationally through GATT, GATS etc., but mainly through the creation of the EU market)
- participation in the internationalization of money and capital markets
- a growing discussion on the relative merits of the Dutch welfare state (as a specific variant of the Rhineland model) in comparison with the more Anglo-Saxon models[4]
- social trends in favour of liberalization and individualization.

In a cultural climate such as this, it is logical that the discussion of whether the special arrangements in the Netherlands in the area of CG are useful and whether they can be retained is gaining momentum. With regard to whether these can be retained it should be said that this is not determined only by political ideas and legal regulations, but also and no less by the power of the markets. In any event, the discussion on the most desirable forms of CG in the Netherlands is very lively. The report, *Corporate Governance in the Netherlands*, by the Peters Committee (October 1996)[5] has acted as a catalyst. It is not my task, however, to give an analysis of this discussion, but to discuss CG within/by the insurance industry. It was necessary, however, to refer to the above (very briefly) as a (dynamic) environmental framework.

Problem Formulation

4. The following problem formulation will apply to the rest of my paper. Given the Dutch context, what can be said of the practice or developments with regard CG in relation to the insurance industry? This relates to two perspectives, namely both (a) CG exercised in relation to insurance companies, and (b) CG exercised by these institutions (even more broadly, including the pension funds). In the first instance, the emphasis is on Financial Governance, in other words, the influence exerted by the providers of capital and credit. In the second instance, the focus is widened to include the aspect of competition and the perspective of the prudential legal supervisor. This is, after all, my daily task.

Outline

5. In the next paragraph a sketch is given of the Dutch insurance industry. Attention is also given to competitive relationships. In paragraph 3 a discussion follows of the possible specific characteristics of CG of insurance companies. The role of insurance and pension funds in CG of other companies is also discussed. In paragraph 4 the related aspects of policy with regard to competition in the insurance sector and supervision in relation to the CG phenomenon are dealt with. Finally, the last paragraph contains a brief summary and conclusions.

2. Sketch of the Dutch Insurance Industry

Data

6. Firstly a table with data on the number of insurers in the Netherlands.

Since the Netherlands is a member of the EU, the legal licensing system applies in accordance with the various European Directives. Our country has traditionally had a very liberal policy with regard to establishing businesses, also for foreign companies. This is partly the reason for the higher density of insurers in the Netherlands, as is illustrated in Table 2.

7. For the positioning of the (life) insurance industry in the Netherlands mention must be made of the pension funds. Although an employer (or, alternatively, via the negotiations regarding the collective labour agreement) is free to promise a pension to employees, or not to do so, approximately 85 per cent of employees has such a promise of a pension. This may be implemented through a life insurer (both by means of a group contract and through indivi-

TABLE 1

Number of insurers in the Netherlands (as at 31 December 1996*)

	Life	Non-life	Total
With a licence:			
– registered offices in the Netherlands	96	266	362
– branch office in the Netherlands	3	22	25
Through a notification procedure			
– ranch office in the Netherlands	3	113	116
– services provided in the Netherlands	98	328	426
	200	729	929

* Number of active small mutual non-life insurance companies exempt from supervision: 251.
Source: Dutch Insurance Supervisory Board.

TABLE 2

Density of insurers in a number of countries (as at 31 December 1995); defined as the number of insurance licences per 1 million inhabitants

	Life	Non-life	Composite	Total
The Netherlands	6.4	25.5	–	31.9
Germany	1.5	4.1	–	5.7
France	2.2	3.4	–	5.7
United Kingdom	2.7	10.2	0.9	13.9

Source: Dutch Central Bureau of Statistics and annual reports of supervisors.

TABLE 3

Pension funds in the Netherlands

	Number of funds as at 31 December 1994	Balance-sheet total as at 31 December 1994 ($\times$ NLG 1 million)
Industry-wide pension funds	82	178,662
Company pension funds	1003	147,598
Pension funds for the professions	11	15,290
Savings funds	6	708
Abp (civil servants)	1	194,044
	1103	536,302

Source: Dutch Insurance Supervisory Board.

dual policies) or by means of a pension fund. Various types of pension funds are important in this regard. The following table contains some relevant data.

In order to complete the above table, it should be mentioned that as at 31 December 1995 life insurance contracts for pension purposes had been entered into with life insurance companies for more than one million people, for a total insured amount of NLG 45 billion. For further data, see Pensioenmonitor, VK-studies, No. 9 (1996; pp. 37–46).

Together with the various mutual funds or unit trusts, insurance companies and pension funds are the most important institutional investors. As an indication of their importance in quantitative terms, the combined balance-sheet total of the insurance companies plus the pension funds as at 31 December 1996 is estimated to be approximately NLG 864 billion, in other words, 130 per cent of GNP of the Netherlands in 1996.

For discussions of CG the fact that adjustments have been made to the investment policy during the past ten years is of considerable importance. Previously the favourites were (government)bonds, private loans, mortgages and direct real estate. At present equities, indirect real estate holdings and financial derivatives are given greater emphasis. In the case of insurers, this is related to the increasing role of unit-linked insurance policies (with no investment risk for the insurer).

In the case of pension funds the aim of indexing accrued pension rights plays a central role. At year-end 1996 the proportion of 'real assets' (equities and real estate) in the portfolios of the abovementioned group of institutional investors was estimated to be 35.2 per cent, as opposed to approximately 16.1 per cent in 1985.

COMPETITIVE RELATIONSHIPS

8. Table 2 showed a high density of insurers in the Netherlands. This is sometimes explained as a sign of limited competition (see, for instance, Drabbe, 1994). The reasoning behind this is that as a result of a well-developed system of self regulation in the industry (in other words, cartel-like agreements!) the premiums and profits are kept so high that a limited market share – albeit in a steadily growing market – results in a sufficient net return on capital. This seems to be a strongly distorted historical picture which urgently needs to be updated.

Due to the easy access, relatively many foreign insurers have been active on the Dutch market since the sixties. Later this was also a strategic choice in order to gain access to Fortress Europe. Furthermore these foreign insurers often did not participate in the process of self regulation. The access was not only *de jure*, but also *de facto*. In this regard the role of the independent

TABLE 4

Number of insurers in the Netherlands (corrected for insurance groups) as at 31 December 1995

Life	Non-life	Total
59	198	257

insurance brokers' network is of crucial importance, so that it is relatively easy to build up a market position. The emergence and growth of direct writers was also an additional stimulus to competition, resulting in a reduction in the value of distribution channels through salaried agents.

As early as in 1988 the well-known Cecchini report pointed out that premium levels in the Netherlands (and the UK) were relatively low. Since then competition has increased. Forms of price leadership in market segments have almost entirely disappeared. Self regulation to the extent to which it occurred has been almost abolished since 1992 (exceptions are very general group exemptions in recommended policy conditions, data collecting and advertising codes). Even in recent years, in which even the non-life insurers reported splendid profit growth, the net return on capital may be characterized as relatively meagre in this subsector.

Studies of the development of the degree of concentration also support the above argument (see also Vermaat, 1992, p. 16 and Nijenhuis, Potjes & Schilder, 1994).With regard to the life insurance business increasing competition is coming from the pension funds. In addition, pension funds are setting up life and non-life insurance subsidiaries. This should, however, be seen in perspective. A significant number of insurers are, after all, part of an insurance group or even of a financial conglomerate. Despite the fact that within such groups competition occurs between sister companies (aimed, in particular, at the various distribution channels), this reduces the number of 'genuinely' independent market players. Table 4 therefore puts Table 1 in perspective:

3. INSURANCE COMPANY OWNERSHIP AND CORPORATE GOVERNANCE

Further Data

9. In this paragraph CG of or by insurers (and pension funds) will be discussed. From the discussion it will emerge that the Financial Governance variant is the most important, and exercised in both directions. In addition to the general influence of Dutch legislation (such as that regarding the structure regime), Informal Governance (not discussed further here) and the role of solvency supervision and the competition policy (see also paragraph 4) are also of

TABLE 5

Types of insurers by ownership characteristics as at 31 December 1995

	Life	Non-life	Total
Public limited liability companies	79	149	228
Mutuals (including class 3 exempted mutual guarantee companies)	13	128	141
Non EU/European Economic Area	4	23	27
	96	300	396
Dutch shareholders	72	245	317
Foreign shareholders	24	55	79
Listed	23	30	53
Non-listed	73	270	343

importance. In order to provide a sketch of Financial Governance within the Dutch insurance industry, the relationships of ownership are, of course, of great importance. For this reason we have provided a number of additional tables in this section. In the following table, a further categorization of the types of insurers is given.

Contractual Governance is relatively unimportant for the insurance industry (for pension funds this is more complicated). Although insurers are also active on the capital markets on the demand side (with a view to optimizing their capital structures) they occupy a relatively strong position. Due to the nature of their very long-term liabilities, insurers and pension funds have better matching than, for instance, banks. The relationship with suppliers/customers is unique. They are, after all, the same policyholders in two different roles. Although large group contracts play a role, this influence is reflected more in the conditions of contracts and less on the governance side. After all, contract renegotiations occur regularly so that a 'hold up' problem does not exist in this respect. Credit providers play a role of little importance. It is for this reason that Financial Governance mainly relates to the role of shareholders. Below some data are given with regard to the distribution of shareholdings in insurance companies.[6] The legal provision that a stake of 10 per cent or more in a licensed insurer requires a declaration of no objection from the supervisor is also important in this regard. In addition, listed companies are subject to the Disclosure of Major Holdings in Listed Companies Act.

Finally, I wish to discuss a few characteristics of the distribution of shares held by insurance companies and pension funds in other companies.

It is not possible at this moment to provide an analogous table for the distribution of shares held by insurance companies and pension funds in other

TABLE 6

Some data on the distribution of shareholdings in insurance companies

(A) Distribution of Dutch listed shares (in %)[7]

	1990	1995
Banks	0.7	0.8
Institutional investors[8]	19.0	19.1
Non-domestic	44.0	39.3
Investment funds	1.5	1.3
Others	34.8	39.4

(B) Percentage of equities in total assets (31-12-1995)

	Total assets (Dfl bn)	% Equities
Life assurance companies	300.9	19.3%
Non-life insurance companies	38.9	21.9%
Pension funds	536.0	22.8%

(C) Classification of life assurance companies established in the Netherlands as at 31 December 1996)

Mutuals	Stock companies controlled by:			Others[10]	Total
	Majority holdings by so-called 'administration offices'	Foreign ownership	Other stock companies		
27	19	13	23	14	96

(D) Mutual holdings[11] between Dutch financial conglomerates[12] (direct and indirect) (31-12-1996)

by: \ in:	ING	ABN AMRO	AEGON	FORTIS	STAD ROTTERDAM
ING	–	16.6	5.3	8.9	19.9
ABN AMRO	0	–	0	0	0
AEGON	6.3	12.9	–	0	0
FORTIS	6.2	5.7	0	–	19.7
STAD ROTTERDAM	0	0	0	0	–

companies. In general the shareholdings of insurance companies and pension funds have the same characteristics as those of any investor. Leaving aside less frequently occurring strategic participations aimed at acquiring control (or defensive participations) the aim is to achieve direct or indirect revenues from

TABLE 7

FDSE-Quotient for Non-Life Insurers, 1990–1994 (the FDSE-Quotient is the freely distributable shareholders' equity divided by the size of the required solvency margin)*

Non-life insurers	1990	1992	1994
Market total	2.4 (2.7)	2.7 (2.8)	2.5 (2.8)
Part of a group			
Yes	2.3 (2.6)	2.5 (2.6)	2.4 (2.7)
No	2.8 (3.6)	3.8 (5.1)	3.4 (4.4)
Origin of shareholders			
The Netherlands	2.6 (2.8)	2.9 (2.7)	2.7 (2.7)
Foreign	2.0 (2.4)	2.1 (3.0)	1.8 (2.9)
Size**			
Large	1.7 (2.2)	2.1 (2.5)	1.9 (2.4)
Small	3.5 (3.9)	3.7 (3.4)	3.8 (4.1)

* The corresponding data for non-life insurers which make regular dividend payouts are given in brackets.
** Criterion: NLG 100 million in annual premium income.

the investment. Tax considerations are mainly the reason for at least a 5 per cent holding by insurance companies, that is, in the fiscal entity. In the case of pension funds this tax incentive does not play a role. Exceptional cases aside, the participations are well diversified.

FINANCIAL GOVERNANCE ON INSURERS

10. On the basis of the above and from the point of view of Financial Governance, the question of whether shareholders manage to attract a larger portion of the net added value is of considerable importance. Given the degree of competition on the insurance market, the conflict is between the shareholders and the interests of those who wish to keep capital growth within the company (management and policyholders: security and profit sharing). In a (brief) study on the basis of data held by the Dutch Insurance Supervisory Board, Bakker (1996) came up with the following results for non-life insurers (see Table 7).

On the basis of the above results, Bakker (1996, p. 59/60) draws the following conclusions.

1. Despite the cyclical character of the market for non-life insurers the FDSE-quotient is fairly stable during the period under review. (The FDSE-quotient may be regarded as a good indication of the degree of solidity of an insurance company.)

TABLE 8

FDSE-quotient for Life Insurers, 1991–1995 (the FDSE-quotient is the freely distributable shareholders' equity divided by the size of the required solvency margin)*

Life insurers	1991	1993	1995	Average dividend (%) 1991–1995
Market total	1.0 (1.1)	1.7 (1.8)	1.9 (2.1)	8.50% (10.21%)
Origin of shareholders				
The Netherlands	1.1 (1.1)	1.9 (2.0)	2.1 (2.2)	8.93% (9.89%)
Foreign	0.8 (0.7)	0.9 (0.7)	1.3 (1.2)	5.92% (14.81%)
Size**				
Large	1.0 (1.1)	1.7 (1.8)	2.0 (2.1)	8.69% (9.29%)
Small	1.2 (1.2)	1.7 (1.2)	1.7 (1.6)	4.54% (10.29%)

* The corresponding data for life insurers which make regular dividend payouts are given in brackets.
** Criterion: NLG 100 million in annual premium income.

2. On average insurance companies which pay out a dividend have a higher FDSE-quotient, particularly if they are foreign companies or are not part of a group.
3. The level of the FDSE-quotient within the group of foreign insurers diverges strongly. This may be due to differences between their respective countries of origin, but also to relative maturity and the market position they have achieved.
4. Insurers which are part of a group have a lower FDSE-quotient. This can be explained by their risk management (or growth strategy) at group level, but also by more active CG by shareholders at this level!

Personally, on the basis of the above, I draw the more general conclusion that since 1990 CG has still had little discernible influence on non-life insurers in the Netherlands. Only weak indications of a movement in this direction can be observed. Possibly this is not only due to the relatively weak or weakly concentrated position of shareholders in the Dutch non-life insurance industry, but also to the moderate returns and the unfavourable tax treatment of dividend payouts. A parallel study was recently carried out in relation to life insurers (see Table 8).

The latter data gives rise to the following additional conclusions.
1. Life assurance companies show steady growth in their FDSE-quotients. This reflects the achieved results.
2. Life insurers in foreign hands have a slightly lower FDSE-quotient.
3. Other differences are not very relevant, with the exception of the fact that the smaller foreign life assurance companies, in particular, pay out an above average dividend to their parent companies.

Finally, I conclude that with regard to CG – despite the less cyclical market position – little difference (as yet) exists between non-life and life insurers.

FINANCIAL GOVERNANCE ON PENSION FUNDS

11. Leaving aside legal prudential supervision, pension funds are usually characterized by internal or internalized discipline. The latter is the result of the composition of the management of pension funds which is (mostly) based on equal representation of employers and employees. This has resulted in combined influence by employers and employees (trade unions). Where previously there was little interest in the investment activities of a fund (in fact their main activity!), this has definitely changed in recent years (*cf.* Goslings, 1996). Sponsoring companies set higher norms for investment returns, while active members and pensioners show greater interest. Added to this the more intense discussion on the desired competition with life insurers and the increasing opportunities to take out additional insurance with pension funds, the above implies stronger Financial Governance pressure on pension funds. This will become more explicit in the coming years. The following are a number of predictable developments in relation to this.
- stricter performance measurement and norms for returns on investment
- an emphasis on the importance of the quality of managers
- heterogeneous financial groups, with pension funds as parts of these
- the emergence of the trust phenomenon as a legal form for a pension fund
- demands for a greater say for those with pension rights and/or profit sharing arrangements a reaction to the need for further independence for funds in relation to the sponsors.

To what extent the last phenomenon will actually have a substantial effect in relation to CG is open to discussion. The interests of the various groups are often opposed, so that the creation and exercize of influence are weakened. Also, in a more general sense, the influence of large constituencies (such as members meetings and shareholders' meetings) without further organizational and accepted concentrations is usually insignificant. Such negative experiences with attempts to democratize pension funds will also stimulate the emergence of the trust phenomenon.

FINANCIAL GOVERNANCE BY INSURERS AND PENSION FUNDS

12. This does not relate to internal group relationships in which, for instance, a subsidiary is directed to a greater or sometimes indeed a lesser extent by controlling top holding companies or sub-holding companies. The influence

on strategic (controlling) participations entered into for commercial motives will not be discussed either. For the rest, Financial Governance by insurers and pension funds may be regarded as cautious. The dominant factor is the aim of the long-term investment.[13] (*Idem* Gelauff & Den Broeder, 1996 p. 77).

However, in recent years there have been noticeable signs that especially the large insurers and pension funds are intending to give more attention to Financial Governance. This is related to several trends indicated earlier. Internationalization of the capital markets, convergence due to EU and EMU, more competition, more interest – from both sides – for investor relations[14] and the public debate in relation to CG are all contributing to this. In addition, the expansion of investment in equities by institutional investors means that 'voting with their feet' (alias the 'Wall Street walk!') is less opportune for a relatively small country like the Netherlands.

In the Netherlands there is also no 'market for corporate control'. Due to the many practised forms of protection (such as preference shares, priority shares, depositary receipts, binding nomination or voting caps) hostile takeovers hardly ever occur. All of these factors imply that the larger investors (have to) seek ways of better protecting their long-term interests in the companies and groups in which they participate. (Frijns *et al*, 1995).

I therefore expect a strong influence in the national CG debate in the coming years from this quarter. This will result in adjustments to Dutch company law in which a new socially acceptable and fruitful balance will be achieved between the various stakeholders, in particular management/shareholders/labour. Furthermore, the increasingly far-reaching and convergent embedding of Dutch company law in EU company law is of crucial importance in this respect.

4 CORPORATE GOVERNANCE, COMPETITION AND PRUDENTIAL SUPERVISION

Trends in CG in the Netherlands

13. Actually putting CG, or other variants of this, into effect assumes that this is possible. If the so-called model of perfect competition applies to a certain market, this would not be possible. After all, the 'entrepreneur' is in that case only a price taker and a pure volume adjuster. Although theoretically oriented economics and legislation lawyers are rather impressed (and apparently normatively enamoured) with this abstract model, this form seldom occurs in practice. In by far the largest number of cases, a given market (which is usually broader than the 'national' domain) is characterized by the monopolistic competition model (actually a confusing name!). This has a number of degrees of freedom for the market behaviour of companies, so that all sorts of dynamics can occur.[15] Furthermore the company also has moments at which it can make

choices which are not directly subject to market confrontations (in particular, in relation to intra-company issues). In a general sense, there is therefore room to influence the company by means of CG and therefore also for influence of and by insurance companies and pension funds.

14. Given the external forces already sketched earlier, CG in the Netherlands is undergoing major changes. For instance, the globalization and internationalization of markets for goods and services – and, in particular, the capital markets – as well as the creation of the EU and EMU provide strong stimuli. The social compromise reached in the seventies in the Netherlands between 'capital' and 'labour' – for instance, through the structure regime for large companies and the role of the works councils – is under pressure. This is partly the result of the reduction in the power of the unions on the labour market as a result of the relative labour surplus. The demands of shareholders with regard to profitability carry more weight since the restructuring of companies in the eighties and nineties when it became apparent that sufficient shareholders' equity was necessary as a buffer. The same empirical experiences have increased the desired level of returns on shareholders' equity – partly because of the unfavourable tax treatment of dividend payouts and certainly now that long-term interest rates have not adequately reflected decreased inflation expectations – and, in doing so, have added to the importance of the capital factor. In line with this, the resistance of groups of investors to protective barriers, which in their view are too high, is understandable. Developments of this sort need time. (Itself another illustration of the fact that markets do not work as perfectly as the textbooks assume!) The trends still have to take shape in a context which is constantly changing. Business cycle and economic structure interfere. Movements involving social pressure groups and the resulting legislation – fortunately – need time. The international dimension sometimes accelerates this and sometimes slows it down.

15. In recent years in the Netherlands the struggle for a greater role for shareholders has flared up. It is not possible to summarize this discussion adequately here. I wish to give only three examples as an illustration of this. Considerable discussion was generated by a proposal to make it compulsory to submit protective clauses for review by a panel of experts (with the possibility of lodging an appeal with the Commercial Chamber of the Amsterdam Court, which may only conduct a limited judicial review) if a shareholder or group of shareholders has acquired a certain percentage of the shares or depository receipts.

The report of the Peters Committee (1996), *Corporate Governance in the Netherlands*, has raised even more dust. This committee made forty recommendations aimed at increasing the degree of CG. The focus was primarily on the soundness and transparency of the role of the supervisory board of the company and, in the second instance, on the possibilities for shareholders to obtain more information. Also, the proxy solicitation instrument was recommended in addition to opening a legal possibility for majority shareholders to claim the remaining shares subject to realistic conditions.

The opinions on this are still very divided. Some regard all of this as an undesirable increase in the influence of the capital factor, although a few union leaders do wish to increase the influence of certain (large) shareholders – in particular, the influence of the pension funds. Others believe that these proposals do not go far enough by any means because, in fact, nothing really changes. In this regard, the opinion that the essence of the discussion on CG in the Netherlands should be the revision of the structure regime is very interesting. In this regard, Boot (1995) has suggested that the right to appoint members on the supervisory board of a company should be given to a special appointment committee – which, in accordance with the articles of association, should consist of (representatives of) shareholders, employees and other interested parties – possibly, for instance, in the ratio of 60 per cent members of the supervisory board and 40 per cent additionally co-opted members, in order to guarantee the role of the independent experts.

An alternative solution would be to hold a vote of confidence in the sitting supervisory board periodically (for instance, every seven years) and/or at request of a qualified majority of shareholders in the general meeting of shareholders. The above is intended to illustrate the proposition that the outcome of the CG debate is still far from clear. In my personal assessment, the new 'solutions' will be determined by (i) the impact of the EU and other international forces, and (ii) the degree to which a shift occurs in the economic influence of labour as opposed to capital. It seems that the importance – and therefore the influence – of the providers of shareholders' equity will increase, both *de facto* and *de jure*. Whether this tendency will continue in the decades to come depends on the race between the decrease in the size of the potential working population due to aging, on the one hand, and the degree of participation of women and the elderly, migration from the South and East, the nature and speed of technological development, the impact of environmental demands and the development of the savings ratio, on the other. From a short-term perspective, however, the influence of shareholders within Dutch management models for companies will increase substantially.

Trends in Competition and Competition Policy

16. In paragraph 2 an indication was given that the insurance market in the Netherlands is characterized, in general, by strong competition. Despite the emergence of concentration phenomena, which has also occurred in other countries, through mergers and takeovers or the creation of insurance groups

and financial conglomerates, the degree of concentration has decreased rather than increased. (Vermaat, 1992). This result can be explained by influences such as the strong growth in the turnover of small and medium-sized insurers, in particular, the impact of direct writers, entry by new foreign players (with the backing of financially strong parent companies) and the erosion of self-regulatory agreements and forms of oligopolistic price leadership. The above development will certainly continue in the coming years. A number of factors play an important role in this. A case in point is the increasing competition between pension funds and insurers, which increasingly are being allowed to enter into each other's traditional areas. This is further intensified by the actual lowering of thresholds to competition through the gradual creation of a genuinely convergent European insurance market through the harmonisation of legislation, cultural convergence, the increasing importance of cross-border service provision (aimed particularly at companies) *et cetera*. No less important in this regard is the competition policy of 'Brussels' and 'The Hague'. EU competition policy has resulted in notification and termination of the traditionally important self-regulatory agreements (in so far as these had not already perished in the face of market forces). The group exemptions which have been granted do not serve as an obstacle to competition. The Dutch own national competition policy has also been considerably tightened up in line with that of 'Brussels'. The new Competition Act goes a step further.

The emphasis here is placed on prohibiting all mutual agreements between companies unless it can be shown in advance that such agreements will be advantageous to the consumer. This modernization and tightening up of Dutch policy on competition in line with the EU is characterized by its juridical flavour. The action taken by Mr Kok's government towards the deregulation of legislation supports the above. An important example in this regard is the intended abolition of the legal provisions in relation to the commission system for insurance intermediaries. In short, the simple conclusion from the above is not only that the Dutch market is characterized by strong competition, but also that a substantial increase in competition may be expected in the future. This will be all the more so if a downward movement occurs in the business cycle or the typical cycle of the non-life industry. As a supervisor, I am concerned about these future developments.[16]

17. Together with other parts of the financial sector, the insurance sector plays an essential part in the economy. Confidence is a keyword. This not only includes confidence in the financial system as such – with regard to both the short and the long term: liabilities over periods of more than thirty years! – but also confidence no less in the individual companies. Long ago the legislator therefore decreed that there should be a prudential supervisor which would supervise solvency and solidity, in particular.[17] In the light of recent experiences, society is absolutely unwilling anymore to accept bankruptcies. For this reason,

a prudential supervisor must be concerned when the balance between market forces, competition policy and supervisory policy is in danger of being disturbed.

My criticism of modern competition policy is twofold. Firstly, the tacit norm of perfect competition is erroneous. In the context of technological growth and dynamic markets, if efficient competition is to be achieved, a form of monopolistic competition is preferable to a legally defined form of so-called perfect competition. Furthermore, the fiduciary character of the financial sector does not benefit from excessive competition with a significant chance of bankruptcies. Without an acceptable level of self-regulatory agreement which can be verified by the government, supervision will be compelled to take on the form of material supervision. This results inevitably in limitations on entrepreneurial behaviour (which competition policy attempts to prohibit by different means).

Instead of normative supervision which only imposes general conditions on the behaviour of the insurer (through, for instance, the solvency requirement), a network of restrictions will be created in relation to products and groups of products. Furthermore, this 'degeneration' of the supervisory system aside, a renewed wave of concentration will sooner occur in the insurance market which will probably also include the insurance brokers. Ultimately, on balance, the consequences of such a J-curve effect will be less genuine competition and therefore higher consumer prices.[18]

Trends in Corporate Governance and the Role of the Prudential Supervisor

18. In the previous section it was explained that the task of the prudential supervisor has been increased considerably as a result of both public feeling and the nature of competition policy. The development of CG methods will have a parallel influence. In my opinion, the trends in CG in the Netherlands described earlier in this paragraph support this assumption. Whatever institutional form this takes, this will result in more and more direct influence on the part of the providers of capital. It goes without saying that a more Anglo-Saxon CG culture will be a strong stimulus for the importance of short-term performance benchmarks and the emphasizing of quantities such as shareholders' value. Such a development will be further stimulated by the growing role of rewards in the form of bonuses and options for management and senior personnel. Insurance companies will also not be able to distance themselves from this. In principle, the mutual insurers may well be able to do so, but in general they have the problem of raising the equity necessary for expansion. Pension funds will also increasingly experience the same pressure to perform; not, it is true, from shareholders, but from sponsors, members and outsiders (for example, politicians, analysts and journalists).

In itself stricter financial checks on institutions need not be disastrous.[19] The matter becomes more serious if insufficient attention is given to such aspects as the neglect of the special nature of pension and insurance business, fixation on short-term effects and the link between the nature of the liabilities and investments.

An example of such an aberration is the intention (of a commercial institution in the Netherlands) to publish *monthly* performance indicators with regard to the investment policies of institutional investors. Such nonsense can do damage to a healthy industry. Nevertheless, if the expectations regarding CG trends in the Netherlands which have been outlined – and in line with these, in the other EU member states – come to fruition this will present prudential supervision with a new challenge. Demands will also be made on other external controllers, such as the external auditor and the actuary.

Since, in my opinion, a more material type of insurance supervision is not desirable from a society perspective (because this would put the economic cart before the horse) other solutions have to be found such as an increase in the required solvency margins and a more prospective definition of normative supervision (through, for instance, profit testing, embedded value calculations and scenario studies). A stronger emphasis on the long-term importance of supervision is important as a countervailing power and as a reaction to increasing manifestations of Anglo-Saxon CG. After all, the prudential supervisor has long been one of the most important CG players! In addition, the assessment of shareholders of insurance companies and perhaps the assessment of the expertise and reliability of the management and supervisory directors are important instruments.

19. From the prudential point of view, the same key, namely a greater emphasis on the long-term perspective, is an eye-opener with regard to the desired model for Financial Governance by insurers and pension funds on other companies (in other words, their investments and participations). In general, the investor role must be and must remain paramount. However, this certainly does not exclude a more active role in Financial Governance.[20] This will perhaps not occur with such activism as, for instance, CALPERS (Crist, 1995), but certainly more actively than at present.

For a responsible exercising of their roles, institutional investors in the Netherlands will have to be given more opportunities for effective Financial Governance. In this respect, I foresee both the reduction and the removal of existing protective constructions and, in time, an amendment to company law but, in the shorter term, I foresee the creation of a special right of access for major shareholders to both strategic information relating to the company and consultation with management. Such intensified communication between these special parties – possibly through special shareholder committees but, if necessary, directly – should serve to shore up confidence in the long-term direction of the company. In this regard, not every shareholder is the same. A further recommendation by the Peters Committee is important in this respect, namely, that sector and company analyses should be stimulated so that more objective information is available for evaluation by institutional investors. It is, after all, a colossal task for an investor to generate such insights himself.

A development such as this in Financial Governance by insurers and pension funds is not only a positive way of disciplining the companies involved, but also has a positive effect on investment behaviour (and the external assessment of this) by the institutions themselves. In time this gives support to the work of prudential supervision.

5. Summary and Conclusions

20. In this paper the importance and the developments in the Netherlands in the area of Corporate Governance, in particular on and by insurance companies (and pension funds), were discussed. The element of Financial Governance – in other words, influence by the company's group of capital providers – is of particular importance in this regard. Following a brief sketch of CG within the Dutch economic order (as a variant of the Rhineland model) and the structure of the insurance market in the Netherlands, the degree to which insurers (and pension funds) actually show signs of CG was discussed. In this respect, it was noted that until now there was relatively little substantial CG *on* or *by* insurers and pension funds. At the same time, signs have been observed which indicate that a considerable increase in Financial Governance in the Netherlands is likely. These developmental trends were then discussed in more detail. In addition, an analogous influence from the domain of European and national competition policy was considered. Both developmental trends were then evaluated from the specific perspective of (legal) prudential supervision.

21. On the basis of the above discussion, I draw the following *conclusions*:
1. Discussions on CG certainly have a substantial significance in addition to their fashionable facets.
2. The CG arrangements in the Netherlands cannot be extricated from the European and other international forces and developments.
3. There is a very real chance that CG of a more Anglo-Saxon guise will become dominant in Europe.
4. CG exercised by insurers and other institutional investors (such as pension funds) – in particular the Financial Governance variant – will manifest itself substantially in due time. This applies primarily to CG within the Netherlands. In so far as institutional investors make use of international (external) investment managers, this effect will be relatively much weaker.

5. In doing so, an emphasis on the long-term investment perspective will be a countervailing force against an undesirable emphasis on short-term benchmarks.
6. An increase in CG of insurers (and perhaps of pension funds) may be accompanied by very undesirable risks. This is all the more so since competition policy in the European Union and, in particular, in the Netherlands is becoming stricter and is defined primarily in legal terms.
7. A considerable effort will therefore be required of prudential supervisors – and of those who play a role in this, such as external accountants and actuaries – with the danger of slipping into systems of supervision which are inferior from the perspective of society as a whole.

Notes

1. A well-known definition is: "Corporate Governance can be defined as the whole system of rights, processes and controls established internally and externally over the management of a business entity with the objective of protecting the interests of all stakeholders." (CEPS 1995 p. 5). In Dutch persistent use is made of the English term CG. This points to the origin of such discussions in the seventies in the USA and later in the UK. With Moerland (FD 16 March 1996) I prefer '*ondernemingsdisciplinering*' (disciplining of companies) as the equivalent Dutch term.
2. In the Netherlands a normative retrospective system of supervision has existed for a long time which has as its main focus the monitoring of solvency (of more broadly, solidity). The Dutch Insurance Supervisory Board (which has been a foundation established under Civil Law since 1992) is responsible for legal supervision and operates as a so-called 'independent public authority'. For a general introduction see Vermaat/Oosenbrug (1994).
3. The so-called 'structure regime' has been applicable since 1971 to companies which meet the following criteria: (1) a subscribed capital of at least 25 million guilders, (2) at least 100 employees employed in the Netherlands, and (3) the presence of a works council in the company. Under the structure regime, the supervisory board is given strong powers, namely (i) it appoints its own members by co-option (with a right of nomination and a right of veto – which may be annulled by a Court ruling – for the general meeting of shareholders and the works council), (ii) it appoints and dismisses the members of the management board and ratifies the annual statements of accounts and (iii) it has to give its approval for important decisions taken by the company. There are two important exceptions. Subsidiaries of a holding company in the Netherlands, of which the latter is subject to the structure regime, are themselves exempted from it. In the case of international holding companies in the Netherlands, where at least 50 per cent of the shares are in foreign ownership, a milder regime applies in which more powers are given to the general meeting of shareholders.
4. It has by no means been established that the Anglo-Saxon model for companies is superior to the Rhineland or German model. De Jong (1996), for instance, argues on the basis of long-term empirical results, that the Anglo-Saxon model in the long run is characterised by (on average) lower labour productivity, lower growth of the total added value and lower employment. The higher pressure exerted by the capital market – resulting in a relatively higher dividend – appears to be counterproductive from a perspective of society as a whole.

According to Scholtens (1996) the differences between the USA, UK, Germany and Japan with regard to their financial systems are, in fact, much less fundamental so that the influence of such systemic differences on the way in which CG operates in these countries cannot be very significant. Other factors would then have to have a greater effect!

5. *Corporate Governance in Nederland.* This is a Dutch echo of such well-known reports as the Treadway Committee (USA 1987), the Cadbury Committee (UK 1992), CEPS (EU 1995) and the ICMG report (International 1995).
6. Pension funds almost exclusively have the legal form of a foundation under Civil Law. See also section 11 of this paragraph.
7. Total value of listed shares as a percentage of Gross Domestic Product: 72,2 per cent
8. Insurance companies and Pension funds.
9. Directly or indirectly listed on the Amsterdam Stock Exchange: 22.
10. For example: Pension funds, Foundations or Family ownership.
11. In the Netherlands these participations usually are so called certificated shares, i.e. without direct voting power.
12. As regards the other important insurance groups: the ACHMEA GROUP is in essence a mutual group, DELTA LLOYD GROUP is a 100 per cent subsidiary of COMMERCIAL UNION (UK), INTERPOLIS GROUP is a 100 per cent subsidiary of the (Mutual) RABO BANK GROUP.
13. This applies less to partial portfolios for which independent (external) fund managers are given responsibility. In such cases, investment behaviour usually is so active that CG pressure is less efficient.
14. *Idem* De Man (1996)
15. And that's a good thing too! After all, from a theoretical point of view, in a pure market form of perfect competition without any exogenous intervention by an 'auctioneer', to use Walras's term, no new equilibrium would arise of its own accord.
16. This is dealt with extensively in Vermaat and Bakker (1994).
17. In the Netherlands – as in the United Kingdom, and currently in all EU countries – a normative system of retrospective supervision has been applied since 1923, in which insurers are free to adjust the way they run their companies, their products and their premium tariffs to market conditions. This promotes very innovative and competitive markets!
18. Another example which typifies the adverse effect of an approach to competition law which is too legalistic is the following. The new Act will impose a variety of far-reaching limitations on voluntary chains in relation to the use of shop formulas. A large retail business is not subject to this (after all, it is one company!). On balance, the consequence will be a weakening of the independent retailer and, in time, a reduction in competition.
19. This paper does not include a comparative discussion of the achievements for society of the Anglo-Saxon and Rhineland models (see footnote 4). Neither is an answer given to the question whether the net returns required by shareholders at present are not too high from the perspective of society as a whole.
20. The question with regard to so-called Chinese walls will again come forcefully to the fore and not only in relation to financial conglomerates!

Index

Page numbers in *italics* indicate tables; references in **bold** indicate figures.

A
ABI *see* Association of British Insurers
accounting conventions 52
acquisitions *see* mergers and acquisitions
AEX *see* Amsterdam Exchanges
allocative efficiency 252, 254
Amsterdam Exchanges (AEX) 141–2, 146–7
Amsterdam Securities Depository (ASD) 142
Amsterdam Stock Exchange (ASE) 141
Anglo-Saxon model of corporate governance 50, 107
 characteristics 89
 shareholder influence 106, 107, 108
 short-term profitability objectives 107, 108
 transparency 89, 106
ASD *see* Amsterdam Securities Depository
ASE *see* Amsterdam Stock Exchange
assets
 allocation of residual rights 92
 asset substitution 58, 178
 control and ownership, separation of 92–3
Association of British Insurers (ABI) 222–3, 232
audit committees 225, 229
auditors 91
Australia 217–18
Austria 141

B
Banca Commerciale Italiana 186
Banca d'Italia 181, 189, 193
Banca Nazionale dell'Agricoltura 189
Banca Nazionale del Lavoro 189
Banca di Roma 23, 189
Banca di Sconto 169
Banking Council [Czech Republic] 78
bankruptcy 57, 239–40
 Czech Republic 78
 Italy 32–3, *33*
 legislation 52, 240
 United Kingdom 105

banks
 and acquisitions and mergers xv
 as debtholders and shareholders xiv, xv, 90, 94, 108, 164, 172–3
 as large shareholders 163–4, 172–8
 bank-based financial systems 48
 board placements 192, 251
 and capital market development 47
 collateralization of loans 35, *36*
 community business and finance 28–9
 conflicts of interest 164, 172–3
 control of voting rights 173
 corporate finance provision 17, 94, 248, 250, 253
 corporate governance role 17, 45, 94, 114, 164, 173, 192, 245–6
 and corporations, long-term relations with 245–6, 250
 debt-driven monitoring 173
 and debt restructuring 35, *35*
 EU banking directives 206, *207*
 foreign bank share ownership xiv
 historic activity 163
 informational advantage xiv, xv, 94, 245–6
 in insurance and investment fund market 45
 investment behaviour 90
 new capital standards, response to 45
 non-financial enterprises, reducing stakes in 45
 portfolio restrictions *53*, *54*
 and privatisation process ix, 188–9
 proxy voting 173, 251
 regulation 52, 240
 rescue finance 246, 252
 and restructuring 35, *35*, 94
 risk aversion 173
 shareholdings, lending, correlated with 178
 and short-term debt 250
 universal bank-based governance 19
 see also 'banks' under individual countries
Becattini, Giacomo 26

Belgium
  banks, investment by 282–3
  corporate governance x
  disclosure legislation 266–8
  insider system 263
  ownership structure 271–87
    complex structures 272, **274**
    concentrated ownership 263, 266–9, 281, 287
    control leverage factor 263, 275, 277–8, 279
    families and individual investors 263, 271, 272, 276, 281
    foreign investors 271, 272, 276, 281
    holding companies 263, 271, 272, 275–6, 281, 287
    industrial and commercial companies 271, 272, 276, 281
    investor categories 263
    large shareholdings, changes in 286–7, 287, 292
    pyramidal structures 263, 267, 271–2, **273**, 275, 276–8, 282, 287
    ultimate shareholders 275–6, 277, 277, 278, 279, 290–1, 296
  shareholder classes 281–4
    employee shareholders 283
    family shareholders 281–2
    financial institutions 282–3
    foreign shareholders 284–6
    the government 283
    holding companies 281–2
    institutional investors 283–4
    insurance companies 283–4
  stock exchanges 142, 151–2
  voting rights and restrictions 266–7, 268–9
    blocking minorities 278–9, 280
    deviation from one share-one vote rule 277, 278
    majorities 278–9, 280
    supermajorities 278, 279, 280, 281
block trading 47
Board of Directors
  accountability 56
  bank placements 192
  board composition and corporate performance 2–3, 7–9, 8, 12
  board size and corporate performance vii, 3, 9–11, 10, 12
  board turnover and corporate performance 242–3
  corporate governance
    association with 237
    monitoring role xxiii, xxiv, 2, 3, 12, 93, 242–3
    working party recommendations 203, 204
  director selection and remuneration 91
  employee-nominated members xii
  executive directors 2, 3, 12
  government-appointed members xii
  institutional investors and 63
  internal governance mechanism 1
  key board committees 225, 229, 232
  non-executive directors xxiv, 2, 3
  outsider-dominated boards and corporate performance 242
  workers' representatives 200
bond finance 248
Brussels Stock Exchange 269

C
Cadbury Committee [UK] xxi, 91 61, 93, 105, 147, 203, 204, 217, 225, 231, 242
Canada: mutual fund portfolios 43, 44
capital adequacy requirements xiv
capital market
  impact of institutional sector on 46
  infrastructure modernization 49
  intermediation 48, 49
  market liquidity 46–7
  modernization 49
  monitoring role 63
  and product market, interrelation 253
CARIPLO 189
Central and Eastern European countries (CEECs) 199, 205–7, 212
  corporate governance problems 206, 212
  cross-border governance ix
  financial market regulation 206–7
  shareholding structure 211, 212
  stock market capitalization 208–9
  transition to market economies ix, 200
Centre for European Policy Studies (CEPS) xxi, 218
CEOs
  pay 241
  turnover 2, 242
China 235
CMF *see Conseil de Marchés Financiers*
Comit 23
commercialisti 34

commitment and trust x, 238, 252
competition 91, 252–5
  and allocative efficiency 252, 254
  barrier to monopoly abuse 253, 256
  and corporate governance 236, 252–5, 256
  and firms̃financial institutions relations 252, 256
  in markets for corporate control 254
  and productive efficiency 252, 254
  product market competition xxvi, 236, 253, 256
Confindustria 24
Conseil de Marchés Financiers (CMF) 153–4, 156
contractual governance 109, 303
Cooke ratio 96
cooptation-system 107, 205
Copeba 272, **274**, 275
Copenhagen Stock Exchange 143, 146, 218
co-regulation 147
corporate failures 91
corporate finance 46, 248–50, 255
  as a management discipline 94
  bank finance 17, 94, 248, 250, 253
  financing patterns, international 248–9
  retained earnings as dominant source 248
  stock market finance 253
corporate governance
  bank role 17, 45, 94, 114, 164, 173, 192, 245–6
  central problem 92, 238
  competition and 236, 252–5
  and corporate performance ix–x, 92, 235–57
  cross-border governance ix
  determinants 52–5
  and differing ownership structures 238
  enhanced understanding, benefits of 41
  external pressures 113
  financial governance *see* financial governance
  government interventions 188
  insurance companies and 308–11
  legal and regulatory framework xvi, xx, 240, 254
    see also European Union
  market indicators 208–11
  matrix of governance by sector vii, xiii–xxiv
  a matter of performance accountability 91
  national characteristics 50–1
  optimal system xxv, 92

  ownership concentration and 243–4, 266
  principal-agent relationship xvii, 2, 56, 92, 93, 237, 238, 239, 240, 241, 301
  prudential supervisor, role of 318–20
  public policy agenda and reforms 91
  public-sector ownership, role of 50
  reallocation ability xxiv
  separation of ownership and control 91
  shareholder influence 57–8, 89, 113, 117–18, 203, 243
  similarities and common features xxv, 50
  system convergence xxv, 89
  systems approach 236
  term explored xi–xii, 42, 89, 92, 301
  topology of 301–3, **302**
  working party reports *see* Cadbury Committee; Centre for European Policy Studies; Greenbury Report; Peters Committee; Viénot Committee
  see also 'corporate governance' under individual countries; institutional investors
corporate governance models
  Anglo-Saxon model viii, 50, 89, 106, 107, 108
  company-oriented system 293
  Dutch model (structure system) 89, 106, 107
  enterprise-oriented system 293
  German (Rhineland) model 89
  insider systems xix, 45, 50, 56, 58, 63, 64, 67, 238, 251, 253, 255, 256, 257, 263
  Latin model 89
  outsider systems 50, 56–7, 58, 63, 64, 238, 251, 254–5, 256, 257, 263
corporate management
  accountability 55–6, 63, 91
  debt as a disciplining device 57, 58, 94, 113
  defensive behaviour xxiv, 57, 64, 67, 94, 268
  entrenchment xxiv, 169, 244
  evaluating xxiii, 2
  external pressures 114
  incentives *see* incentives
  monitoring and disciplining x, xxiii, xxv, 3, 56, 57, 93, 239, 242, 245
  moral hazard 121, 170, 182, 183–4
  performance and remuneration, relation between xxiii, 116, 176, 240–1
  remuneration *see* incentives
  short-term decision-making 91

corporate performance
  board turnover and 242–3
  cross-firm and cross-country variations 235
  and governance, relation with ix–x, 92, 235–57
  monitoring xx
  ownership structure and 243, 244
  variables affecting 165
corporations
  accountability 60
  concepts of 164–5, 237–8
  insider-managers 165
  inter-firm relationships 250
  legal and regulatory framework 240
  life-cycle development 253
  listed companies and market capitalization 47, 48
  listed company ownership in major industrial companies 30–1, 30
  outsider-managers 165–6
  ownership structures see ownership structures
  principal–agent relationship xvii, 2, 56, 92, 93, 237, 238, 239, 240, 241, 301
  separation of management and ownership xvii, 1, 91, 217
  shareholder model 238
  stakeholder approach 164, 238
  transfer of control xv
Crédit Agricole 189
Crédit Lyonnais 189
Credito Italiano 186
cross-border activities
  by institutional investors 45, 46, 205, 218
  governance ix
  relaxation of constraints on 45, 200
Cuccia, Enrico 23
Czech Republic
  bankruptcies 78
  banks
    conflict of interest problem 206
    non-performing loans 79
    and privatizations 79, 206
    prudential rules 207
    return on average assets 79
    shareholding 211
  corporate governance 79, 206
  corporations
    domestic outside ownership 206
    management and employee ownership 205–6
    post-privatization 206
  insurance companies 207
  pension funds 207
  privatization viii, xvi, 73, 74, 75, 76–9, 77, 83
    investment privatization funds (IPFs) 77, 78
  state influence in enterprise sector 77–8
  stock market capitalization 208–9

D
DB see Deutsche Börse
debt as a disciplining device 57, 58, 94, 113
debt-equity swaps 74
debt restructuring 35, 35
Denmark
  derivatives exchange 143
  stock exchange 143, 146
  supervisory boards xii, 200
  voting rights 202
deregulation 45, 55, 67, 108, 236
derivatives 67
Deutsche Bank A.G. 163
Deutsche Börse (DB) 141
Deutscher Kassenverein AG 141
Deutsche Telekom 191
Deutsche Terminbörse GmbH (DTB) 141
disciplining x, 239, 255
  debt as a disciplining device 57, 58, 94, 113
  'exit and voice' framework 46, 229, 239
disclosure requirements viii, xviii, 47, 52, 58, 220, 240, 266–8
disintermediation 47
DTB see Deutsche Terminbörse GmbH
Dutch Association of Stockbroking 105
Dutch Central Bank 100

E
EASDAQ 152, 213
economic and monetary union (EMU) 203, 205
electricity companies 191, 191
employee legislation 52
Employee Retirement Income Security Act (ERISA) [USA] 61
employee shareholders 283
EMU see economic and monetary union
ENI see National Hydrocarbon Agency
Enti pubblici 20, 21, 22, 24, 36, 37
entrenchment xxiv, 169, 244

Index

EOE *see* European Options Exchange
equity culture 45, 49, 55
European Company Statute 199
European Options Exchange (EOE) 141, 142
European Union (EU)
  corporate governance framework
    banking directives 206, *207*
    board structure 203, *204*, 205
    company law 200–5
    financial market regulation 206–7
    harmonization, attempts at 202, 203, 213
    insurance directives 206–7, *207*
    pension funds directives 200, 207, *207*
    sensitive issues 200
    single market legislation and 203
    stock exchange governance 135–58, 149–57
    on voting rights 201–2
  domestic listed companies 208
  ownership concentration, variance in 211
  shareholding structures, variance in 210–11
  stock market capitalization 208, *209*, **210**
'exit and voice' 46, 229, 239

F

fiduciary character of the financial sector 60–1, 318
financial governance
  direct control via debt 42, 45, 56, 58, 60
  direct control via equity 42, 45, 49, 56, 57–8, 59
  impact of financial systems changes on viii, 41, 42, 45, 55
  impact of institutional investors on 55–6
  market control via debt 56, 57, 59, 63
  market control via equity 56, 57, 58, 63
Financial Reporting Council 61
Finland 201
Floridienne **272**, 272, 277, 278
France
  banks
    active shareholders 189
    corporate finance 248
    government reform of 189
    privatization 189
    state-owned 188
    targeting of small and medium enterprises 189
  Belgium, investment in 284–6, *285*
  corporate governance

  insider system 251
  Viénot Report xxi, 203, *204*, 212
  corporations
    government intervention in privatized firms 190
    inter-company holdings 63, 251
    large shareholders 265
    market capitalization 264, *264*
    ownership of common stock *51*
    ownership structure viii, 63, 95, *95*, 118, *119*, *210*, 211, 250, 251, 265
    voting rights 201
  foreign investors 211
  institutional investors 211
  'noyaux durs' (core investors) 52, 251
  pension systems 48–9
  regulated market concept 142
  stock exchanges 142
    domestic listed companies 206
  takeover activity *64*
France Telecom 191
Frankfurt Stock Exchange (FWB) 141
free-rider problem 2, 93, 94, 165, 166, 167, 171, 172, 243
fund management 49
FWB *see* Frankfurt Stock Exchange

G

German Options and Futures Exchange 141
German Securities Deposit 141
Germany
  banks
    as large shareholders 163
    corporate finance provision 173, 248, 253, 255
    corporate governance role xiv
    and corporations, long-term relations with 250
    proxy voting 173
    restructuring finance 246, 255
    shareholders and debtholders 173
    voting power 173, *177*
  Belgium, investment in 284
  corporate governance
    concentrated ownership and 244
    incentives and disciplining 255
    insider system 45, 56, 251
  corporate management 176, 242
  corporate performance, ownership structures and 244, 245

Germany (*cont.*)
  corporations
    capital structure 127, *127*
    dividend pay-out ratios 249
    equity investors, nature of 250
    market capitalization 208, 264, *264*
    mergers and acquisitions 63, 64, *64*
    proxy voting xxii
    shareholder information flows 238–9
    shareholding turnover 245
    voting rights restrictions 269
    workers' board representatives 200
  institutional investors
    growth in shareholding 211
    historic experience 163
    ownership of listed companies 30–1, *30*
  mutual fund portfolios *43*, 44
  ownership structures 95, *95*, 96, 118, *119*, 168, 210–11, *210*, 244, 250, 251, 265
    foreign investors 211
    industrial parent companies xviii
    interlocking shareholdings 251
    large shareholders 163, 168, 265
    listed company ownership 30–1, *30*
    non-financial corporations, ownership concentration in 119, *119*
    ownership of common stock *51*, *179*
  pension funds 47, 48–9, 60
  stock exchanges 141
    domestic listed companies 208
golden parachutes xxiv, 57
golden shares 190–1, 254
Greenbury Report xxi, 61, 217, 225, 231
Grossbanken 163

H
Hungary
  banks
    foreign investment 206
    prudential rules *207*
    shareholding 211
  corporations
    foreign ownership 206
    state ownership 206
  insurance companies *207*
  pension funds *207*
  privatization xvi, 74, *75*, 76, 83
  stock exchange 209

I
IBIS 141
incentives x, xxiv, 1, 93, 113, 239, 240–2, 255
  governance and pay, relation between 241, 242
  options as a form of remuneration xxiii, 92, 116, 241
  pay and performance, relations between xxiii, 116, 176, 240–1, 242
  reputation as an incentive mechanism 116
incorporation xx
Indosuez 189
industrial companies
  financial structure 52, *52*
  parent companies xviii
information technology ix, 45, 46, 140
insider trading xviii, 122, 147, 148, 240
institutional investors
  annual rate of growth in OECD regions 42–3, *44*
  boards, influence on 63
  capital market operations 41
  coalition forming 247–8
  cross-border activity 45, 46, 205, 218
  EMU, impact of 203, 205
  fiduciary responsibilities 59, 60–1
  and financial governance 55–6
  foreign assets holdings 43–4
  governance role ix, xxv, 42, 44, 56, 59–60, 62, 217, 237, 247
  growing influence of viii, 41, 42–4, *43*, 218
  growth of managed assets 45
  impact on financial markets 46–50
  investment strategies 49–50, 61–2, 249
  liberalization of activities 45
  and the market for corporate control 42, 63–7
  modus operandi 42, 44–6
  in outsider systems of governance 58
  ownership of common stock 172
  passive investors 59
  performance measurement systems 49
  portfolio composition (OECD countries) **65–6**, 68
  portfolio restrictions 52, *53–4*
  pressure-resistant institutions 172
  pressure-sensitive institutions 172
  professional management 46
  and restructuring 239–40
  role xxi–xxii
  shareholder activism 62
  short-term versus long-term strategies 61–2
  and takeover activity 59, 63, 64, 67

institutional investors (*cont.*)
   total assets in OECD area 42, *43*
   voting behaviour xxi–xxii, 172, 199, 205
   see also banks; 'institutional investors' under individual countries; insurance companies; pension funds
insurance companies
   as a large shareholder *175*
   EU directives 206–7, *207*
   governance and 308–11
   holdings in OECD region 42–3, *43*, **44**
   increasing shareholdings 45, 90
   international diversification 44
   portfolio composition **65**
   portfolio restrictions *53, 54*
   see also 'insurance companies' under individual countries
Internal Market Programme xvi
internationalization of businesses 55
investment privatization funds (IPFs) [Czech Republic] 77, 78
investor capitalism 217
Ireland 202
IRI 20, 21, 22, 24
ISD ix, 140, 142
Italy
   bankruptcies 32–3, *33*
   banks
     and acquisition finance 33
     bank/firm relations 20–2, 32–3, 34, 36
     bias against long-term financing 31
     collateralization of loans 31, 35, *36*
     corporate changes, involvement in 32, 33, 34, *34*
     corporate finance provision 30
     corporate governance role vii, 25, 28, 31–2
     current account lending 31
     debt restructuring 35, *35*
     and distress finance 26, 32–3, *33*
     entrepreneurs, role in relation to 28, 29
     informational advantage 28
     local banks and small firm development viii, 18, 26, 28, 29, 34–6
     and market for corporate control 29–36
     multiple bank borrowing 31
     non-financial firms, shareholding in 30–1
     privatization 189–90, 193
     regulation 193
     shareholding *30*, 31
     state-owned 189

corporate control, universal bank-based governance 19
corporate governance
   coalition control models 28
   Enti pubblici, role of 18, 19, 20, 21, 22, 24, 36, 37
   family and coalition devices 36
   informal corporate governance 28
   large firms, governance of 18
   post-war model 17–18, 19–20, 24–5
   pre-war model 19
   private corporate governance 25
   small firms, governance of 18, 28, 29, 36, 37
   two-tier model viii, 37
   worker and community monitoring 28
corporations
   entrepreneurial activity 182–3, 184
   flexible specialization model 27
   informal shareholder relations 180, 181, 184, 185
   moral hazard opportunities 182, 183–4
   non-financial corporations, ownership concentration in 119, *119*
   ownership of common stock *51, 179*
   ownership structure and control xviii, 95, *95*, 96, 118, *119*, 182, 183, **184**, 184, 185, 186–7, *210*, 211, 265
   privatization programme 186–7, *187*
   pyramidal groups 63, 182, 183, *183*, 184, 185
   separation of ownership and control 182, *183*, 185
   small- and medium-sized enterprises (SMEs) 26–8, 26–9, 29
   stock market capitalization 208
   union militancy 27
pension systems 47, 48–9
privatization 181, 186–7, *187*
regulated markets, reform of 142–3
state central role in capitalism vii–viii, 18, 19, 24, 25, 36, 181, 211
stock exchanges 142–3, 147

J
Japan
   banks 126–31
     board placements 123–5, 131, 176, 178
     corporate banking relations 130–1, *130*
     corporate finance 114, 128–30, *128*, 132, 240, 248

Japan, banks (*cont.*)
    and corporate financial distress 246
    corporate shareholdings 131
    and corporations, long-term relations with 250
    governance role viii–ix, xiv, 114, 125, 126, 132
    and the *keirestu* 180
    main bank system 114, 126, 130–2, 178, 185
    restructuring finance 239, 255
    shareholders and debtholders 173, *176*
Belgium, investment in 284
'bubble' years 120, 128, 129, 131
corporate governance 112–34
    bank governance role viii–ix, xiv, 114, 125, 126, 132
    Board of Directors
        bank nominees 123–5, 133–4, 176, 178
        composition of 122–3, *123*
        corporate directors 123, 125
        external directors 123–5, *123*, 133–4, 176
    control via debt 42, 58, 60
    disciplining 113
    elements of economic inefficiency 114
    external pressures 113, 114
    insider model 56, 58
    institutional investors and 42, 114, 122, 132
    inter-corporate ownership, negative effects of 122
    large shareholders, influence of viii, 121–2, 132
    ownership and management, separation of 115
    reputation as an incentive mechanism 116
    shareholder role and influence 113, 117–20, 122, 125, 132
corporate management
    incentives 113, 114, 116
    moral hazard 131
    remuneration 116, 132, 133, 242
corporations
    anti-trust laws 180–1, 186
    Board of Directors 122–5
    capital costs 248, 249
    capital structure 127–30, *127*
    corporate banking relations 130–1, *130*
    downsizing and layoffs 124
    executive turnover 125
    keiretsu 120, 125, 173, 179–80, *180*, 181, 253, 265
    legal structure 114–16
    leverage 127
    listed companies and capitalization 115, *115*
    market capitalization 115, *115*, 208, 264, *264*, 265
    monopoly abuse 253
    number of companies by size and status *115*
    post-war reform 180–1
    Presidents' Clubs 180, 181
    quoted companies 264, *264*
    shift to market forms of finance 129
financial governance 58
institutional investors
    governance role 42, 114, 122, 132
    ownership of listed companies 30, *30*
    positive effects of ownership 122
    shareholdings 118, 119
mergers and acquisitions 63, *64*, 116–17, *117*
mutual fund portfolios *43*, 44
ownership structures 63, 95, *95*, 96, 117–20, **118**, *119*, 179–80, *179*, 185, 186, *186*, *210*, 211, 255, 265–6
    cross-shareholding 114, 120–1, *121*, 132
    inter-corporate shareholdings 122, 179–80
    mutual ownership structures 181
    ownership of common stock *51*, 119–20, *119*, 179, *179*
pension funds 60
shareholder litigation system 126
shareholders
    informal shareholder relations 181
    information flows 238–9
    large shareholders 114, 119, *120*, 121–2
    shareholder rights, changes in 125–6
junk bonds 67

K
keiretsu 120, 125, 173, 179–80, *180*, 181, 253, 265
Københavns Fondsbørs A/S 143

L
Lamfalussy, Alexandre x
leveraged buy-outs (LBOs) 59
London Metal Exchange (LME) 151

London Stock Exchange (LSE) 144, 150–1, 264
  governance 152, 153
Luxembourg
  Belgium, investment in 284
  supervisory boards xii

M
Madrid Stock Exchange 3
management buy-outs xvii, 73, 74, 75, 81, 91
market capitalization
  as percentage of GDP 264, *264*
  international overview 47, *48*
market for corporate control 1, 29–36, 42, 56, 63–7, 167, 168, 170, 185, 245, 254
  see also takeovers
market exposure 49
market liquidity viii, 46–7, 61, 62, 170
matrix of governance by sector vii, xiii–xxiv
Mattei, Enrico 21
Median Voter Theorem 145–6
Mediobanca 18, 23, 36
Mellen, Charles 163
Menichella, Donato 20
mergers and acquisitions xii, 63, *64*, 252
  banks and xv
  Third Company Law Directive xxii
  see also 'mergers and acquisitions' under individual countries; takeovers
Metallgesellschaft 239
monopoly abuse 246, 253, 254, 256
moral hazard opportunities 121, 170, 182, 183–4
mutual funds xviii, 45, 168, 188
  governance guidelines 60
  as large shareholders *174*
  portfolio diversification 44
  portfolio restrictions 53, *54*
  stated investment policy 61

N
NAPF *see* National Association of Pension Funds
NASD *see* National Association of Securities Dealers
Nasdaq 154–6, 264
National Association of Pension Funds (NAPF) [UK] 61, 222–3, 232
National Association of Securities Dealers (NASD) [US] 154, 155–6
National Hydrocarbon Agency (ENI) [Italy] 21, 22, 24
National Investment Funds (NIFs) [Poland] 81
nationalization programmes xvii
National Property Fund (NPF) [Czech Republic] 77, 78, 84
Netherlands
  banks
    'certificates of no objection' 100, **101**, 102–3
    financial institutions, investment in 100, 102, *102*, 103, 104
    non-financial institutions, investment in 100, 102, *102*, 103, 105, 108
    participations 103–5, *104*
    risky assets, investment in 96, 100
    shareholdings viii, 96, **99**, 100
  Belgium, investment in 284
  bond investment 96, **98–9**
  corporate governance xviii, x, 105–8, 303–21
    boards of directors and supervisory boards 106, 107, 108
    cooptation-system 107, 205
    insider model 56
    Peters Report 91, 105–6, 107, 203, *204*, 212
    prudential supervisor, role of 318–20
    scarcity of evidence on 90
    shareholder role and influence 106, 107, 315–16
    trends 314–16, 318–20
  corporations
    stock market capitalization 208
    voting rights 201
    workers' representatives 200
  financial governance, by insurers and pension funds 313–14, 319
  institutional investors 96, **97**
  insurance companies 305–21
    as large shareholders *175*
    competitive relationships 307–8, 316–18
    contractual governance 309
    and corporate governance 308–11
    deregulation 317
    FDSE-quotient for life insurers 312, *312*
    FDSE-quotient for non-life insurers 311–12, *311*
    financial governance by 313–14, 319

Netherlands, insurance companies (*cont.*)
    financial governance on 308, 309, 311–13
    foreign insurers 307, 317
    need for long-term investment perspective x
    number and density of insurers 305, *306*, 307, *308*
    ownership characteristics *309*
    pension funds, competition from 308, 317
    self-regulation 308
    shareholding distribution *310*
  mergers and acquisitions 314
  ownership structures 95–100, *95*, **97–9**, 108
    foreign shareholding viii, 89, 96, **97–9**, 100, 108
    institutional investors 96, **97**
  pension funds 48, 60, 305, *306*, 307, 308, 313–14, 317, 318
  stock exchanges 141–2, 146–7
new equity issues 248
New York Stock Exchange 264
non-financial companies xvii, xviii, xix 119, *119*
'noyaux durs' (core investors) 52

O

OECD countries
  concentration of institutional assets in 59
  corporate governance: differences and convergence 50–2
  equity holdings of institutional investors 64, **65**
  growing role of institutional investors viii, 41, 42–4, **44**
  mutual funds 44
  ownership of common stock 50, *51*
OM Group 143, 144, 146
Oslo Stock Exchange 218
ownership structures 250–1
  Chicago view 188
  concentrated shareholdings x, 56, 118, 165, 167, 168, 169, 182, 183, 185, 239, 243, 250–1, 252, 255–6, 266
  cross-shareholdings xix, 56, 120–1, *121*, 238, 251, 253, 288–90
  dispersed shareholdings 118, 165, 168, 170, 251, 263, 266
  domestic outside ownership 206
  dynamic evolution 244
  endogeneity 186, 192
  family holdings 253, 256
  foreign ownership viii, 89, 96, **97–9**, 100, 108, 206, 211, 218, 284–6
  individual investors xix, xx, 218, 238
  insider system 238
  institutional investors *see* institutional investors
  inter-corporate holdings 122, 238, 256
  management and employee ownership 205–6
  mixed structures xii–xiii
  non-voting shares 202
  outsider ownership 205
  relation of differences to corporate control 252, 266
  stable shareholdings 119–20
  state ownership 205
  structural differences (Europe) *95*, 210–11, *210*, 218
  transition economies 205

P

Paribas 189, 272, 275, 277, 278, 286
pension funds 60, 188, 218
  as large shareholders 168, *175*
  asset allocation 49
  contractual governance 309
  and equity market development 47–8
  EU directives 200, 207, *207*
  governance role 218
  holdings in OECD region 43, *43*
  internal governance structure xxii
  pay-as-you-go (PAYG) system 49, 55, 207
  pension reform 55
  portfolio composition **65**
  portfolio restrictions *53*, *54*
  rate of growth in OECD regions *44*
  shareholdings 45
  and takeover activity 59
  voting behaviour xxi
  see also 'pension funds' under individual countries
Peters Committee [Netherlands] 91, 105–6, 107, 203, *204*, 212, 315–16, 320
Poland
  banks
    foreign investment 206
    prudential rules *207*
  corporate governance 81–2, *82*, 207

Poland, corporate governance (cont.)
  corporations
    domestic outside ownership 206
    employee ownership 206
    foreign ownership 206
    insurance companies 207
    pension funds 207
    privatization viii, 73, 74, 75, 76, 79–83, 83, 84
  stock exchange 209
Polish Workers' Council 80
portfolio management 49
  average holding periods 62
  core portfolio 62
  diversification xx, xxi, 49
  indexed portfolios 62
  restrictions 52, 53–4
  satellite portfolio 62
price manipulation 147, 148
principal/agent relationship xvii, 2, 56, 92, 93, 237, 238, 239, 240, 241, 301
privatization 55, 72–85
  capital privatization 74, 75, 76, 80
  and choice of ownership structure 185, 188, 190, 192
  'commercialization' stage 79–80, 85
  cross-country variations 75, 76, 83
  degree of control exercised by owners 74, 75, 76
  effective governance structure 83–4
  and equity culture development 49
  EU provisions xvi
  foreign investment xvi, 73, 76
  'golden shares' 190–1, 254
  government intervention in privatized corporations 190–1, 192
  incentives 78, 79, 83, 84
  insider privatization viii, 73, 74, 76, 81
  'liquidation' route 73, 74, 75, 80
  management/employee buyout 73, 74, 75, 81
  mass privatization xvi, xix, 73, 74, 75, 76, 80–1, 83–4
  outside ownership 74, 75, 76, 81
  role of banks in ix, 188–9
  speed of 74, 75, 76, 83, 84
  state influence 77, 78, 79
  voucher privatization xix, 73, 74, 76–7, 78, 84
  see also 'privatization' under individual countries

Privatization Investment Funds (PIFs) xix
Prix Marjolin (L. Renneboog) x
productive efficiency 254
product market competition xxvi, 236, 253, 256
proprietary trading systems (PTSs) ix, 47, 140
proxy voting xxii, 31, 60–1, 63, 93, 106
pyramidal groups 63, 182, **183**, 183, 184, 185, 263, 267, 271–2, **273**, 275, 276–8, 282

R
regulation 52, 207, 240, 256–7
  co-regulation 147
  public regulation 147, 148
  self-regulation 147–9, 155, 157, 174–9
  two-tier systems 149, 154
relationship investing 62, 63
remuneration committees 225, 229, 241
reputation as an incentive mechanism 116
restructuring x, xii, 67, 94, 239–40
Rudman Report 155
Russia, asset stripping 164

S
San Paolo di Torino 189
SEC *see* Securities and Exchange Commission
Securities Commission (Consob) [Italy] 143, 158
Securities and Exchange Commission (SEC) [US] 60, 154, 155
Securities and Investments Board [UK] 151
securities markets 46, 47
  regulation 207
securitization 67
self-regulation 147–9, 155, 157, 174–9
shareholder activism 56, 59, 60, 61, 62, 69
shareholders
  coalition formation 243
  employee shareholders 283
  free-rider problems 2, 93, 94, 165, 166, 167, 171, 172, 243
  governance role and influence 1, 57–8, 89, 93, 113, 117–18, 167, 203, 243
  informal relations among 178–9, 185
  information flows 238–9
  the large shareholder (LSH)
    agency problems 93, 118
    banks as 163–4, 172–8
    governance role 1, 114, 167, 168, 170, 172, 237

shareholders (*cont.*)
    impact on managers' discretion and initiative 169–70
    insider LSH 165, **166**, 169, 170, *171*
    outsider LSH 165, **166**, 167, 169–70, 170, *171*, 172
    and privatizations 188
    pros and cons of presence of 165–6, **166**, 167, 168–70, 170–1, *171*, 172, *174–5*, 179
    and reduction in market liquidity 170
    and takeovers 166–7, *171*
    typically institutional investors 172
    risk sharing 239
    voting behaviour (Europe) 205
    see also ownership structures
shareholders' meetings xx, xxii, 63, 106
share repurchase schemes 268
SIB *see* Securities and Investments Board
Slovak Republic
    banks: prudential rules 207
    corporations
        domestic outside ownership 206
        management and employee ownership 205–6
    insurance companies 207
    pension funds 207
    stock market capitalization 208–9
Slovenia *207*, 209
small- and medium-sized enterprises (SMEs) 26–8, 29, 49, 83, 247–8
Société de la Bourse de Luxembourg SA 144
Société Générale de Belgique 189, 286
Spain
    banks 188
    corporate performance 3–12
    market capitalization 264, *264*
stakeholders xii, xix–xxi, xxvi, 91, 92, 107–8, 109, 164, 238
STET 191
stock exchange governance 138–58
    Belgium stock exchanges 151–2, 153
    conflicts of interest 157
    EASDAQ 152, 213
    in the EU ix, 139–58
    French model 153–4, 156
    LSE review 150–1, 152
    Nasdaq 154–6
    regulation ix, 52, 147, 240
        co-regulation 147
        self-regulation and surveillance 147–9, 157
    two-tier system 154

surveillance and management, separation of 153–4, 156, 157
stock exchanges
    ancillary services 139
    capital intensive nature 145
    clearing and settlement services 139
    competition ix, 140, 145, 146, 157
    cross-border transaction activity ix
    economies of scale 145
    investor-owned exchanges ix, 144, 145–6, 149, 156
    member-owned exchanges ix, 144–5, 146, 148–9, 156, 157
    minority shareholdings, offers of 146–7
    mixed model 146, 149
    outside ownership 144, 145, 146, 149
    ownership costs 145
    ownership structures xiv, 144–7, 156–7
    privatization 143
    stock market capitalization to GDP ratios 208, *209*, **210**
    transaction costs 148
    transaction services ix, 139
    treated as firms 140, 143
    see also 'stock exchanges' under individual countries
Stockholms Fondbors AB 143
Stockholm Stock Exchange 143, 146, 218
stock options as remuneration xxiii, 92, 116, 241
Sweden
    foreign investors 211
    insider model of corporate governance 56
    ownership of common stock *51*, 211
    pension systems 60
    shareholder voting rights 201, 202
    stock exchange 143, 146
    stock market capitalization 208
Switzerland 56, 208, *264*

T
takeovers
    anti-takeover instruments xxiv, 57, 64, 67, 94, 268
    in closed markets 210
    disciplinary device 57, 63, 113, 257
    EU proposals xv–xvi
    hostile takeovers xix, 64, 67, 93–4, 239, 245, 254, 314
    institutional investors and 59, 63, 64, 67

takeovers (*cont.*)
  large shareholder benefits 166–7
  in open stock market situations 209
  regulation 52, 240
  takeover boom (1980s) 67, 91
technological advances, impact of 45, 46–7, 55, 252
telecommunication companies xvi, 191
Third Company Law Directive xxii
Tokyo Stock Exchange 248, 264
trading costs 47
transaction costs 46, 47, 69, 92, 251
transition economies xiv, xxv
  ownership structures 205
  see also Central and Eastern European countries (CEECs)
transparency xviii, 52, 89, 105, 106
Transparency Directive xviii

U
United Kingdom
  bankruptcies 105
  banks
    corporate governance 223–5, *224*
    merchant banks' board size 225, *226*
    relationship with institutional investors 231, 232–3
  Belgium, investment in 284
  corporate finance 248, 249, 255
  corporate governance
    adoption of 12 month service contracts 223
    banks 223–5, *224*
    of financial institutions 223–9
    government intervention in privatized firms 190–1
    guidelines 61
    incentives and disciplining 240, 255
    key board committees 225, 229, 232
    outsider system 251
    roles of Chair and CEO, separation of 223
    shareholders and 93
  corporate performance 90, 244
  corporations
    board sizes 223, 224, *224*
    capital structure 127, *127*
    dividend pay-out ratios 249
    equity investors, nature of 250
    'golden shares' 190–1

  market capitalization 264, *264*
  mergers and acquisitions *64*
  quoted companies 264, *264*
  stock market capitalization 208
  takeovers against utilities 191, *191*
institutional investors 217–33, 238
  bank shareholdings 222, *222*
  coalition formation 247
  corporate governance structures 223–9, 231–2
  and corporate restructuring 239–40
  disclosure obligations 220
  dominant role 210, 211
  financial institutions ownership 220–3, *221*
  financial institutions, relationship with 229–33
  listed company ownership 30, *30*
  rise in shareholding 211
  total investment 219–20, *219*
  voting behaviour 232
insurance companies xiv, xviii, 219, 225, *227–8*, 229
life assurance companies 229, *230*, 232, 247
mutual fund portfolios *43*, 44
ownership structures xviii, 95, *95*, 118, 119, *119*, 210, *210*, 211, 238, 247, 250, 265
  dispersed shareholdings 239, 251
  dynamic evolution of ownership patterns 244
  foreign investors 211
  individual ownership 238
  the large shareholder *120*
  ownership of common stock *51, 119, 179*
  shareholders' voting rights 201
pension funds xiv, xviii, 47, 218, 247
privatization 190–1
  golden shares 254
stock exchanges 140, 144, 150–1, 152, 153, 264
takeover activity 63, *64*, 94, 191
United States
  corporate finance 248
  corporate governance
    guidelines 61
    and incentives 240, 255
    outsider system 58, 251
    shareholder influence 89, 93
  corporate management, pay and performance 176, 242

United States (*cont.*)
  corporate performance 242, 244
    ownership concentration and 243
  corporations
    capital costs 248–9
    capital structure 127, *127*
    domestic listed companies 208
    equity investors, nature of 250
    market capitalization 206, 264, *264*
    quoted companies 264, *264*
  institutional investors 217–18, 238
    and corporate governance 247
    and corporate restructuring 239–40
    historic experience 163
    ownership of common stock 172
    ownership of listed companies 30, *30*
  insurance companies xiv, 247
  investor capitalism 217
  mergers and acquisitions 63, 64, *64*, 67, 94, 117
  mutual funds *43*, 44, 247
  ownership structures 95, *95*, 96, 118, *119*, *210*, 211, 217–18, 238, 247, 264–5
    dispersed shareholdings 239, 251
  individual ownership 238
  large shareholders 119, *120*, 265
  non-financial corporations, ownership concentration in 119, *119*
  ownership of common stock *51*, *179*
  pension funds xiv, 47, 69–70, 205, 218, 247
  US Private Securities Litigation Act 60

V
venture capital 52
Vienna Stock Exchange 141
Viénot Committee xxi, 203, *204*, 212
voting rights
  double or multiple rights 201–2
  in the EU 201, *201*
  non-voting shares 202
  one-share, one-vote principle 106, 201
  ordinary rights xv
  proxy voting xxii, 31, 60–1, 63, 93, 106

W
warrants 268
Wiener Börse AG 141
work governance 109, 303

FINANCIAL AND MONETARY POLICY STUDIES

* 1. J.S.G. Wilson and C.F. Scheffer (eds.): *Multinational Enterprises.* Financial and Monitary Aspects. 1974   ISBN 90-286-0124-4
* 2. H. Fournier and J.E. Wadsworth (eds.): *Floating Exchange Rates.* The Lessons of Recent Experience. 1976   ISBN 90-286-0565-7
* 3. J.E. Wadsworth, J.S.G. Wilson and H. Fournier (eds.): *The Development of Financial Institutions in Europe, 1956–1976.* 1977   ISBN 90-286-0337-9
* 4. J.E. Wadsworth and F.L. de Juvigny (eds.): *New Approaches in Monetary Policy.* 1979   ISBN 90-286-0848-6
* 5. J.R. Sargent (ed.), R. Bertrand, J.S.G. Wilson and T.M. Rybczynski (ass. eds.): *Europe and the Dollar in the World-Wide Disequilibrium.* 1981   ISBN 90-286-0700-5
* 6. D.E. Fair and F.L. de Juvigny (eds.): *Bank Management in a Changing Domestic and International Environment.* The Challenges of the Eighties. 1982   ISBN 90-247-2606-9
* 7. D.E. Fair (ed.) in cooperation with R. Bertrand: *International Lending in a Fragile World Economy.* 1983   ISBN 90-247-2809-6
  8. P. Salin (ed.): *Currency Competition and Monetary Union.* 1984   ISBN 90-247-2817-7
* 9. D.E. Fair (ed.) in cooperation with F.L. de Juvigny: *Government Policies and the Working of Financial Systems in Industrialized Countries.* 1984   ISBN 90-247-3076-7
 10. C. Goedhart, G.A. Kessler, J. Kymmell and F. de Roos (eds.): *Jelle Zijlstra, A Central Banker's View.* Selected Speeches and Articles. 1985   ISBN 90-247-3184-4
 11. C. van Ewijk and J.J. Klant (eds.): *Monetary Conditions for Economic Recovery.* 1985   ISBN 90-247-3219-0
* 12. D.E. Fair (ed.): *Shifting Frontiers in Financial Markets.* 1986   ISBN 90-247-3225-5
 13. E.F. Toma and M. Toma (eds.): *Central Bankers, Bureaucratic Incentives, and Monetary Policy.* 1986   ISBN 90-247-3366-9
* 14. D.E. Fair and C. de Boissieu (eds.): *International Monetary and Financial Integration.* The European Dimension. 1988   ISBN 90-247-3563-7
 15. J. Cohen: *The Flow of Funds in Theory and Practice.* A Flow-Constrained Approach to Monetary Theory and Policy. 1987   ISBN 90-247-3601-3
 16. W. Eizenga, E.F. Limburg and J.J. Polak (eds.): *The Quest for National and Global Economic Stability.* In Honor of Hendrikus Johannes Witteveen. 1988   ISBN 90-247-3653-6
* 17. D.E. Fair and C. de Boissieu (eds.): *The International Adjustment Process.* New Perspectives, Recent Experience and Future Challenges for the Financial System. 1989   ISBN 0-7923-0013-0
 18. J.J. Sijben (ed.): *Financing the World Economy in the Nineties.* 1989   ISBN 0-7923-0090-4

FINANCIAL AND MONETARY POLICY STUDIES

19. I. Rizzo: *The 'Hidden' Debt.* With a Foreword by A.T. Peacock. 1990
ISBN 0-7923-0610-4

*20. D.E. Fair and C. de Boissieu (eds.): *Financial Institutions in Europe under New Competitive Conditions.* 1990   ISBN 0-7923-0673-2

21. R. Yazdipour (ed.): *Advances in Small Business Finance.* 1991   ISBN 0-7923-1135-3

*22. D.E. Fair and C. de Boissieu (eds.): *Fiscal Policy, Taxation and the Financial System in an Increasingly Integrated Europe.* 1992   ISBN 0-7923-1451-4

23. W.C. Boeschoten: *Currency Use and Payment Patterns.* 1992   ISBN 0-7923-1710-6

24. H.A. Benink: *Financial Integration in Europe.* 1993   ISBN 0-7923-1849-8

25. G. Galeotti and M. Marrelli (eds.): *Design and Reform of Taxation Policy.* 1992
ISBN 0-7923-2016-6

*26. D.E. Fair and R. Raymond (eds.): *The New Europe: Evolving Economic and Financial Systems in East and West.* 1993   ISBN 0-7923-2159-6

27. J.O. de Beaufort Wijnholds, S.C.W. Eijffinger and L.H. Hoogduin (eds.): *A Framework for Monetary Stability.* Papers and Proceedings of an International Conference (Amsterdam, The Netherlands, 1993). 1994   ISBN 0-7923-2667-9

*28. D.E. Fair and R. Raymond (eds.): *The Competitiveness of Financial Institutions and Centres in Europe.* 1994   ISBN 0-7923-3131-1

29. A.F.P. Bakker: *The Liberalization of Capital Movements in Europe.* The Monetary Committee and Financial Integration, 1958–1994. 1996   ISBN 0-7923-3591-0

30. H.A. Benink: *Coping with Financial Fragility and Systemic Risk.* 1995
ISBN 0-7923-9612-X

31. K. Alders, K. Koedijk, C. Kool and C. Winder (eds.): *Monetary Policy in a Converging Europe.* Papers and Proceeding of an International Workshop. 1996
ISBN 0-7923-3746-8

*32. F. Bruni, D.E. Fair and R. O'Brien (eds.): *Risk Management in Volatile Financial Markets.* 1996   ISBN 0-7923-4053-1

---

*Published on behalf of the *Société Universitaire Européenne de Recherches Financières* (SUERF), consisting the lectures given at Colloquia, organized and directed by SUERF.

Kluwer Academic Publishers – Dordrecht / Boston / London